Global Power Shift

Comparative Analysis and Perspectives

Ample empirical evidence points to recent power shifts in multiple areas of international relations taking place between industrialized countries and emerging powers, and between states and non-state actors. Yet there is a dearth of theoretical interpretation and synthesis of these findings, and a growing need for coherent approaches to understand and measure the transformation. This edited series aims to bring together scholars from all major world regions as well as different disciplines in order to discuss and possibly blend their different approaches and provide new frameworks for the understanding of global affairs and the governance of global power shifts.

For further volumes:
http://www.springer.com/series/10201

Enrico Fels • Jan-Frederik Kremer •
Katharina Kronenberg
Editors

Power in the 21st Century

International Security and International Political Economy in a Changing World

Springer

Editors
Enrico Fels
Bonn University
Center for Global Studies
Institute for Political Science
and Sociology
Bonn
Germany

Jan-Frederik Kremer
Bonn University
Center for Global Studies
Institute for Political Science
and Sociology
Bonn
Germany

Katharina Kronenberg
Bonn University
Center for Global Studies
Institute for Political Science
and Sociology
Bonn
Germany

ISBN 978-3-642-25081-1 e-ISBN 978-3-642-25082-8
DOI 10.1007/978-3-642-25082-8
Springer Heidelberg Dordrecht London New York

Library of Congress Control Number: 2012935687

Printed on acid-free paper

Springer is part of Springer Science+Business Media (www.springer.com)

Preface

Power has no limits.
(Tiberius Caesar)

For millennia the study of power has been an essential part of human philosophical endeavours. Already in ancient times Greek and Indian philosopher as well as Roman and Chinese statesmen tried to answer questions regarding the essential nature of power, its sources and how to use power wisely in order to keep and increase it. However, despite these efforts power in essence remains to some extent a mystery. In International Relations (IR) myriads of researcher have tried to understand what power in IR might look like, which shapes it can take and how they work and interact.[1]

At the beginning of the second decade of the 21st century there is a great debate going on that deals with the question whether there is a power shift taking place between the developed countries and the so called emerging or reemerging powers (mainly China, Brazil, India and Russia, but also other countries like Indonesia or South Africa). This debate is not only taking place in academic circles, but has also largely influenced public discourses around the globe. While there is a lot of academic work on the empirical implications of a perceived power shift between the western world and emerging powers (e.g. Rachman 2008; Grevi 2009; Stephens 2009; Zakaria 2009), a comparable debate has not taken place on questions connected with these implications, e.g. how power shifts in international relations can actually be captured methodological in the 21st century – comprised of an arena that is largely characterized by a complex economical, political, financial and ecological interdependence. Likewise, questions regarding the changing nature of power as an ability or function in such an environment are barely debated on a theoretical level. Especially when it comes to answer the questions of what the nature of power in today's interstate relations might look like, which forms it might

[1] For a longer discussion on the debate see Chap. 1 from Fels in this volume.

take, which new sources it can be based upon or which ways may have become more effective than others for exercising it internationally, one discovers both theoretical confusion and cacophony. Various concepts and approaches that were developed in the decades after the Second World War compete for explanatory power. On a general level Realist and Neo-Realist scholars regard hard power capabilities (military and economic resources) as the most important sources of power in IR (cf. Waltz 1990; Mearsheimer 1995; Grieco 1995). Joseph Nye, on the other hand, argues for soft power, as the ability to attract others and win their support for own positions, or smart power, a combination and application of soft and hard power resources in a 'smart' way, as the most important sources and ways for exercising power in international affairs (Nye 1990a, b; 2011).

David Baldwin (2002: 178–179) again introduced a multi-dimensional concept of power; power in his concept can be analyzed in terms of its scope, weight, means and domain. To understand power in its total character, Barnett and Duval (2005) also developed a multi-level approach towards power: They presented an approach which combined material, relational and structural components of power. Barnett and Duval distinguished on an analytical level between compulsory, institutional, structural and productive power, asserting that those four forms would be able to explain the whole picture of power in IR (Barnett/Duval 2005).

Other scholars – most prominently Stephen Krasner (1985) and Susan Strange (1987, 1988, 1996) – have argued for structural power as being the most important source of power in IR. Additionally, other scholars have brought power concepts from the field of sociology into the debate and argued for non-intentional, institutional, impersonal or discursive power as important power variants (cf. Guzzini 1993, 2005). Lukes for example pointed out the importance of the relationship between power and interests, as well as the importance of winning the "hearts and minds" of another actor in order to successfully exercise power (Lukes 2005). Other authors in IR – especially postmodern and critical scholars – understand power as being productive in terms of creating subjectivity, norms and discourses. Power in this understanding constitutes subjects by normalizing them throughout the overt and covert effects of norms and discourses (cf. Focault 1972). These effects cannot be controlled by a single actor or small group of actors. Furthermore, norms and discourses become own sources of power, controlling the behaviour and belief-system of human beings. Power in this understanding is "making up people" (Hacking 1986). Proponents of Max Weber's definition of power as a relational concept have followed another, quite different idea on power (Weber 1947; Baldwin 1979, 1980, 2002; Dahl 1957). Thus, every interested observer of the debates on power in IR will recognize that power in IR seems to have not only a Janus face as a defining characteristic feature, but – to stick to the image – should best be understood to have the polycephalic countenance of Hekate, Brahma or Svantovit. There is now such a variety of concepts and understandings of power in our discipline that someone might find it quite hard to stay informed and not to lose his head in the discussion. The aim of this book is therefore twofold: first, to shed some light onto the discussion on this important topic by outlining the competing strands and concepts in the literature, second – and with respect to the altered international environment of the 21st century – to contribute to the debate by introducing novel approaches and understandings or new applications of older concepts in order to show how scholars might understood power in our changing world in this new century.

The concept of power is still today "one of the most troublesome in the field of international relations" (Gilpin 1981: 13) and a useful definition of power in IR "remains a matter of controversy" (Waltz 1986, 333). Indeed, this book likewise will not be able to give a conclusive answer towards the question "What is power?". However, by providing approaches and studies for perhaps the two most important sectors of IR –International Security and International Political Economy (IPE) – the volume seeks to widen the understanding of power in our discipline with regards to developments at the dawn of the 21st century. To do so, on the one hand, the book focuses primarily on international relations and on power in the stricter IR sense. Accordingly, concepts of power which have been developed under the prime objective to understand power in sociological and linguistic terms (Focaultian, discoursive, impersonal and other postmodern approaches), on the other hand, will not be explored in this volume.

In order to achieve these aims, this volume brings together scholars working in the fields of IR, IPE, economics and finance as well as security studies. By approaching the subject from a variety of angles and introducing new theoretical designs and empirical analyses, they seek to foster the debate particularly in those realms that continue to be important for modern nation states: security and economics. Furthermore, this book not only includes contributions from authors with different academic backgrounds, but – even more important – very different ontological, epistemological and theoretical perspectives. Due to this basic feature, the volume is not designed to develop one specific and exclusive concept for understanding the nature of power in IR. In fact, it intends to combine the work of scholars working on issues within the fields of security and economic into a single volume in order to outline both differing and similar understandings of power (and its multiple facets) within the academic community working on the international realm, tackle different aspects, combine existing theoretical considerations with empirical evidence and present novel ideas for grasping power in the modern world.

The book's first part, *Theoretical Considerations about Power*, deals with the various theoretical aspects of power. The contributions concentrate not only on power discourses within IR on a general level and possible shifts of it among international actor, but discuss established and novel understandings of power in its various dimensions and present possibilities for adapting them to the 21st century. The volume's second part, entitled *International Security and Power*, encompasses contributions that deal with power developments in one field of IR, which has probably gained the most attention since the establishing of our discipline. The section assesses old and new sources of international power and analyses implications they have in the currently changing global environment. *International Political Economy and Power*, the final part of the book, contains contributions, which deal with power in the realm of trade, finance and economics. The authors examine how economic power should best be understood, in which ways economic interdependence and the governance of the global economy affect the international power status of states, and how economics has been used in recent times to gain and exercise power in a globalized world.

The volume's first chapter, *Power Shift? Power in International Relations and the Allegiance of Middle Powers*, starts with a general overview of the competing understandings of power in IR. Enrico Fels argues that one can distinguish three power concepts: power-as-resources, relational and structural power. Combining the allegiance of middle powers and a relational understanding of power, Fels proceeds and analyses Australia's allegiance as a case study in order to give an example for measuring a possible power shift between the United States and China. Whereas in economic terms Australia's relationship with China became much more interdependent in the last decades, Canberra continues to strengthen its security ties with Washington, demonstrating the limited fungibility of power between power areas.

Cornelia Beyer continues the theoretical debate in Chap. 2, *Hegemony and Power in the Global War on Terrorism*, by using the US hegemony between 2001 and 2008 as well as US leadership in the Global War on Terror as an example in order to debate a modern concept of hegemony, combining realist, constructivist and critical IR perspectives while distancing her concept from the simple realist notion of unipolarity. She finds that the US hegemony is based on material and ideological power and validates her thesis with a qualitative analysis of interviews conducted with scholars and practitioners from the the EU und ASEAN and their evaluation of US dominance.

Gitika Commuri critically discusses Joseph Nye's well-known concept of soft power in Chap. 3. In *Are you Pondering what I am Pondering? Understanding the Conditions Under which States Gain and Loose Soft Power* she uses Nye's original articulation of the concept – in terms of persuasion and attraction of others and hence without the gradual inclusion of economic power Nye himself added later. She concentrates on the conditions in which states may gain or lose soft power and investigates the relationship of these conditions with hard power capabilities, the role of the international structure and, particularly interesting, to a relational understanding of power. The article finishes by clarifying why states can gain and lose soft power in another state at the same time, since a state's soft power often only intentionally aims one group, i.e. certain elites or the population in the targeted state. Commuri argues that besides the internal conditions of nation states and the structure of the international system, historic conditions are responsible for significantly shaping the ability of states to possess and project soft power.

In Chap. 4, *Towards a New Understanding of Structural Power – "Structure is What States Make of it"*, Andrej Pustovitovskij and Jan-Frederik Kremer develop a new understanding of structural power after discussing existing approaches of structural notions of power, including Susan Strange's concept. By pointing out the importance of states' needs and goods for their structural power position in international relations and by introducing an approach for linking these to the exercise of power in structural terms they explore the very sources of structural power. They show that by influencing their baskets and the likelihood of becoming credible outside options for other actors in international negotiations, states can gain structural power in international affairs.

Stephan Frühling and Andrew O'Neil commence the volume's second part, which concentrates on aspects of power in the field of security. In Chap. 5, *Nuclear Weapons and Power in the 21st Century*, they deal with probably the most destructive weapons mankind has so far developed and discuss possible effects of novel developments in the field of nuclear arms on future power relations. The two authors show that although nuclear weapons make massive destruction possible, states managed in the past to find a delicate balance of terror that brought stability during the Cold War. With the technological advancement of many nations especially from the Global South, however, the main pillar of the previously quite successful nuclear order – the Non-Proliferation Treaty (NPT) – comes under rising pressure from latent nuclear powers. Frühling and O'Neil argue that while one should not conclude that latent nuclear powers will turn into de facto ones quickly, their new nuclear capabilities will nevertheless have wider systemic effects as a new type of power resource.

Sarah Kirchberger shows in Chap. 9, *Evaluating Maritime Power: The Example of China*, that in order to measure and compare national naval strength it is essential to employ an innovative multi-facet framework that goes beyond the traditional consideration of numbers, vessel types and employed personnel. After outlining the concept of sea power she proceeds with a closer look at China's naval modernization strategy and the impact the Chinese naval build-up has on the Asian naval balance of power. Following her critical assessment of the Middle Kingdom's maritime capabilities, Kirchberger concludes that although China's maritime power might be growing, it is – especially if compared to some neighbouring nations – relatively weak considering its high dependency on maritime transport, its vast coastline and the size of its Exclusive Economic Zone.

In Chap. 8, Roxana G. Radu draws attention to the increasing importance of information and communication technology both as a source of national power as well as a threat to it. After conceptualising cyber security and the novel vulnerabilities states face in an increasingly digitalized national and international environment, Radu concentrates on the role that informational power plays in trans-national relations. She concludes *The Monopoly of Violence in the Cyber Space: Challenges of Cyber Security* by using the empirical cases of Estonia, Georgia and South Korea to outline policy responses by countries that experienced critical cyber attacks in the recent past.

In Chap. 10, *Drones as Future Air Power Assets: The Dawn of Aviation 2.0?*, Louis-Marie Clouet concentrates on the important tactical and strategic impacts of Unmanned Arial Vehicles (UAVs) for 21st century power relations. Taking recent military experiences as a starting point, he outlines how UAVs are already changing the ways air power is gained and exercised by Western and non-Western militaries, e.g. by using drones for better battlefield awareness. He sketches out likely future developments within this important field and shows that drones are set to fundamentally alter the traditionally air power hierarchy as they allow for military air assets that are cheaper (compared to the costs of traditional jets and bombers) and easier to manufacture (particularly due to dual-use technologies) – something that particularly benefits developing countries. Given the rising global demand for drones and the increasingly tougher industrial competition, Clouet concludes with a call for a stronger European cooperation in order to avoid falling behind militarily and technologically.

Following a reflection of the European discourse's development on traditional power politics in the decades after the end of the Cold War, Magnus Christiansson delves into the concept of military balancing and shows in Chap. 7, how this particular concept, which was long absent in the European security debate, continues to be relevant when it comes to certain European sub-complexes such as the Baltic Sea region. He proceeds in *The Military Balance in the Baltic Sea Region – Notes on a Defunct Concept* by concentrating on military capabilities of regional states, sorts their various balancing patterns into three basic strategies – assurance, avoidance or self-realization – and examines the impact the Russian-Georgian war in August 2008 had in altering these strategies. The results of his analysis show that balancing theory helps to get a better grasp of regional state's security behaviour and compensates for blind spots of theories dealing with governance or complex interdependence.

In the book's 6th Chapter Jost Wübbeke uses a constructivist approach to address the question of how important natural resources serve as tools or sources of power in the 21st century. After examining existing approaches towards resource power and offering an insightful assessment of todays distribution of key resources, Wübbeke analyses in *Three Worlds of Natural Resources and Power* the importance of resources in international relations by using Wendt's conceptions of three different ontological perceptions of world politics that form three idiosyncratic role models of interstate relations: Hobbesian, Lockean, Kantian. He points out that depending on the ontological perception of international relations by the international actors involved and the role model applied by them, the importance of resources as sources of power varies significantly and therefore there is neither an automatic link between natural resources and power nor between scarcity and conflict.

Benjamin J. Cohen starts the volume's third part, which concentrates on international economic aspects of power, by closer examining monetary power in international affairs. In Chap. 11, *The International Monetary System: Diffusion and Ambiguity*, he addresses the question of the ontology of power and rule-setting in the international monetary system. By distinguishing between two dimensions of monetary power – autonomy and influence – Cohen offers an innovative approach towards power in the international monetary system. Within this context he examines and analyses different developments, outlining a diffusion of power among states as well as between states and non-state actors rather in the dimension of autonomy than in the dimension of influence. Cohen introduces the concept of *leaderless diffusion*, meaning that leadership in the system has been more scattered than relocated. He argues that a power shift has taken place from few very powerful states towards a growing number of autonomous actors, especially when it comes to rule-setting abilities within the monetary system. Furthermore, he outlines that on the level of governance, a distinction should be made between the individual state and the global system and thus offers an elaborated approach towards understanding monetary and economic power in the 21st century.

In *Leaders in Need of Followers: Emerging Powers in Global Governance* Stefan A. Schirm shows how regional and emerging powers such as Brazil and Germany strive to exercise leadership in international negations. By looking at negations within the World Trade Organisation (WTO), the founding of the G20 and both countries bids for permanent seats in the UN Security Council, Schirm explores in Chap. 12 the necessary conditions for regional powers to gain followership in the international community. In concentrating on followership as a core condition for success and failure of emerging and regional power's leadership in global governance, he succeeds in developing a thoughtful methodology that facilitates analysing the exercise of power by middle and great powers.

In Chap. 13, *A Power Through Trade? The European Union and Democracy Promotion in ACP States,* Dennis Nottebaum tests whether the EU, which he defines as a trading power, has the ability to exert power and to influence the internal development (especially the promotion of democracy) of its trading partners from Africa, the Caribbean and the Pacific (ACP states) by using the access to its internal market as a bargaining chip. Nottebaum assesses the European impact on trade relations operationalized as trade openness by using a two-stage least squares model (2SLS) with panel data covering the years from 1991 to 2008. Thereby he provides evidence that the EU has considerable success in linking trade issues with issues of democracy promotion in the ACP states.

Maaike Okano-Heijmans outlines in *Power Shift: Economic Realism and Economic Diplomacy on the Rise*, the book's 14th Chapter, how latecomer countries are much more willing to use economic tools for strengthening their position in international negotiations and for intervening in their domestic economies to achieve political goals than economically developed countries in Europe and North America. To do so she reconceptualises the economic dimension of power by adjusting existing theoretical concepts that link economics and politics, to current realities and contemporary debates. In analysing Chinese foreign policies she is able to validate her initial assumptions and confirms concerns of the future success of foreign policies from European countries.

In the last chapter of this volume, *Exploring China's Rise as a Knowledge Power*, Maximilian Mayer uses China as a case study in order to point to an often neglected aspect of national power: knowledge und technology. He argues that a truly comprehensive understanding of how China could (again) become a hub of world politics requires an historical exploration of the Chinese position within the global political economy of knowledge. Drawing from the ideas of Susan Strange, Robert Gilpin, and Joseph Schumpeter, he explores the global knowledge power politics in which China's rise is embedded and concludes that, in sum, China's knowledge power has obviously increased. However, China largely relies on creeping processes of knowledge creation that neither reduce its technological dependence nor result in a sharp increase of knowledge power. On a theoretical level, Mayer's case study illustrates that, despite the alleged conceptual elusiveness of knowledge, a reasonably coherent and differentiated assessment of qualitative and quantitative alternations of knowledge power is possible.

Finally, carrying out this book project benefitted from the support, ideas and work of many individuals and institutions. First and foremost we would like to thank the authors not only for participating in the project and presenting fresh ideas and concepts, but also for their patience and efforts during its various stages. Furthermore, we are particularly grateful to Prof. Dr. Xuewu Gu, director of the Center for Global Studies (CGS) at the University of Bonn, for supporting the project right from the start with great enthusiasm, productive discussions and financial backing. Thanks are furthermore due to our other colleagues at the CGS – Maximilian Mayer, Andrej Pustovitovskij, Pavlina Schmitz, Ben Behschnitt, Tschen-Ing Liu, Markus Nagel, Katharina Below, and Jan-Paul Franken – for their helpful suggestions and assistance. We are also grateful to the International Studies Association (ISA) for allowing us to present our papers at its 52nd Annual Convention in Montreal (Canada) in March 2011 and discuss selected analyses and views expressed in this volume with scholars from all over the world. For a very friendly and professional cooperation we furthermore wish to express our gratitude to the economics and political science section of our publisher Springer, particularly to Barbara Fess. Finally, we would like to extent thanks to our colleagues at the Department for Political Science and Sociology at the University of Bonn – not only for providing a fruitful working environment, but also for personal and academic encouragements during the many phases of this book project.

Enrico Fels, Jan-Frederik Kremer,
Katharina Kronenberg

Bonn, Spring 2012

References

Baldwin, D. A. (1979). Power analysis and world politics: New trends versus old tendencies. *World Politics 31*(2), 161–194.

Baldwin, D. A. (1980). Interdependence and power: A conceptual analysis. *International Organization, 34*(4), 471–506.

Baldwin, D. A. (2002). Power and international relations. In W. Carlsnaes, T. Risse, B. Simmons (Eds.), *The handbook of international relations* (pp. 177–191). Thousand Oaks: Sage Press.

Barnett, M., & Duvall, R. (2005a). Power in international politics. *International Organizations, 59* (Winter), 39–75.

Dahl, R. A. (1957). The concept of power. *Behavioral Science, 2*(3), 201–215.

Foucault, M. (1972–1977). *Power/knowledge: Selected interviews and other writings 1972–77.* Brighton: Harverster.

Gilpin, R. (1981). *War and change in world politics.* Cambridge: Cambridge University Press.

Grevi, G. (2009). *The Interpolar world: A new scenario.* Occasional Paper – No. 79, European Union Institute for Security Studies.

Grieco, J. M. (1995). The Maastricht treaty, economic and monetary union and the neo-realist research program. *Review of International Studies*, *21*(1), 21–40.

Guzzini, S. (1993). Structural power: The limits of neorealist power analysis. *International Organization*, *47*(3), 443–478.

Guzzini, S. (2005). The concept of power: A constructivist analysis. *Millennium – Journal of International Studies*, *33*, 495–522.

Hacking, I. (1986). Making up people. In T. Heller, M. Sosna, & D. Wellbery (Eds.), *Reconstructing individualism.* Stanford: Stanford University Press.

Krasner, S. D. (1985). *Structural conflict: The third world against global liberalism.* Berkley: University of California Press.

Lukes, S. (2005). Power and the battle for the hearts and minds. *Millennium: Journal of International Studies, 33*(3), 477–493.

Mearsheimer, J. J. (1995). The false promise of international institutions. *International Security*, *19*(3), 5–49.

Nye, J. S. Jr. (1990a). The changing nature of world power. *Political Science Quarterly*, *105*(2), 177–192.

Nye, J. S. Jr. (1990b). Soft power. *Foreign Policy*, *80*, 153–171.

Nye, J. S. Jr. (2011). *The future of power*. Public Affairs, 2011.

Rachman, G. (2008). Is America's new declinism for real? *Financial Times* (November 24).

Stephens, P. (2009). Financial crisis marks out a new geopolitical order. *Financial Times* (October 9).

Strange, S. (1987). The persistent myth of lost hegemony. *International Organization*, *41*(4) (Autumn), 551–574.

Strange, S. (1988). *States and markets – An introduction to international political economy.* London: Pinter Publishers.

Strange, S. (1996). *The retreat of the state: The diffusion of power in the world economy.* Cambridge: Cambridge University Press.

Waltz, K. (1990). Realist thought and neorealist theory. *Journal of International Affairs*, *44*, 21–37.

Waltz, K. N. (1986). Reflections on theory of international politics: A response to my critics. In R. O. Keohane (Ed.), *Neorealism and its critics.* New York: Columbia University Press.

Weber, M. (1947). *The theory of social and economic organization.* New York: The Free Press.

Zakaria, F. (2009). *The Post-American world: And the rise of the rest.* London: Penguin Books.

Contents

Contributors

Dr. Andrew O'Neil Professor and Director of the Griffith Asia Institute, Griffith University, Brisbane. Editor-in-chief of the Australian Journal of International Affairs and ex officio member of the National Executive of the Australian Institute of International Affairs. Chief Investigator on the Australian Research Council's Linkage Project Australian Nuclear Choices

Andrej Pustovitovskij Lecturer and Ph.D. Candidate, Center for Global Studies, University of Bonn, apust@uni-bonn.dein

Benjamin J. Cohen Louis G. Lancaster Professor of International Political Economy at the University of California, Santa Barbara. He is a member of the Editorial Board of Review of International Political Economy and – among the many other positions he held during his career – also served as member of the Editorial Board of International Organization (until 2010) and member of the Advisory Board of the Princeton Encyclopedia of the World Economy (2005–2009)

Dr. Anna Cornelia Beyer Lecturer at the Department of Politics and International Studies, Faculty of Arts and Social Sciences, University of Hull, c.beyer@hull.ac.uk

Dr. Louis-Marie Clouet Associate Research Fellow, Institut français des relations internationales (Ifri), Paris. Director of Research in Intercultural Management, Institut de Management et de Communication Interculturels (ISIT), Paris

Magnus Christiansson Associate Lecturer at the Department for Security and Strategy, Swedish National Defence College, Stockholm, magnus.christiansson@fhs.se

Dr. Gitika Commuri Associate Professor, School of Social Sciences and Education, Department of Political Science, California State University Bakersfield, gcommuri@csub.edu

Enrico Fels Lecturer, Managing Editor of the series "Global Power Shift – Comparative Analysis and Perspectives" (Springer) and Ph.D. Candidate, Center for Global Studies, University of Bonn

Dr. Stephan Frühling Senior Lecturer, Strategic and Defence Studies Centre, Australian National University. Deputy Director of Studies, Military Studies Program, Australian Command and Staff College. Managing editor 'Security Challenges'. Chief Investigator on the Australian Research Council's Linkage Project on Australian Nuclear Choices, stephan.fruehling@anu.edu.au

Dr. Sarah Kirchberger Assistant Professor, Department for Chinese Language and Culture, Asien-Afrika-Institut, University of Hamburg

Jan-Frederik Kremer Lecturer, Center for Global Studies, University of Bonn and Ph.D. Candidate, Institute of Development Research and Development Policy, Ruhr-University Bochum

Katharina Kronenberg Lecturer and Ph.D. Candidate, Center for Global Studies, University of Bonn

Maximilian Mayer Lecturer and Ph.D. Candidate, Managing Assistant of the Center for Global Studies, University of Bonn

Dennis Nottebaum Ph.D. Candidate at the Centre for Interdisciplinary Economics (CIW) and member of the Graduate School of Politics, University of Münster

Dr. Maaike Okano-Heijmans Research Fellow, Netherlands Institute of International Relations 'Clingendael', The Hague. Visiting Fellow, Asia-Pacific College of Diplomacy (APCD), Australian National University

Roxana Radu Research Fellow, Center for Media and Communication Studies, Central European University Budapest, and Ph.D. Candidate, Graduate Institute of International and Development Studies, Geneva, roxana.radu@graduateinstitute.ch

Dr. Stefan Schirm Professor of Political Science and Chair for International Relations, Ruhr-University Bochum. Fellow at the Transatlantic Academy and Visiting Scholar at the School for Advanced International Studies (SAIS), John Hopkins University, Washington D.C. (2010–2011)

Jost Wübbeke Ph.D. candidate at the Graduate School of Global Politics and the Environmental Policy Research Centre, Free University Berlin, j.wuebbeke@gmail.com

Part I
Theoretical Considerations About Power

Chapter 1
Power Shift? Power in International Relations and the Allegiance of Middle Powers

Enrico Fels

Within the last two decades, China has been the most seriously debated emerging power seen by academics, politicians and large parts of the public alike to be able to effectively challenge the dominant position of the United States of America (US) in global as well as Asian-Pacific affairs.[1] Indeed, after having enjoyed a brief moment of global unipolarity following the demise of the Soviet Union in the early 1990s, Washington's current situation has changed remarkably. Some points are particularly worth mentioning. To begin with, the world's former *hyperpuissance* (Hubert Védrine) has to recover from the worst global economic crisis since 1929. The US unemployment rate is up to almost 10% (far away from the 4% in 2000), its federal budget deficit was estimated at 1.4 trillion USD in 2011 (Younglai 2011) and total outstanding public debt skyrocketed to 14.7 trillion USD in September 2011 (US Treasury 2011). Secondly, the US continues to be heavily engaged in large military operations in Iraq and Afghanistan. The military missions in these two war-torn countries do not only continue to cost US tax payers a great deal of money[2] and account for the death of hundreds of US soldiers and local

---

I am grateful to Robert Ayson, Hugh White, Frans-Paul van der Putten, Yusuke Ishihara, Jared Sonnicksen, Gudrun Wacker and Maximilian Mayer for earlier discussions on this topic. All remaining errors are my own. This chapter is based on a paper presented at the 52nd Annual Convention of the International Studies Association in Montreal (Canada) on March 16th 2011. See Fels 2011a.

[1] See for instance: Abeysinghe and Lu 2003; Vaughn and Morrison 2006; Christensen 2006; Deng and Moore 2004; Friedberg 2005 and Wagener 2011.

Although being frequently referred to in academic and popular debates, Asia-Pacific is not a fixed region but comprises around 42 states from East Asia, Southeast Asia and Oceania in the Western Pacific Ocean. Often (though not always) the US, Russia and India are – due to their respective strategic relevance – also included as regional actors. This paper follows that understanding.

[2] According to the liberal think-tank *National Priorities Project* the costs for both wars have summed up since 2001 to more than 1.27 trillion USD until September 2011. See National Priorities Project 2011.

E. Fels et al. (eds.), *Power in the 21st Century*, Global Power Shift,
DOI 10.1007/978-3-642-25082-8_1, © Springer-Verlag Berlin Heidelberg 2012

civilians, but – more important from a strategic perspective – have bogged down the US military for some years to come. Finally, Washington is confronted with an increasingly assertive and economically rising China in Asia-Pacific, a region that according to high-ranking US politicians has "become more closely interlinked than ever before" (Obama 2009) with the fortune of America, "is a key driver for global economic growth" (Kirk 2009) and a place, "where much of the history of the 21st century will be written" (Clinton 2010).

Without any doubt, China's development is crucial for understanding the changing perceptions of the region's importance in wider global affairs as well as the shifting power structure within the region itself.[3] China has experienced astonishing growth rates of about 8–12% over the last 30 years. This development has increased the Chinese gross domestic product (GDP) in real terms to more than half of the American GDP and may overtake the United States within the next two decades.

China has furthermore integrated itself in the US-led global economic system and has gained considerable economic weight within the Western Pacific. In fact, due to the astonishing development of the Chinese economy, Asia-Pacific's regional economic structure has become much more Chinese-centred in the last years (Gaullier et al. 2007; Drysdale 2010b). Additionally, while growing economically, China has succeeded in building an impressive technological capacity as well as a strong domestic innovation system (Mayer 2011; CGS-Forschungsgruppe Wissensmacht 2011). Its long-lasting economic progress has furthermore allowed Beijing to finance an impressive military build-up, permitting the People's Liberation Army (PLA) to gain operational abilities to likely prevail in a military encounter with US forces close to Chinese borders, e.g. over the status of Taiwan (Office of the Secretary of Defence 2010). Thus, China's reappearance as a major power in the Western Pacific combined with its growing military posture may mark, as some authors have noted, the end of the 'Vasco da Gama-period' of Western dominance in the Western Pacific (e.g. White 2005).

Most of the above mentioned facts and developments are widely acknowledged. Over the last years, China's rise in the key region of international affairs in the 21st century has triggered a lot of research and writing on transitions, power shifts and changes in balance.[4] Indeed, after the passing of US primacy in regional economic affairs as well as Beijing's historic position in the region, it is only logical to assume that important changes in the economic basis and military capabilities of China cannot go without effect on the region's security and power structure.

This chapter, however, argues that in order to assess potential power shifts in Asia-Pacific it is important to rely on a measurement of power in international affairs that differs from the traditionally used equalization of rising resources and rising power. After taking a closer look at some important theoretical aspects of the

---

[3] On the importance of studying the regional level of international relations see Fawn 2009 as well as Buzan and Waever 2008.

[4] See for instance Goh 2004; Medeiros 2005; Power 2005; Ross 2006; Shambaugh 2004/05, 2005; Gill 2007 or Levin 2008.

nature of power in international relations, the chapter will outline why the allegiance of certain regional states – states, which cannot be attributed great power status but are still relevant for the overall system they are embedded in – should be seen as a telling factor in regional power relations. Following a detailed account of the attributes of that group of states, this new measurement of power is applied to the case of Australia, one of Washington's oldest allies in the region and a very close trading partner of Beijing.

Power in International Relations

Most scholars of International Relations (IR) as well as political practitioners agree that "power is the platinum coin of the international realm, and that little or nothing can be accomplished without it" (Gelb 2009: 26). As Alexander Wendt has shown, basically all IR theories have the underlying assumption that power is important in international relations (Wendt 1999: esp. 97). However, studying power in political science is a very arduous task. Twenty-five years ago, Kenneth Waltz noted that even defining power "remains a matter of controversy" (Waltz 1986: 333). So far, this controversy has not been resolved; instead, it is likely to continue for some time to come. Many approaches have been developed in IR in order to gain a better understanding of power in international affairs, its underlying mechanisms, the ways different actors use power as well as the varying importance of its sources.[5] All this has contributed to making research on this topic "one of the most troublesome in the field of international relations" (Gilpin 1981: 13).

On the whole, it is possible to distinguish between three main understandings of power in international relations: power-as-resources, relational power and structural power. The first strand is reflected by Waltz' (1979) emphasis on "capabilities" and "attributes of units" and Morgenthau's (1954) approach towards "elements of national power".[6] According to this power-as-resources understanding, certain material and immaterial factors within/of a state can be used to measure national power.[7] Power is thus basically seen as a possession of states. Proponents of this perception of power argue that adding up these different factors not only equals a state's national power, but does subsequently allow the power distribution among states in the international arena to become visible and is to be taken as the structure of international power. This notion of power continues to be very popular among political scientists and practitioners and is probably the main lens through

[5] Good overviews are provided by Wrong 1979; Clegg 1994; Baldwin 2000; Mattern 2008.

[6] However, Morgenthau's landmark book also shows that he has a relational understanding of power as he defines power as a "psychological relation between those who exercise is and those over whom it is exercised". See Morgenthau 1954: 25.

[7] Waltz, for instance, mentions population, territory, economy, resource endowment, military strength, political stability and competence. See Waltz 1979: 131. For Robert Gilpin only three resources (military, economic and technological means) indicate power. Gilpin 1981: 13.

which China's re-emergence is seen today (e.g. Treverton and Jones 2005). Joseph Nye rightfully argues that this view is fostered by believing that equalling power with possession of certain resources "makes power appear more concrete, measurable, and predictable" (Nye 1990a: 26).

The second understanding of power perceives it as a causal relationship between actors in international affairs in which one state affects the behaviour of another state by using own material and immaterial resources. Max Weber was probably the first political scientist to understand power in this regard. He described power as "the probability that one actor within a social relationship will be in a position to carry out his own will despite resistance" (Weber 1947: 152). His understanding of power strongly influenced Robert Dahl's more popular definition according to which "*A* has power over *B* to the extent that he can get *B* to do something that *B* would not otherwise do" (1957: 202f). Power thus comes from an actual or potential (social) engagement between two or more actors, it is therefore not equal to a state's resources, but based on a state's ability to effectively use own material and non-material[8] attributes in a specific context to gain power over another actor. As this shift from a concept of power-as-resources to a relational understanding allows for a more complex understanding of power, some authors have noted that it constituted a revolution in power analysis (Baldwin 2000: 178).

The third major understanding depicts power in structural terms. Proponents of this approach see power mainly related to the establishment of or control over structures in international relations. According to Susan Strange, structural power is the ability "to decide how things shall be done, the power to shape frameworks within which states relate to each other, relate to people, or relate to corporate enterprises" (Strange 1988: 25). Also Christensen (1978) emphasises the need to consider a situation's setting in which the interactions between two or more actors occur and Stephen Krasner proposes a structuring 'meta-power', which is "the ability to change the rules of the game" (1985: 14). Strange holds that "the possessor of [structural power] is able to change the range of choices open to others, without apparently putting pressure directly on them to take one decision or to make one choice rather than others" (1988: 31).[9] Others add that structural power in international politics is the combination of "the effects of positions of a state in a given structure that work conductively to its benefit in interaction with

[8] Also Joseph Nye's 'soft power' approach is based on a relational understanding of power. See Nye 2004. It should be noted, however, that 'soft power' is difficult to generate and even harder to wield *intentionally* in order to influence another actor. In Chap. 3 of this volume Commuri deals more closely with this kind of power.

[9] Other (post-)structural approaches argue that A's ability to influence the relevant elites of B as well as the influence of discourses, role models and social structures within states ('third' and 'fourth' face of power) should be seen as separate forms of power. See for instance Lukes 2005; Chase-Dunn 1989; Digeser 1992; Campbell 1998. However, while both 'faces' can indeed be seen as exercises of power, a relational conception of power can nevertheless very well capture most (if not all) of these aspects. See Guzzini 2000: esp. 62ff.

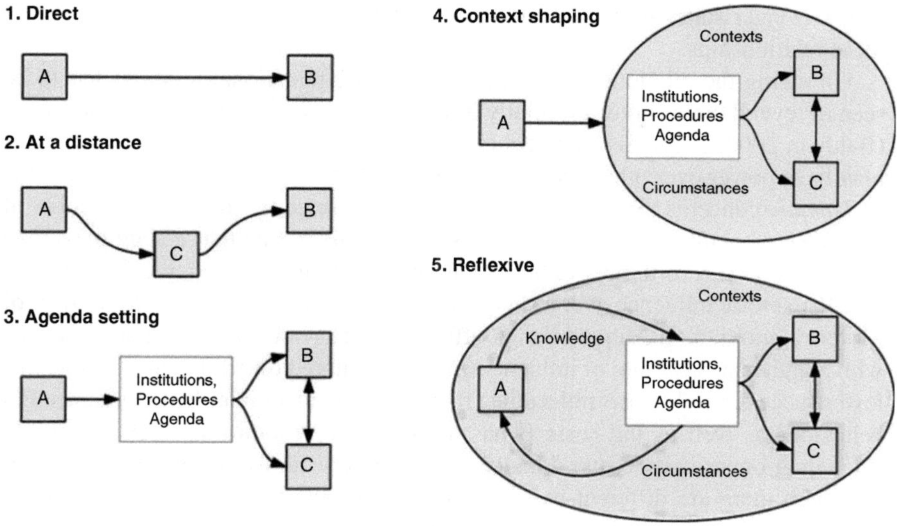

Fig. 1.1 Forms of relational power (Lebel 2006)

other states, regardless of whether this state is aware of the existence of these positions or not" (Gu 2010: 198).

Indeed, such a structural notion of power presents a formidable theoretical challenge to the relational concept of power *if* the international power structure in question is to be understood as solid, one-dimensional, all encompassing, basically unchangeable and ignorant of involved actors' behaviour. However, as Susan Strange has noted in her writings, there should be at least four different important structures in international affairs, all equipped with a separate (but interlinked) power structure of their own and different actors competing for a place at the top of the hierarchy.[10] In consequence, proponents of structural power have to explain why these international structures "defined as persistent patterns of power relationships in specified scope and domains, cannot be usefully studied using the relational concept of power" (Baldwin 2000: 185).

It is obvious that a relational understanding of power is capable of explaining power structures in various issue-areas between several actors, involved in interactions overlapping in time, space and taking shape in several forms (see Fig. 1.1). Strange herself in fact adopts a relational conception of power when describing a security structure as "a framework of power created by the provision of security by some human beings for others" (1988: 45). Thus, *structures in international affairs can be understood as repeated interactions between states*, enabling

[10] According to Strange, these four structures are within the issue areas security, production, finance and knowledge. See Strange 1989.

some stronger states to consistently gaining advantages over weaker ones within these relationships.

Following the relational conception, power in international relations has to be seen in several dimensions, especially in *scope*, *domain*, *reliability*, *costs* and *means* (Baldwin 2000: 178f). *Scope* refers to different issue-areas, meaning that an actor may have power over other actors in issue-area X, but not necessarily in issue-area Y. *Domain* concerns the number of other actors affected by state A (the number of Bs under A's influence) or the size of state B. This means that a state may have power in one part of the world but not automatically in another region or that it is able to exercise influence over a small state but not over a bigger one. *Reliability* of power refers to the likelihood that A affects the behaviour of B. Evidently, a state with a higher success rate of influencing others is more powerful than a state with a lower success rate.[11] *Costs* reflect the efforts A has to incur in order to influence B's behaviour as well as the costs B has to bear while submitting to A's demands (including opportunity costs). Finally, *means* are crucial for understanding power. Although there are different ways of categorizing the various means relevant in international relations, the most important are probably symbolic, economic, diplomatic and military means (e.g. Baldwin 1985). The first includes A's appellation to some shared norms, symbols and/or values in order to shape B's behaviour (e.g. the rights of asylum seekers, acceptance of peaceful protests or respect of national sovereignty). Economic means are characterized by ways of influencing the flow of goods, services and currencies (this may include sanctions on one end of the spectrum as well as preferential trade agreements and economic aid at the other end). Thirdly, practical diplomatic engagement is a useful means for exercising power, e.g. by negotiation or provision of valuable information. Finally, military means encompass the use – or threat of use – of military force. For good reason, this component has gained the most attention by writers on power in the international realm. Additionally, it is key for understanding the Sino-American competition in Asia-Pacific and the region's security affairs. The ability to apply as well as to resist military force – especially under the current semi-anarchic international system – continues to be the *ultima ratio* of international politics (Gelb 2009: 163; Carr 1964: 109).

However, as shown above, it is important not to equate a nation's military forces with its military power. Power only comes from influence and therefore capacities have to be seen on an issue-to-issue basis to gain that influence. Being able to field troops equipped with sophisticated weaponry is barely half of the story; what matters more is being able to use ones' military means to change the other side's behaviour. This is the lesson Washington had to learn in Vietnam, the experience

[11] Interestingly, Waltz also acknowledges this. Despite dismissing the relational concept of power, he agrees that "the stronger get their way – not always, but more often than the weaker" (1993: 169). Surprisingly, this closely reflects – unintentionally? – a position of Immanuel Wallerstein, who held some years before Waltz that "the stronger 'get their way' more frequently than the weaker" (1986: 331).

Moscow made in Afghanistan and the task with which the world's largest military alliance is currently struggling with in the exact same country. Additionally, what is valuable within a certain domain and scope can be less useful in another theatre and different issue-area. For instance, armed forces designed to fight a conventional large-scale military conflict in middle Europe may prove less capable of defeating Islamic warlords in Somalia or Mujahedeen across the Hindu Kush – and vice versa. And military troops are likewise not very useful in negotiations on international climate change cooperation, currency issues or debt relief programs. Power in politics is simply much less fungible than e.g. money in everyday economics. Actor A equipped with conventional military means can thus be more or less powerful – depending on the concrete issue area and B's attributes.

Ranking of States

Considering the importance of the relational aspect of power, it becomes clear that hierarchies of states face some difficulties.[12] Scholars have nevertheless tried to rank powers from lowest to highest, labelling some nations as great powers and other as middle or minor ones (see Fig. 1.2).

Usually, hierarchies follow the power-as-resources understanding and base their grading on material (and sometimes also non-material) attributes of states.[13] Such an approach is plausible as it allows for a putative 'objective' measurement of national power. Critics have rightly noted, however, that this approach threatens to be a "lump concept of power which assumes that all elements of power can be combined into one general indicator" (Guzzini 2000: 55). Additionally, as shown above, the fundamental problem remains: How to compare (and combine) the

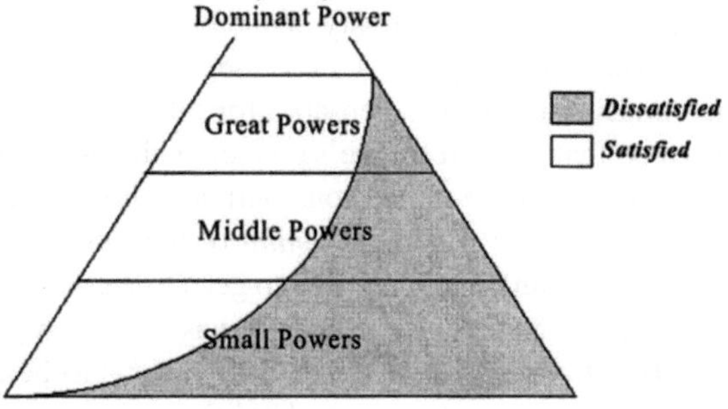

Fig. 1.2 Example of a hierarchisation of states according to their accredited power (Kugler and Tammen 2004) (It is of course possible that there is more than just one dominant power at the top of a hierarchy)

[12] A comprehensive theoretical discussion of hierarchy is presented by Lake 2009. See Scholvin (2011) for a valuable overview of current hierarchisation models.

[13] See for instance Cline 1977; Tellis et al. 2000; Virmani 2005; Merrit and Zinnes 1989; Taber 1989; Kugler and Arbetman 1989; Noya 2005; Nolte 2006; Casetti 2003.

power *relations* among different actors? In this context, Dahl noted, that "it is difficult enough to estimate relative influence within a particular scope and domain; it is by no means clear how we can 'add up' influence over many scopes and domains in order to arrive at total, or aggregated, influence" (1991: 27). Thus, indices, which treat power only as those resources a national government has command of, obviously do not present the whole picture.

On the other hand, measuring power in relational terms is not only more complex but seems to be less feasible for analytic enquiry. Proponents of the relational power approach rightly stress that political outcomes are the key to identifying power relations. Baldwin, for instance, holds that in order to measure the power of A (domain) over B within a certain issue area (scope) one has to look at seven aspects: "(1) the probability of B's compliance; (2) the speed with which B complies; (3) the number of issues include [...]; (4) the magnitude of positive or negative sanctions provided by A; (5) the costs to A; (6) the costs to B; and (7) the number of options available to B" (2000: 181). Obviously, such a meticulous relational approach is hard to apply for making general statements on international politics (see Keohane 1986: 187). With regard to regional security, how can IR scholars possibly add up the political outcomes of every political interaction between states in a certain region in order to get a general understanding of the region's power distribution (and rank states accordingly) when it comes to security affairs?

There is, of course, a solution to this. Critics of a power-as-resource approach have – for good reason – pointed to the fact that "what constitutes a 'good hand' in card games depends on whether one is playing poker or bridge" (Baldwin 2000: 179). However, even with a relational understanding of power, it is still very useful to take into account the tangible and intangible resources of states, simply because in the international arena states – or better: their governments – cannot only play several card games at once, but (even more important) also *know* which of these card games are more significant to them than others. Dismissing resources and taking a minimalist 'policy-contingency approach'[14] would mean to neglect the obvious differences between nations and their resource basis as well as losing the academic ability to reduce reality's complexity to some extent for the sake of a greater analytical understanding of general processes and relations. Power resources *are* the raw materials that are indispensable for later power relationships. Thus, while keeping in mind that every resource's de facto value for gaining power (by using or not using it) depends on the dimensions outlined above, it is useful to roughly classify states according to the general *potential* of their resources identified to be relevant in the respective 'card game' in order to get a first good grasp of a region's affairs. As White has noted: "No country in history has exercised great power without great wealth" (2010: 19). Indeed, historically there seems to be a causal relationship between the quantity of some resources and political outcomes in certain international issue-areas such as military and security affairs (see Mearsheimer 2001: 55–67).

[14] This captious approach would basically mean to judge power relations on a case-by-case basis without being able to interconnect the various cases. See Sprout and Sprout 1965.

Great Powers in the Regional Power Hierarchy

With regard to Asia-Pacific's security 'card game', this means first to have a look at the distribution of resources understood to be relevant for the provision of national (and regional) security. Subsequently, regional states in Asia-Pacific can then be ranked into three categories: great, middle and small powers. Labelling some states as great powers has a long tradition (see Buzan and Waever 2008: 33f). Additionally, most writing in IR has been concentrated on the influence of great powers and superpowers (see Danilovic 2002). It is important to distinguish between both types: While the first have great weight in many scopes in their regional domain, the latter are also able to continuously influence other regions as well. The category of superpower thus only seems to be useful for a global perspective and will not further be considered here.[15] In the field of security, great powers are largely identified by their conventional military capabilities. Among many other authors, Mearsheimer has noted that in order "to qualify as a great power a state must have sufficient military assets to put up a serious fight in an all-out conventional war" (2001: 4). Additionally, he emphasises the need for great powers to have a nuclear deterrent in order to prevent nuclear blackmailing by other actors (ibid.). Obviously, his understanding clearly takes into account relational effects of military resources. A power-as-resources ranking of great powers would therefore identify five great powers in Asia-Pacific: the US, China, Russia, India and Japan (see Fig. 1.3).

Yet, a relational understanding of power demands some important changes to that list of five great powers. Looking at Beijing's and Washington's influence in regional security relations makes clear that both have to be attributed great power status. For the other three, such a ranking is not that easy. Considering Russia's political influence in Asia-Pacific, for instance, it is hard to see Russia as a great power in Asian-Pacific security affairs (see Amirov 2010). Russia is much more engaged in Europe and Central Asia – militarily, economically and strategically (Fels 2009; Rozman 2010). Given its status as the world's largest country, Russia has officially been a part of Asia-Pacific since 1689, when it signed the Treaty of Nerchinsk with the Middle Kingdom. However, the shape of the Russian armed forces in this part of the world, the economic (and demographic[16]) development of the Russian Far East (RFE) and – as Russian Premier Vladimir Putin has noted – the "poor links [of the RFE] to the economic, information and transportation network to the rest of Russia" (cited in Nation 2010: 51) raise serious doubts about a Russian great power status in regional security affairs even if one takes a power-as-resources

[15] Currently, there are only one and a half super powers on the global level. The US continues to be able to exercise relevant influence on many issue-areas in all world regions. Within the last two decades, China indeed expanded its ability to change the behaviour of other states especially in the field of economics in many regions such as Africa, Central Asia and South America. It largely replaces the Soviet Union/Russia in this role.

[16] The population of the Russian Far East Federal District has declined to only 6,5 Mio. – as much as Laos or Papua New Guinea (RIA Novosti 2010).

	United States	China	Russia	Japan	India
Total area	9,826,675 km²	9,596,961 km²	17,098,242 km²	377,915 km²	3,287,263 km²
Population (July 2010)[a)]	307,212,123	1,338,612,968	140,041,247	127,078,679	1,156,897,766
GDP (2009)[1)]	US$ 14.26 trillion	US$ 4.909 trillion	US$ 1.255 trillion	US$ 5.068 trillion	US$ 1.236 trillion
Defense budget (2009)	US$ 693.6 billion	US$ 70.3 billion[b)]	US$ 41.05 billion	US$ 52.6 billion	US$ 35.88 billion
Arms export[c)] (2009)	US$ 6,795 million	US$ 870 million	US$ 4,469 million	–	US$ 22 million
Soldiers (2009)	1,580,255	2,285,000	1,027,000	230,300	1,325,000
Nuclear forces operational/ total inventory	2,468 / 9,600	~180 / 240	4,650 / 12,000	virtual capability	n.a. / 60 – 80
ICBM[d)]	Minuteman III (13,000 km)	DF-5A (13,000 km)	Satan (16,000 km)	virtual capability	Agni-V (5,000 km, in development)
Aircraft carriers	11	program + renovation of former Soviet Kuznetsov class aircraft carrier	1	1 (helicopter carrier)	1

Central Intelligence Agency 2010a-e; IISS 2010: 31, 33, 222, 225, 359, 361, 398-399, 408-409; Federation of American Scientists 2010; SIPRI 2010.
a) Estimate.
b) Official defense budget at market exchange rates
c) Figures are SIPRI trend indicator values (TIVs) expressed in US$ millions at constant (1990) prices
d) Example

Fig. 1.3 Power-as-resources ranking of probable great powers in Asia-Pacific (Wagener 2010: 6)

approach. This does not mean to dismiss Russia's regional abilities entirely – but one should not overstate them either. Moscow simply cannot successfully engage in a major confrontation with China or the US in Asia-Pacific, rather, its economical and technological resources[17] gives Moscow the "role of a spoiler" (Nation 2010: 50) in some regional security relations such as the Korean question – something that is important to keep in mind for other regional actors, but not sufficiently for Russia to be ranked at the regional top. Additionally, due to the RFE's internal problems it is very likely that even in the next one or two decades Russia cannot influence other actors in regional military affairs more that it can now. On the contrary. Given its

[17] Arms and energy deals rather than pro-active and resourceful diplomatic activities will continue to be the main expression of Moscow's regional engagement.

situation, Moscow "will remain a second tier player" (Ibid.: 53) in Asia Pacific's post-Cold War security environment for many years to come.

Japan is another example of the importance of a relational understanding of power. Despite having the necessary military resources identified to be relevant for security relations, Tokyo has not acted as a great power in the security domain since losing World War II (see Maull 1990; Samuels 2007; Aoi 2004). Ever since then Japan has exercised an impressive restraint in the field of security (in stark contrast to its behaviour in regional and global economics). It is certainly true that Japan has developed capable armed forces regardless of Article IX of its constitution. However, by taking a relational understanding of power, it becomes obvious that Tokyo has not only aligned itself very closely with Washington, but has – so far – shown an extremely strong reluctance to take on a more assertive role in regional security affairs as well and acted more like a much smaller state (Hatch 2009). Thus, considering Japanese behaviour towards the field of security, Japan should – despite being an economic giant – currently not be placed at the top of the regional security hierarchy (see also Yoshihide 2009).

India, finally, is a more tricky case. In the past, New Delhi has barely been involved in Asian-Pacific security affairs, but was concerned with internal challenges and its relationships with Islamabad and Beijing. This, however, has changed considerably within the last decade. After its economic integration with Asia-Pacific, New Delhi has – with some delay – not only acquired quite impressive military capabilities, but has also begun to become strategically more committed to the region (Fels 2011b). This change of mind can be exemplified by joint statements regarding strategic cooperation with Japan (December 2006, October 2010) or Indian participation in the Malabar naval exercises since 2003. Of course, Pakistan and China, two important Indian neighbours, still capture most of New Delhi's attention. Nevertheless, India has not only developed a much more self-confident approach towards Asian-Pacific security affairs in recent years, but also its traditional sphere of influence – the Indian Ocean – is gaining more importance due to rising energy dependence of countries in Asia Pacific (see Cook et al. 2010: 31). All in all, this allows India to be considered in the top tier.

Identifying Middle Powers in Asia-Pacific

Middle powers have been significantly less studied in IR than great powers and their relations. In fact, the concentration of mainstream literature in the field of security on great powers has led to an almost general dismissing of the role that other states in international relations play; non-great powers are and were mostly considered to be part of 'the rest'. Such thinking, however, not only neglects important aspects of the relational understanding of power, but also dismisses essential components of the international system itself. As one scholar argues, "a different approach to theory development, such as that illustrated by middle-power theory, might lead us to theories [...] that actually reflect reality in its greater complexity" (Neack 1995: 227). Additionally, for a relational understanding of power it is particularly important to concentrate on middle powers for assessing power relationships (and power shifts) as competing great powers often seek support from middle powers in their quest for regional influence (Wight 1978: 50–52, 63–65).

Only few scholars have paid attention to middle powers (or second-tier countries, as they have sometimes been called) within the last decades. One of them, Carsten Holbraad, argues that "given that the existing state system, in common with many earlier systems of modern history, contains a substantial number of units which obviously are neither great nor small states, a study of the role of middle-sized powers seems a natural complement of the traditional concern with great powers" (Holbraad 1984: 3). Interestingly, in his extensive work on the topic, Holbraad also shows that notable authors like Thomas Aquinas (1225–1274), Bartolus de Saxoferrato (1313–1357), Giovanni Botero (1544–1617), Gabriel Bonnot de Mably (1709–1785), Adam H. D. von Bülow (1757–1807), Carl von Clausewitz (1780–1831), Hans Christian Ernst von Gagern (1766–1852), Friedrich Ludwig Lindner (1772–1845) and Heinrich von Treitschke (1834–1896) were in one way or another concerned with the role of second-ranked powers in international affairs (Ibid.: 10–45). Summing up their different findings and ideas, Holbraad concludes that in history, though middle powers were largely understood as materially less well-equipped than great powers, they were nevertheless viewed as defenders of the balance of power as well as providers of peace and order (Ibid.: 41). He furthermore outlines that accrediting middle powers with an international legal status of their own (comparable to that of great powers) was attempted by second-ranked powers during the Congress of Vienna, the German Customs Union (*Zollverein*), the Versailles Peace Conference, the League of Nations as well as in the United Nations (Ibid.: 45–66). From time to time middle powers were successful in gaining special recognition (such as in the League of Nations), mostly, however, they failed in light of the fierce resistance by the primary powers (and even the smaller ones, too).

Within the last decades, a couple of definitions of "secondary regional powers" (Huntington 1999: 47) have been suggested in order to characterise middle powers' role in international relations. Following Chapnick (1999) one can sort the various approaches towards these second-ranked powers into three basic understandings: the *hierarchical*, *functional*, and *behavioural* model. To begin with, the *hierarchical* understanding of middle powers in the literature closely resembles the notion of historic writers on this group of states. Holbraad summarizes that "middle power, or its synonyms, has been a relational concept, in the sense that it has been defined or described with reference to other classes of the system, especially that of the principal powers" (Holbraad 1984: 42). Others add that these historic authors on the subject "saw a hierarchical, stratified international system in which objective capability, asserted position, and recognized status combined to produce three classes of states" (Dewitt and Kirton 1983: 22) – great, middle and small powers. The problem with such an understanding is that it basically equates status with material capabilities – the same misleading notion as the power-as-resources understanding. It is, however, useful in pointing out that some states below the great powers are equipped with sufficiently more material and immaterial capabilities than smaller states – which in turn allow them to act more self-sufficient in the international arena than the smaller ones.

The *functional* model rests on the assumption that middle powers perform – just like great powers – special functions in international relations due to their material capabilities and political willingness to engage in the international arena. In this regard, Gelber (1946) observed that "since major powers are differentiated by their greater functions from the rest, the Middle Powers [sic] ask that they be distinguished from the lesser ones by the same criteria". The functional approach towards second-tier states dates back to Canadian diplomat Hume Wrong, who based his understanding on three 'functional criteria': the extent of a state's involvement in an issue, its interests, and its ability to contribute to the situation in question (cited in Chapnick 1999: 74). Later authors added that "informally, middle powers have often come to assume such responsibilities, and to gain special influence in functional areas where their interests have appeared strongest" (Wood 1988: 4). Unfortunately, with the exception of Hume Wrong, no other author specified the functions they attributed to middle powers. Wrong's understanding, however, has certain strength as it outlines the importance of those states other than great powers that also have capabilities to influence relations among states in some issue-areas and in specific situations. In turn, this perspective also includes a relational understanding of power.

The *behavioural* model links middle power status to a variety of specific behaviours in international affairs. According to Andrew Cooper and his colleagues, second-tier states can best be identified by "their tendency to pursue multilateral solutions to international problems, their tendency to embrace compromise positions in international disputes, and their tendency to embrace notions of 'good international citizenship' to guide their diplomacy" (1993: 19). Other authors have defined middle power behaviour as that of conflict managers, moral powers and status seekers (Wood 1988: 19f).[18] Robert Keohane added that a middle power is "a state whose leaders consider that it cannot act alone effectively, but may be able to have a systemic impact in a small group or through an international institution" (1969: 296). Robert Cox observed that second-tier states are committed to "orderliness and security in interstate relations and to the facilitation of orderly change in the world system" (Cox 1989: 826). Such a strategic behaviour was understood to be essential to their national interest (Pratt 1990: 151). It was furthermore seen as a way to avoid being totally dominated by great powers (Glazebrook 1947). Interestingly, a behavioural understanding of middle powers was sometimes combined with a functional one (see for instance Lyon and Tomlin

[18] This is quite closely related to a functional understanding of middle powers.

1979: 12f). Indeed, as both strands emphasise the need to look at the foreign policies of those countries understood to be middle powers, they seem rather close. However, a general problem of this third approach is that the (normative) behavioural characteristics identified as relevant for middle power status vary through the literature.[19]

A useful behavioural understanding is presented by Nolte (2007), who refers to 'leadership' (understood as relevant political influence in diplomatic fora) as a behaviour that middle powers can exercise on some issues despite being less well-equipped with resources than great powers.[20] Additionally, with regard to security issues, another behavioural ability was claimed to be important. As Hugh White rightly emphasises, in the field of security it comes down to the ability of a middle power not to necessarily win against a great power in an all-out war, but to considerably raise the costs and risks for great powers to engage in such a military engagement (2010: 68). He furthermore holds that "middle powers can influence what happens around them so as to protect their interest. They can negotiate with great powers, not simply obey them" (Ibid.: 67). Both components allow for being combined with a relational power approach towards second-tier states.

After reviewing these three different strands in the literature on middle powers, it is possible to define middle powers according to the strengths and weaknesses of the different concepts and combine it with a relational understanding of power. First, just like great powers middle powers also must have sufficient control over material (and non-material) resources. Secondly, middle powers must be willing to exercise some form of responsibility in regional affairs, e.g. by successfully taking a diplomatic lead on some important issue areas or using their means to shape other nations' behaviour in order to contribute to regional stability. Finally, with regard to security and related to the first point, a middle power must be militarily self-sufficient enough to inflict great costs even on a major state attacking it. Interestingly, these three criteria come very close to a definition of second-tier states suggested by R.G. Riddell more than 60 years ago. He recommended that in order to identify states as middle powers one has to compare "their size, their material resources, their willingness and ability to accept responsibility, their influence and their stability" (1984: 68f) to other international actors. Following the first criteria allows for a first portrayal of plausible second-tier states in Asia-Pacific (see Fig. 1.4).

Of course, only an in-depth analysis of the countries' specific behaviour can show whether all of these states can, first, indeed be considered middle powers in

[19] In this regard, Chapnick rightly notes that the behavioural approach risks being tautological when scholars set up a list of behavioural characteristics taken from likely middle powers such as Canada and use these characteristics to subsequently identify Canada as a middle power. See Chapnick 1999: 76. However, deducting behavioural features from a group of states is possible as long as no small n-design is used for deducing these features in the first place, a test group is included and, most importantly, the states under examination were not grouped together by indicators which were designed to identify relevant states a priori as the relevant group to look at.

[20] On 'leadership' as a tool for measuring power see also Schirm's contribution in Chap. 12 in this volume.

	South Korea	Australia	Indonesia	Malaysia	Thailand	VietNam
Total area	99,720 km^2	7,741,220 km^2	1,904,569 km^2	329,847 km^2	513,120 km^2	331,210 km^2
Population[a)]	48,754,657	21,766,711	245,613,043	28,728,607	66,720,153	90,549,390
GDP (2010), PPP, bio US $[b)]	1,467	889.6	1,033	416.4	580.3	278.1
GDP (2010), exchange rate, bio US $[b)]	986.3	1,220	695.1	219	312.6	102
Defence budget bio US $ 2010	25.4	24.5	4.47	2.81	4.81	2.41
Capabilities active (reserve)	655,000 (4,500,000)	56,552 (20,440)	302,000 (400,000)	109,000 (51,600)	305,860 (200,000)	482,000 (5,000,000)
Nuclear forces or ability for entire nuclear fuel cycle	Yes	No	No	No	No	No
ICBM	–	–	–	–	–	–
Aircraft carriers	1 helicopter carrier	2 helicopter carriers planned	–	–	1 helicopter carrier	–

CIA World Factbook 2011; IISS 2010: 195–292; IAEA 2011; Republic of Korea Navy 2011; Royal Australian Navy 2011; Royal Malaysian Navy 2011; www.naval-techonology.com 2011.
a) Estimate for July 2011
b) Estimate

Fig. 1.4 Power-as-resources listing of likely middle powers in Asia-Pacific (Fels 2011a)

regional security affairs and, secondly, in combination with a relational understanding of power highlight, whether there is a power shift taking place between China and the US. What such a relational power analysis may look like is subsequently exemplified by taking a closer look at Australia as a case study.

Australia and the Case for Middle Power Allegiance

By looking at the three criteria set out above, Australia is a middle power *par excellence*. Australia's resources are a good starting point. Australia has managed to run one of the most productive economies – not only by regional but also by global standards (e.g. IMF 2011: 172). Additionally, it has one of the world's best education systems and was ranked first in the 2010 United Nation's Human Development Index out of 172 countries (UN 2011). Furthermore, the Australian continent is extremely rich in natural resources such as coal (biggest exporter, fourth largest global reserves), iron ore (second largest producer), nickel (largest reserves, second largest producer), zinc (third largest producer), gold (second largest producer) and uranium (third largest producer, largest world reserves). Its wealth of important minerals relevant for high- and low-tech industries makes Australia an important trading partner also for many nations outside of Asia-Pacific.

Secondly, within the last decades, Australia has been very active in regional and global diplomacy and for instance took a lead in the establishment of some regional and global institutions. The most notable achievements in this area are probably the *Cairns Group* (which brings together 19 agricultural exporting countries and was quite successful in the past in WTO trade negotiations), the Australia Group (which fights the spread of biological and chemical weapons) and the *Asia-Pacific Economic Cooperation* (APEC). Thus, Canberra has traditionally pursued a very active regional diplomacy. Combined with the size of its economy this is one of the major reasons for Australia being included in the G20.

Regarding the third criterion, the Australian Defence Force (ADF) is certainly a capable security actor equipped with modern weapon systems. In terms of personnel size the ADF may be smaller than the armed forces of most other regional actors. However, considering the ADF's advanced weapons technologies (and the force multiplication they provide), the ratio of soldiers to the countries overall population is comparable to modern European armies. Over the last decades, Australia has maintained a capable navy, air force and army (IISS 2010: 394ff). Currently, Canberra has the 14th largest defence budget in the world and is actively involved with 3,300 soldiers in various military operations in other countries. With regard to an attack by a great power, also other factors beyond defence spending and operational readiness are relevant. Most importantly, Australia's geographic location works in its favour. While it is necessary to note that defending a whole continent is a difficult task for every armed forces with the size of the ADF, it is even more important to realize that Australia in operational terms 'only' has to defend its northern approaches while any would-be attacker actually needs to control them – a much more difficult task to achieve (White 2010: 68). Every major power willing to attack the Australian continent needs to overcome this so-called 'air-sea-gap', meaning that Australia can use a strategy of denial (not unlike the one China currently employs towards the US), layered defence and self-reliance to ensure its own security (Dibb 1986). Additionally, Australia is geographically distant from the three regional great powers India, China and the US – the lines of supply of any attacking nation would be very long and vulnerable to Australian countermeasures. Taking all three criteria into account, Australia thus qualifies a middle power.

Australia Between China and the US

As has been mentioned above, China has managed to increase its economic standing in most Asian-Pacific countries. This trend is very likely to continue and China is set to be the most important trading partner to every single nation in the Western Pacific by 2020 (Drydale 2010a). Its economic growth is considered the key driver of a perceived power shift in regional and global affairs, a development largely seen in China's favour. Some authors summed up this logic very aptly: "As China rises in most facets of national power, the United States' relative power will

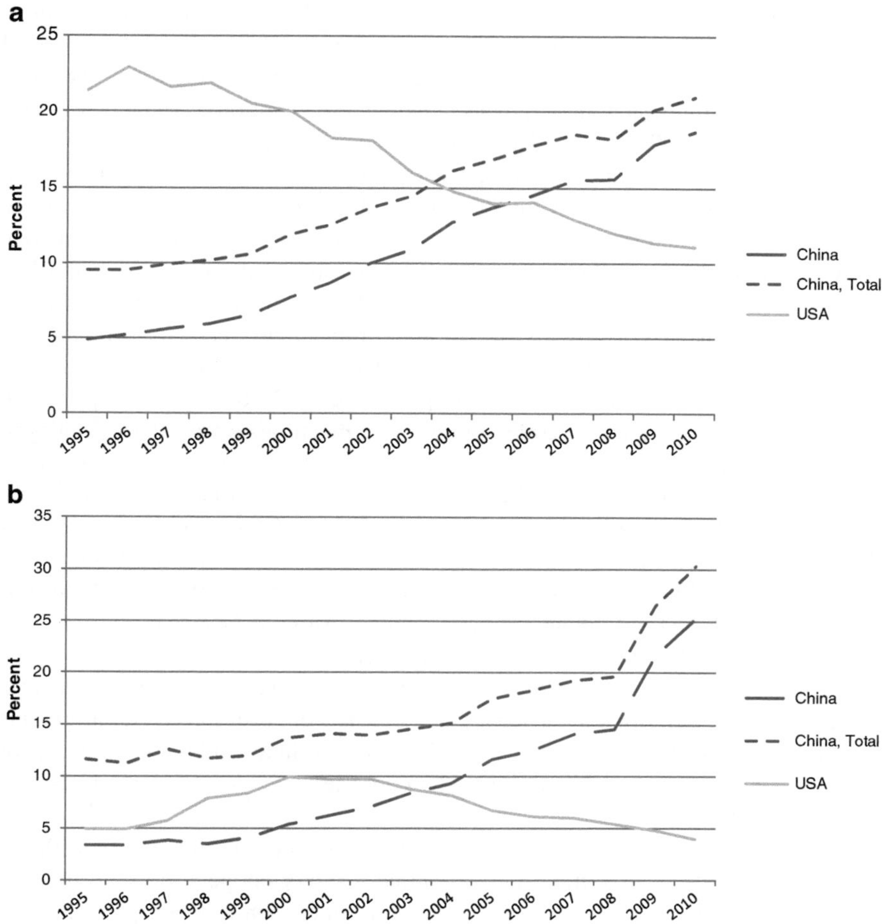

Fig. 1.5 (**a**) Import share of China (mainland), China (total incl. HK & Macao) and US to Australia (data obtained from: UNCTADstat.org 2011). (**b**) Share of Australia's exports to China (mainland), China (incl. HK & Macao) and the US (data obtained from: UNCTADstat. org 2011)

naturally decline, and over time even US alliance partners in Asia will seek to become more autonomous from the United States and develop strong ties across the board with China" (Cook et al. 2010: 15). With regard to Australia, China overtook the United States as Australia's most important trading partner in 2004 and gained a strong footing in the Australian economy (see Fig. 1.5a,b). In fact, "Australia is profiting strongly from China's economic boom, probably more than almost all other Western states" (Schörnig 2010: 8).

Interestingly, however, China has failed to gain influence in Australia on security affairs. Quite the opposite, Canberra has strengthened its security ties with Washington despite Beijing's increasing importance to Australia's economy.

Its allegiance towards Washington did not change. Although China's resources in various fields grew a great deal, Beijing was – from a relational understanding of power – not able to wield power over Australia in the field of security (i.e. to change Australian security behaviour with respect to Chinese intentions). To be precise, for a brief moment in 2004, it looked as if China indeed had gained some security clout in Australia when Alexander Downer, Australia's then-foreign minister, mentioned shortly after a meeting with Chinese leaders that there would be no automatic Australian military support to the US in a conflict between China and Taiwan. Downer's remarks faced huge criticism within Australia as well as from the US. Shortly afterwards, then-prime minister John Howard made clear that Australia would stick to the ANZUS treaty (the military alliance between Australia and the US), Downer distanced himself from his remarks and felt misquoted. According to cables from the US embassy in Canberra published by Wikileaks, then-opposition leader Kim Beazley stated in 2006 not only that the alliance with the US enjoyed broad bipartisan support, but also that "in the event of a war between the United States and China, Australia would have absolutely no alternative but to line up militarily beside the U.S." (cited in Wikileaks 2011a). Other cables revealed that then-prime minister Kevin Rudd floated the idea of an Asia Pacific Community (APC) in early 2009 "mostly as an effort to ensure Chinese dominance of the East Asia Summit (EAS) did not result in a 'Chinese Monroe Doctrine' and an Asia without the United States" (cited in Wikileaks 2011b).

Apart from the Downer incident 2004, Australia thus seeks to maintain its close allegiance to the US. Looking at security-related acts of Australia can highlight this as well. In terms of arms purchases, Washington continues to be *the* single major weapons supplier to the ADF (followed by countries also closely aligned with the US; see Fig. 1.6).

Aside from buying American arms and thus ensuring interoperability with US forces, Canberra has also intensified its actual military cooperation with the US. Since 2005, both countries have participated in more than a dozen joint military operations ranging from large-scale naval exercises like *RIMPAC* to smaller field combat trainings such as *Talisman Saber*. In addition to maintaining its military cooperation with the US, Canberra also began to internally balance against China's rise, i.e. by laying out a strategic framework to ensure national security for potential cases in which the US might not be able to come to its direct aid or in case of a future US retrenchment (Australian Government 2009; Kelly 2010). In fact, China's future military capabilities are already seen as a rising challenge to Australian sovereignty (Babbage 2011: vii). New weapon systems to be acquired for the ADF serve the double task of ensuring interoperability as well as self-reliance. Obviously, instead of bandwagoning with a rising China in security affairs, Australia is committed to both sticking with its old US ally and preparing for times when the US, e.g. due to its financial problems, may not be able to act as a powerful partner. In this context, Australia has also begun to strengthen its security ties with other regional (middle) powers such as Indonesia, South Korea and Japan.

There are four main reasons why Beijing was not able to weaken Canberra's allegiance towards Washington in the last years. Firstly, following a relational

	'95	'96	'97	'98	'99	'00	'01	'02	'03	'04	'05	'06	'07	'08	'09	*Total*
Canada	85	21				40		1	27	37	18					229
France		20		20	15		35	5	20	28	56	64	55	90	113	519
Germany		236		236			236	236	236	236	236	238	5	25	23	1,939
Israel								15	13	13	5	18	19		30	112
Italy					110	55	55	110								330
Norway							17	24	23							63
Japan												30				30
Sweden		247		247	240		487	7	251	11	11	11	4			1,517
UK		6				63	279	111	31	17	8					514
US	64	52		21	268	206	83	138	198	164	138	322	547	266	592	3,084

Figures may not add up due to conventions of rounding. Source: SIPRI Arms Tranfers Database 2011.

Fig. 1.6 Arms exports measured in SIPRI Trend Indicator Values (TIVs) to Australia, 1995–2009 (in US$ in 1990 constant prices) (TIVs do not represent the financial value of military goods transferred, but are an indication of the volume of arms transferred. Hence, TIVs can be used to measure trends in international arms transfers, such as changes in the total flow of weapons and the geographic pattern of arms exports or imports. See SIPRI 2011)

understanding of power as well as reflecting the role of middle powers in international relations, Canberra has sufficient military potential to raise the costs for Beijing if the latter attempts to change Australian behaviour in the field of security by force. Thus, great powers in the region have to convince Canberra that closer cooperation in the field of security is in Australian interests – or be willing to commit a high amount of military resources in subduing Canberra. As Joseph Nye and Edward H. Carr have rightly noted, in a relational context also the ability to get other actors "to want what you want" (Nye 1990b: 167f) and the "power over opinion" (Carr 1964: 108) are important facets of power (and affect the dimension of reliability). In this context, it clearly works in America's favour that the ties between the US and Australia have evolved over a very long time (2011 marked the 60th anniversary of the ANZUS treaty) and are backed by both nations' Anglo-Saxon roots and shared liberal political values. Such traditional bounds are hard to change and provide a good basis for US 'soft power' over Australia. As one scholar notes: "Even baby steps away from the alliance will meet powerful political and ideological resistance" (Heinrichs 2011).

Secondly, security cooperation with the US offers Australia benefits that China can hardly substitute – changing its allegiance from Washington to Beijing would be very costly for Canberra. The benefits Australia gains by its allegiance towards the US range from access to high technology (e.g. the advanced Aegis combat system) and sensitive intelligence (especially via the UKUSA Community ('Echelon')) to America's extended nuclear deterrence. Despite the Chinese advancements in the fields of military technology and intelligence gathering in recent years, Canberra cannot be sure about possible gains from closer security cooperation with China.[21] Neither has China shown willingness to share vital intelligence with other countries, nor could Australia trust that Chinese military technology and intelligence would match accustomed US quality. Accordingly, Australia would face high opportunity costs if it were not to cooperate with the US.

Thirdly, Washington has changed its security attitude towards regional actors quite a bit and has become less bilateral than during the Cold War. While the US 'hub-and-spoke system' continues to be Washington's main security framework in the region, the US promoted security multi- and mini-lateralism in Asia-Pacific and is pursuing an "enhanced bilateralism" (Cook et al. 2010: 30) by interconnecting the 'spokes'. As a middle power with an active regional diplomacy, this works in Australia's favour. Washington's new stance can be highlighted by the US' push for a stronger role of APEC in regional security affairs, the establishment of the *Trilateral Coordination and Oversight Group*, which deepens the relations between Japan and South Korea, or the *Trilateral Strategic Dialogue* between Tokyo, Washington and Canberra. (Of course, this also allows Washington to ensure some stronger burden sharing in its current alliance system.)

Finally, as outlined above, Australia has strongly benefitted in the past from US security engagement in the region and Australian-American security cooperation. In this context it is unclear to Canberra and other regional middle powers whether a stronger China would also act as benevolently as the US. Recent incidents with Japan, where Beijing used its economic power to change Toyko's behaviour, cast some doubts about Beijing's future intentions. This notion is also fuelled by an increasingly harder stance from China in territorial disputes in the South China Sea. China's new assertiveness is furthermore one of the major reasons why Canberra invited Washington in November 2011 to set up a new military base in Darwin.

In sum, Australian behaviour in the field of security follows the logic of a relational understanding of power: *A* (China) faces higher costs when trying to subdue *B* (Australia) due to *B's* relatively sophisticated military capabilities as a regional middle power. Next to raising the costs for *A* in their mutual interaction, *B* also faces high opportunity costs when giving in to the demand of *A* in this particular scope (security) due to the attractive outside-option of continue cooperating with *C* (the US). Additionally, *B* is not willing to become too dependent on *C*, so it continues to increase its own military abilities. Whether this has decreased the actual reliability of *B* towards *C* remains to be seen.

[21] Apart from establishing a security dialogue and some minor military-to-military relations.

Conclusion

The discussion on power in international affairs has shown that a relational understanding of power is important in order to differentiate between a rise in resources with a rise in actual power. With regards to the evaluation of international power as well as power shifts, statistics obviously only provide half of the picture. As outlined on a theoretical level, scholars need to look at the allegiance of middle powers in specific fields in order to fully capture possible power shifts among great powers. Analysing the allegiance of this class of states seems to be useful as they have sufficient capabilities to act as 'swing states' in specific scopes such as security affairs in times of great power rivalry – something that is altering the regional balance of power in favour of one great power or another.

The chapter's empirical part identified Australia as such a middle power. Furthermore, the analysis of Canberra's relations to Beijing and Washington showed that China's economic development and rise in military resources could not be transferred by Beijing into an ability to influence Australia in the field of security. This, of course, does not mean that China's economic resources will play no role in Beijing's security relations with Australia and other regional middle powers or their strategic planning. Like many other regional states Australia certainly tries to have both – good economic relations with China and strong security ties with the US. However, when the chips are down, it is very likely going to be Washington, which can rely on Australian allegiance. Considering the data provided, Canberra (and probably other middle powers as well) is – even if the Middle Kingdom tries to exercise economic power for security purposes – likely going to stick with its allegiance to the US as a source of various strategic and security-related benefits as well as an extra-regional counterweight to a China that grows economically and militarily.

Thus, as long as the great powers in Asia-Pacific do not manage to establish a concert between each other (which would be a considerable setback for the diplomatic influence of second-tier countries), middle power behaviour will be an important indicator for the de facto influence of great powers in regional affairs and the distribution of power on various scopes in the system.

References

Abeysinghe, T., & Lu, D. (2003). China as an economic powerhouse: Implications on its neighbors. *China Economic Review, 14*(1), 164–185.

Amirov, V. B. (2010). Russia's posture and policy towards Northeast Asia. In S. Blan (Ed.), *Russia's prospects in Asia* (pp. 1–28). Carlisle: Strategic Studies Institute.

Aoi, C. (2004). Asserting civilian power or risking irrelevance. In S. N. Katada, H. W. Maull, & T. Inoguchi (Eds.), *Global Governance. Germany and Japan in the international system* (pp. 111–126). Aldershot & Burlington: Asgate.

Australian Government. (2009). Defending Australia in the Asia Pacific Century. Force 2030. Defence White Paper, Commonwealth of Australia, 2009. http://www.defence.gov.au/whitepaper/docs/defence_white_paper_2009.pdf

Babbage, R. (2011). Australia's strategic edge in 2030. *Kokoda Papers*, No. 15, February 2011.

Baldwin, D. A. (1985). *Economic statecraft*. Princeton: Princeton University Press.

Baldwin, D. (2000). Power and international relations. In W. Carlsnaes, T. Risse, & B. Simmons (Eds.), *The handbook of international relations* (pp. 177–191). Thousand Oaks: Sage.

Buzan, B., & Waever, O. (2008). *Regions and powers. The structure of international security*. Cambridge: Cambridge University Press.

Campbell, D. (1998). Why fight: Humanitarism, principles, and post-structuralism. *Millenium: Journal of International Studies, 21*, 497–521.

Carr, E. H. (1964). *The twenty years' crisis, 1919–1939. An introduction to the study of international relations*. New York: Harper and Row.

Casetti, E. (2003). Power shifts and economic development: When will China overtake the USA? *Journal of Peace Research, 40*(6), 661–675.

CGS Forschungsgruppe Wissensmacht. (2011). Sind die BRIC-Staaten aufstrebende Wissensmächte? Herausforderungen für die deutsche Wissenspolitik. *CGS-Discussion Paper*, No. 3, January 2011. http://www.cgs-bonn.de/pdf/DP-3_BRIC_Wissensmacht_Final.pdf

Chapnick, A. (1999). The middle power. *Canadian Foreign Policy, 7*(2), 73–82.

Chase-Dunn, C. (1989). *Global formation: Structures of the world-economy*. Oxford: Blackwell.

Christensen, C. (1978). Structural power and national security. In K. Knorr & F. N. Trager (Eds.), *Economic issues and national security*. Lawrence: Regents Press of Kansas.

Christensen, T. J. (2006). Fostering stability of creating a monster? The rise of China and U.S. policy toward East Asia. *International Security, 31*(1), 81–126.

Clegg, S. R. (1994). *Frameworks of power*. London: Sage.

Cline, R. S. (1977). *World power assessment. A calculus of strategic drift*. Boulder: Westview.

Clinton, H. R. (2010). Speech of US Secretary of State at Honolulu, 28th Oct 2010. http://www.state.gov/secretary/rm/2010/10/150141.htm

Cook, M., et al. (2010). Power and choice: Asian security futures. Report of the Lowy Institute for International Policy, 2010. http://lowyinstitute.org/Publication.asp?pid=1306

Cooper, A. F., Higgott, R. A., & Nossal, K. R. (1993). *Relocating middle powers: Australia and Canada in a changing world order*. Vancouver: UBS.

Cox, R. W. (1989). Middlepowermanship, Japan, and the future world order. *International Journal, 44*(4), 822–862.

Dahl, R. A. (1957). The concept of power. *Behavioral Science, 2*(3), 201–215.

Dahl, R. A. (1991). *Modern political analysis*. Englewood Cliffs: Prentice Hall.

Danilovic, V. (2002). *When the stakes are high*. Ann Arbor: University of Michigan Press.

de Glazebrook, G. T. (1947). The middle powers in the United Nations system. *International Organization, 1*(2), 307–315.

Deng, Y., & Moore, T. G. (2004). China views globalization: Toward a new great-power politics? *The Washington Quarterly, 27*(3), 117–136.

Dewitt, D. B., & Kirton, J. (1983). *Canada as a principal power*. Toronto: Wiley.

Dibb, P. (1986). *Review of Australia's defence capabilities*. Canberra: Australian Government Publishing Service.

Digeser, P. (1992). The fourth face of power. *Journal of Politics, 54*, 977–1007.

Drysdale, P. (2010a). Preparing for the rise and rise of Asia. East Asia Forum, 19th July 2010a. http://www.eastasiaforum.org/2010/07/19/preparing-for-the-rise-and-rise-of-asia-%E2%80%93-weekly-editorial/

Drysdale, P. (2010b). China and Japan in landmark shift in Asian economic power?. East Asia Forum, 6th Sept 2010b. http://www.eastasiaforum.org/2010/09/06/china-and-japan-in-landmark-shift-in-asian-economic-power-weekly-editorial/

Fawn, R. (2009). 'Regions' and their study: Wherefrom, what for and whereto? *Review of International Studies, 35*, 5–34.

Fels, E. (2009). *Assessing Eurasia's powerhouse: An inquiry into the nature of the Shanghai Cooperation Organisation*. Bochum: Winkler.

Fels, E. (2011a). Inde: Entre partenariat et concurrence avec l'Europe. In L.-M. Clouet & A. Marchetti (Eds.), *L'Europe et le monde en 2020. Essai de prospective franco-allemande* (pp. 129–144). Villeneuve d'Ascq: Septentrion.

Fels, E. (2011b). Middle power allegiance and power shift in Asian-Pacific security affairs – the case of Australia. In *Paper presented at 52nd Annual Convention of the International Studies Association*, Montreal (Canada).

Friedberg, A. L. (2005). The future of U.S.-China relations. Is conflict inevitable? *International Security, 30*(2), 7–45.

Gaullier, G., Lemoine, F., & Ünal-Kesenci, D. (2007). China's emergence and the reorganisation of trade flows in Asia. *China Economic Review, 18*(2), 209–243.

Gelb, L. H. (2009). *Power rules. How common sense can rescue American foreign policy*. New York: Harper Collins.

Gelber, L. (1946). Canada's new stature. *Foreign Affairs, 24*(2), 277–289.

Gill, B. (2007). *Rising star – China's new security diplomacy*. Washington, DC: Brookings Institution.

Gilpin, R. (1981). *War and change in world politics*. Cambridge: Cambridge University Press.

Goh, E. (2004). The US-China relationship and Asia-Pacific security: Negotiating change. *Asian Security, 1*(3), 216–244.

Gu, X. (2010). Soft, hard and structural power and global power shift. ZEI discussion paper, No. 198, 2010.

Guizzini, S. (2000). The use and misuse of power analysis in international relations. In R. Palan (Ed.), *Global political economy: Contemporary theories* (pp. 55–67). London: Routledge.

Hatch, T. (2009). Japan, the middle power. Why it's acting like smaller states, Newsweek, 3 rd Oct 2009. http://www.newsweek.com/2009/10/02/japan-the-middle-power.html

Heinrichs, R. (2011). Relying on a great power for defence is foolhardy, Canberra Times, 19th Feb 2011, p. 23.

Holbraad, C. (1984). *Middle powers in international politics*. London: Macmillan.

Huntington, S. (1999). The lonely superpower. *Foreign Affairs, 78*(2), 35–49.

International Institute for Strategic Studies (IISS). (2010). The military balance 2010.

International Monetary Fund (IMF). (2011). *World economic outlook tensions from the two-speed recovery: Unemployment, commodities, and capital flows*. Washington, DC: International Monetary Fund.

Kelly, P. (2010). US debt a threat to security. The Australian, 17th July 2010.

Keohane, R. O. (1969). Liliputians' dilemmas: Small states in international politics. *International Organization, 23*(2), 291–310.

Keohane, R. O. (1986). Theory of world politics: Structural neorealism and beyond. In R. O. Keohane (Ed.), *Neorealism and its critics* (pp. 158–202). New York: Columbia University Press.

Kirk, R. (2009). Speech of US Trade Representative Ambassador at the US-Korea Business Council, 5th November 2009. http://www.america.gov/st/texttrans-english/2009/November/20091106140537xjsnommis0.3027002.html

Krasner, S. (1985). *Structural conflict: The third world against global liberalism*. Berkley: University of California Press.

Kugler, J., & Arbetman, M. (1989). Choosing among measures of power: A review of the empirical record. In R. J. Stoll & M. D. Ward (Eds.), *Power in world politics* (pp. 49–77). Boulder & London: Lynne Rienner.

Kugler, J., & Tammen, R. L. (2004). Regional challenge: China's rise to power. In J. Rolfe (Ed.), *The Asia-Pacific: A region in transition* (pp. 33–53). Honolulu: Asia-Pacific Center for Security Studies.

Lebel, L. (2006). Reflections on power. USER Weekly Research Updates No. 125. Unit for Social Environmental Research, Chiang Mai. http://www.sea-user.org/uweb.php?pg=170

Levin, M. L. (2008). *The next great clash – China and Russia vs. the United States*. Westport (Connecticut)/London: Praeger Security International.
Lukes, S. (2005). *Power: A radical view*. New York: Palgrave Macmillan.
Lyon, P. V., & Tomlin, B. W. (1979). *Canada as an international actor*. Toronto: Macmillan.
Mattern, J. B. (2008). The concept of power and the (un)discipline of International Relations. In C. Reus-Smit & D. Snidal (Eds.), *The Oxford handbook of international relations* (pp. 691–698). Oxford: Oxford University Press.
Maull, H. W. (1990). Germany and Japan: The new civilian powers. *Foreign Affairs, 69*(5), 91–106.
Mayer, M. (2011). Chine: l'affirmation d'une puissance. In L.-M. Clouet & A. Marchetti (Eds.), *L'Europe et le monde en 2020. Essai de prospective franco-allemande* (pp. 129–144). Paris: Septentrion.
Mearsheimer, J. J. (2001). *The tragedy of great power politics*. New York: W.W. Norton.
Medeiros, E. S. (2005). Strategic hedging and the future of Asia-Pacific stability. *The Washington Quarterly, 29*(1), 145–167.
Merrit, R. L., & Zinnes, D. A. (1989). Alternative indexes of national power. In R. J. Stoll & M. D. Ward (Eds.), *Power in world politics* (pp. 11–28). Boulder/London: Lynne Rienner.
Morgenthau, H. J. (1954). *Politics among nations: The struggle for power and peace*. Chicago: University of Chicago Press.
Nation, R. C. (2010). Russia in East Asia: Aspirations and limitations. In S. Blank (Ed.), *Russia's prospects in Asia* (pp. 29–62). Carlisle: Strategic Studies Institute.
National Priorities Project. (2011). Cost of war to the United States. September 2011. http://costofwar.com/en/
Neack, L. (1995). Linking state type with foreign policy behaviour. In L. Neack et al. (Eds.), *Foreign policy analysis: Continuity and change in its second generation*. New Jersey: Prentice Hall.
Nolte, D. (2006). Macht und Machthierarchien in den internationalen Beziehungen. Ein Analysekonzept für die Forschung über regionale Führungsmächte. *Working Paper at the German Institute of Global and Area Studies (GIGA)*, No. 29. http://duei.de/index.php?file=workingpapers.html&folder=publikationen#29
Nolte, D. (2007). How to compare regional powers: Analytical concepts and research topics. In *Paper prepared for delivery at the ECPR Joint Session of Workshops*, Helsinki, 7–12th May 2007.
Noya, J. (2005). The symbolic power of nation. Working Paper at the Real Instituto Elcano de Estudios Internacionales y Estratégicos, No. 35. http://www.realinstitutoelcano.org/wps/portal/rielcano_eng/Content?WCM_GLOBAL_CONTEXT=/elcano/elcano_in/zonas_in/usa-transatlantic+dialogue/dt35-2005
Nye, J. S. (1990a). *Bound to lead: The changing nature of American power*. New York: Basic Books.
Nye, J. S. (1990b). Soft power. *Foreign Policy, 80*, 153–171.
Nye, J. S. (2004). *Soft power: The means to success in world politics*. New York: Public Affairs.
Obama, B. (2009). Speech of US President at Suntory Hall (Tokyo, Japan), 14th November 2009. http://www.whitehouse.gov/the-press-office/remarks-president-barack-obama-suntory-hall
Office of the Secretary of Defence. (2010). Military and security developments involving the People's Republic of China. Annual report to Congress. http://www.defense.gov/pubs/pdfs/2010_CMPR_Final.pdf
Power, J. (2005). The so-called rise of China – Asia's power game. International Herald Tribune, 8 April 2005. http://www.iht.com/articles/2005/04/07/opinion/edpower.php
Pratt, C. (1990). Has middle power internationalism a future? In C. Pratt (Ed.), *Middle power internationalism: The north south dimension*. Kingston and Montreal: McGill-Queen's University Press.
Riddell, R. G. (1948). The Role of Middle Powers in the United Nations, Statements and Speeches, Canadian Department of External Affairs, *48, 40*

RIA N. (2010). Medvedev concerned by falling population numbers in Russia's Far East, news report, 3rd July 2010. http://en.rian.ru/russia/20100703/159674420.html

Ross, R. S. (2006). Balance of power politics and the rise of China: Accommodation and balancing in East Asia. *Security Studies, 15*(3), 355–395.

Rozman, G. (2010). Russian repositioning in Northeast Asia: Putin's impact and current prospects. In S. Blank (Ed.), *Russia's prospects in Asia* (pp. 63–96). Carlisle: Strategic Studies Institute.

Samuels, R. J. (2007). Securing Japan: The current discourse. *The Journal of Japanese Studies, 33*(1), 125–152.

Scholvin, S. (2011). Emerging non-OECD countries: Global shifts in power and geopolitical regionalization. *Economics, Management and Financial Markets, 6*(1), 19–43.

Schörnig, N. (2010). The roo and the dragon. Australia's foreign policy towards China during the Rudd era. PRIF Report, No. 99, Frankfurt/M., 2010. http://www.hsfk.de/Publikationen.9.0.html?&no_cache=1&detail=4230&cHash=f332396cab

Shambaugh, D. (2004/05). China Engages Asia – Reshaping the regional order. *International Security, 29*(3), 64–99.

Shambaugh, D. (Ed.). (2005). *Power shift – China and Asia's new dynamics*. Berkley: University of California Press.

Sprout, H., & Sprout, M. (1965). *The ecological perspective on human affairs: With special reference to international politics*. Princeton: Princeton University.

Stockholm International Peace Research Institute (SIPRI). (2011). Explanation of the TIV tables. www.sipri.org/databases/armstransfers/background/explanations2_default

Strange, S. (1988). *States and markets*. London: Pinter Publishers.

Strange, S. (1989). Toward a theory of transnational empire. In E.-O. Czempiel & J. N. Rosenau (Eds.), *Global changes and theoretical challenges: Approaches for the world politics of the 1990s* (pp. 161–176). Massachusetts/Toronto: Lexington Books.

Taber, C. S. (1989). Power capability indexes in the third world. In R. J. Stoll & M. D. Ward (Eds.), *Power in world politics* (pp. 29–48). Boulder/London: Lynne Rienner.

Tellis, A., et al. (2000). Measuring national power in the postindustrial age. Analyst's handbook. RAND Corporation report. http://www.rand.org/pubs/monograph_reports/MR1110z1.html

Treverton, G. F., Jones, S. G. (2005). Measuring national power. RAND Corporation report. http://www.rand.org/pubs/conf_proceedings/CF215.html

United Nations (UN). (2011). Regional and national trends in the human development index 1970–2010. http://hdr.undp.org/en/data/trends/

US Treasury. (2011). The daily history of the debt results, Result for 2nd September 2011. http://www.treasurydirect.gov/NP/BPDLogin?application=np

Vaughn, B., Morrison, W. M. (2006). China–Southeast Asia relations: Trends, issues, and implications for the United States. Congressional research service report for Congress, 4 April 2006. http://www.fas.org/sgp/crs/row/RL32688.pdf

Virmani, A. (2005). Global power from the 18th to 21st century: Power potential (VIP2), strategic asses & actual power (VIP). In *Working paper at the Indian Council for research on international economic relations*, No. 175, Nov 2005.

Wagener, M. (2010). The US military presence and the future of security partnerships, paper presented at the 5th Berlin Conference on Asian Security (BCAS), organized by Stiftung Wissenschaft und Politik (SWP, Berlin), German Federal Ministry of Defences and Center for Strategic and International Studies (CSIS, Jakarta), Oct 2010, p. 6. http://www.swp-berlin.org/fileadmin/contents/products/projekt_papiere/bcas_wagener101215_ks.pdf

Wagener, M. (2011). Die aufgeschobene Konfrontation: Warum die USA mit China (noch) kooperieren. In *Internationale Politik*, Nr. 2 (pp. 112–119).

Wallerstein, I. (1986). Walter Rodney: The historian as a spokesperson for historical forces. *American Ethnologist, 12*(2), 330–336.

Waltz, K. N. (1979). *Theory of International Politics*. New York: McGraw-Hill.

Waltz, K. N. (1986). Reflections on theory of international politics: A response to my critics. In R. O. Keohane (Ed.), *Neorealism and its critics* (pp. 322–346). New York: Columbia University Press.

Waltz, K. N. (1993). The emerging structure of international politics. *International Security, 18*(2), 44–79.

Weber, M. (1947). *The theory of social and economic organization.* New York: The Free Press.

Wendt, A. (1999). *Social theory of international politics.* Cambridge: Cambridge University Press.

White, H. (2005). The limits of optimism: Australia and the rise of China. *Australian Journal of International Affairs, 59*(4), 469–480.

White, H. (2010). Power shift: Australia's future between Washington and Beijing. *Quarterly Essay, 39*, 1–74.

Wight, M. (1978). *Power politics.* Leicester: Leicester University Press.

Wikileaks. (2011a). Cable 77562, 9/8/2006 6:10, 06CANBERRA1366.

Wikileaks. (2011b). Cable EO 12958, 28/03/2009 02:24, STATE 030049.

Wood, B. (1988). *The middle powers and the general interest.* Ottawa: The North–South Institute.

Wrong, D. H. (1979). *Power. Its forms, bases and uses.* Oxford: Blackwell.

Yoshihide, S. (2009). Comments at the 2009 Japan-US future leaders policy dialogue. http://www.tokyofoundation.org/en/articles/2008/japans-middle-power-diplomacy

Younglai, R. (2011). Economist list US budget deficit as No. 1 worry. Reuters, 28th Feb 2011. http://www.reuters.com/article/2011/02/28/us-usa-economy-survey-idUSTRE71R1LF20110228?feedType=RSS&feedName=topNews

Chapter 2
Hegemony and Power in the Global War on Terrorism

Anna Cornelia Beyer

This chapter discusses the role and power of the United States in a world of globalisation and global governance after 9/11, and specifically in the years 2001–2008. Theoretically and empirically, the Global War on Terrorism served as the background to analyze how the United States uses its power in different forms to 'govern' the world in a hegemonic manner. While this governance is not comprehensive and all-encompassing, it is important in creating and influencing world affairs; it sets agendas and influences policy-making. Hegemonic governance and the use of a superior unipolar position in the international system are based on both material and ideological power. Both dimensions are needed to govern within the context of the Global War on Terrorism. This chapter will first discuss the interrelated role of ideas and matter generally, and for hegemony specifically. It will then discuss United States hegemony more broadly, and conclude with a presentation of how this hegemony was utilised to achieve participation in the GWOT by the EU and ASEAN. Parts of this chapter have been published in a former version in "Hegemony, Equilibrium and Counterpower", which appeared in *International Relations* (Beyer 2009).[1]

Hegemony in Mind and Matter

In this section, I will give an example of theory synthesis, which will serve as the background for the following analysis of US power in a globalised world. Here, a synthetic perspective on unipolar power is discussed and it is argued that a realist and constructivist and critical perspectives have to be combined in order to understand US unipolar power and its application. It is therefore argued that we have to reconcile realist and other approaches if we are to understand the multidimensional

---

[1] I would like to thank the publishers of International Relations for their generous acceptance to republish parts of a former article.

E. Fels et al. (eds.), *Power in the 21st Century*, Global Power Shift,
DOI 10.1007/978-3-642-25082-8_2,

reality of US predominance (Moravcsik 2003). In my view, the opposition between a focus on ideas or on material factors is an unnecessary one (Keohane 2000): whereas realism argues for 'reality' being presented in material terms, such as military strength and economic power, constructivism, for example, highlights the importance and shaping power of ideas, with norms being particularly significant. The opposition between the 'material' and the 'ideational', however, is a false one: human affairs are structured by both; each is 'real', 'true' and 'important'. One can regard the material and the ideational as quite distinct; they are, however, closely interrelated and partly interdependent. Material factors have fundamentally shaped human affairs from the beginnings of our existence. While life historically has been constrained by material natural conditions such as water, mountains, and deserts and so forth, ideas (in particular, norms) also have a constraining power on individuals, societies and states. For material change to occur, ideas have to be expressed in creative or destructive action. Humans therefore act as the creators of ideas and as the mediators between ideas and the material. Regarded by realists as material facts (population) and in constructivism as bearers of ideas (agents), humans operate in both dimensions, able to transform the ideational into the material, and vice versa. On the one hand, ideas can develop in response to the material world (Chirot 2000); modern science, ideologies and arguably even religions refer in one way or other to matter, trying to explain it (through science), change it (through ideology) or transcend it (through religion). Non-natural matter (such as the UN building in New York, weapons arsenals, border fortifications, the means of production or the international transport system), on the other hand, is dependent on ideas, as there is no matter, apart from nature itself, which would exist in its particular realization without ideas. Every non-natural material 'particle' of the state and the international world is the outcome of preceding ideas, which have resulted in human actions in order to create these 'facts'. Non-natural material facts are therefore the accumulated result of ideas. States and institutions can be regarded as material facts, as they only exist so long as they are represented in matter (infrastructure, government buildings, the police, the media and so forth), but they are the result of ideas and continue to exist because of these ideas. The 'state', historically, had to be invented (Chirot 2000: 11), and it continues to exist only due to the shared belief in its reality and feasibility. In the words of Alexander Wendt: 'Sovereignty is an institution, and so it exists only in virtue of certain inter-subjective understandings and expectations' (Wendt 1992: 412). Ideas are needed for creating and changing material facts. The state, the European Union (Parsons 2003), the United Nations, transnational enterprises – none of these would be in existence without preceding ideas. Wars, revolutions (Philpott 2001; Galtung 1978: 298) and even terrorism depend on a preceding ideology, or an idea. Change, therefore, creative and destructive, is first and foremost the result of ideational factors, but it has to be realized by affecting the material. Ideas can also serve as stabilizing factors, such as in the case of national identities, and international and societal norms. The third element which is needed for explaining the interrelated nature of the material and the ideational, and which both realist and constructivist approaches regard as important, is agency (the human factor), which represents a two-way transmission belt between the material and the ideational. Agency is directly contemplated by constructivism, in terms of (other-regarding) active and reactive behavior. In structural realism it is understood indirectly, in the form of (self-regarding) reactive behavior, in Waltz's defensive version (Wendt and Waltz in interview with the author 2007). In the international world, for example, it is to be found in the processes of exercising policies of conflict and cooperation: internal and external balancing, diplomacy, economic interaction, the creation of institutions, or military interventions. Policies are the product of ideas, but material change only happens after action by the agent, usually involving the use of other non-natural material elements (such as weapons or the means of production) and resulting in material change (such as a shift in polarity, the accumulation of wealth, and the destruction or creation of state entities or institutions) (Dessler 1989). Even the most appealing idea cannot be realized without successful agency; the latter, however, is itself dependent on material potential, such as weapons and energy resources held by states. Wars, revolutions, the creation of new political entities, and political discourse via the media are all highly dependent on material resources, and all are realized via agency. For example, violence depends on financial and energy resources and weaponry, politically creative acts need an economic backing and an infrastructure, and even political discourse is dependent on media.

It should now be apparent that material and ideational factors are both necessary for understanding international relations more broadly and the predominant position of the United States in the world more specifically. The United States are not the only great power, but they are the most dominant in both the ideational dimension (its discourse and ideology) and in the material dimension (its economy, armaments) which together combine into 'thick hegemony'. US hegemony, then, rests on material foundations, but is created and maintained via ideas.

Unipolarity and Hegemony

In this section, I will describe the term hegemony to larger extent in order to be able to discuss the bases of hegemony and how we can understand the United States as a hegemon. Here, I will try to show how hegemony has been conceptualized in the past by using the synthesised perspective described above. Both dimensions – material and ideational – have been used to understand hegemony better. First, I will discuss how hegemony is essentially being understood in Realist terms as unipolarity. Then I will discuss the broader hegemony term introduced by Gramsci.

'Polarity' as a feature of international relations was brought into the discussion by Waltz (1979) in his new version of Realism, structural realism. He assumed that we had to look at the configuration of the 'international system' in order to understand world affairs. This configuration was characterized in terms of the distribution of power between the states, involving big – or powerful – states ('poles') and medium and minor powers. What then made a state a powerful state? For Waltz, all one had to count were the capabilities – material markers of international power such as the economic strength of a country, the size of its military and geographical and population figures. All these criteria are ultimately material in nature, and this is the basis for measuring power for Waltz. Ideological aspects do not feature heavily here. For Waltz, it is only the 'stuff that one can count' that matters for describing a polar state.

For describing the configuration of the international system, there are different possibilities. One could imagine a system in which there are many powerful states of more or less equal power, such as in the twentieth century in Europe. The second possible configuration of the international system would be 'bipolar'. This would be a system as we have observed it in the era of the Cold War with two major states – the US and the USSR – competing for power. Interestingly, Waltz in his *Theory of International Politics* did not think about a third possibility of configuration of the international system, the configuration that most scholars think we live in today: 'unipolarity'. Unipolarity denotes the situation that within the international system – or a regional framework – one state is the leading state in terms of capabilities, one state therefore in material terms dominates the international system.

The United States in the analyzed period 2001–2008 (Beyer 2010) dominated the international system in material terms. It had the strongest economy on a global scale; it had the only military with truly global reach, for example. Also, its positioning between two oceans makes it less vulnerable to conventional attacks than most other states. And finally, it provides over a large, oftentimes very well educated population. Many scholars have proclaimed the unipolarity of the United States (p.e. Kapstein 1999). Some, however, have doubted it. For example, Mearsheimer (2008) and Huntington (2008) suggested that the United States is just one pole among many and that we are already living in a multipolar world. For them, mainly the BRIC states (Brazil, Russia, India and China) account for powers that need to be counted in, with an economically emergent China and a resource-strong and militarily strong Russia, they would argue, we are already living in a multipolar world where no state solely dominates. They do not consider the European Union as a pole, though. This is interesting, as in economic terms the EU as a whole is similarly strong as the United States. Globally, it is the only match to the United States in economic terms. However, particularly Mearsheimer, being a Realist, probably does not see the EU as a unit or an actor in its own right. For them, the EU rather resembles an alliance, and can therefore not be counted in the systemic distribution of power. The difference between these critical voices and the general opinion, though, in my view is rather one of definition. I doubt that Mearsheimer and Huntington would go as far as arguing that the United States is not the most dominant power in international relations currently. Rather, they want to point out that there are other strong powers present which should not and cannot be ignored. It remains to be seen and is too early to judge yet what the current economic crisis in the United States will bring forward as results for the overall power of the US.

In conclusion, the United States in the time of interest here was the strongest power in terms of capabilities on a global level. It was and is not the only strong power globally, neither in military terms nor economic terms, which are the main categories for measuring power according to Realists assumptions. But, particularly in military terms they are the strongest power and they dominate all other – weaker – states. Militarily, no state has the chance to challenge the United States.

According to the Realist paradigm, this constellation should also indicate how unipolarity (or hegemony) is exercised: in terms of military and economic power. This perspective excludes other aspects of interaction, such as discourse. Material strength, according to this perspective, is used to control other states for the hegemon's benefit. This might happen particularly by the use of force or the threat of force, less so by using economic power. A differing perspective here was introduced by Gilpin (1981), who argued that the hegemon would attempt to control the international realm by providing public goods, thereby using its economic power. We will see later on, that the latter aspect seems particularly important for hegemony.

But, as pointed out above, when we speak of power of a state over others, we cannot only regard the pure material point of view and count capabilities. We also have to take other elements into account, for example the exercise of power and soft power issues – such as ideology and ideas. If we regard these as important, we take a more critical or constructivist turn. Here, I would like to focus on the critical scholarship, which has termed the United States a hegemon.

Hegemony derives from the Greek word 'egemon', which denotes the domination or leadership of one state over another, and thereby already indicated an interactional dimension. The term has been applied in political science writings early on by Gramsci, who used it in a Marxist perspective to describe the hegemony of the bourgeoisie, and how a hegemony of the working class could be achieved. He described hegemony as 'a relation, not of domination by means of force, but of consent by means of political and ideological leadership. It is the organisation of consent' (Simon 1991: 22). Already we see the strong role that ideas and ideology play for hegemony. Consensus is being based on shared understandings and priorities. Later on, Gramsci discussed the issue of force, stating that a dominant relationship which was mainly based on oppression and coercion could not be counted anymore as a hegemony but rather resembled dictatorship, or in our terms imperialism. 'It is one of the cases in which these groups have the function of "domination" without that of "leadership": dictatorship without hegemony' (Cuneo 2007). For him, hegemony needed to be based on a combination of 'force and consent' (Engel 2006: 2). This consent is therefore a central feature of hegemony, and it relates the issue of hegemony back to the ideational dimension of international relations which was pointed out in the beginning of this essay. As Gramsci already indicates, hegemony is more than just material predominance. It is the will to exercise the resulting power, first, and the success in acquiring ideological support from the subordinates for this role, second. A social relational aspect is therefore implied.

Gramsci, however, used the term hegemony to analyze and describe relations only within the national state; he did not initially apply the term to international relations and systemic descriptions. This, however, was later on achieved with the neo-Gramscian approach by Cox (1996). Cox transferred the notion of hegemony to the international level, and applied it to the United States. 'Cox sees the current global hegemony as an outwards expansion of an American historical bloc, which he labels *pax Americana*. The legitimating ideology of *pax Americana* is, of course, neoliberalism', and 'Cox also identified a range of ways in which hegemony is expressed by international organizations as both the products of the hegemonic world order and institutions that facilitate the expansion of the rules of that order, in this case neoliberalism' (Engel 2008: 162ff). As Cox himself asserts, he used Gramsci's ideas to describe a leading role of the United States in both material and ideational dimensions: 'Antonio Gramsci used the concept of hegemony to express a unity between objective material forces and ethico-political ideas – in Marxian terms, a unity of structure and superstructure – in which power based on dominance over production is rationalized through an ideology incorporating compromise or consensus between dominant and subordinate groups' (Cox 1977: 387).

By bringing in Gramsci's analysis to the domain of International Relations, Cox again referred to consensus as the important criterion for analyzing hegemony: 'In the hegemonic consensus, the dominant groups make some concessions to satisfy the subordinate groups, but not such as to endanger their dominance. The language of consensus is a language of common interest expressed in universalist terms, though the structure of power underlying it is skewed in favor of the dominant groups' (Cox 1977: 387). He thereby criticized the neorealist use of the term as too one – dimensional and lacking soft-power aspects, such as ideology and consensus:

> Indeed, in neorealist discourse the term "hegemony" is reduced to the single dimension of dominance, i.e., a physical-capabilities relationship among states. The Gramscian meaning of hegemony which I have used and which is important in distinguishing the *pax britannicana* and *pax Americana* from the other world orders in the sequence suggested above, joins and ideological and intersubjective element to the brute power relationship. In a hegemonic order, the dominant power makes certain concessions or compromises to secure the acquiescence of lesser powers to an order that can be expressed in terms of a general interest. It is important, in appraising a hegemonic order, to know both (a) that it functions mainly by consent in accordance with universalist principles, and (b) that it rests upon a certain structure of power and serves to maintain that structure. The consensual element distinguishes hegemonic from nonhegemonic world orders. (Cox 1996: 55f)

This analysis of the United States as a hegemon in both material and ideational terms was novel at the time and challenged fundamentally the neo-realist understanding of hegemony. However, even Gilpin used in part Gramsci's ideas when writing about hegemony and empire. For him, it was perceptions and prestige that mattered for hegemons. He concurs with the Gramscian understanding that consensus is important as the basis for hegemony when he writes:

> the ruling elites and coalitions of subordinate states frequently form alliances with the dominant powers and identify their values and interests with those of the dominant powers. Empires and dominant states supply public goods ... that give other states an interest in following their lead. Finally, every dominant state, and particularly an empire, promotes a religion or ideology that justifies the domination over other states in the system. (Gilpin 1981: 30)

However, coming from the Realist perspective, he qualifies this perception on the same page:

> Ultimately, however, the hierarchy of prestige in the international system rests on economic and military power. Prestige is the reputation for power, and military power in particular. Whereas power refers to economic, military, and related capabilities of the state, prestige refers primarily to the perceptions of other states with respect to a state's capacities and its ability and willingness to exercise its power. (Gilpin 1981: 31)

Gramsci's ideas obviously had influenced Gilpin to a certain degree, even if he still remained in the Realist perspective, describing material power as the dominant element in hegemony.

The Gramscian assumptions on hegemony came back more recently and were particularly presented in Hobson's work. Hobson (2000) utilized Gramsci to describe a number of criteria for measuring hegemony. A hegemon, according to him, must:

- Be economically and militarily dominant over other states, have preponderant power.
- Be a state committed to liberal principles, 'because only liberal states have the will to pursue hegemony: authoritarian states prefer imperialism, moreover, liberal states are concerned to create an open and liberal world order' (Hobson 2000: 39).
- Have a rudimentary consensus among those states which it dominates.
- Pursue a long-term perspective or strategy on setting up regimes, and thereby creating a sort of world order (Hobson 2000: 40).

Therefore, Hobson also mentions that for hegemony not only the dominance in power counts, not only a unipolar position within the world system. Hegemony also needs to be based on consensus of the subordinated.

This consensus, in my and Hobson's view, is based on 'soft power' and what has been called 'sticky power', or the application of ideological influence and economic capability. The ideological influence is needed to create the perspectives and images that are necessary to make hegemony appear beneficial and to create an idea of legitimacy. Economic capability is needed to create a functioning world economy, in which many states fare better than they would without the hegemon's contribution to this economy. This also makes hegemony seem beneficial. Finally, even military power can be used to create consensus, when the hegemon uses the military power – or promises to use it – for the protection of its subordinates. It therefore depends on the way the different capabilities are used if we could term a unipolar state a hegemon. Military and economic power in particular can also be used in quite different ways, to exercise control and to exploit and pressure other states. If this would be the dominant mode of interaction between the unipolar power and the subordinates, we would probably not speak of hegemony, at least not a benign hegemony.

It seems important to me to include these additional aspects into the understanding of hegemony, as the one-dimensional perspective of Realism on unipolarity (and therefore hegemony) does not give us much insights on how domination is functioning, what social processes it is based on. Calculating power and predicting behavior from establishing polarity-configurations of the system is certainly a minimalist way of understanding international affairs. If we regard ideas and interactions as important, though, we can better explain issues of stability and cooperation, or potentially conflict and change, in a hegemonic international setting. This is what Gilpin sensed when he wrote about war and change under hegemony and discussed interactional and perceptional features.

Power and Its Exercise of the United States

While the past parts introduced the assumption that hegemony in general is based not only on material factors, but on ideational factors as well, this part is testing this assumption at the example of the US hegemony over ASEAN and the EU. The following discussion summarizes the results that have been found in a previous study on US hegemony within the Global War on Terrorism (Beyer 2010). We will see, again, that not only material power counts for US hegemony, but that it is largely dependent on the exercise of soft power and ideological factors underpinning it.

For discussing aspects of power and in order to differentiate between different forms of power, Wartenbergs distinctions are helpful. Wartenberg describes dominance as a situation in which we find 'not to a single exercise of power but to a relationship between two social agents that is constituted by the existence of a power differential between them' (1990: 117). Power then, which rests on a dominant position within any system, can be exercised in three different forms: *influence*, *coercion* and *force*. A hegemon, according to the definitions above, will make predominant use of influence in order to create consensus. It might, at times, also use coercion, but will be less inclined to use force.

In my previous study (Beyer 2010), I have argued that the mode of conduct between the United States and two selected regions – namely the EU and ASEAN – in the period 2001–2008 was based predominantly on the exercise of influence and the shaping of discourse, but also on the use of economic and hard power, but in a less controversial way. For this study, I interviewed scholars and practitioners of the EU and ASEAN to single out the reasons for these regions to participate in a US-led Global War on Terrorism (GWOT). Participation in the GWOT was understood as cooperation with and as therefore an effect of US hegemony. The causes for participation would therefore indicate the ways in which hegemony was exercised. The interviewees responded to a large extent that the states in the regions went along with what the United States did in part because terrorism is understood to be the, or a, main threat towards the EU and ASEAN. This means that the elites in both regions accepted the dominant discourse promoted by the United States that international terrorism is to be seen the main threat to international security in our times. Without this shared 'ideology', I argue that not as much participation in the Global War on Terrorism would have to be observed. Therefore, the leading role of the United

States, and their effect in inspiring participation in global counterterrorism measures, is to be explained partly by the power of discourse, by their ideological influence.

The interviews in the EU and ASEAN were subjected a textual analysis. Questioning on the international distribution of power, the interviewees were asked if the United States was a dominant power, at least compared to their own region. This would imply that, in accord with the Realist perspective, the materially dominant position of the US in the world could have contributed to participation of the regions in the GWOT. The second set of questions involved the issue of pressure, which would imply that there was diplomatic pressure exercised towards the governments within the region to go along with the United States policies. With regards to economic relations, it was asked if economics played any role in the decisions to participate in the Global War on Terrorism. The confirming answers would indicate that due to economic interdependence the states possibly did cooperate as they were dependent on the US and it would have negative repercussions on them not to comply with its policies. When ‘authority’ was asked for, the question involved if the US was seen as a leading state and as a legitimately leading state. Authority here was understood to be a marker of consensus. With questions involving the perception of threat, finally, influence was measured to account for the basis of this consensus. When threat was confirmed, this implied that the discourse of the United States was accepted, including a perception of a major threat to the world’s states from terrorism. Threat discourse as a measurement of United States hegemony was highlighted by Steger (2005) and Jackson (2004), who both described the dominant terrorism discourse as an element of United States globalism, and a marker of their hegemonic position. While Steger compares this to former discourses on globalization, Jackson particularly analyzed the discourse within the Global War on Terrorism.

For both ASEAN and the EU the dominant power position of the United States, compared to ASEAN and the EU, was confirmed. As we can assume that the EU with its strong economic power is among the major powers in the world, we can take this as an indicator for unipolarity of the United States, or at least great power status. Apart from that, the indicators for both regions differ slightly. For ASEAN, the main motivator for participation in the Global War on Terrorism was the interdependence with the United States. This was mentioned openly in the interviews, with statements such as Ramakrishna’s:

> ASEAN governments recognize that if they are seen not to be taking a firm stand against terrorism, there will be a negative political impact, both domestically as in terms of foreign direct investment, and this is very important to ASEAN, especially because it sees itself in competition with other Asian regions and states. So they have to show that they are serious in dealing with terrorism. (Ramakrishna, interview with the author 2006)

It was mentioned that in case of non-compliance there would be important political and economic repercussions, which the ASEAN states feared. Also, the role of the United States as a security provider could be compromised in case of non-cooperation. Therefore, participation was motivated by interdependence, a relationship in which a certain pressure might have been exercised, actively or passively. Some pressure in the relationship was mentioned; some scholars indicated that pressure was exercised on a bilateral level to make the states go along with the policies of the United States to counter terrorism, but only informally. The leadership role of the United States was not questioned, which indicates that the support for hegemony of the US was still strong. The presence of consensus was confirmed by the majority of interviewees. However, interestingly, the threat of terrorism was not seen as a major one in ASEAN (even though ASEAN is much more affected by terrorism than the EU, for example). This could potentially mean a lack of consensus underlying the US hegemony, as their dominant discourse – that terrorism is the major threat we currently have to counter – was not agreed with. However, as the responses for authority were strong, we can assume that the US hegemony was still supported. This was particularly indicated by some respondents who claimed that the leadership role of the United States was not doubted. Overall, the results indicated that the factors most dominantly influencing participation in the Global War on Terrorism – apart from the US being the dominant state internationally – were dependence on, and influence of, but also authority of the United States. In conclusion, many interviews confirmed that the United States was seen as a leading state, and legitimately so, and that particularly economic repercussions were expected in case of non-participation. On the other hand, there was not a full confirmation of the influence hypothesis for ASEAN, as not all respondents confirmed that ASEAN views international terrorism as a main threat to the region. But most respondents acknowledged that the terrorism discourse was shared to large degree. However, consensus also seems to be present in ASEAN, even if this is not as strongly based on discursive influence as in the case of the EU. It can therefore be argued that while the dominant position of the US materially is the strongest factor for hegemony, other aspects do contribute significantly to hegemony and cannot be ignored. These aspects also challenge the Realist perspective, as unipolar power was not majorly utilized in terms of pressure or open coercion, but rather due to dependence and by the provision of goods. This is probably the basis for US hegemony in ASEAN being accepted as legitimate. As this legitimacy in this case is not based on a strongly shared discourse on terrorism, it could be based on the economic relationship which was observed, meaning that the US is perceived as a benefactor and a security guarantor. In Realist terms, this could be explained by an alliance between the ASEAN states and bandwagoning from their part with the US. However, it can also be interpreted as shedding light on the fact that additional aspects count towards hegemony, such as economic interactions and the perception of the US as legitimately leading, hence consensus. Overall, this would indicate that here we have stronger support for the interpretation of hegemony in Gilpin's sense, meaning that material power and the provision of goods is most causal for the stability and functioning of hegemony.

For the EU, also a dominant power position of the United States was confirmed, but less so than for ASEAN. Here, however, interdependence did not play a role at all. The interviewees responded that economic interdependence did not contribute to the decisions to participate in the Global War on Terrorism. The EU member states in combination are economically too strong to make interdependence work as a compelling factor for them to cooperate with the US's policies. On the other hand, the responses on authority and influence were highly positive. This means the EU did not only see the US as a legitimate leader, it also accepted their version of describing international terrorism as a dominant threat to their security. In particular, the study indicated that the US is understood as exercising a legitimate leadership role, and providing this function as an important role in the world. More importantly even, the discourse promoted by the United States on terrorism was shared in the EU, according to the statements of the interviewees. All of them stated that terrorism was understood as representing the main threat to international security in this period. While the European Union is not obviously a primary target of international terrorist attacks (very few Islamist attacks have been counted, it is unclear, however, how many attacks have been prevented), this indicates that the discourse on the threat is shared among the US and the EU and therefore there is a high level of ideological influence in this relationship to be found. For example, Kuhne argued that it is essentially the factor of a shared threat that compels the EU to participate in the Global War on Terrorism. More than the assumption of the United States as a leading state, and even more than the mere material power of the US, this shared ideology of terrorism as the main threat was cited as contributing to participation of the EU. This form of influence was thereby receiving stronger support from the respondents as a cause for participation than the material dominance of the US, including pressure. Both aspects indicate a hegemonic relationship here, in which the United States makes use of their dominant power, particularly through soft power, particularly discursive power, and is accepted as a legitimate leader, a role which found a relatively strong consensus in the European Union. The findings do not contradict Realist interpretations, as the materially dominant role of the US still is to be understood as being important. Also, the relationship and the cooperation of the EU can be explained in terms of alliance and bandwagoning. However, the internal processes of this relationship and the interactions are interesting, as apparently they are based more on soft power and influence, indicated by the commonality of interest, rather than on threats and power calculations.

Conclusion

This article tried to show that the United States acted – at least in the period of the Global War on Terrorism – as a hegemon in international relations. This hegemony was in part based on its predominant power position within the world, on economic and military capabilities. On the other hand, also interactional and ideological factors contributed to the leading position of the United States as a hegemon. The discourses they promoted brought the world together under common ideas and assumptions about the world, about goods to be pursued and threats to be countered.

The case studies mentioned in the third part of this chapter illustrated that the United States can lead by applying ideological power and combining this power with the effects of their unipolar position. In the case of ASEAN, economic power is dominant, but also are the United States believed to be a legitimate leading state.

For the EU, the effects of soft power exercise in hegemony are even stronger, as the EU not only accepts the leading role of the US; it also accepts the US dominated discourse on contemporary security threats, terrorism being the major issue among them.

This implies that indeed the US leads by utilizing both material and ideological aspects of power. They could not lead by military and economic power alone, as then their leadership would have difficulty to create consensus, which hegemony is based on. This consensus, which is created via the promotion of compelling ideas and discourses, is needed to keep hegemony stable. If the domination of the United States would exist without consensus to be based on, probably there would be more opposition towards the leading state and less willingness to comply and go along with their policies.

An interesting fact is the difference in findings for the two case studies: ASEAN being more economically dependent but less under the rhetorical influence of the US, while the EU being not economically dependent but highly under the rhetorical influence of the US. The explanation for this difference most likely lies in the additional factors not researched in the study, such as traditional affiliations, economic strength of the EU, alliances, and a shared culture. It remains an open research question if more generalizable statements about differences of strong and weak actors under hegemony and how they behave towards the hegemon. Could it be that weaker, more dependent actors buy less into the ideological dimension of hegemony? What would that mean, and what kind of implications would it have? It would be interesting to compare further cases of exposure to hegemony and how states and other actors react to it.

Hegemony, however, is not necessarily global. I have discussed hegemony here in abstract terms and looked empirically only at the cases of South-East Asia and Europe. It can be assumed that in other parts of the world, such as China, for example, the hegemonic discourses are perceived in a much different way. How far-reaching hegemony and the consensus-shaping powers of hegemonic discourses really are is hard to discern from these results. More research is needed to determine this. However, it can be assumed that in large parts of the world the United States do indeed make good use of their leading position by creating hegemony and therefore leading the world with surprisingly few opposition. For future research, it will be interesting if the hegemonic role has changed under the new presidency of Obama, in which a new leadership style is to be found, the Global War on Terrorism has been partly abandoned and reframed. Also, the current economic difficulties of the United States might have an impact on the capability of the United States to provide with hegemonic leadership in the future. It, however, is beyond the scope of this article to speculate on this.

References

Beyer, C. (2009). Hegemony, equilibrium and counterpower: A synthetic approach. *International Relations, 23*(2), 411–427.

Beyer, C. (2010). *Counterterrorism and international power relations: The EU, ASEAN and hegemonic global governance*. London: IB Tauris.
Chirot, D. (2000). *How societies change*. Thousand Oaks: Pine Forge Press.
Cox, R. (1977). Labor and hegemony. *International Organization, 31*, 385–424.
Cox, R. (1996). Gramsci, hegemony, and international relations: An essay in method. In R. Cox & T. Sinclair (Eds.), *Approaches to world order* (pp. 49–66). Cambridge: Cambridge University Press.
Cuneo, C. (2007). Hegemony in Gramsci's original prison notebooks. http://socserv2.mcmaster.ca/soc/courses/soc2r3/gramsci/gramheg.htm. Accessed 21 Jan 2007.
Dessler, D. (1989). What's at stake in the agent-structure debate? *International Organization, 43*(3), 441–473.
Engel, S. (2008). The world bank and neoliberal hegemony in Vietnam. In R. Howson & K. Smith (Eds.), *Hegemony. Studies in consensus and coercion* (pp. 159–183). New York & London: Routledge.
Engel, S. (2006). Where to neoliberalism? The World Bank and the post-Washington consensus in Indonesia and Vietnam. In *Paper presented to the 16th Biennial Conference of the Asian Studies Association of Australia*, Wollongong, Australia, 26–29 June 2006.
Galtung, J. (1978). *Peace and social structure. Essays in peace research* (Vol. 3). Copenhagen: Ejlers.
Gilpin, R. (1981). *War and change in world politics*. New York: Cambridge University Press.
Hobson, J. (2000). *The state and international relations*. Cambridge: Cambridge University Press.
Huntington, S. (2008). The lonely superpower. In: Foreign Affairs, March/April, http://www-stage.foreignaffairs.org/19990301faessay966/samuel-p-huntington/the-lonely-superpower.html. Accessed 05 March 2008.
Jackson, R. (2004). *Writing the war on terrorism: Language, politics, and counterterrorism*. Manchester: Manchester University Press.
Kapstein, E. (1999). *Unipolar politics: Realism and state strategies after the cold war*. New York: Columbia University Press.
Keohane, R. (2000). Ideas part-way down. *Review of International Studies, 26*, 125–130.
Mearsheimer, J. (2008). Conversations in international relations: Interview with John J. Mearsheimer (Part I). *International Relations, 20*(1), 105–124.
Moravcsik, A. (2003). Theory synthesis in international relations: Real, not metaphysical. *International Studies Review, 5*(1), 131–136.
Parsons, C. (2003). *A certain idea of Europe*. Ithaka: Cornell University Press.
Philpott, D. (2001). *Revolutions in sovereignty: How ideas shaped modern international relations*. Princeton: Princeton University Press.
Simon, R. (1991). *Gramsci's political thought: An introduction*. London: Lawrence and Wishart.
Steger, M. (2005). From market globalism to imperial globalism: Ideology and American power after 9/11. *Globalizations, 2*(1), 31–46.
Waltz, K. (1979). *Theory of international politics*. New York: Random House.
Wartenberg, T. (1990). *The forms of power: From domination to transformation*. Philadelphia: Temple University Press.
Wendt, A. (1992). Anarchy is what states make of it: The social construction of power politics. *International Organization, 46*(2), 391–425.

Interviews with the Author

Kenneth Waltz (2007, New York)
Alexander Wendt (2007, Ohio)
Kumar Ramakrishna (2006, Singapore)

Chapter 3
"Are You Pondering What I Am Pondering?" Understanding the Conditions Under Which States Gain and Loose Soft Power

Gitika Commuri

Given the ubiquity of the term 'soft power' it is clear that the concept represents, without doubt, one of the key elements of international relations.[1] The strength of the concept lies in the fact that it allows theorists and practitioners to think about power in more complex and dynamic ways – at least in ways more complex than some Realist assertions of hard power.[2] And yet the manner and conditions under which soft power is manifested makes it one of the most nebulous and ambiguous concepts within the field of International Relations [IR], granted that the field of IR is rife with ambiguous concepts. Even though the concept is frequently used, the fact is that it is one of those terms that defy generalization – one of the elements of theory building. Scholars are puzzled by the processes through which soft power unfolds and its impact on bringing about the desired policy change. Intuitively we understand that soft power must exist and yet our attempts to grasp it leave us with some clarity but much confusion as well.

In this chapter, I acknowledge the scholarly work that has sought to extend the applicability of the concept in different cases, attempted to extend our understanding of the relationship between resources of soft power and outcomes and others who have pointed to the analytical weakness of the concept. While these are the dominant strands of theoretical discussion and practical application, they are not necessarily mutually exclusive. I draw on this literature and posit another line of reasoning vis-à-vis the concept – one that is less explored. Perhaps, a rigorous

I owe this quote to the Animaniacs cartoon series 'Pinky and the Brain'.

[1] The term has existed both in the public and academic discourse for about two decades now. There are countless articles and books on soft power of various states and international organizations; United States, China, Turkey, Russia, Japan, India and European Union (see Nye 2002, 2004, 2010; Fraser 2005; Rugh 2006; Watanabe and Mc Connell 2008; Bell 2009; Wang and Lu 2008; Cho and Jeong 2008; Hunter 2009; Li 2009; Ding 2008; Oguzlu 2007; Tsygankov 2006; Parmar and Cox 2010; Kurlantzick 2005; Kurlantzick 2007 others).

[2] It must be noted though that while the concept of soft power seems to have captured our attention in a significant manner – the idea in itself may be seen in Gramsci's articulation of the concept of hegemony. Zahran and Ramos (2010) discuss the resemblance between the two concepts.

E. Fels et al. (eds.), *Power in the 21st Century*, Global Power Shift,
DOI 10.1007/978-3-642-25082-8_3,

attempt to lay out the conditions under which states may lose or gain soft power will give us a better grasp of the concept and its applicability. It will also allow us to think about shifts in power – that is conditions under which power will shift from one state to another or one region to another.[3] In the sections that follow, I define the concept, present a brief review of previous research, and lay out the conditions under which states are likely to gain or lose soft power.

Thus this paper is an attempt to return to the discussion begun by Nye's seminal work on soft power and other scholars who followed his lead in examining the impact and implications of soft power. Nye defines soft power as "getting others to want the outcomes you want" (Nye 2004: 5). Nye contends that soft power is the ability to get others to do what you want through persuasion,[4] and attraction – thus the emphasis is on cooptation not coercion. Nye's articulation of the concept has not remained consistent, and this becomes particularly noticeable in his discussion of resources of soft power.

Nye claims there are three main resources in a state for soft power, which are Its culture (in places where it is attractive to others), its political values (when it lives up to them at home and abroad), and its foreign policies (when they are seen as legitimate and having moral authority) (Nye 2004). These resources may be deployed by state or non-state actors. Nye is careful to distinguish these resources of soft power from those of hard power – sticks and carrots. He recognizes that there is a relationship between soft power and hard power, but argues that this relationship is not necessary and that states can exhibit soft power without having the requisite hard power. And yet, we see in Nye's conceptualization a gradual inclusion of economic power – thus the carrots he seeks to avoid, emerge for instance in the form of foreign aid. Preferences of states are thus shaped by persuasion that takes the form of attraction [wherein one imitates the other because of some innate intrinsic value of the others mode of existence] as well as inducements [wherein certain economic and political benefits flow directly to the object of soft power]. The initial definition and sources of soft power as set forth by Nye have remained essentially uncontested by other scholars who have followed Nye's line of reasoning – though some have focused more on the intangible elements of soft power than others.[5] In this study, the concept is understood in its original articulation – in terms of persuasion and attraction and hence without inducements.

[3] Typically this discussion plays out in the context of hard power capabilities of states. Changing economic and military indicators are used to understand and evaluate shifts in power. Even Nye who focuses on soft power, considers these material shifts significant. That said, this is an attempt to integrate material and less tangible shifts in power.

[4] Lebow (2005) makes a distinction between two kinds of persuasion; dolos and peitho, wherein the former is persuasion through deceit and false logic and the latter involves building a friendship and is based on common identities, mutually valued norms and practices. Peitho has the potential to foster cooperation, and is clearly the better of the two.

[5] By uncontested I do not mean to suggest that critics have not sought to question the usefulness of the concept. There is ample critique of the concept itself and the difficulties associated with identifying the specific outcomes related to soft power resources. What I do suggest, in this context, is that the initial definition set out by Nye has been used by a number of scholars.

The discussion so far has focused primarily on either: (a) the extension of the concept of soft power in the context of different countries and various tools, (b) specified the causal pathways between input and output or (c) critiqued the concept for its analytical weakness.[6] The first examines the thesis within certain issue areas and in specific countries – a test so to speak of whether and to what extent soft power tools work. This literature focuses on specific tools of soft power such as popular culture, exchange programs, radio as a tool of public diplomacy, development assistance, disaster relief and so forth. The second discussion extends Nye's initial argument by specifying the connection between input and outcomes. That is, it focuses on helping us understand the processes through which soft power is realized.[7] Both these thematic explorations of the concept of soft power are critical to the theoretical and practical understanding of the term – particularly since these discussions provide us insight into the tools and conditions of soft power. Lastly, scholars have focused on the ambiguity inherent in the concept of soft power making it a problematic concept.[8] While the critique is valid, the fact is that the concept of soft power has only come into more usage, not less. We must grapple with the concept, no matter how slippery, and that is what I hope to do in this paper – but by treading a different path – one that attempts to lay out the conditions under which states may gain or lose soft power.

In the section that follows, I reflect back on some of the observations made by the various scholars and ruminate over the possible conditions under which states lose or gain soft power. I must acknowledge here that this attempt to set out these conditions is problematic to the extent that states may constantly be in the position of losing and gaining soft power – that their actions may in a sense be contradictory. Given that states may be gaining and losing soft power at the same time in different issue areas and in different parts of the world, it becomes important to move beyond an examination of soft power in specific contexts and to think about broad conditions. This discussion must also be sensitive to the idea that the question of soft power must really be explored in the context of state in question and the extent to which the state seeks to extend power. Hence *capabilities* (tangible and intangible) and *intentions* become relevant, to the extent that they shape the degree to which states can and will extend

[6] While I have sought to distinguish these three broad strands of literature, I understand that these strands overlap in some instances.

[7] Seiichi (2008) and Ding (2008) focus their efforts on clarifying the relationship between inputs and outcomes, by examining the processes through which inputs are translated into outcomes.

[8] For instance, an issue of concern is that states may be engaging in hard (economic/military) and soft power tactics at the same time. In that case how are we to distinguish between actions of state A that may be shaped by carrots for instance, or by possible military repercussions and not necessarily by attractiveness to other states. How do we know that state A is not able to realize its policy because of poor extension of soft power as opposed to state B's receptivity to soft power, but necessity to respond to more strategic concerns? See critiques and attempts to refine the concept in the edited book by Parmar and Cox (2010). In particular see Layne (2010) for a trenchant critique of the concept, the relationship between resources and outcomes and more importantly how we measure outcomes.

soft power. States that may qualify as great states with the possibility of being hegemonic are more likely to seek to extend global influence, whereas smaller states will have a different set of capabilities and perhaps agenda. Furthermore the object of soft power will shape the extent to which outcomes are realized.

Before venturing in this direction, I would like to clarify some concerns regarding the term 'conditions'. First, we must differentiate between conditions and tools. Often these two terms are used interchangeably, causing considerable confusion. I define conditions as *circumstances* under which states will lose or gain soft power – context that makes it more likely for one or the other to happen. Tools on the other hand, are action oriented events or processes undertaken by the state or non-state actors. Tools are specific resources that are used to affect the outcome – in terms of shaping state behavior to one's own interests. Thus having a broad national agenda, diverse and broadly appealing wide reaching media outlets, student exchange programs, elements of popular culture are treated as tools or strategies of extending soft power. In the context of this discussion, the focus is not on the specific tools used by states but the context within which these tools are used since that is what will assist us in understanding when states gain and lose soft power. Second, we may see certain conditions relevant for both loss and gain (thinking of it along a continuum – one end of which will create opportunities for gaining power and the other end, for loss), while others may be specific to loss of power. Third, the articulation of conditions, is limited to the following: relationship between hard and soft power, international structure (economic, cultural and political), relational power, moral authority (includes the acquiring of this authority through values, institutions and actions, as well as provision of public goods, state-society relations and hubris), and historical conditions. I have not delineated internal and external conditions – essentially they emerge together in the discussion that follows.

Conditions Under Which States Will Gain or Loose Soft Power

Hard power: Economic and military: While Nye suggests that soft power is not dependent on hard power, he does acknowledge that the two are related. In fact Zahran and Ramos contend that hard and soft power, are linked in interesting ways. They point out that "it is possible for command power behavior to utilize intangible soft power resources in the same sense that co – optive power behavior can make use of tangible hard power resources. . .Actually it is even possible that command power creates soft power resources, or that co-optive power creates hard power resources" (2010: 17–18). This line of reasoning is persuasive and shows us the complex relationship between hard and soft power.[9] It is reasonable to assume that

[9] Nye agrees that this articulation of the relationship between command power and co-optive power is important contribution to our understanding of soft power (Nye 2010). It is noteworthy

hard power resources of a state – its material well being, military capacity, are seen as attractive qualities in other states. The state in question does not necessarily have to extend this power, its very existence becomes attractive to those that aspire the same or even to those that have no such aspirations. In fact, the question of extension of hard power resources is perhaps key in this regard – illegitimate use of hard power, as in show of force, will actually result in the diminution of soft power. So the state has to maintain a fine balance. That said, we can hypothesize that the states ability to extend soft power depends on hard power especially if we consider the extent to which the state seeks to extend its soft power – that is if the state seeks global influence, it must have the requisite hard power resources for it to appear attractive to other states.[10] Why? From a realist standpoint, one could make the argument that states aspire to acquire power (military and economic) and will imitate the ideas and practices of great states [to the extent possible]. To an extent this adoption of practices/principles/ideas may be seen as an extension of soft power, but then there is always the concern whether attraction equals interest. In fact the state in question (object of power) may adopt practices of the other state, without complying with the interests of the agent state.

However Oguzlu[11] suggests, that major powers (US, EU) "are likely to act as hard powers, simply because they have strong agency" and more likely to securitize issues of concern. He contends that Turkey is more able to extend soft power in part because it lacks significant hard power resources. This is an interesting reversal of the argument that hard power resources make possible the extension of soft power. While Oguzlu's argument bears further consideration, it is possible to argue that the question of hard power is a relative question, relative to other states and to the extent one wants to extend power. This takes us back to the condition of capabilities and intentions.

The question of international structure: Can 'attractiveness' or 'persuasion' be a structural condition? That is, can certain values, institutions and actions become dominant mode of engagement within certain structures? The three possibilities

that while Nye states that soft power is not dependent on hard power, he also finds that the two are inexorably intertwined (2004: 30). In 'The Paradox of American Power' Nye seems to consider the relationship between hard and soft power a tad more seriously – for instance his discussion of the closest competitors (China, Russia, India, Japan) of the US hinges on their economic and military capacity. Furthermore he states "if our economy fails, we will lose the basis for our hard power as well as our soft power" (2002: 111).

[10] Geiger (2010: 88) states "American soft power is not just the innocent product of the attractiveness of American values, democracy and capitalism, but rather arises from the USA's superior power resources and its ability to augment its power by constantly renegotiating the terms of domination and subordination."

[11] Oguzlu (2007: 82) argues that middle sized countries are more likely to use soft power (no choice) for non-securitized issues. He examines the case of Turkey to understand the conditions under which middle sized countries "could be considered as acting as a soft power." It could be argued that the Feminist theoretical tradition would agree with this line of reasoning, in the sense that feminists would argue that women by their subordinate position and so also weak states, are more likely to use soft power as a means to their goal. This certainly needs further consideration.

discussed below extend across economic, cultural and political realms, ideally compelling us to think in a comprehensive way about the structural conditions under which soft power may be extended.[12] It is the combination of these various structural level powers that will provide the necessary ambient conditions for the state to extend soft power.[13]

Economic: The dominant mode of production – as a global economic structure will shape the ability of the state to extend soft power. Hence a capitalist world economy will allow certain ideas [those related to the generation and distribution of wealth] to be more attractive, acceptable, and dominant. This means that it is going to be easier for some states within the system to be able to exercise this kind of dominant power. It is not so much the purposeful extension of state power, rather the inherent nature of the system that allows for the state to extend its power. States that constitute the core will inevitably attract the attention of those in the semi-periphery or periphery, both of which might seek to imitate the core not only because formal institutional structures encourage such behavior through inducements – carrots and sticks, but also because the core states emerge as model states.[14] Thus the crucial elements of soft power – attraction and emulation – as identified by Nye, shape state interests. The classic instance in the modern context is the emergence of a liberal economic order that is underpinned by a capitalist mode of production. This does not mean that conceptions of growth within a mode of production will not be challenged – however these challenges, so long as they remain on the margins of the system, will not significantly alter the structure. There are possibly two concerns with perceiving such structural conditions as relevant to the extension of soft power. One, that, structures evolve and change over a period of time and further that states may rise or decline within a certain economic structure. Second, that states in the core might have certain interests in common – in which case how do we know that the soft power strategies of state A are successful as opposed to state B. To some extent, this problem may be mitigated in a unipolar structure but less so in a multipolar structure.

[12] The question of structure can be seen to be drawn from at least four theoretical traditions: Realism, Marxism and Constructivism and Liberal Institutionalism.

[13] In this regard the argument forwarded by Susan Strange is very prescient. Strange distinguishes between relational and structural power and defines the latter as a power "that confers the power to decide how things shall be done, the power to shape frameworks within which states relate to each other, relate to people or relate to corporate enterprises" (Strange 1994: 25). Strange distinguishes between four interrelated sources of structural power; security, production, finance and knowledge/ideas/beliefs.

[14] I borrow the concepts of core, periphery and semi-periphery from Wallerstein's (1974) work on world systems. As Wallerstein suggests there is mobility between the core and the semi-periphery and this mobility might explain the shifts in global power- for instance the rise of China within the capitalist world system.

Cultural: Increasingly there is an effort in IR, to conceptualize and understand the implications of culture at a structural level.[15] Constructivists in particular have persuasively argued about the prevalence of norms and identity that shape interaction. For instance, norms of Christendom created certain affinity among medieval European states, thus shaping their interaction to some extent.[16] Similarly the states that were a part of the 'umma' the Islamic community of states – could be seen to have certain modes of engagement in common.[17] Within a structure where religion is the dominant cultural mode of engagement and its influence extends to social, economic, political realms – in that context states must draw on their religious sensibilities to be able to extend soft power. Thus states that had similar moral order and values would be more effective and receptive to soft power. Clearly, this would work only if there is acceptability to that specific religious articulation. It would be counterproductive otherwise. In the more modern context, we see the proliferation of secular ideas, and norms,[18] thus enhancing the appeal of secular states. Take for instance, the argument that there is consensus of norms and values between Europe and North America [particularly Canada and the United States]. Such a consensus allows, for example, an acceptance of human rights regime; the understanding that genocide constitutes a violation of moral code. In this context, I also think that it is important to have agreement among the core powers in the international system.[19] Significant dissent is an indication that

[15] While clearly constructivists have engaged more thoroughly in examining the significance of identity and norms in international relations, the idea that the international system may have some common norms of operation goes back to some of the arguments of the English school – specially their articulation of international society (see Bull 1977). More recently constructivists have indicated the presence of global norms (Price 1997; Tannenwald 2007).

[16] Hedley Bull (1977: 27–33) notes this engagement in his discussion of the Christian international society that mitigates anarchy.

[17] Mustafa Dhada notes that the concept of 'ummah' or an Islamic community of states evolved outside of statecraft. It was a community of faithful "sharing a cardinal set of norms and values grooved around monotheism". The concept was useful in the context of inter-tribal warfare and functioned with qualified success during the first four caliphs. Eventually it fell prey to "tribalism, sectarianism and ethnocentricity". However it was retrieved by some scholars such as Ibn Khaldun who revived notions of soft power in the context of relations between the world of peace (primarily inhabited by the Muslim faithful) and Darul Jihad (Place of war). This was seen as a tactical compromise (personal communication with Dr. Dhada, May 13, 2011).

[18] It is possible that certain religious traditions will become more acceptable that others in a secular structure. Buddhism with its meditative traditions might become more culturally acceptable in a secular world – how this necessarily translates into extension of soft power is a problematic issue.

[19] Ikenberry and Kupchan (1990: 283) examine how hegemonic power is sustained not only by the use of material incentives but more importantly at the level of substantive beliefs. Acquiescence of leaders in secondary nations is achieved through socialization. Elites in these states consent to the norms articulated by the hegemon and pursue policies consistent with the hegemon's preferences. An interesting argument forwarded in this context is that of John Owen (2001: 121) who contends that the presence of political liberalism as a transnational movement explains the acceptance of the hegemonic power of the United States. Thus hegemonic power is sustained because liberal states do not challenge the hegemon.

soft power of a state may be diminishing. This also depends on the context and the degree to which the agent wants to extend soft power. If the intention is to have a global appeal, in the modern context an argument can be made that secular states are more likely to be appealing.[20] However if the focus of one's attention is regional or more localized, then perhaps religion becomes important.

Political: Lastly, the political structure of the international system and whether that system is unipolar, bipolar, or multipolar, would shape the context and degree to which the state in question could extend soft power. Perhaps we can think in the following manner:

- *Unipolar*: The hegemon is able to extend considerable soft power – especially if the hegemon is not perceived as threatening.[21]
- *Bipolar*: Two great powers extend their influence in different realms and are thus able to constrain each other. Obviously, the US-SU relationship comes to mind, with one extending over the other eventually.[22]
- *Multipolar*: Here soft power becomes more fragmented as different states have the capacity to extend their power within certain zones of influence.[23] A multipolar system will make it more difficult to extend soft power, in the sense that there will be too many states competing to extend soft power. Furthermore a multipolar world might present alternative models of growth – social, political and economic – thereby diminishing the appeal of a single model. Perhaps we can see the beginnings of this in the increasing debate about the influence of Beijing consensus as opposed to a Washington consensus (Cho and Jeong 2008: 461–466).

[20] Of course it does not necessarily have to be one or the other – states may be able to balance their appeal. For instance, there has been some conversation about the emergence of Turkey as a model state for states that are experiencing civil unrest in the North African and Middle Eastern region (early 2011). Turkey is seen by some to have balanced the demands of secular and religious traditions without significantly sacrificing one for the other. For states with large Muslim populations, Turkey presents a more appropriate model of statehood than the classic liberal Western states. Nevertheless, this may not be the perception of states within the European Union that see Turkey as an 'other' and not quite a state that has managed to overcome or balance its Islamic heritage (see Neumann 1999).

[21] In this regard, Ikenberry's (2001) argument about 'binding institutions' becomes relevant to the extent that the winning state is not perceived as a threat and is able to create conditions for cooperation with and amongst other states in the international system. Similar arguments may be seen in Owen (2001).

[22] I disagree with Nye that the Soviets did not have soft power – I think that depends on which part of the world one is looking *from* and *at*.

[23] Nye (2004: 73–89) discusses the extension of soft power by other states such as Soviet Union, France, Japan among others. However he contends that the United States has the most appropriate resources for the extension of soft power. That said, Nye makes a reference to 'soft balancing' (2004: 26–27) wherein states will align with each other and extend their power in such a manner as to make it difficult for the United States to use hard power. He discusses this in the context of denial of legitimacy to the US for actions against Iraq.

Relational power: Power may be understood as a structural or relational concept. While we focused on structures in the preceding section, the concern in this section is with relational power. Relational power may be understood in terms of agent-subject relations; that is relationship between the state that is extending soft power and the receptive state.[24] In order to understand this relationship it is important not only to understand (a) the structural location and positioning of these states vis-à-vis each other (b) but also in the context of regional or other power configurations (c) as well as the internal power dynamics within the state that is at the receiving end of soft power. Thus, the ability of state A depends on the structural position of that state vis-à-vis the target state – the discussion in the preceding section is useful here. Regarding regional or other power configurations, it is possible that soft power deployed positively in one state or region, may be perceived negatively in another.[25] Thus when a state allies, assists or is seen to have a close relationship with a state that is deemed a pariah state, it risks its ability to extend soft power vis-à-vis other states in the region. America's close relationship with Israel is a case in point to the extent that it complicates American relationships with other Arab states in the region and restricts extension of soft power in those states.[26]

Lastly, the question of power dynamics within the state; internal relations between elites [defined as those who hold political/economic and cultural power] and masses within a particular target state shape the receptivity of soft power. Nye and others discuss to some extent the idea of soft power impacting the elites and masses in a different way.[27] Hence the resources of soft power (cultural attractiveness, political values and foreign/diplomatic policy) as conveyed through a series of tools may be received differently. Since there is no systematic discussion of this aspect of soft power, it is to our advantage perhaps to think along the following lines:

---

[24] Edward Lock (2010: 42) persuasively argues that one of the problematic elements of soft power is its inability to account for relational and structural power. In essence, Lock argues that to understand power we have to understand not only how the agent extends power, but also how receptive the subject is to the extension of that power. "The successful exercise of power, by definition, requires the subject of power to decide to act in a manner consistent with one's intention."

[25] Oguzlu (2007: 85) seems to support this argument. He argues that Turkey lost soft power in the Middle Eastern region when it was seen to be an extension of NATO, which was viewed as an agent of imperial powers.

[26] However it is not clear whether this is a general condition. Consider a similar situation with China having a close relationship with North Korea, another pariah state. It appears that China is able to use this relationship to its advantage – in the sense that it does not seem to have adversely affected the extension of Chinese soft power in a significant manner, though it is also a fact that China's neighbors (South Korea and Japan) are cautious. Perhaps the difference lies in the perception that the US is having an enabling affect on Israel, whereas China is seen as having a moderating effect on North Korea.

[27] Nye (2010: 4) states "soft power is a relationship of attraction that *depends on the eyes of the beholders*" (emphasis added). Wang and Lu also raise the question of the target audience – elites or masses and control over policy formulation. They argue that during the Cold War, citizens in Eastern Europe might have found Western culture attractive, but not the elites (see Wang and Lu 2008: 446).

- *Situation 1*: The soft power influence of state A is received *positively* [+] in state B both by *elites and masses*.
- *Situation 2*: The soft power influence of state A is received *negatively* [−] in state B both by *elites and masses*.
- *Situation 3*: The soft power influence of state A is received *positively [±] by the elites but negatively [−] by the masses*.
- *Situation 4*: The soft power influence of state A is received *negatively [−] by the elites but positively [±] by the masses*.
- *Situation 5*: The soft power influence of state A is received *negatively and positively*.
- *[−/+] by the elites and the masses*: In this scenario elites and masses may be reacting to various tools of soft power with varying intensity of negative and positive reaction.

Thus if we have a sense of state/society relations [assessing the degree of disjuncture between state and society], we might be in a better position to understand how relations between elites and masses will affect the receptivity of power and hence whether the agent (in this context a state) is gaining or loosing soft power. This basic framework can be further complicated by adding other states to the picture. That is extension of soft power is not restricted to state A, but may be simultaneously extended by state C, and so forth.

Moral authority or legitimacy: Nye contends that states that are seen to have legitimacy or moral authority are more likely to exert soft power.[28] In the post second world war context, such legitimacy is seen to be derived from values, institutions and multilateral action. Nye makes the argument that states that undertake unilateral action are likely to find their ability to extend soft power constrained. In fact there has been considerable focus on the loss of American soft power during the actions undertaken by the American administration after September 9/11 – in particular the attack on Iraq. *Legitimacy may thus be seen as a consequence of internal and external attributes* in so far as states must be seen as legitimate internally and externally. That is, under certain structural conditions (economic, political and cultural), certain kinds of actions will be considered legitimate as opposed to others – as discussed previously. That said, there are some other actions of states in the international arena that will grant greater or lesser moral authority to these states. In the sections that follow I discuss two of these; failure to provide public goods and hubris.[29]

[28] Notions of moral authority and legitimacy again are not without contention, even as they are deployed in the scholarly world and the practical arena of international relations. They raise significant questions regarding 'who' bestows moral authority (civil society, state, non-governmental organizations, international organizations like the UN) or recognizes actions as legitimate or illegitimate.

[29] While Nye does refer to hypocrisy (understood as the difference between rhetoric and action) as one of the criteria for loss of soft power, it is not included in this specific discussion since almost all states are hypocritical. The question is: At what point does hypocrisy become damaging to soft power? And who is recognizing the hypocrisy of the nation, because obviously nations get away with a lot of hypocrisy unless they are called on it, and it depends a lot on who is doing the calling.

Failure to provide public goods: States, especially great states derive their power not only from economic and military resources, but also from their ability to undertake some tasks in the international system that do not directly result in tangible rewards for the state, but that do shape the image of the state and thus make it more or less appealing. Typically this may relate to the assistance by the state to others in times of crisis – such as natural calamities [earthquake, tsunami, drought, and epidemics], other humanitarian crisis [as in genocide, civil war] securing international waters and so forth. It is plausible to argue that it is not so much the routine provision of public goods [as perhaps in a domestic arena] but the more urgent, context-specific crisis reaction that constitutes the defining moment. Small states, as minor players in the international system are not required to provide public good – that is, it is does not damage their legitimacy or credibility if they do not provide these goods. But the expectation from major powers is different. An example in this instance can be the actions taken by China in the wake of the Asian financial crisis in 1997 or those of the US after the tsunami in Asia in 2001. When major powers do not react to such events in a positive manner, there is a significant loss of soft power.

Hubris: There is an old saying – 'power corrupts'. Essentially one of the challenges of existence as individuals and collectives [states] relates to the question of power. Invariably power has a corrupting influence to the extent that we [individuals and states] are persuaded of our invincibility and ability to shape the world as we may. In the context of discussions in IR we can retrieve the insights offered by Thucydides regarding the pitfalls and misfortunes of actions that are motivated by hubris – which in turn may be driven by a sort of moral narcissism. When states are seen as projecting their power regardless of dissent, or tout their values as exceptional, they run the risk of reducing their soft power. Interestingly enough, while civilizational/national pride is deemed intrinsic to collectives and enhances their power both internally and externally, such pride may have counter-productive consequences. The argument in this regard, is that such action will breed dissent and suspicion of the state in question. Once again though, it seems to matter a lot as to who is doing the distrusting. It seems that losing the trust of key allies is more damaging to a state's soft power than the distrust of states ideologically different to unfriendly.[30]

Regarding internal attributes, Nye indicates the relevance of values and institutions. The argument for the extension of soft power clearly hinges on the internal political, social, and economic institutions of the state. It is these institutions and the principles they embody that emerge as significant resources that are and can be mobilized by the state. Clearly for a state to be regarded as attractive – these are crucial factors. That said, it could be argued that it is the *nature of state-society relations* that are more fundamental. Thus the degree of closeness

[30] North Korea having distrust of the US obviously doesn't matter much at all regarding US soft power, but losing the trust of Britain would probably have a significant impact.

between state and society will affect how states are perceived.[31] Invariably, those states that have significant disjuncture between state and society are states that may be unstable and less likely to draw positive attention. At the extreme end are the failed states. However these are rare and mostly the international system consists of states that have varying degree of state-society relations, some more close than others. States can extend soft power when there is a close fit between the two. But when there is a significant disjuncture between state and society – states lose soft power. Typically, those states that have stable ethnic/national relations,[32] no significant disparity of wealth, and are democratic – are more likely to have stable state-society relations. The underlying assumption in this context is that civil society institutions do not aggressively challenge the state – thus even in stable states it is the degree to which civil organizations support or challenge the state – that allows for the extension of power. The challenge posed by civilians in the United States regarding its actions in Vietnam severely damaged the reputation of the state and may be seen as having impacted its moral legitimacy.[33] Thus when members of the civil society engage in open and mass dissent through demonstrations and riots, the perceived legitimacy of a state is damaged. Conversely, when there is a close nexus between public and private institutions, this appears to bolster the soft power appeal of the state – especially when the state appears to be absent. Parmar (2010) argues that the efforts of philanthropic organizations such as the Ford Foundation were significant in bolstering the soft power of the United States, essentially because it took the form of non-propoganda propaganda.[34] It is when such civil institutions support the ideological foundations of the state, and its actions, that the state is likely to gain soft power. Further, civil society institutions can and do create their own soft power, sometimes this power extends the influence of the state, but it also has the capacity of damaging the soft power of the state. Popular culture for instance has been perceived as a tool of soft power. However, popular culture can be perceived in both negative and positive

[31] However, it is important to clarify that this degree of closeness really depends on whether the state in question is democratic or not. Totalitarian states exhibit a fusion of state and society, but that is not seen as a legitimate mode of governance.

[32] In this regard, Miller's (2005) state-to-nation balance or imbalance becomes a key factor. Miller argues in a different context that the greater the state-to-nation imbalance in a region, the greater the war propensity within the region. It could be argued that Miller's ideas may be applied within the context of the state – those states that are challenged by demands for secession where there are several national articulations are less likely to have cohesive state-society relations.

[33] Nye (2004) discusses the challenge within the US from the media and other organizations, to the war in Vietnam. It made the actions of the state less legitimate.

[34] Parmar (2010) observes that institutions like the Ford foundation were significant in promoting Americanism and combating Anti-Americanism, as they worked through elite universities such as Harvard. In particular he refers to the success of Henry Kissinger's Harvard and Salzburg Seminar Series, where in elites from other states were invited to the United States, exposed to the institutions and principles of the United States, along with the experience of living in the country – so that they may appreciate the unique nature of the American system.

ways within the target state and hence may not always be to the advantage of the state that seeks to extend soft power.

Historical conditions: Are significant for understanding the situations under which states may gain or lose power because they provide the contextual environment within which states function. In this regard, it is possible to distinguish between *historical junctures and historical events*. Historical junctures are the consequence of a series of historical events that trigger distinct and significant shifts in the historical trajectory of states or the international system. For instance, historical junctures are conditions wherein certain dramatic events or crisis allow for the emergence and acceptance of power of certain states.[35] An example in this context may be the emergence of the United States and the Soviet Union at the end of the Second World War. Both these states had certain degrees of soft power because of the devastation in much of the world, collapse of the existing colonial states and different ideological orientations that were appealing. These historical junctures and the subsequent emergence of powerful states create a degree of path dependency to the extent that dominant states that do emerge have a significant level of power and attraction for the other states in the system at least until the other states begin to rival the dominant powers. Another instance of an historical juncture is colonialism, and in this context it is possible that soft power may both, be extended or limited. Post-colonial literature indicates that erstwhile colonized states incorporate some of the aspects of the colonizing power.[36] Clearly post-colonial states have inevitably adopted similar political, economic and even cultural institutions.[37] That said, it is also a fact that it is these post-colonial states or elites within them who were trained in the classic colonial tradition that overthrew the erstwhile colonizers.[38] Perhaps we can think of three possibilities in this context:

[35] Ikenberry and Kupchan (1990: 284) discuss the socialization of norms thus ensuring the extension of hegemonic power. They hypothesize that one of the first conditions is that "socialization occurs primarily after wars and political crisis, periods marked by international turmoil and restructuring as well as the fragmentation of ruling coalitions and legitimacy crises at the domestic level. The simultaneity of international and domestic instability creates the conditions conducive to socialization."

[36] Ashis Nandy (1988) discusses the complex identity constructions in colonizing and colonized states in the context of relationship between Britain and India.

[37] Post-colonial states are not merely at the receiving end of the extension of soft power by the erstwhile colonizing state. For instance, the United States may be seen as a post-colonial state of sorts – but one which is able to extend power in the international system because it is a beneficiary of the legacy of British colonialism in terms of language, political structures and liberal philosophy. It is also possible that erstwhile colonizers are able to extend power when their rule over the colonized state lasted for a substantial period of time, was accompanied by significant structural change within the state and allowed for the embedding of the colonized state in an international structure that favored the imperial states. The difference between the European and the Japanese imperial expansions comes to mind in this regard.

[38] Ferguson (2003) writes that it was the archetype Bengali babu quoting Shakespeare and working for the British, that was the bane of the British empire in India (see also the discussion in Ikenberry and Kupchan 1990). In the context of Turkey, Oguzlu (2007: 85) points out that the imperial legacy of the Ottoman empire has made the other states suspicious of Turkey.

- *Situation 1*: Colonialism leads state A (the erstwhile colony) to be receptive to state B (colonial power). This may be seen as a *positive* [+] from the perspective of state B.
- *Situation 2*: Colonialism leads state A to reject [−] soft power tools extended by state B.
- *Situation 3*: Colonialism leads state A to respond *positively and negatively* to the attempts of state B to extend soft power.

This discussion of historical events and junctures is necessarily brief and I have not included other conditions such as internal and external conflict, revolutions, significant natural disasters, diaspora and other such phenomena.

Conclusion

In the preceding discussion, I have attempted to lay down some conditions that may shape a state's ability to gain or loose soft power. A state's ability to extend soft power depends on both internal and external conditions – some of which are more critical than others. Clearly the ability to extend power depends on capabilities (as in requisite political, economic and cultural power) and intentions of states, but more importantly on the external conditions such as structure of the international system and historical conditions within which the state is embedded. This is necessarily a preliminary attempt at understanding these conditions and much work needs to be done to examine each of these conditions in greater detail and to understand how they relate to each other.

Acknowledgements I would like to acknowledge the assistance of Robert Etcheverry in the preparation of this paper.

References

Bell, D. (2009). War peace and China's soft power: A Confucian approach. *Diogenes, 56*, 26–40.
Bull, H. (1977). *The anarchical society: A study of order in world politics*. New York: Columbia University Press.
Cho, Y. N., & Jeong, J. H. (2008). China's soft power: Discussions, resources and prospects. *Asian Survey, 48*, 453–472.
Ding, S. (2008). *The dragon's hidden wings: How China rises with its soft power*. Lanham: Lexington Books.
Ferguson, N. (2003). Think again: Power. *Foreign Policy, 134*, 18–24.
Fraser, M. (2005). *Weapons of mass distraction: Soft power and American empire*. New York: Thomas Dunne Books.
Geiger, T. (2010). The power game, soft power and the international historian. In I. Paramar & M. Cox (Eds.), *Soft power and US foreign policy: Theoretical, historical and contemporary perspectives*. New York: Routledge.
Hunter, A. (2009). Soft power: China on the global stage. *The Chinese Journal of International Politics, 2*, 373–398.
Ikenberry, J., & Kupchan, C. (1990). Socialization and hegemonic power. *International Organization, 44*, 283–315.

Ikenberry, J. (2001). *After victory: Institutions, strategic restraint, and the rebuilding of order after major wars*. Princeton: Princeton University Press.
Kurlantzick, J. (2005). The decline of American soft power. *Current History, 104*(686), 419–424.
Kurlantzick, J. (2007). *Charm offensive: How China's soft power is transforming the world*. New Haven: Yale University Press.
Layne, C. (2010). The unbearable lightness of soft power. In I. Parmar & M. Cox (Eds.), *Soft power and US foreign policy: Theoretical, historical and contemporary perspectives*. New York: Routledge.
Lebow, R. (2005). Power, persuasion and justice. *Millennium, 33*, 551–582.
Li, M. (2009). *Soft power: China's emerging strategy in international politics*. Lanham: Lexington Books.
Lock, E. (2010). Soft power and strategy: Developing a 'strategic' concept of power. In I. Parmar & M. Cox (Eds.), *Soft power and US foreign policy: Theoretical, historical and contemporary perspectives*. New York: Routledge.
Miller, B. (2005). When and how regions become peaceful: Potential theoretical pathways to peace. *International Studies Review, 7*, 229–267.
Nandy, A. (1988). *The intimate enemy: Loss and recovery of self under colonialism*. Delhi: Oxford University Press.
Neumann, I. (1999). *Uses of the other: 'The East' in European identity formation*. Minneapolis: University of Minnesota Press.
Nye, J. (2002). *The paradox of American power: Why the world's only superpower can't go it alone*. New York: Oxford University Press.
Nye, J. (2004). *Soft power: The means to success in world politics*. New York: Public Affairs.
Nye, J. (2010). The future of soft power in US foreign policy. In I. Parmar & M. Cox (Eds.), *Soft power and US foreign policy: Theoretical, historical and contemporary perspectives*. New York: Routledge.
Oguzlu, T. (2007). Soft power in Turkish foreign policy. *Australian Journal of International Affairs, 61*, 81–97.
Owen, J. (2001/2002). Transnational liberalism and US primacy. *International Security, 26*, 117–152.
Paramar, I. (2010). Challenging elite anti-Americanism in the Cold War: American foundations, Kissinger's Harvard seminar and the Salzburg seminar in American studies. In I. Paramar & M. Cox (Eds.), *Soft power and US foreign policy: Theoretical, historical and contemporary perspectives*. New York: Routledge.
Price, R. (1997). *The chemical weapons taboo*. Ithaca: Cornell University Press.
Rugh, W. (2006). *American encounters with Arabs: The soft power of US diplomacy in the middle East*. London: Praeger Security International.
Seiichi, K. (2008). Wielding soft power: The key stages of transmission and reception. In Y. Watanabe & D. McConnell (Eds.), *Soft power superpowers: Cultural and national assets of Japan and the United States*. Watertown: East Gate Books.
Strange, S. (1994). *States and markets*. Kingslynn, Norfolk: Biddles.
Tannenwald, N. (2007). *The nuclear taboo: The United States and the non-use of nuclear weapons since 1945*. Cambridge: Cambridge University Press.
Tsygankov, A. (2006). If not by tanks, then by banks? The role of soft power in Putin's foreign policy. *Europe-Asia Studies, 58*, 1079–1099.
Wallerstein, I. (1974). *The modern world system: Capitalist agriculture and the origins of the European world economy in the sixteenth century*. New York: Academic.
Wang, H., & Lu, Y.-C. (2008). The conception of soft power and its policy implications: A comparative study of China and Taiwan. *Journal of Contemporary China, 17*, 425–447.
Watanabe, Y., & McConnell, D. (2008). *Soft power superpowers: Cultural and national assets of Japan and the United States*. Watertown: East Gate Books.
Zahran, G., & Ramos, L. (2010). From hegemony to soft power: Implications of conceptual change. In I. Parmar & M. Cox (Eds.), *Soft power and US foreign policy: Theoretical, historical and contemporary perspectives*. New York: Routledge.

Chapter 4
Towards a New Understanding of Structural Power: "Structure Is What States Make of It"

Andrej Pustovitovskij and Jan-Frederik Kremer

res tantum valet quantum vendi potest–
a thing/good is worth only what someone else will pay for it
(Ancient Roman Saying)

Introduction

The study of power in International Relations (IR) can be seen as the search for the cornerstone of our discipline. Hardly any theory or approach of IR can claim evidence and explanatory power without at least implicitly addressing the question of the ontology of power. In this article we will, by introducing our concept of structural[1] power, offer a new path towards understanding a concept famously introduced in the 1980s by Susan Strange (1987, 1988a, 1988b), but still lacking clarity in operationalization and application. By addressing the questions: "How does structural power work?/How does structural power change the rules of the game?/How is structural power constituted?/Through which kind of transmission channels does structural power affect the power position of states?/What are the underlying power resources of structural power? What is the relationship between structural power and other forms of power?", our approach to structural power will, by answering these questions, offer a new approach towards the study of power in IR and will foster the understanding of a concept which can help to understand international relations in an interdependent age. By doing so, we will present a concept of structural power which differs from the concept of Susan Strange, but which is also able to enclose her ideas about power structures in world politics, by examining the importance of states' needs and goods for their structural power position in international relations. The aim of this article is to foster a new understanding of structural power, by introducing a concept of structural power

[1] Here we define structure as the interrelation or arrangement of parts in a complex entity.

E. Fels et al. (eds.), *Power in the 21st Century*, Global Power Shift,
DOI 10.1007/978-3-642-25082-8_4, © Springer-Verlag Berlin Heidelberg 2012

independent from the assumed, but empirically not proofed existence of a specific number of dominant power (sub-)structures and certain resources, but based on a model of structure able to enclose changes in power structures in international affairs.

To lay the foundation, we first give a brief overview of the existing approaches and debates on structural power in IR. Secondly, we present our core assumptions and propositions. In a third step, we introduce our theoretical framework of structural power. We then will also address the question of how structural power can be understood and how its effects can be explained. Furthermore, it will be shown how structural power works and how a state might be able to improve its own position in terms of possessing structural power.

Discussion: Power and IR

In the field of IR, a variety of approaches have been developed to understand what power in international affairs actually means, how it is used, what sort of overt or covert mechanisms it relies on and what kind of power sources should be considered more important than others (see Baldwin 1979; 2002).[2] Typically, realist and neo-realist theories conceptualize power as the overall amount of capabilities possessed by a state. They regard hard power, mainly military might and pure economic power, as dominating other means of power application (Waltz 1979; Walt 1991; Gilpin 1981).

In this understanding, the possession of a larger number of relevant resources (like GDP, territory, population, size of the military, etc.) transforms more or less automatically into more power and therefore into more security for the state in an anarchic international system (Baumann et al. 1999: 250). According to the neo-realist school in international relations, the amount of resources possessed by a state (power-as-resources understanding) constitutes its hard power capabilities and is therefore essential for identifying its power position in the international structure. It is assumed that the larger a state's power resources are, the greater is the probability of its ability to achieve the superior national preference (Waltz 1990; Mearsheimer 1995; Grieco 1995: 27). However, empirical evidence and various studies have shown that the mere possession of hard power capabilities is not sufficient for a state to govern outcomes in an effective and preference-satisfying way on the international level.

For instance, the United States of America today hold an undisputed pre-eminence in the international system with regards to hard power capabilities (Norrlof 2010; Joffe 2006), especially when it comes to military power – a pre-eminence which is almost second to none in historic comparison (Ferguson 2005, BPSM).

However, although these hard power capabilities should allow the U.S. to shape outcomes in a way that matches their preferences in international politics, as the

[2] For a longer discussion on different concepts of power in IR see Chap. 1 of Enrico Fels in this volume.

hard power approach would assume, empirical research has shown that over the last decades the USA have had increasing difficulties satisfying their preferences unilaterally in many sectors.[3]

Also Nye's concept of soft power (Nye 1990a, 1990b, 2004a, 2004b) is short-coming, when it comes to explaining the whole range of international relations and advocates of soft power have so far failed to clarify when and where governments of great and middle powers changed their position on major issues due to the ideational attractiveness and normative persuasion of other countries. While there are cases in history in which hard power played a crucial role in allowing one party to coerce another to subdue, proponents of soft power theory found it much harder to present such examples and to present an analytical framework which allows us to operationalize soft power in international relations (see Kagan 2002).

A second school of scholars in political science has introduced a concept of power, seeing power as a relational concept. Based on Max Weber's definition, defining power as "the probability that one actor within a social relationship will be in a position to carry out his own will despite resistance" (Weber 1947, Dahl 1957 also uses this concept), power derives from the relationship between two or more actors and the context the actors are imbedded in and not only from capabilities themselves. The value of capabilities in this concept is determined by the relational context (cf. Baldwin 1979).

The third widely debated understanding of power in international relations depicts power in structural terms. Proponents of this understanding see power as mainly related to the establishment of structures, or the control over structures, in international relations. The concept of structural power became popular with the writings of Susan Strange (see Ward 1987; Lawton et al. 2000). Strange defines structural power as the power "to decide how things shall be done, the power to shape frameworks within which states relate to each other, relate to people, or relate to corporate enterprises" (Strange 1988a: 25). She adds that structural power "means rather more than the power to set the agenda of discussion or to design" (ibid.). Strange emphasizes that "power over structures" is more important than "power from resources", thus arguing for a reconsideration of the actual value of economic resources and military capabilities for the outcomes of divergences between great powers in the modern world (Strange 1996: 25–30). In Strange's understanding, power cannot only settle outcomes within interstate relations due to material or ideational factors but, "even more importantly", power can shape and define the structures or tacit bargains states are actually embedded in and these structures become a resource of power by framing the rules of the game in favour of

[3] Take for example the problems of the U.S. to achieve its preferences in the disputes with North Korea and Iran as well as in the sphere of international trade (e.g. implementing the Singapore topics into the WTO regime). The more general question whether U.S. hegemony is in decline or remains unchallenged still mainly depends on structural factors in terms of institutions, military and economics (Ikenberry 2003, 2004; Katzenstein 2005; Ferguson 2003; Mann 2003; Bacevich 2008; Joffe 2006; Zakaria 2011).

the actor. States that have the ability to exert control over these international relevant power structures (security, finance, production, knowledge) thus influence the framework defining their relations with other states. This comes close to what Steven Krasner (1985: 14) calls meta-power, i.e. the power "to change the rules of the game". Guzzini (1993) describes that other authors have tried to distinguish different categories of power, related to the control or effect of structures (indirect institutional power, non-intentional power, impersonal power), but failed to offer a way for application of these concept in IR.

Looking back, it can be said that numerous scholars of IR have undertaken remarkable efforts to address ontological questions, the causes and the effects of structural power in international relations. However, the existing approaches fall short when it comes to the operationalization of the concept of structural power for the analysis of international relations and when it comes to the theoretical explanation of the causal mechanisms of structural power. Sticking to specific and restricted ontological prepositions existing approaches are unsuitable to explain structural changes. Having discussed the existing approaches in political science/IR towards power/structural power we will present our approach towards structural power, starting with the prepositions and assumptions of our concept in the following chapters.

Prepositions and Assumptions

We agree with a broad range of scholars assuming deep interdependence of international relations (most famously Keohane and Nye 1977, 2001; Keohane 1984; Baldwin 1980). This means that the actors are to an increasing extent not able to satisfy the full range of their own needs themselves and are therefore dependent on cooperation, trade and negotiations. The actors' only, yet limited, alternative might be war (we consider states as the primary, though not sole, agents of IR). However, this alternative becomes more and more costly and unattractive, especially when nuclear powers are involved and/or it comes to negotiations between strategic partners. Accordingly, actors try to satisfy their own needs in ongoing negotiations with each other. They act boundedly rational, which means that they are comprehensively – but not fully – informed. Therefore the distribution of information can be significant in negotiations.

Furthermore, we assume that *goods* satisfy the *needs* of states. Theoretically, any need may be completely satisfied (a satisfaction of 100%) or not at all (a satisfaction of 0%)[4] and the state of interest will be located some place between these two theoretical poles. We define *goods* more widely, as anything that may meet a need and can hypothetically be exchanged for other goods. We also follow the

[4] The quality of needs stated in percentages is used in this paper for the purpose of better illustration and exemplification and not for analytical purpose.

assumption that needs of states accumulate from the needs of different groups (social, economic, etc.) and that we are able to identify these needs through analysis and to rank needs, like e.g. Moravcsik (1991, 1993, 1997), Schirm (2005, 2009, 2011), Dür (2007) and others have shown. It is not the objective of this paper to develop a method to measure the needs in qualitative terms, but it is important to note that it is possible to elaborate and rank the needs by using analytical tools, which are already well introduced (Moravcsik 1997). Needs as well as goods differ in quality, as we will show below.

Goods and Types of Goods

First, let us clarify the difference between resources and goods. Resources are anything an actor can theoretically access freely within his cruising radius. These resources turn into goods, when another actor articulates a corresponding need and an exchange with another good becomes possible. As a result, material and positional goods exist physically as resources, but only turn into goods when they are related to a need. Ideational goods, however, are only materialized when they are met by a need.

We basically distinguish three types of goods: *material*, *positional* and *ideational* goods. Examples for material goods are money, manufactured products etc. The term positional goods refers to a convenient positioning, may it be in geographical terms, e.g. a passage for transport, or in terms of negotiation, e.g. a certain asset in an IGO such as the IMF. Ideational goods are more problematic to define. These goods do not per se exist as mentioned above, but arise only from a specific need for them. In contrast to material or positional goods, ideational goods are of a virtual nature; they only exist as long as there is a need for them. Without the idea of general human rights, for example, there can be no need for the good "human right". Should an adequate need for the idea of universal human rights arise in a country such as Germany, then good governance or human rights in China could be seen as an ideational good which would be suitable for satisfying Germany's ideational need. Moreover, a state's need for greater recognition or legitimacy may be satisfied by a good, e.g. in the form of a visit by the U.S. President. Such a wide conceptualization of goods allows us to include a full range of IR-issues in our analysis.

Since we assume that goods can generally be exchanged in any combination, this distinction is primarily made for the subsequent operationalization.

Availability of Goods

More important than the distinction between the different types of goods is the aspect of *availability*. Basically, we distinguish three levels of availability – goods of *general* availability (e.g. soil, wind, low-tech products, etc.), goods of *limited* availability (e.g. oil, rare earths, know-how, UN Security Council membership, key markets, etc.) and goods of *exclusive* availability (such as certain patents and technologies, access to certain geographic areas like the Panama Canal, certain raw materials and ideational goods, etc.). As a measure of scarcity, availability of the goods is not primarily dependent on the number of goods potentially available but on the amount of goods *actually* available for exchange. A raw material may be widespread, i.e. a *general* good, but if it is extracted only in relatively small amount, without an option to increase its amount in the short term (e.g. due to long development terms of new fields, etc.) it becomes a *limited* good. This implies that the availability of goods may be artificially limited by the actors or may generally be very limited due to an actor's strategy. Know-how is in principle unlimitedly reproducible, but is usually spread by the owner in a very limited way.

Since a vast number of goods falls in the categories of limited or exclusive goods because of their quantitative limitations or limited provision, actors permanently compete for goods, especially in those cases where the needs of two or more actors overlap. Goods inevitably become objects of trade if one actor needs them and is not able to produce them himself or to substitute them at acceptable costs. Consequently, players are at any given time engaged in different negotiations with states and non-state actors to satisfy their own needs via acquisition or exchange of goods.

Critical to the significance of goods is not only their availability, but the correlation of the characteristics of the goods themselves and the nature of actors' needs in the particular constellation.

Needs

Needs differ in their *relevance* and *urgency*. Here we partly follow the concept introduced in bargaining theories (see Muthoo 2000; Schneider 2005). The relevance of the needs of an actor depend on the accumulation of the relevance and the urgency by endogenous groups trying to shape the government's policy – the more a group is able to push its needs, or the more groups share common needs, the stronger their relevance.[5] The urgency of the needs depends on the discrepancy between the extent to which an actor has already satisfied a need and the (theoretical) possible maximum coverage. For example, in a fictional case, the need for security in Germany may be covered at 80%, in contrast to Israel's at only 40%. Hence, the urgency in Israel in this area is much higher. We can derive the relevance and urgency of the actor's needs, for example by analyzing the preference of the state (for example through the interpretation of strategy papers, government files, news coverage, interviews, documents, speeches, etc.).

[5] Cf. e.g. Moravcsik (1997).

Rare Goods

The significance (as a quality) of goods is the combination of their availability on the one hand, and the relevance and urgency (as well as their accumulation among the actors) on the other hand. A combination unfavourable for an actor (low availability on the one side and/or high relevance and urgency of the needs on the other) leads to *rarity* of goods, which is why we speak of *rare* goods. Hence "rare" does not mean scarcity of goods per se, but a high demand in contrast to the amount of goods available. Rare goods are by virtue of their quality more important than non-rare goods.

Basket

The total of all goods that can be offered by an actor for exchange is his *basket*.

Structural Power

After these preliminary considerations, we will introduce the core of our approach to structural power. Let us look at the outside option variable.

Player A can strengthen his position vis-à-vis actor B if he can boast an outside option (OO) in a negotiating situation.[6] This OO (player C) possessses a good that meets the needs of A and is offered under comparable or better conditions. Player C has to be apparent as an (willing and able) OO for B. Since B's perception of C being an OO for A is crucial, it gives A the possibility to bluff. It also makes a situation possible where B is aware of C being A's OO, but does not realise A's non-awareness of C being an OO. In this case, the structural power of A has a non-intentional character.

Goods that C will be offered by A in exchange do not need to be the same goods as offered to B. The more OOs actor A is able to accrue, the weaker is B's position in negotiations with A in this round, since we assume the power relation here to be a zero-sum game. In addition, A may be an OO for C in some other bargaining situation. Accordingly, this may mean a power gain for C in a parallel negotiation round. Due to the fact that a reasonable alternative exists, A now possesses (structural) power (e.g. A may play C off against B), even though A's capability endowment remains unchanged. Only the specific situational context, namely the emergence of one or possibly even several OO gives A (structural) power (Fig. 4.1).

---

[6] Likewise connected to this consideration is the lack of structural power in the case of martial conflicts, in which no negotiations of any kind take place. Here the resources are only used for one's own needs (for attacking or defense), so that in this case any measurement results in measuring resource power.

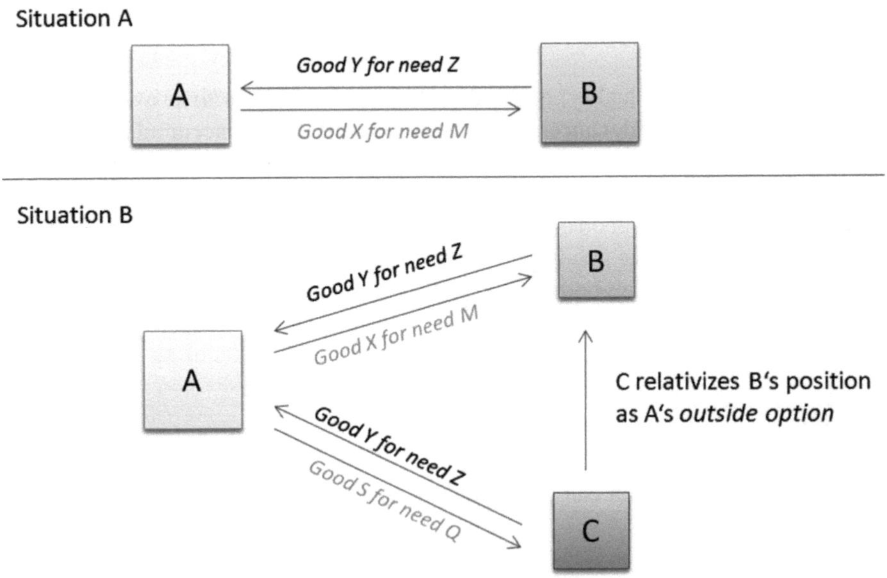

Fig. 4.1 The importance of outside options in international affairs

The ability to attract OOs and also to become an OO for third actors depends on how *rare* the goods in the basket of an actor are. Basically, the rarer the goods in the basket the higher is the probability of attracting OOs or of becoming an OO for other actors. The main point for our considerations is that the combination constituted from the needs of all players and all goods offered by them for exchange constitutes a structure which may provide actors with structural power in negotiations. Accordingly a state has structural power if:

> A state possesses a specific set of goods (basket) which it may offer for exchange in an international bargaining situation and parts of the composition of his basket meet the demand of other actors particularly well AND his own needs are highly compatible with the range of supply (baskets of all other actors) in the system the state is embedded in. Due to the former aspect, the possibility rises to be an OO for other players, because of the latter aspect the number of potential OOs for the actor himself rises.

Based on these prepositions, let us have a closer look of how this concept works: On the one hand it can be stated that an actor (actor A) holds power over another actor (actor B), if he is the only one able to offer goods desperately needed by B. B does not have any OO and thus holds a much less favorable bargaining position. If, however, one or more actors appear who offer B the same good – provided that the vendors have not formed a syndicate – B now has several OOs apart from A. His bargaining position has improved drastically.

On the one hand the power of those actors who are now able to serve as OO has increased, on the other hand B's power has been extended since he can from now on in any bargaining situation realistically threaten to choose an OO. The position of the actor who can now act as OO – which he could not do before – as well as that of the actor in

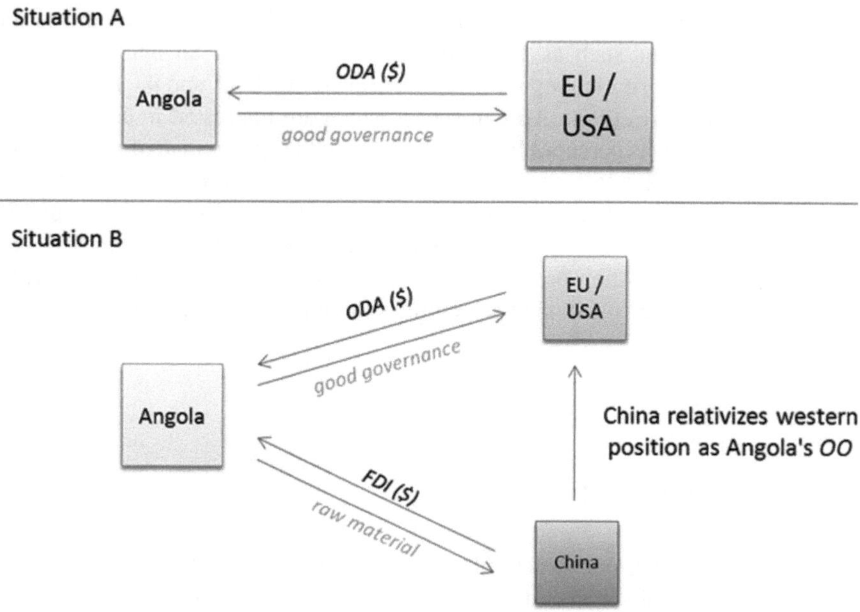

Fig. 4.2 The emergence of China as outside option (OO)

need of the good have improved in relation to A (gain of power). Actor A has suffered a loss in structural power in relation to B due to the emergence of credible OOs for B.

Let's have a closer look at this situation using the theoretical example of Official Development Assistance (ODA) and investments for Africa[7]: Before China presented herself as a donor country in Africa, the African states had mainly been dependent on ODA from the USA and the EU. Those two actors had agreed to their payments under very similar terms (good governance, transparency, human rights, etc.) – one might say they had based their conditions on their (EU and USA) mutual understanding. Apart from a very few exceptions (geo-strategically important countries, which were able to offer goods to the USA and the EU such as stability, efforts to fight terrorism, oil, etc. and thus held a favorable positions themselves) the African states had had to accept those terms if they had wanted to receive the good ODA. Due to the lack of OOs, there had been no alternative for those countries than to accept the terms. The structural position of the USA and the EU had been strong (quasi a monopoly on the needed good ODA), that of the recipient had been weak (no OOs). When China presented herself as donor country, the situation changed radically. China refused to join the "condition-syndicate" and assigned her ODA to African states without any general conditions[8]. China thus became an OO for the

[7] cf. Tull 2006; Brookes/Shin 2006; Kappel/Schneidenbach 2006; Woods 2008.

[8] China bases her promise of payment on terms such as supply of raw materials.

African countries. They were now able to receive ODA without having to meet "tedious" conditions such as good governance or others – an interesting option especially for authoritarian regimes. The position of the USA and the EU in relation (within the structure) to the African states, which are interested in achieving their own preferences, was perceptibly weakened due to the appearance of a realistic OO. The US and the EU lost structural power since they were no longer the only provider of a desperately needed good. China could for the first time act as provider of these goods and thus as OO, and may be able to use this OO in other bargaining situations in favor of their preferences. The African states also gained power; they are now able – due to the new structural situation – to choose between several options (Fig. 4.2).

Understanding of Structure

It becomes clear that our structural concept varies greatly from Strange's idea of structure: Hyperbolically said, in Strange's concept the structure resembles a labyrinth in which the powerful actor opens and closes doors and even moves walls for the mice that are inside. He is thereby able to determine the routes they take and to shape the labyrinth according to his wishes.[9] According to Strange's understanding of structure the structure is established throughout the interplay of the four main power structures in world politics (security, production, finance and knowledge) and these four separate structures influence each other. Therefore a state holds structural power, first: if he possesses important capabilities related to the main power structures and second: if he is able to exercise authority/control over the structures.

Our understanding of structure and structural power follows a different concept. We understand structure as a fluid, emergent network of interactions and relations of the actors involved, which is constituted by the goods or rather their attributes as well as by the needs of the actors and thus determines the quality of the goods contained in the actors' baskets. The quality of the goods can be influenced by all actors, both directly and indirectly, and provides the context for power-as-resource. The resources, and accordingly the resource power, influence the structure, but are located on a different level (see Fig. 4.3) than the structure and the structural power. Resources and resource power influence structural power without being an immediate part of it.

The implicit logic of this understanding of structure resembles Adam Smith's notion of a market: The market is constituted by simultaneous actions of

[9] For example, consider the principle of "Kompetenz-Kompetenz" (having authority to determine – also one's own – authorities) within the EU.

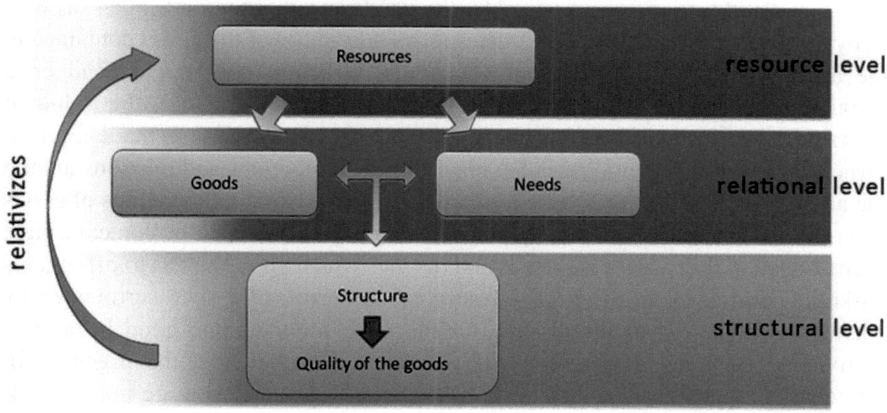

Fig. 4.3 Interaction of the three types of power

self-interested actors that do not fully control their actions' effects; it influences the actors' further actions (Balaam and Veseth 2008).

The advantage of this concept of structure and structural power is that the relation of goods and needs forms a structure, which is not dependent on highly disputable ontological prepositions. Take for example Strange's ontological preposition that there are four main power structures in world politics. Without a doubt, there might be something like a security structure and most scholars will also agree that there might be something like a production and finance structure and you might find some scholars agreeing on Strange's notions of what a global knowledge structure might look like, but her decision of choosing four main power structures and not three or five is mainly a deductively determined ontological statement without explicit empirical justification. Marxists and Neo-Marxists would argue that there is only such a thing like a production structure, which is more important than all other structures and determines world politics. Realists and mercantilists would argue for the security structures (and maybe the finance structure) as being the most important one(s). By conceptualizing structure and structural power resources/capabilities bound to a specific ontological statement about the character of the structure which consists of deductively determined 'power structures' and by arguing that control over structures is also a resource of power, the concept runs the risk of becoming tautological and of failing to encompass changes in structure on a meta level (What's exactly the relation between 'control over' and 'possessing resources'?). When there are only four (or even two, three, or whatever number of) superior 'power structures' with different relevant power-resources, and relevance of the resources is defined by the specific character of the structure itself, there remains no room for explaining changes in structure "outside" these four (like the occurrence of a new 'power structure' (e.g. the "digital structure") or the descent of a existing one, due to the empirical reality of facts). Our concept of structure and structural power offers a way to overcome these problems. Just to remind us, in our understanding structure is an emergent network of interactions and relations of the actors involved, which is constituted by the goods or rather their attributes, as well as by the needs of the actors. It thus determines the quality of the goods contained in the actors' baskets. Therefore our concept of structure does not depend on a disputable ontological statement about the character of structure, the value of different resources and/or goods in specific sectors and its relation, made a priori. Structure in our understanding is the result of the interactions and relations among the actors which take place on the fundament of the existing relationships of goods and needs of the actors and the urgency of these needs. The specific context a state is embedded in determines his needs and decides which goods he has to offer in his basket. The urgency of the need of the good 'security' of a state surrounded by enemies is higher, than the urgency of the need for the same good by a state surrounded by long lasting allies. If you have a broken leg, the urgency for 'crutches' is much higher, than without a broken leg and if you are not yourself able to produce crutches, you will have to trade them – what your needs are and what the urgency of these needs is, is determined by the goods you are able to hold at hand yourself (your basket) and by the context you live in.

Other concepts of structural power follow the logical conception of determining a priori that a specific kind of resources in a specific kind of context are of relevance and importance for exercising structural power while others are not. They therefore argue for an ex ante deductively defined structure-resources relation.

We propose a different conception. In our opinion, you cannot a priori make a general ontological statement on which kind of resources are in any situation within a specific power structure of higher relevance and importance than other ones. In an international environment characterized by high and complex interdependence and complex interactions among the states in various spheres and sectors of affairs, you can just forecast trends. Like in Adam Smith's market model, where the price for a good is determined by the market itself and where you are not able to recognize and determine its value a priori and out of the context of the market, you are also not able to determine the value of a resource/good in interstate power relations a priori. Since in the case of international relations and interstate bargaining processes, structure is the result of the relation between goods and the needs of the states, the importance and relevance of goods themselves must be defined by this relation, if we want to avoid tautology. Or to say it more literally "the price of a good is determined by the market" or, other words "res tantum valet quantum vendi potest".[10]

This shows that structural power possesses a resource-based as well as a relation-based character. Resource-based, because – according to our concept – resources have a major influence on the composition of a state's basket: The possession of resources correlates, as expected, strongly with the availability of material and positional goods for the actors – the more resources are available to an actor, the more goods he potentially has to offer, the greater is the statistical probability that a

[10] Ancient Roman saying: a thing/good is worth only what someone else will pay for it.

larger number of *rare* goods is among them (furthermore a great concentration of resources in one spot may also be a rare good). At the same time, as mentioned above, our concept of structural power also contains an important relational aspect: Resources in general are of limited value. Their value is significantly influenced by the relation between resources (the own as well as the competitor's ones) and the needs which in turn in their totality (in a global context) constitute a structure. This structural context codetermines the value (rarity) of the resources and significantly influences their quality as goods.

This structural context is also the reason why we talk of *structural* instead of relational power. This nomenclature is based on the assumption that although relations determine the quality of an actor's goods, this determination can only be carried out by including the entire "market"/structure with all its elements and their causal relations, that is all baskets noticed by the actors with all the contained goods as well as adjunctive needs. The said determination positions an actor within the structure. In the end, resource- as well as relation-related aspects are inextricably linked to this structure, yet they are conceptionally situated on a different level than the structure formed by them (see Fig. 4.3). Moreover, this structure is not monolithic but contains substructures, as will be shown later.

At this point, it is justified to ask if it is really necessary to introduce a further structural level similar to the relativizing effects of the relational concept of power. Looking closely at the concept of relational power, certain shortcomings become obvious. A relation requires the interaction of two or more actors; it is constituted by interaction. The relation between this limited number of actors results into an ad-hoc structure which only exists for the limited duration and scope of this specific action. Therefore the effect is purely linked to the intention of the actors involved (because a relation needs an active start by the actors), as well as restricted to specific duration of the process. This concept implies the isolation of the actors involved from all other previous, simultaneous and subsequent interactions on a temporal and spatial level. It is therefore unable to offer an understanding of a structural meta-level independent from the specific interactions of a limited number of actors. In contrast, our concept of structure offers a context which logically connects the multiple relations taking place under the conditions of interdependent anarchy by focusing on a meta-level. Effects caused by interaction may be intentional or non-intentional, as shown above, and unfold independently from the rigid borders of a specific relation.

Again, structural power does not operate per se but through relativization. It influences the value of a possession in a specific context either positively or negatively. Whenever state A has access to more OOs than B to satisfy its needs and therefore possesses more structural power, the value of the resources B owns is relativized. Due to the existence of alternatives, B is no longer able to use these resources effectively as a coercive means towards A. Structural power influences A's resource power relativizingly, by weakening or strengthening it with respect to actor B.

Even in a constellation in which only actor A and actor B enter negotiations (as for example in the case of exclusive goods), and in which OOs are available to none of the actors, structural power is present. In this case, however, structural power is located at two extremes: One actor (A) – the actor who possesses the exclusive goods and whom the other actor (B) is dependent on if he wants to satisfy his need for these goods – holds 100% of structural power, whereas B has 0% structural power. If no OOs exist, actor A possesses all the structural power and actor B none.

It is important to note that zero denotes an actual power level and therefore has to be a feature of power in theoretical considerations. A relationship in reference to power becomes an empty vehicle if a constellation in which one actor holds 100% of the power and the other holds 0% power is not possible. For a relation to work out, both sides need to have a "value" – without countervalue, the power position is inevitably absolute and tautologic. At a proportion of 100% versus 0%, the structure works completely in favor of the player who possesses 100% of the power. Here, the structure itself does not have a relativizing effect because one counterpart does not possess anything that could relativize resources of the other player and consequently its power position.

A very similar situation is to be found in constellations of 50% versus 50%, that means in case of a par situation. Due to the fact that structural power takes effect with the same intensity on both sides, the relativizing effects negate each other. However, as soon as the constellation is 50.1–49.9%, structural power acts minimally in favour of the actor holding 50.1%. As a result, in any negotiating situation neither structural power nor resource power can exist on their own – they influence each other and are conceptionally inextricably linked.

To sum up, the concept presented above works as follows:

> Goods that an actor can offer in exchange as well as the actor's needs are derived from his resources which can become material, positional or ideational goods. These resources turn into goods whenever another actor articulates a corresponding need, and the resources can be exchanged for other goods.
>
> The relations between the goods and needs of all actors constitute a structure. This structure, at the same time, determines the quality (more or less rare) of the goods. The quality of the goods and therefore availibility of OOs determine the actor's structural power. Structural power can influence the actor's (resources) power by relativizing it.

Coming back to the labyrinth allegory mentioned above, any actor here is simultaneously both designer of the labyrinth and "mouse", competing against other actors in creating the most favorable structure (the shortest possible way to the cheese). The following paragraph will sketch how actors are able to influence the structure, and hence their structural power.

Influencing Structural Power

In the previous paragraph, we addressed the link between the possession of resources and the possession of goods. There are basically two possibilities to influence one's own structural power or that of the competitor, or rather to change one's position within the structure in relation to the latter – by manipulation on either the resource- or the relational level. By manipulating his own basket or that of another, or by manipulating his own need for goods or that of another, any player can to a certain extent influence his structural power level.

Greater rarity can be achieved by an actor manipulating his own basket or that of another, or by manipulating his own needs for goods or that of another. This may be done by any actor by upgrading own products (e.g. technological improvements, changes in conditions, occupation of important positions, limitation of the *availability* of goods, etc.) or the degradation of the goods of other actors (such as downgrading of nuclear threat by a missile shield, implementation of new practices, new way of goods delivery, etc.), or also by manipulating the availability of OO's by creation of a "cartel".

In this context, any race for technology and production advantages – may it be in terms of exercising control over raw materials or in terms of competitiveness, key patents or military strength – is nothing but an approach to relatively improve one's own basket in comparison to those of other players. Hence, any effort in this direction does not only contribute to – more obvious – hard and soft power, but also to structural power.

However, an increase in structural power in one area does not imply that the state in general becomes (structurally) stronger. Even though we assume that all goods are principally exchangeable, we do not deny that negotiations and the exchange of goods are usually limited to particular sectors. The reason may be that trade patterns have long been established, or else linked to the problem of weighting the value of goods against each other precisely. It is for example easier to calculate the value of a barrel of oil in US$ than in the range of concessions in the field of TRIPS. This semi-permeability of sectors is, due to reasons of practicability, not the logic of the structure. This is also one of the reasons why a large amount of structural power in one area – e.g. security or environmental technologies – does not automatically imply that the actor holds a large amount of structural power in general.

However as sectors differ regarding their urgency and the relevance of adjunctive needs, the probability that they contain rare goods can also vary greatly. As rare goods are more uncommon in the textile than in the semiconductor sector, the importance of the actors' positioning within the latter substructure is more important for their general structural power.

In addition, players can create new needs for other actors in their own interests or modify existing ones, making their goods more attractive and rare, e.g. through technological progress, framing, etc. Apart from influencing the competitors' needs, an actor can also try to manipulate his own needs – either by reducing them to a minimum or by substituting them with other needs that the state is able to satisfy by itself. An extreme example of this is North Korea:

The continuing conflict on the Korean peninsula and the insensitivity of the North Korean regime towards the pressures and sanctions of states superior in hard and soft power (e.g. the USA, South Korea, Japan and even to some extent the PR China) can well be explained in terms of structural power. On the one hand, North Korea profits from limiting the material needs of its population and from substituting needs that cannot be met for ones that can be met on the basis of a government ideology. On the other hand, Pyongyang creates a strong need for security and normalization among its neighboring states and other actors by keeping up a constant threat. With regard to South Korea and Japan, this threat can be defined as the danger of a military conflict, which North Korea would not be able to win but which would cause a large number of casualties. From an American perspective, the threat is the danger that military technology could be sold for example to Iran. From a Chinese perspective, the North Korean threat can be seen as the danger of large numbers of North-Korean refugees crossing the Chinese border. From a general western perspective, the threat lies in a continued "hostage-taking" of the North Korean people by its own government.

Only Pyongyang is able to deliver the goods needed to satisfy the other players' needs for security and normalization without an armed conflict. In this constellation, North Korea has few, yet exclusive goods in its basket and needs only a limited number of widely available goods – food and energy supplies. Pyongyang therefore holds a relatively large amount of structural power compared to its own resources.

Another already mentioned possibility to improve the own structural position is to form syndicates/cartels. This enables actor B, by making special agreements with A's OOs, to deprive the later of his OOs and thus to prevent himself from being played off against them. It is obvious that this strategy helps – under normal circumstances – all actors (B und A's potential OOs) not only to gain a stronger position within the structure, but also to increase their profit. Accordingly, it is not surprising that such a behavior is often to be witnessed in the field of IR (where no antitrust laws exist), whenever the interests of pooling actors match. A virtual syndicate like that was, for instance, formed by the representatives of the EU and the USA when it came to dictating terms for granting ODA to African states in the example given above.

A further prominent example is the OPEC[11]. It was founded in 1960 as a response to the inability of the oil-producing states to stand up to the so-called seven sisters, the largest western oil-companies, which had oligopolistically dominated the oil market since the early twentieth century and had thus formed a de facto syndicate themselves. During the 1960s, oil was the primary – and in most cases the only – relevant good which the oil-producing states in the Middle East, Africa and South America had to offer. At the same time it was only conditionally *rare* due to the fact that, although oil already made up a large amount of the energy sources of the world's economy, there was no scarcity of the black gold produced and sold by the seven sisters, so that due to the excess production the actors were able to satisfy their needs without difficulty. In addition, the oil-producing states themselves had no OOs, because of the absolute dominance of the seven sisters on the oil market and their close relations to each other as well as to the western states. Despite their resources their structural position was accordingly weak and their efforts to renegotiate certain concessions and oil prices were mostly without success.

[11] cf. for the OPEC Case Rose 2004 and Witte and Golldthau 2019.

The foundation of the OPEC-syndicate, however, improved the structural position of the oil producers. This new situation already became apparent when the new calculation formula for the dues on income tax of the oil companies was negotiated between 1962 and 1964. At first the oil companies, aware of the weakening of their position, refused to accept the OPEC as an actor and insisted on bilateral negotiations with the individual members in order to play them off against one another. Despite the oil-producing states' threats of taking unilateral measures the oil companies were only willing to make minimal concessions. Only when the individual OPEC-members refused to enter into negotiations outside the OPEC, they were accepted. Afterwards, however, the seven sisters still tried to isolate single members from the OPEC-front. Although the oil companies eventually succeeded in reaching an individual agreement with Iran and even though the remaining OPEC-members disagreed about their attitude, the latter still managed, despite their unfavorable structural position, to achieve a moderate success (Witte and Goldthau 2009) – they had increased their structural power by forming a syndicate.

A few years later, the structure was changed by a serious shortage of the good 'oil'. The worldwide rapidly increasing demand as well as the destabilization in the Middle East, caused by a series of political changes, turned the relation between availability of and demand for the good into reverse. In addition, a breakup of the seven sisters' syndicate by several independent oil companies offered the producing states a number of OOs. Those factors turned oil into a relatively *rare* good and strengthened the structural position of the OPEC-members and accordingly weakened the position of the West. However, during the oil embargo of 1973 the OPEC still did not manage to turn its new power position into political concessions regarding US and European politics on Israel. The main reason for that was that the OPEC was de facto unable to persuade its members to reduce the oil production. On the contrary, a few members hardly reduced their production, while others actually increased it in order to take advantage of the price rise for obtaining the desperately needed foreign currency. The OPEC thus merely succeeded in taking 14% of its output off the market with the result that no significant supply gap occurred in the West. It is evident that the OPEC-members were, despite their noticeably improved structural position in this specific area of the structure, not willing or – as a consequence of the very limited number of *rare* goods in their basket – not able to refrain from offering the good 'oil' in order to maintain the syndicate. Their structural position was *altogether* still weak and without the syndicate it was even weaker. It must, however, not be overlooked that the OPEC managed for the first time to dictate prices, without having agreed on them with the oil companies beforehand, and, thus induced a power shift on the oil market (Witte and Goldthau 2009). But, in the end this increase of the price for oil was primary caused by the changed quality of the good 'oil' which became considerably more rare than it had been 10 years before.

Apart from these considerations, the resolutions we mentioned prove another point. Whenever an existing interdependency is questioned, for example by threatening to withdraw it, the goods in question are once again put up for bargaining.

It can usually be assumed that the party calling this constellation into question expects its counterpart to have no convincing OO. Even the act of threatening is a negotiation conducted one-sidedly by the threatening party, based on its own assessment. Of course, the players may bluff with regard to available OO or their own needs, as already mentioned above. Taking into account common trade conflicts, it becomes clear that such situations constitute a large part of the daily routine of IR.

Conclusion

In this paper, we have tried to address deficits of power research and to present an approach for a solution by answering the key-questions we introduced above. We have shown how structural power works, how it is constituted and which transmission channels it uses to affect the power position of states. We have traced the underlying resources of structural power and explained the relationship between resources and structural power. Structural power is intertwined with the two other levels of power. Hence we can speak of a complex system in which the effect is more than just a sum of its parts. Our concept of structural power is not limited to a deterministic understanding of the effects of resources on a state's power position. It is also not restricted to a relational context shaping the value of power resources logically restricted to the duration of the specific relation. Instead, the structural context or the structure the actors are embedded in exercises considerable relativizing influence on the resource level. The effect of the structure is not limited to a specific interaction of actors. Therefore we have been able to present a concept, which is able to enclose other concepts of structural power (e.g. Strange) and which is able to analyze the sources and effects of structural power in 21st century international relations characterized by complex interdependence and its implications for the states.

References

Bacevich, A. (2008). *The limits of power: The end of American exceptionalism*. New York: Metropolitan Books.

Bailer, S. (2004). Bargaining success in the European Union: The impact of exogenous and endogenous power resources. *European Union Politics, 5*, 99–123.

Balaam, D. N., & Veseth, M. (2008). *Introduction to international political economy*. Upper Saddle River: Pearson/Prentice Hall.

Baldwin, D. A. (1979). Power analysis and world politics: New trends versus old tendencies. *World Politics, 31*(2 (January)), 161–194.

Baldwin, D. A. (1980). Interdependence and power: A conceptual analysis. *International Organization, 34*(4 (Autumn)), 471–506.

Baldwin, D. A. (2002). Power and international relations. In W. Carlsnaes, T. Risse, & B. Simmons (Eds.), *The handbook of international relations* (pp. 177–191). Thousand Oaks: Sage.

Baumann, R., Rittberger, V., & Wagner, W. (1999). Macht und Machtpolitik Neorealistische Außenpolitiktheorie und Prognosen über die deutsche Außenpolitik nach der Vereinigung. *Zeitschrift für Internationalen Beziehungen, 2*, 245–286.

BPSM – Bonn Power Shift Monitor, accessible via: http://www.cgs-bonn.de/monitor/monitor.htm

Brookes, P., & Shin, J. H. (2006) China's influence in Africa: Implications for the United States (The Heritage Foundation Backgrounder, No. 1916, 22.2.2006). http://www.heritage.org/research/reports/2006/02/chinas-influence-in-africa-implications-for-the-united-states. Accessed 15 Dec 2011.

Dahl, R. A. (1957). The concept of power. *Behavioral Science, 2*(3), 201–215.

Dür, A. (2007). EU Trade Policy as protection for exporters: The agreements with Mexico and Chile. *Journal of Common Market Studies, 45*(4), 833–855.

Ferguson, N. (2003). Think again: Power. *Foreign Policy, 134*(March–April), 18–24.

Ferguson, N. (2005). *Colossus. The rise and fall of the American Empire*. London: Penguin.

Gilpin, R. (1981). *War and change in world politics*. Cambridge: Cambridge University Press.

Grieco, J. M. (1995). The Maastricht Treaty, economic and monetary union and the neo-realist research program. *Review of International Studies, 21*(1), 21–40.

Guzzini, S. (1993). Structural power: The limits of neorealist power analysis. *International Organization, 47*(3 (Summer)), 443–478.

Ikenberry, G. J. (2003). Is American multilateralism in decline? *Perspectives on Politics, 1*(3 (September)), 533–550.

Ikenberry, G. J. (2004). Illusions of empire: Defining the new American order. *Foreign Affairs, 83* (2 (March – April)), 144–154.

Joffe, J. (2006). *Die Hypermacht. Warum die USA die Welt beherrschen*. Bonn: Hanser Verlag.

Kagan, R. (2002). Power and weakness. *Policy Review*, No. 113.

Kappel, R., & Schneidenbach, T. (2006) China in Afrika: Herausforderungen für den Westen (GIGA Focus, Nr. 12). http://www.giga-hamburg.de/content/publikationen/pdf/gf_global_0612.pdf. Accessed 15 Dec 2011

Katzenstein, P. J. (2005). *A world of regions. Asia and Europe in the American imperium*. Ithaca/London: Cornell University Press.

Keohane, R. (1984). *After hegemony: Cooperation and discord in the world political economy*. Princeton: Princeton University Press.

Keohane, R., & Nye, J. S., Jr. (1977/2001). *Power and interdependence: World politics in transition*. Boston: Addison Wesley.

Keohane, R., & Nye, J. S., Jr. (2001). *Power and interdependence*. New York: Longman.

Krasner, S. D. (1985). *Structural conflict: The Third World against global liberalism*. Berkley: University of California Press.

Lawton, T. C., Rosenau, J. N., & Verdun, A. C. (2000). *Strange power. Shaping the parameters of international relations and international political economy*. Aldershot: Ashgate.

Mann, M. (2003). *Incoherent empire*. London: Verso.

Maslow, A. H. (1943). A theory of human motivation. *Psychological Review, 50*, 370–396.

Mearsheimer, J. J. (1995). The false promise of international institutions. *International Security, 19*(3), 5–49.

Moravcsik, A. (1991). Negotiating the single European Act: National interests and conventional statecraft in the European Community. *International Organization, 45*(1), 19–56.

Moravcsik, A. (1993). Preferences and power in the European Community: A liberal intergovernmentalist approach. *Journal of Common Market Studies, 31*(4), 473–524.

Moravcsik, A. (1997). Taking preferences seriously: A liberal theory of international politics. *International Organization, 51*(4), 513–553.

Muthoo, A. (2000). A non-technical introduction to bargaining theory. *World Economics, 1*(2 (April–June)), 145–166.

Norrlof, C. (2010). *America's global advantage. US hegemony and international cooperation*. Cambridge: Cambridge University Press.

Nye, J. S., Jr. (1990a). The changing nature of world power. *Political Science Quarterly, 105*(2), 177–192.

Nye, J. S., Jr. (1990b). Soft power. *Foreign Policy, 80*, 153–171.
Nye, J. S., Jr. (2004a). *Soft power: The means to success in world politics*. New York: PublicAffairs.
Nye, J. S., Jr. (2004b). The decline of America's soft power: Why Washington should worry. *Foreign Affairs, 83*(3 (May–June)), 16–20.
Petersen, N. (1986). Bargaining power among potential allies: negotiating the North Atlantic Treaty, 1948–49. *Review of International Studies, 12*, 187–203.
Rose, E. A. (2004). OPEC's dominance of the global oil market – the rise of the world's dependency on oil. *Middle East Journal, 58*(3), 424–443.
Schirm, S. (2005). Der Einfluss von Interessen und Normen auf nationale Positionen zur Global Economic Governance. *Zeitschrift für Politikwissenschaft, 15*(3), 825–847.
Schirm, S. (2009). Ideas and interests in global financial governance: Comparing German and US preference formation. *Cambridge Review of International Affairs, 22*(3), 501–521.
Schirm, S. (2011). Varieties of strategies: Societal influences on British and German responses to the global economic crisis. *Journal of Contemporary European Studies, 19*(1), 47–62.
Schneider, G. (2005). Capacity and concessions: Bargaining power in multilateral negotiations. *Millennium – Journal of International Studies, 33*, 665–690.
Strange, S. (1987). The persistent myth of lost hegemony. *International Organization, 41*(4 (Autumn)), 551–574.
Strange, S. (1988a). *States and markets – An introduction to international political economy*. London: Pinter Publishers.
Strange, S. (1988b). The persistent myth of lost hegemony – Reply to Milner and Snyder. *International Organization, 42*(2 (Autumn)), 751–752.
Strange, S. (1996). *The retreat of the state: The diffusion of power in the world economy*. Cambridge: Cambridge University Press.
Tull, D. M. (2006). China's engagement in Africa: Scope, significance and consequences. *Journal of Modern African Studies, 44*(3), 459–479.
Volgy, T. J., & Lawrence, I. E. (2000). The faces of hegemonic strength: Structural versus relational capabilities. *International Interactions, 26*(3), 229–251.
Walt, S. M. (1991). The renaissance of *security studies. International Studies Quarterly, 35*(2), 211–239.
Waltz, K. (1990). Realist thought and neorealist theory. *Journal of International Affairs, 44*, 21–37.
Waltz, K. N. (1979). *Theory of international politics*. New York: McGraw-Hill.
Ward, H. (1987). Structural power – A contradiction in terms? *Political Studies, 35*, 593–610.
Weber, M. (1947). *The theory of social and economic organization*. New York: The Free Press.
Wendt, A. (1999). *Social theory of international politics*. Cambridge: Cambridge University Press.
Witte, J. M., & Goldthau, A. (2009). *Die OPEC – Macht und Ohnmacht des Öl-Kartels*. München: Carl Hanser Verlag.
Woods, N. (2008). Whose aid? Whose influence? China, emerging donors and the silent revolution in development assistance. *International Affairs, 84*(6), 1205–1221.
Zakaria, F. (2011). The Post-American World: Release 2.0, New York: W. W. Norton & Company

Part II
Power and International Security

Chapter 5
Nuclear Weapons and Power in the 21st Century

Stephan Frühling and Andrew O'Neil

On 16 July 1945, the nuclear age was heralded by the successful *Trinity* test explosion at Alamogordo, New Mexico. Robert Oppenheimer later wrote that the sheer force of this new weapon made him think of the *Bhagavad Gita* verse "Now I am become Death, the destroyer of worlds" (Hijiya 2000: 123–167). Villains in countless movies seek nuclear weapons for their evil schemes, and only the philosopher's stone and other imaginary items rival them as sources and symbols of power in popular imagination. During the Cold War, their mere existence seemed to threaten the survival not only of opposing armies, but of civilization itself.

And yet, more than 60 years after the invention and first use of nuclear weapons, less than a dozen out of close to 200 states worldwide have acquired them.[1] In 1945, the United States rushed to use its only two atomic bombs on Hiroshima and Nagasaki within a few days of confirming that the devices functioned as intended. But two generations later, those two explosions remain the only actual use of the new weapon in anger, notwithstanding several close calls throughout the Cold War. In Fred Iklé's words, they remain "encapsulated . . . in a cocoon of non-use (1997: 11). Nuclear weapons are unique in their physical destructiveness, but the influence of that destructive force on international affairs to date remains indirect and latent. Whether this will remain the case in the 21st century is of great consequence for the future relationship between nuclear weapons and 'power', and indeed for the future of humankind itself.

This chapter examines the power that nuclear weapons will bestow on the states that possess them in the 21st century. It focuses on the nature of this power itself, rather than the future distribution of power and nuclear arsenals among specific states. Therefore the chapter begins by examining the relationship between nuclear

[1] The United States, Russia, United Kingdom, France and China are recognized as nuclear powers under the Nuclear Non-proliferation Treaty. Israel is widely suspected of having an undeclared nuclear arsenal. South Africa abolished its nuclear weapons before the end of Apartheid. India, Pakistan and North Korea have tested nuclear devices. Ukraine, Kazakhstan and Belarus 'inherited' nuclear warheads from the Soviet Union but handed them over to Russia.

E. Fels et al. (eds.), *Power in the 21st Century*, Global Power Shift,
DOI 10.1007/978-3-642-25082-8_5, © Springer-Verlag Berlin Heidelberg 2012

weapons and power as it has developed since 1945 in more detail, focusing on the importance and limits of deterrence as the exercise of coercive power. It will argue that the extent to which nuclear weapons bestow power on states which possess them is largely determined by the wider nuclear order as it has developed over the second half of the twentieth century. Judgments about the future of the relationship between nuclear weapons and power therefore depend on how this nuclear order will evolve in the 21st century.

Nuclear Weapons, Power and Twentieth Century Nuclear Order

States' decisions on whether to acquire nuclear weapons, or how to convert their possession into meaningful power in the international system, are not taken in a vacuum. The nuclear order – which states possess nuclear weapons, their respective force structures and employment doctrines, and more generally the 'accepted' international norms of nuclear weapons possession and employment – is the context within which states perceive the power of nuclear weapons, and conditions the way in which they can be used. At the same time, states' decisions on nuclear weapons also determine and change this order over time. What, then, are the core elements of nuclear order in the early 21st century?

Deterrence: Harnassing the Power of Nuclear Weapons

There is no question that nuclear weapons allow the release of tremendous amounts of power in the physical sense – certainly far more so than conventional explosives based on chemical reactions. In the same manner in which the latter underlie 'conventional' military forces, nuclear warheads in conjunction with delivery vehicles, command and control systems, trained personnel and employment doctrine, constitute nuclear forces.

Nuclear weapons are thus a special form of military capability. Like conventional, general purpose forces, they form a power resource that can be assessed and compared between states and across time by drawing on summaries of numbers and physical attributes in the *IISS Military Balance* and similar publications. But while most other power resources, such as population, gross national product, the attractiveness of culture and values, or mineable deposits of minerals and hydrocarbons, are a by-product of normal and everyday societal activity, military forces are not. Rather, they are purposefully created to give states the option to use force, or to threaten the use of force, in international affairs. In doing so, states seek power defined, in Lawrence Freedman's words, as the "*capacity to produce effects that are more advantageous than would otherwise have been the case*" (2008: 30).

The link between military forces in general, and nuclear forces in particular, on the one hand, and power thus defined on the other hand, is neither a direct nor a simple one. The immediate effect of using military force is purely physical: killing people and destroying things. Developing and successfully implementing a strategy that translates this capacity for harm into the desired political effect is difficult, and an uncertain proposition at the best of times. Violence and the threat of violence can be used for coercion, or to seek to impose outright control, and the capacity to employ violence can be an asset that potential allies find attractive. Indeed, there can be times when the survival of the state depends on it. But by their very nature, military forces are nevertheless a specialized form of power that can only influence others in a way that has very limited relevance to most problems confronting humankind and international relations, most of the time. The sheer destructiveness of nuclear warheads accentuates this problem manifold.

Immediately after the Second World War, the implications of atomic bombs for strategy and world order were far from clear. Most commentators were concerned about the advantage that the 'absolute weapon' was seen to bestow on 'aggressors'. When the existence of the atomic bomb was revealed, there was little expectation that the US monopoly on the new weapon would last long.[2] Attention therefore quickly turned to examining the strategic consequences of eventual proliferation of the atomic bomb, and to the methods that could be used to meet the threat of atomic bombs being used to support wars of territorial aggression like the ones the Allies had just overcome.

Through deterrence, nuclear weapons became a solution to the threat of large-scale conventional aggression, as well as to that of their own existence. Deterrence itself has a tradition in strategic thought that can be traced back centuries, even millennia, but its perceived utility as a strategic concept peaked in the wake of the nuclear revolution. As early as 1946, Bernard Brodie wrote that

> the first and most vital step in any American security program for the age of atomic bombs is to take measures to guarantee to ourselves in case of attack the possibility of retaliation in kind (1946: 76).

Fearful of threatened American nuclear retaliation in response to an unwanted act, the idea of deterrence goes, the adversary would desist from undertaking it in the first place. The more the sheer destructive power of nuclear weapons raised the potential costs of war, the greater the incentive to avoid it.

The ultimate weapon, it was assumed, would thus be the ultimate deterrent to war. As long as deterrence worked, the physical power inherent in the nuclear arsenal would thus not even have to be used to achieve the desired effect. As Glenn Snyder observed at the height of the Cold War, the most striking distinction between the nuclear and the pre-nuclear age was "the possibility that deterrence would be maintained by weapons which would have no rational use for defense should deterrence fail" (Snyder 1961: 9). But successful deterrence implies the

[2] See, for example Castex (1945: 466).

recognition by the adversary of the deterrer's will, and a conscious subjugation to it. Hence, although they are not used in combat, nuclear weapons in a deterrent role exercise power in a most direct, immediate, and politically decisive way (see Freedman 2008: 30).

The Imperative of Stability: The Paradox of Nuclear Weapons' Power

The clear US nuclear superiority over the Communist bloc, and the essential safety of the North American continent from Soviet attack well into the 1960s, gave the United States the means and confidence to oppose communist expansion in Europe. In Asia, the United States explicitly and repeatedly threatened the use of nuclear weapons against China in Korea and the Taiwan Strait, and issued thinly veiled threats against North Vietnam and North Korea. The number of US nuclear weapons skyrocketed, driven by the growth in 'tactical' warheads, and peaked in 1966 (Global Nuclear Stockpiles – 1945–2006: 66).

While Soviet domination of Eastern Europe relied on the force of conventional arms, the military and geostrategic strength of the United States relied on nuclear weapons – a basic pattern that continued until the end of the Cold War (see Gaddis 1982). The 'nuclear umbrella' providing 'extended nuclear deterrence' remains an essentially American phenomenon. It is central to US alliance relationships in Asia and Europe, as it continues to provide US allies with nuclear deterrence, without having to maintain nuclear forces of their own (Yost 2009: 755–780; Tertrais 2010).

But when both superpowers achieved the capacity in the 1960s to strike the homeland of the other *after* absorbing a first strike (a so-called 'second strike capability'), the traditional nexus between the use of force and policy was broken. Nuclear warheads launched on ballistic missiles made it possible to destroy an enemy state's infrastructure and society, without first having to destroy the latter's military forces. One of the key questions for policy makers flowing from this was: What possible policy aims could justify the use of a weapon which not only had the capacity to obliterate another country, but could not prevent the same from happening to one's own?

The fundamental paradox of the nuclear revolution was that the ability of one superpower to deter the use of nuclear weapons by the other was essentially predicated on conveying a credible intent that they themselves would respond to a nuclear attack by using nuclear weapons. By their sheer physical power, nuclear weapons led to the inescapable nature of assured destruction between the superpowers (see Jervis 1989). But in a variation on his earlier observation on the imperative of avoiding war in the nuclear age, Brodie commented during the late 1950s that:

> Deterrence now means something as a strategic policy only when we are fairly confident that the retaliatory instrument upon which it relies will not be called upon to function at all (1959: 272–273).

Given the existential threat of warfare between two nuclear armed superpowers, the possibility that nuclear deterrence threats may ever have to be realized thus cast doubt on the extent to which the use of armed force remained feasible and sensible. The introduction of nuclear weapons into national armories had become a 'Faustian bargain' (Thayer 1995: 149–163): the power of nuclear deterrence to prevent conventional or nuclear aggression was purchased at the price of potentially catastrophic damage, should war nevertheless break out.

One consequence of mutual nuclear deterrence was thus an imperative to maintain stability in the relations between nuclear powers, at least to the point that escalation of hostilities towards nuclear war is avoided. During the Cold War in particular, maintaining the 'delicate balance of terror' became an international military and diplomatic objective in its own right (Wohlstetter 1959: 231–244). It was based on the recognition that adversaries armed with thermonuclear weapons had mutually shared interests, exactly by virtue of their adversarial relationship. In the now classic definition of Thomas Schelling and Morton Halperin, these interests lay "in the avoidance of war that neither side wants, in minimizing the costs and risks of arms competition, and in curtailing the scope and violence of war in the event it occurs" (1961: 1).

This aim for stability is not to be confused with an aim for disarmament, let alone of the unilateral kind: Strategic stability during the Cold War was ultimately dependent on a robust mutual deterrence relationship (Freedman 2003: 184–195). But it meant that nuclear forces "were not being used to compel a change in the status quo but only to contain an enemy"(Freedman 2004: 11), reinforcing the concept of deterrence as the main and only justifiable use of nuclear weapons. Nuclear deterrence, with its threat of overwhelming punishment, imposed caution not only on the adversary, but on both sides, as the risk of catastrophic conflict served to promote restraint in the strategic behaviour of all the main actors. Deterrence, as an instrument of coercion, ultimately proved the only feasible way of harnessing the physical power of nuclear weapons for political goals. But just like war itself it is a force that is difficult to control once unleashed, the power of nuclear weapons constrains not only those against whom they are directed, but also those seeking to use it.

The Exclusive Club of Nuclear Powers

Only when the new condition of mutual assured destruction led them to realize the constraints and dangers imposed by nuclear deterrence, did both superpowers turn their attention towards addressing the rise of new nuclear states in the 1960s. Widely held predictions in the 1960s and 1970s converged on the assumption that dozens of nuclear weapons states would inevitably result from the spread of uranium enrichment and plutonium separation technologies across the international system.[3] Successive US National Intelligence Estimates (NIE) identified more than a dozen "countries of proliferation concern" (including Australia, Japan, Sweden, and West Germany), with the 1966 NIE warning that proliferation would accelerate if the United States and the Soviet Union were "not prepared to give non-proliferation priority over other policy objectives" (Lavoy 2004).

The entry of the United Kingdom and France into the nuclear club (in 1952 and 1960, respectively) was of concern to the Soviet Union in particular, but it was China's nuclear test in 1964 that really served to focus the minds of policy makers in Washington and Moscow. A shared concern that other states were also on the cusp of going nuclear resulted in a joint US-Soviet draft non-proliferation treaty, which was formally opened for signature as the Nuclear Non-proliferation Treaty (NPT) in 1968.[4] The United States, Soviet Union, United Kingdom, France and China entered the treaty as recognized nuclear powers,[5] while all other signatories committed themselves to eschew the development and acquisition of nuclear weapons.

Many states, especially nuclear-capable ones, remained uneasy about acceding to a treaty that seriously inhibited their latitude to acquire for themselves the power of deterrence that nuclear weapons could provide. As William Walker has pointed out, the regime was founded "on two interlinked systems: a managed system of deterrence and a managed system of abstinence". Under this binary system, "the possession of nuclear weapons by the acknowledged nuclear weapon states was a temporary trust, and a trust which could not be extended to other states" (Walker 2007: 436). In a number of cases, it was only after concerted pressure from Washington, coupled with reassurances about extended deterrence guarantees, that these states decided to come on board.[6] Non-members of superpower alliances in the developing world were hardest to convince, and remained cynical about what they saw as the establishment of a 'nuclear condominium' on the part of the five 'legitimate' nuclear powers under the NPT.

Support for nuclear non-proliferation does not mean sacrificing the logic of nuclear deterrence: It continues to be the bed-rock of national security in all the nuclear weapons states. Non-nuclear allies of the United States in NATO Europe, Japan, South Korea and Australia also continue to rely on extended nuclear deterrence. For them, US nuclear weapons provide critical reassurance against conventional and nuclear threats from regional adversaries. The United States continues to station nuclear weapons in five European countries – each of whom is a non-nuclear weapon state under the NPT – and strongly reaffirmed the extension of its nuclear umbrella to Japan and South Korea in the wake of North Korea's nuclear tests in 2006 and 2009. Despite exhortations for global powers to move to 'no first use' doctrines (Sagan 2009: 163–182), nuclear deterrence remains an

[3] See, for example Beaton (1966) and Wohlstetter et al. (1976).

[4] For background see the collection of essays in Barnaby (1969).

[5] Under article 9 of the NPT, 'a nuclear weapon state is one which has manufactured and exploded a nuclear weapon or other nuclear explosive device prior to January 1, 1967'.

[6] For discussion, see Gavin (2004/05: 116–117).

attractive response to conventional threats for nuclear powers, including Russia and Pakistan, and aspiring nuclear powers alike. North Korea and Iran are not seeking to emulate or match America's nuclear capability; they see nuclear weapons as a key strategic equalizer against conventional military threats from the United States.[7]

Despite commitments under article VI on all member states to work towards nuclear and general disarmament, the NPT is not a disarmament treaty (Krause 2007): Its aim is non-proliferation and perpetuation, as long as is necessary, of the unequal and discriminatory situation where a few select nuclear weapons states have 'legitimate' access to the power of nuclear weapons, and a host of states that do not. Nuclear weapons states promise ultimate disarmament and access to civilian nuclear technology to all other signatory states, but the value of arresting non-proliferation is shared by all members of the international community – non-nuclear weapons states have just as strong an interest in other non-nuclear weapons states remaining non-nuclear as do the five recognized nuclear powers.

Despite misgivings over the structural inequities of the NPT, and notwithstanding the widely canvassed imperfections of the non-proliferation regime more generally, it remains the single most popular treaty in the international system with over 190 member states. Only Israel, Pakistan and India have not signed the treaty, and North Korea remains the only country to have formally withdrawn from the NPT. Overall, the NPT has been more successful than many believed possible in broadly preserving the basic traits of the nuclear order of 40 years ago.

Will the Genie Escape the Bottle?

At the beginning of the 21st century, the question then is whether the current structure of the nuclear order can persist, or whether the relationship between nuclear weapons and power might change in a way that would fundamentally alter its three paradigmatic elements: nuclear deterrence as the near-exclusive way in which the physical power of nuclear weapons is used for political purpose; universal recognition of the imperative of stability between nuclear-armed states; and the exclusive nature of the nuclear weapons 'club'. Continuity in the essential elements of the nuclear order does not mean that these three essential principles cannot find expression in a new context. The general shift of the global centre of economic and military gravity from the North Atlantic to East Asia will also have consequences for the global distribution of nuclear weapons, and the relative importance of Asian states for setting global nuclear norms. Pakistan, for example, is rapidly expanding its nuclear force and now may have more warheads than France or the United Kingdom (DeYoung 2011). China is engaged in major program to modernize its nuclear warheads and delivery vehicles, and North Korea

[7] For discussion of the drivers of both states' programs and their likely future trajectory, see Pollack (2007) and Fitzpatrick (2006).

is widely estimated to construct additional warheads from its limited polutonium stocks (Fravel and Medeiros 2010; Nitkin 2011). In general, Asian nuclear powers have shown a greater tolerance for asymmetrical deterrence relationships, relying on much lower warhead numbers than the Cold War antagonists, but have also been much less willing to seek stability through binding and verifiable arms control agreements.[8]

Notwithstanding these differences, there is little indication that an 'Asian nuclear order' will not share the essential elements of order identified above. More worryingly, there are three additional factors that could potentially undermine some, or all three of these elements. These factors could thus profoundly change the way in which the power bestowed by nuclear weapons is distributed and expressed in the 21st century. It is to these that the remainder of this chapter will now turn.

Technology Diffusion and 'Latent Arsenals' as a New Form of Power?

Mastering nuclear technology remains difficult, but the general level of industrial ability around the world is increasing. 'Technology diffusion' (Moodie 1995)[9] is reducing the difficulty of developing and building simple, fission-based nuclear warheads for an increasing number of states. It is a little appreciated fact that, while it was far more difficult 60 years ago to build a nuclear weapon than to develop and build a competitive fighter aircraft, the situation today is the reverse. Advanced microelectronics and materials have made the technology of modern fighter aircraft increasingly complex and expensive. In contrast, the design of a simple but effective nuclear warhead remains the same, and constructing one is becoming easier, rather than more difficult, with the improvement of manufacturing technology and ancillary systems.

The same is also true for the production of fissile material (highly enriched uranium or plutonium). The so-called global 'nuclear renaissance', which has seen states in the developed and developing worlds approve the significant expansion of their civilian nuclear energy sectors to underpin economic growth and reduce carbon emissions, is therefore of particular concern. One study has cited an expected doubling or tripling of global nuclear energy capacity by 2050, and identifies more than 30 states that have plans to construct nuclear power plants for the first time (Squassoni 2008: 1). While these figures may change in the wake of recent events in Japan, it is highly likely that energy hungry states like China and India will push ahead with their plans to significantly build up their civil nuclear capacity. Some states may abjure the construction of (expensive) proliferation-resistant reactors in

[8] See for example Alagappa (2008) and Lyon (2009).

[9] For example, the A.Q. Khan network procured rotors for uranium centrifuges from a Malaysian company. See Albright and Hinderstein (2005).

favour of reactors that are able to serve a dual civilian-military purpose. Others may struggle to institute appropriate nuclear security measures to prevent the leakage of material and expertise from their borders. And if nuclear power production expands significantly, demands for the national control of the more sensitive parts of the fuel cycle uranium enrichment and plutonium separation may also increase despite international efforts to limit the spread of these capabilities.

That said, caution is warranted in assuming that an expanding nuclear power sector will necessarily lead to more nuclear weapon states. There have been well over 1,000 nuclear reactors operating across the globe since the 1940s, and only ten states have acquired nuclear weapons. So far, global proliferation dynamics have remained essentially disconnected from the civil nuclear industry, as every nuclear weapons program has been the product of dedicated military reactors or enrichment facilities, rather than an offshoot of civilian programs (Braun 2006: 637).

Of course, past precedent is no reason to assume that this must remain so in the future, as 'latent arsenals' spread. General technology diffusion and the increased use of civilian nuclear power will make it technically possible for increasing numbers of states to compensate for weaknesses in conventional military forces with relatively simple but effective nuclear weapons, if they choose to do so. Already, Japan is a country which has developed an effective latent arsenal that would allow it to build nuclear forces relatively quickly (Yoshihara and Holmes 2009: 59–78), and Iran may well achieve a similar status (Fitzpatrick 2007: 33–57). Moreover, should the dream of nuclear abolition ever become reality, the result would be a world in which the knowledge of nuclear weapons would continue to exist, even if warheads themselves are dismantled.

Latent arsenals may thus come to define a new type of power resource in the international system. An explicit or implicit threat to convert a latent arsenal into an actual one is, of course, a very different threat to that of actually using a nuclear weapon. Hence, the power bestowed by latent arsenals would not be a weaker form of classic nuclear deterrence, but a new form of power. It would be less immediate than that of nuclear weapons themselves, but it would be no less real for it. For example, a country for whom the acquisition of nuclear weapons is solely a question of intent, and not of capability, would have to be shown much greater deference by other states in the design of regional security architectures, or the avoidance of provocative arms build-ups, than one without that option. If nuclear weapons have been the great equalizer between states in terms of military capabilities, latent arsenals may well become the great equalizer in questions of wider international (security) order.

Bringing the 'Aggressor' Back into the Picture: Nuclear Genocide and Terrorism

If some states may develop latent arsenals as a more subtle and indirect kind of power bestowed by the existence of nuclear weapons, there is also a persistent fear and possibility that someone, somewhere, may want to use their immense physical power directly, to destroy things and kill people. Nuclear deterrence has been credited with preventing the use of nuclear weapons for 'aggression', which had been a fear of the late 1940s, and is a cornerstone of today's nuclear order. But deterrence is not infallible.

Deterrence hinges on the ability to threaten something that a potential aggressor values enough for them to take a 'rational' decision to desist, and it is by no means certain that all future leaders with access to nuclear weapons will fulfill that requirement. Deterrence can break down for many reasons other than an unshakable will for aggression,[10] but it will break down if faced with a leader determined at all cost to use nuclear weapons for their direct, physical power. Luckily for humankind, leaders thus disposed only seldom achieve unquestioned power within any state. But sometimes they do, in which case they can cause unprecedented carnage and unleash state power for genocidal purposes.

Should a 'new Hitler' come to power in a nuclear weapons state, the relationship between nuclear weapons and power would assume a much more direct, physical and dangerous aspect than the one of today, which is moderated by the concept of deterrence. In short, the physical power of nuclear weapons could be used to cause unprecedented destruction and death, before the offending state and its society would in all likelihood also reach the end of its history as a field of radioactive rubble.

The question remains, however, whether one state's use of the physical power of nuclear weapons for genocidal purposes would change the relationship between nuclear weapons and power more generally. Deliberate nuclear use would remain an aberration, and as Bernard Brodie pointed out in the quote cited above, the only sensible answer to the possibility of nuclear aggression is an attempt at nuclear deterrence. Should a genocidal leader with nuclear weapons need to be stopped, nuclear weapons would probably play a role, but there is little reason to suspect that even if deterrence should fail in specific instances, the principal link between nuclear weapons and deterrence would be broken in the relationships between other states.

Similar considerations also apply to the specter of nuclear terrorism. Whether acquisition, let alone construction, of a nuclear weapon by a terrorist group is a realistic proposition, is strongly disputed among experts and policymakers (see Masse 2010). But deterrence may be especially likely to fail if nuclear weapons were somehow to be accessed by terrorist groups such as Al Qaeda. Leaving aside any ideological predilection for inflicting mass casualties, they would be difficult to target for deterrence due to the pressure to 'use or lose' a nuclear weapon (Van de Velde 2010: 682–699). In the worst case, a terrorist nuclear strike in the context of a tense nuclear deterrence relationship between two or more states, such as that which persists on the Indian subcontinent, might even have catalytic effect and trigger a state-based nuclear exchange (Ayson 2010).

---

[10] See for example Payne (1996).

Terrorists or genocidal state leaders may have goals that allow them to directly use the physical power of nuclear weapons. And yet, it is difficult to conclude how nuclear terrorism, demonstrating as it would the damage from using nuclear weapons and probably increasing the stigma attached to their use, could lead other states to lessen the paradigm of deterrence in the way they think about their nuclear arsenals. Unless genocidal aims become commonplace, there is little reason to suppose that the threat, as distinct from the use, of nuclear weapons will not remain the primary way in which states seek to use these weapons' power for political ends.

'Tipping Points' and the Prisoner's Dilemma of Nuclear Weapons Power

One of the most consistent trends in discussion of nuclear weapons since 1945 has been the resilience of predictions that their proliferation among states – and, most recently, among non-state actors – will accelerate. Today, fears that the world is fast approaching, or has already reached, a 'nuclear tipping point' enjoy widespread currency among scholars and practitioners alike (see Campbell et al. 2004). The heady optimism of the post-Cold War period, when many assumed the gradual depreciation of nuclear weapons would lead to a peripheral role for them in international relations, was replaced in the 2000s by a realization that nuclear weapons remain prized strategic assets for states. More recent commentary, particularly within American circles, suggests that unless concerted steps are taken towards nuclear disarmament, the international system will be characterized by the rapid spread of nuclear weapons in coming decades.[11]

Fears that the international system is on the cusp of a major escalation in nuclear proliferation have been stoked by two contemporary developments: The first is the global 'nuclear renaissance' and technology diffusion already mentioned; the second development is the increasing fragility of the international non-proliferation regime, whose structural compact between nuclear and non-nuclear weapons states has been subjected to severe stress since the end of the Cold War. It is increasingly difficult to maintain even the semblance of unity among NPT member states about the relative importance of addressing the emergence of three new nuclear weapons states – India, Pakistan, and North Korea – the rapid rise of Iran's nuclear aspirations, demands for sharing of sensitive aspects of the nuclear fuel cycle, or about the sincerity of the disarmament pledge in the treaty (Leslie 2008).

These developments could certainly provoke a proliferation 'breakout' internationally. Were it to occur, such a break-down of the NPT regime would raise acute challenges for policy makers, not just in terms of their capacity to manage what would be a major shift in regional security dynamics. Once the nuclear 'club' ceases

[11] For the most prominent statement of this position, see Schultz et al. (2007).

to be an exclusive one, many more countries would come to enjoy the benefits and power of sovereign nuclear deterrence. But at the same time, they would also be faced with the difficulty of maintaining stability in the face of existential nuclear threats from a much larger number of sources than is the case in the current order.

That said, recent decades have seen a theoretical challenge to the notion that a proliferated world would indeed be a less safe one. Kenneth Waltz in particular has argued that as long as countries possess a safe, minimum second strike capability, the threat of nuclear weapons would almost automatically ensure a safe balance even in a world with numerous nuclear weapons states. This assumption then leads him to the conclusion that nuclear proliferation could even have positive implications for regional stability – a judgment that is fiercely disputed by 'proliferation pessimists', such as Scott Sagan, who argue that the risk of 'accidental' war by technical error or human miscalculation outweighs any such benefits (Sagan and Waltz 1995).

But the fact that most states around the world have faithfully adhered to the NPT over 40 years demonstrates that, at least so far, they regard the 'Faustian bargain' of nuclear acquisition in such a proliferated world as one that is not worth entering into. If power is the 'capacity to produce effects that are more advantageous than would otherwise have been the case', proliferation pessimists essentially argue that the world has so far avoided a prisoner's dilemma: In a proliferated world, many countries would be worse off not to follow suit, but overall their situation would still not be 'more advantageous' than it is in the current order of an exclusive nuclear club.

Conclusion

After nearly 70 years, and despite revolutionary advances in conventional and biological weapons systems, nuclear weapons remain in a class all of their own. They have thwarted attempts by some military strategists to 'conventionalise' them, and the taboo of the use of nuclear weapons has strengthened, rather than weakened, over time since 1945. Despite the norm of non-use, however, history has also shown that nuclear weapons confer upon states an important deterrent capability. This is the most important reason why no nuclear weapons state today – including the world's greatest conventional military power, the United States – is willing to seriously embark on a process of nuclear disarmament. The future of 21st century global security environment is unclear, and policy makers in nuclear weapons states remain unwilling to dispense with their nuclear inventories for that very reason. Tony Blair's justification of his government's decision to renew the UK's commitment to its nuclear arsenal in 2006 captures the essence of this perspective:

> in the final analysis, the risk of giving up something that has been one of the mainstays of our defence since the [Second World] War, and moreover doing so when the one certain thing about our world today is its uncertainty, is not a risk I feel we can responsibly take (Blair's Trident Statement in Full 2006).

The central role of deterrence in the calculations of nuclear weapons states, along with those states that benefit from extended deterrence guarantees, has been a major thread running through international relations and global security dynamics since the middle of the last century.

But as Bernard Brodie foreshadowed in the aftermath of Hiroshima and Nagasaki, avoiding a deterrence failure has become almost as important for policy makers as ensuring that threats of nuclear punishment remain credible in the eyes of adversaries and would-be adversaries. Even those nuclear weapons states that were characterized as 'rogue' and 'irrational' when they crossed the threshold – China and North Korea – have exercised restraint in their nuclear policies thus far and (along with India) are the only nuclear powers to have committed formally to a no-first use doctrine. The emergence of additional nuclear weapons states in the 21st century may, of course, alter this general historical trend of responsible strategic behavior on the part of the small minority of states that possess nuclear weapons. But it is worth bearing in mind that the many predictions that Hobbesian nuclear anarchy, a "war of all against all", resulting from proliferation over the past seven decades has failed to materialize.

Converting the awesome physical power of nuclear weapons into material influence in international relations will remain problematic for those states that possess nuclear weapons. This realization may prove to be one of the most useful non-proliferation tools in the 21st century. Acquiring nuclear weapons is a risky and expensive process for states fraught with technical and political difficulty. Of course, in certain instances, policy makers press on towards acquisition regardless of the opportunity costs, sometimes even when benefits to national security and prestige are far from guaranteed. But the fact that only a handful of states so far have embarked on the journey to acquiring nuclear weapons should tell us something about the disjunction between the sort of strategic role these weapons play in international relations, and the capacity of states to achieve their national policy objectives in the face of opposition from others. As this chapter has argued, there is no reason to suggest this dynamic will undergo any real change in the 21st century.

References

Alagappa, M. (2008). *The long shadow: Nuclear weapons and security in 21st century asia.* Stanford: Stanford University Press.

Albright, D., & Corey, H. (2005). Unraveling the a.Q. Khan and future proliferation Networks. *The Washington Quarterly, 28*(2), 111–128.

Ayson, R. (2010). After a terrorist nuclear attack: Envisaging catalytic effects. *Studies in Conflict and Terrorism, 33*(7), 571–593.

Barnaby, F. (1969). *Preventing the spread of nuclear weapons* (Pugwash monograph, Vol. 1). London: Souvenir Press.

Beaton, L. (1966). *Must the bomb spread?* Middlesex: Penguin.

Blair's Trident Statement in Full *BBC News Online*, 4 Dec 2006. http://news.bbc.co.uk/2/hi/uk_news/politics/6207584.stm. Accessed 16 Mar 2011).

Braun, C. (2006). The nuclear energy market and the nonproliferation regime. *The Nonproliferation Review, 13*(3), 627–644.
Brodie, B. (1946). Implications for military policy. In B. Brodie (Ed.), *The absolute weapon*. New York: Harcourt, Brace and Company.
Brodie, B. (1959). *Strategy in the missile age*. Princeton: Princeton University Press.
Campbell, K., et al. (2004). *The nuclear tipping point: Why states reconsider their nuclear choices*. Washington: Brookings Institution.
Castex, A. (1945). Aperçus sur la bombe atomique, *Revue de défense nationale*, 1, Oct 1945.
DeYoung, K. (2011). New estimates put Pakistan's nuclear arsenal at more than 100, Washington Post, 31 Jan 2011.
Fitzpatrick, M. (2006). Assessing Iran's nuclear programme. *Survival, 48*(3), 5–26.
Fitzpatrick, M. (2007). Can Iran's nuclear capability be kept latent? *Survival, 49*(1), 33–57.
Fravel, M. T., & Medeiros, E. S. (2010). China's Search for assured retaliation: The evolution of chinese nuclear strategy and force Structure. *International Security, 35*(2), 7–44.
Freedman, L. (2003). *The evolution of nuclear strategy*. Basingstoke: Palgrave MacMillan.
Freedman, L. (2004). *Deterrence*. Cambridge: Polity Press.
Freedman, L. (2008). 'Strategic studies and the problem of Power', reproduced. In T. G. Mahnken & J. A. Maiolo (Eds.), *Strategic studies*. Routledge, Abingdon: A Reader.
Gaddis, J. L. (1982). *Strategies of containment: A critical appraisal of postwar american national security*. Oxford: Oxford University Press.
Gavin, F. (2004/05). Blasts from the past: Proliferation lessons from the 1960s. *International Security, 29*(3), 100–135.
Global Nuclear Stockpiles (1945–2006). *Bulletin of the Atomic Scientists*, July/Aug 2006.
Hijiya, J. A. (2000). The gita of J. Robert Oppenheimer. *Proceedings of the American Philosophical Society, 144*(2), 123–167.
Iklé, F. C. (1997). The next lenin. *The National Interest, 47*, 9–19.
Jervis, R. (1989). *The meaning of the nuclear revolution: Statecraft and the prospect of armageddon*. Ithaca: Cornell University Press.
Krause, J. (2007). Enlightenment and nuclear order. *International Affairs, 83*(2), 483–499.
Lavoy, P. (2011) Predicting nuclear proliferation: A declassified documentary record. *Strategic Insights, 3*(1), 2004. http://www.ccc.nps.navy.mil/si/2004/jan/lavoyJan04.asp. Accessed 16 Mar 2011.
Leslie, R. (2008). The good faith assumption: Different paradigmatic approaches to nonproliferation issues. *Nonproliferation Review, 15*(3), 479–497.
Lyon, R. (2009). *A delicate issue: Asia's nuclear future*. Canberra: Australian Strategic Policy Institute.
Masse, T. (2010). Nuclear terrorism redux: Conventionalists, skeptics, and the margin of safety. *Orbis, 54*(2), 302–319.
Moodie, M. (1995). Beyond proliferation: The challenge of technology diffusion. *The Washington Quarterly, 18*(2), 181–202.
Nitkin, M. B. (2011). North Korea's nuclear weapons: Technical issues *Congressional Research Service Report*, 20 Jan 2011.
Payne, K. B. (1996). *Deterrence in the second nuclear Age*. Lexington: The University Press of Kentucky.
Pollack, J. (2007). North Korea's nuclear weapons program to 2015: Three scenarios. *Asia Policy, 3*, 105–123.
Sagan, S. (2009). The case for No first Use. *Survival, 51*(3), 163–182.
Sagan, S., & Waltz, K. (1995). *The spread of nuclear weapons: A debate*. New York: W.W. Norton & Co.
Schelling, T., & Halperin, M. (1961). *Strategy and arms control*. New York: Twentieth Century Fund.
Schultz, G., William, P., Henry, K., Sam, N. (2007). A world free of nuclear weapons. *The Wall Street Journal*, 4 Jan 2007.

Snyder, G. (1961). *Deterrence and defense: Toward a theory of national security*. Princeton: Princeton University Press.

Squassoni, S. (2008). Nuclear renaissance: Is it coming? Should it?. *Carnegie Endowment for International Peace Policy Brief, 69*, Oct 2008.

Tertrais, B. (2010). *Perspectives on Extended Deterrence*. Recherches & documents 03/2010, Fondation pour la Recherche Stratégique, Paris, 2010.

Thayer, B. (1995). Nuclear weapons as a faustian bargain. *Security Studies, 5*(1), 149–163.

Van de Velde, J. R. (2010). The impossible challenge of deterring "nuclear terrorism" by Al Qaeda'. *Studies in Conflict and Terrorism, 33*(8), 682–699.

Walker, W. (2007). Nuclear enlightenment and counter-enlightenment. *International Affairs, 83* (3), 436.

Wohlstetter, A. (1959). The delicate balance of terror. *Foreign Affairs, 37*(2), 231–244.

Wohlstetter, A., et al. (1976). *Moving toward life in a nuclear armed crowd*. Los Angeles: Pan Heuristics.

Yoshihara, T., & Holmes, J. R. (2009). Thinking about the unthinkable: Tokyo's nuclear option. *Naval War College Review, 62*(3), 59–78.

Yost, D. S. (2009). Assurance and US extended deterrence in NATO. *International Affairs, 85*(4), 755–780.

Chapter 6
Three Worlds of Natural Resources and Power

Jost Wübbeke

Introduction

The supply of natural resources can be a decisive element of 21st century international relations. A world with dwindling resources and environmental degradation poses serious challenges to the global economy and politics. Supply hardly can keep up with the demand of an increasing and prospering population. After several years of wallflower existence, energy security today again appears in the notepads of leading politicians, not least because the rising demand of emerging powers. The social turmoil in Haiti in 2008 and recent unrests in Maghreb countries demonstrate the relentless consequences of rising food prices for political stability. Conflicts over water in Middle East or South East Asia, though not insoluble, are a prevalent phenomenon of our time (Delli Priscoli and Wolf 2009; Grover 2007). Industrialized countries started to worry about the dependence on raw materials, previously virtually an exclusively economic issue (European Commission 2011; U.S. Department of Energy 2010).

History is littered with examples of political disputes including resources. Since the turn of the century, however, people share a sentiment that resources could be the crux of power and conflict in the prospective international system. Yet, the linkage between natural resources and power, scarcity and conflict is not carved in stone (Dalby 2010). How natural resources interact with power is totally unclear. As the recent literature on energy security documents, perceptions of what energy consumption actually means and whether and how it is linked to power vary significantly among people. Sovacool (2011) lists alone 45 definitions of energy security. This suggests that the linkage between natural resources and power is a dynamic one which depends on social contexts. Not only might states have different approaches and perceptions of resource policy, but also different paradigms and logics of resource supply can dominate at different points in time. This analysis explores which form natural resources and power might take under different kinds of contextual knowledge. It sets off with some conceptual notes on resources and power and then outlines the major changes in the resource sector. In the

E. Fels et al. (eds.), *Power in the 21st Century*, Global Power Shift,
DOI 10.1007/978-3-642-25082-8_6, © Springer-Verlag Berlin Heidelberg 2012

final section, I promote the argument that the structural and productive power determine the meanings of natural resources and power and thus shape the future resource system. In three different future "worlds" – the Hobbesian, the Kantian and the Lockean world – states perceive the international system, power and the allocation of resources in different terms.

Natural Resources and Power

Natural resources can be both source and effect of power (Ebel et al. 2000: 9). This mutual relationship is reflected in the three different but compatible forms of comprehensive power, institutional power, and structural/productive power (Barnett and Duvall 2005).[1] Comprehensive power is power which actors possess and employ to manipulate social interaction. This behavioral conception refers to the ability of A to get B what it would otherwise not desire to do (Dahl 1957: 202). Natural resources are one element of comprehensive power, in addition to economic development, population, and military capability (Morgenthau 1948; Cline 1975). Exporters can make a fortune from selling their resources, whereas importing states feed the development of their industries.[2] The power balance between consumers and producers is follows the prices fluctuations of resources. Thus control over natural resources influences the international balance of power (Müller-Kraenner 2008: 1).

Most natural resources are rather uninteresting for politics. Depending on their economic value, military relevance, estimated scarcity, and concentration of supply, however, political actors might designate some of them as "critical" or "strategic" commodities which are essential to national power and security. Linking supply and security occurs through intersubjective processes of "politicization" or "securitization" (Buzan et al. 1998). Oil, the most essential good to the modern industrial age, even appears to be in a natural liaison with national power and security (Kalicki and Goldwyn 2005: 9). Other materials such as rare earth elements, key to many efficient high-technologies, suddenly entered the spotlight of securitization moves by mid-2010 (The Economist 2010). Although raw materials are still much less of a powder keg than fossil fuels, the growing importance of other materials is making the world of resources more complex since power no longer rests only on the control of oil and steel. Elements such as rare earth, indium and tantalum, though used in small amounts, are now central to many progressive technologies.

Power relations between states also influence the availability of resources (Ebel et al. 2000). Governments at times employ "critical" resources as instrument to exert

---

[1] Different from Barnett and Duvall, I consider structural and productive power together as constitutive of social relations.

[2] Many resource-rich countries, however, fail to translate natural richness into economic richness and national strength. According to the "Resource Curse" and the "Dutch Disease" resource-rich countries are prone to social conflicts and build a weak industry (Auty 1993; Corden 1984).

political pressure. Control over natural resources, in these terms, is not an end in itself but connected to general foreign affairs and interstate relations. The security dimension of supply comes principally up in bilateral relations with strategic mistrust. Venezuela uses its oil to counter U.S. hegemony and China allegedly temporarily halted rare earth exports to Japan in the dispute over the Diaoyu/Senkaku Islands. In the view of U.S. officials, dependence on oil imports is eroding American power and limits its scope of action (Deutch et al. 2006: 3). To minimize vulnerabilities to political disruptions of supply, importers engage in a lively strategic mix of diversifying sources, redirecting energy flows and saving resources. Shortly speaking, due to the highly interdependent global resource trade, the effects of comprehensive power are everywhere. However, because some resource markets are globally integrated, as in the case of oil, political intervention can be less effective and costly for the own economy. The economy of Russia and other states are dependent on the "security of demand" (Elhefnawy 2008: 43). The recent boykott of Iranian oil by the U.S., E.U., and Japan demonstrates that consumers can sometimes turn the table and might use the exporter's reliance on oil revenues to apply pressure.

Actors enforce their interests more indirectly through institutional power. By shaping the norms, rules and procedures and expectations of institutions (Krasner 1982: 186), states can influence the behavior of others (Barnett and Duvall 2005: 51). High interdependence of resource trade, common interests in supply and the need for managing scarce resources has caused the emergence of various international institutions in the sector. The Organization of the Petroleum Exporting Countries (OPEC) coordinates production quotas of its members, whereas the IEA realizes policy coordination of strategic oil reserves in order to defy vulnerability to political use of resources (Keohane 1984: 217).

The recent WTO dispute settlement on raw materials is a particular case of institutional power. The US, EU and Mexico charged China with its export restrictions on various raw materials including Bauxite, Coke, Magnesium, and Zinc (World Trade Organization 2011). Through the provisions of GATT and the Chinese accession protocol, the complainants were able to exact free flow of resources. The dispute settlement panel ruled mostly in favor of them, but it remains to be seen whether China will comply. Further mechanisms to ensure the free flow of resources to importers are the Energy Charter Treaty, particularly focusing on transit countries (Selivanova 2010).

Finally, structural and productive powers constitute the social relations and subject positions of the actors (Barnett and Duvall 2005: 52). To this effect, they are also constitutive of comprehensive and institutional power. What possession of comprehensive power means, how the power of other actors is interpreted, how it can and should be used, depends on the specific knowledge, which the structural and productive powers produce. As will be argued below, this knowledge determines in which kind of world we live.

The produced knowledge regulates whether people think that the quest for resources is a political competition and a matter of survival or whether it is an economic activity with economic risks. Structure and productive power assign subject positions to actors (Davies and Harré 1990). They create a dualism of "consumers" and "producers" and distinguish "newcomers" and "established consumers". The latter distinction refers not only to the time of arrival to international resource trade, but defines as well what actors can claim and what they are allowed to do and what not. Positioning states as "consumers" and "producers" is part of the diffuse ability to control, direct, and attract resource flows through financial power, International Resource Companies and technological supremacy. As Stokes and Doug (2010: 43) argue, the U.S. hegemony promotes the openness of oil-rich developing countries in a liberal order and ensures this, if necessary, through military or other coercive measures. This a mixture of coercive comprehensive power and, as they call it "derivative structural power" of controlling access to global oil stocks.

Structural and productive power also produce the meaning of resources. Resources are not resources in themselves. Things become resources when human beings assign a function which they are supposed to fulfill in human economy. As economist Erich Zimmermann (1983: 7) recognized in the 1950s, "The word 'resource' does not refer to a thing or a substance but to a function which a thing or a substance may perform or to an operation in which it may take part, namely, the function or operation of attaining a given end such as satisfying a want." The definition and redefinition of resources – through research, registering patents, developing demand markets – can be a diffuse power and even change fundamental principles of the system. New resources can promote partial shifts of comprehensive power such as LNG strengthens supply of states like Japan and South Korea which are not connected to pipeline networks. Moreover, new resources such as renewable energy can as well change the meanings of power.

Changes in International Resource Supply

Five major changes are occurring in relation to natural resources and power: scarcity, the rise of emerging powers, changing rules of supply, destabilization of major supply regions, and the emergence of environmental concerns. First, insatiable demand will sooner or later deplete many resources and thus complicate customary material foundations of power. For example, economically and technically recoverable reserves of nickel, copper, and tungsten will run out in 50, 40, and 48 years respectively. Although reserves will extend due to price increases, new technologies, and recycling, remaining reserves will be geographically more concentrated. OPEC's share of world oil production will rise from currently 40% to about 50% by 2035 (International Energy Agency 2010: 119). Remaining reserves will also be more difficult to access, and more expensive to extract. The sunken Deepwater Horizon drilling rig and the subsequent oil spill demonstrate that oil development accepts more and more operational and environmental risks. Unconventional oil resources such as heavy oil in Venezuelan tar sands raise hopes of a prolonged oil age because they top conventional reserves by far. They might contribute about 10% to global oil demand. But their extraction is less efficient, more expensive at comes at higher environmental costs. Whether an ice-free Arctic, which presumably contains 30% of undiscovered gas and 13% of undiscovered oil (Bird et al. 2008), or the deep sea can become an important supply source remains to be seen. Including unconventional oil, current IEA scenarios expect oil production not to peak before 2035 (International Energy Agency 2010).

Geological scarcity, however, often matters less than the discourse that makes sense of the material world Castree 2001, p. 13. This discourse currently creates the image of a shrinking world. Because there is uncertainty about the exact amount of reserves in the earth's crust and the ability to extract them, estimating the volume of reserves becomes also a political activity. Oil peak is probably the most controversially hypothesis about future availability of oil (Sieminski 2005). Connected to this talk of scarcity is the discursive element of supply risk, which is quite ordinary for oil, but is also an increasing concern for central raw materials. For many metals and non-fuel minerals, the degree of import dependence and reliance on a single customer is often much higher than with regard to energy, but has also often less political consequences than in the case of oil. Supply of rare earth elements, antimony, and tungsten is particularly striking because China provides nearly for all of global production. The nervousness of market participants and political actors has aroused the interest of speculators in recent years, driving prices up even more and making them more volatile. The following Table 6.1 and Map 6.1 show raw materials which many states see as "critical" and important import sources of selected materials for the U.S. and Europe. The U.S. and Europe have a particularly high import dependence for many raw materials.

The rise of emerging powers is the other great shift in global resource trade. China's enormous development is underlined by its new status as the world's second largest consumer of total primary energy and oil. Between 2000 and 2008, China contributed 40% to the growth of global oil demand, and will do so with 60% until 2035 (IEA 2010). The country is now the world's largest consumer of iron, copper, zinc and other raw materials. The general redistribution of power thus also impacts on the distribution of resources. The newly capability of emerging powers to attract massive amount of resources, has incited more intensive competition for resources particularly with the US, European states, and Japan. Western nations express concerns about Asian "resource mercantilism" and fear of China striving to "lock up" oil supply through strategic investments (U.S.-China Economic and Security Review Commission 2005: 171). Among other reasons, commentators see the new demand of global resource prices increases as a culprit for skyrocketing market prices (see Graph 6.1).

This observation, although partly accurate, tells only half of the story. Through developing resource projects abroad, emerging powers have also made a contribution to increasing global supply. Investments of Chinese and Indian oil companies turned Sudan from an oil importer to a net exporter (Downs 2007). The kind of these investments does not suggest the existence of a national grand strategy to lock up resources, nor does the fragmented domestic policy apparatus in China (Moran 2010: 12; Downs 2010). China and India transfer large amount of their equity oil to international markets (Agrawal 2009: 51). The low environmental and labor costs of mining operations in China also guaranteed very low prices for many raw

Table 6.1 Reserve-to-production ratio, application, and import dependence of important raw materials (Sources: United States Geographical Survey 2011; European Commission 2010; Department of Defense 2009)

	Reserves/ production[a]	Major applications	Defined by EU as "critical"	U.S. strategic stockpile	U.S. import dependence	EU import dependence
Antimony (Sb)	13	Flame retardants, batteries, chemicals	☒		93%	100%
Bauxite (Al*)	133	Aluminium			100%	95%
Beryllium (Be)	Na	Computer and telecommunications	☒		47%	100%
Chromium (Cr)	16	Supperalloys in turbines		☒	39%	46%
Cobalt (Co)	83	Batteries, steel, cutting tools	☒	☒	75%	100%
Fluorspar (CaF_2)	45	Chemicals	☒		100%	69%
Gallium	Na	Electronics	☒		99%	Na
Germanium (Ge)	Na	Fiber-optics, catalysts, electronics	☒	☒	90%	100%
Graphite (C)	65	Foundry, steelmaking, refractories	☒		100%	95%
Indium (In)	Na	LCDs			100%	100%
Iron (Fe)	75	Steel			Net exporter	85%
Magnesium (Mg)	430	Chemistry, refractories	☒		53%	100%
Manganese (Mn)	49	Construction, machinery		☒	100%	91%
Molybdenum (Mo)	42	Steel, superalloys			Net exporter	100%
Nickel (Ni)	50	Steel, batteries, superalloys	☒		18%	55%
Niobium (Nb)	46	Steel, super alloys	☒		100%	100%
Platin Group Metals	174	Catalysts, electronics	☒	☒	94%	100%
Rare Earth (REE)	846	Magnets, phosphors, electronics	☒		100%	100%
Tantalum (Ta)	164	Capacitors in electronics	☒	☒	100%	100%
Tin (Sn)	20	Containers, construction		☒	80%	Na
Titanium (Ti)	110	Aerospace applications, chemistry	☒		81%	100%
Tungsten (W)	48	Cutting tools, electrodes, wires	☒	☒	63%	73%
Zinc (Zi)	21	Galvanizing, alloys		☒	76%	64%

[a]The reserves-to-production indicator includes only current reserves. Because these are likely to increase for many materials, they will be longer available than this indicator suggests

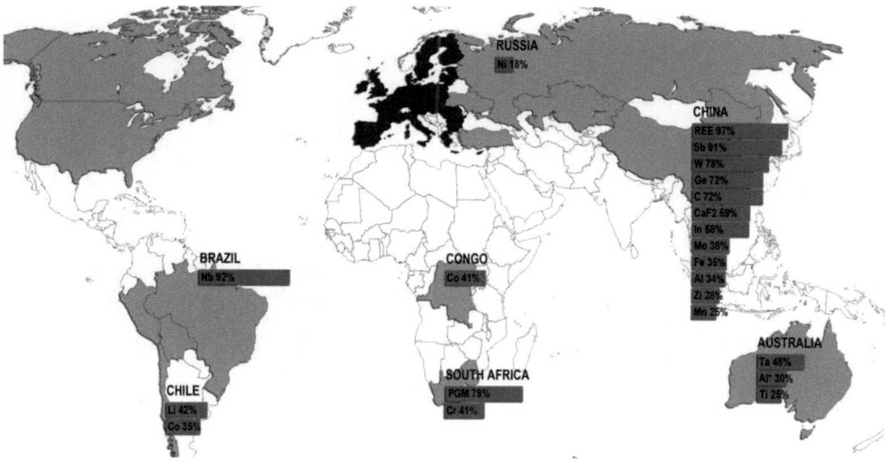

Map 6.1 Source countries of selected European raw materials imports as of 2008/2009. *Grey* colored countries are important suppliers for the EU. The *grey bars* indicate the most important import partner for a particular resource and its relative share of EU imports. Li = Lithium, Cu = Copper, Al = Aluminium (Source: European Commission 2010)

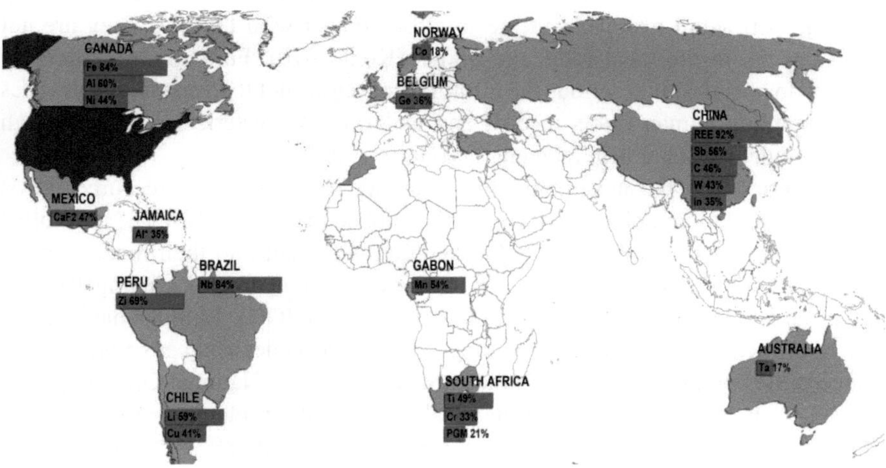

Map 6.2 Source countries of selected American raw materials imports (2006–2009). *Grey* colored countries are most important suppliers. The grey bars indicate relative share of the most important source of overall imports. Source (United States Geographical Survey 2011)

materials for a long time and they use much of the resources for end-products that will be sold to foreign markets.

The rise of emerging powers is particularly challenging to the informal and formal rules of established international energy regimes. Whereas the International Energy Agency represented the most important consumer states, the giants China

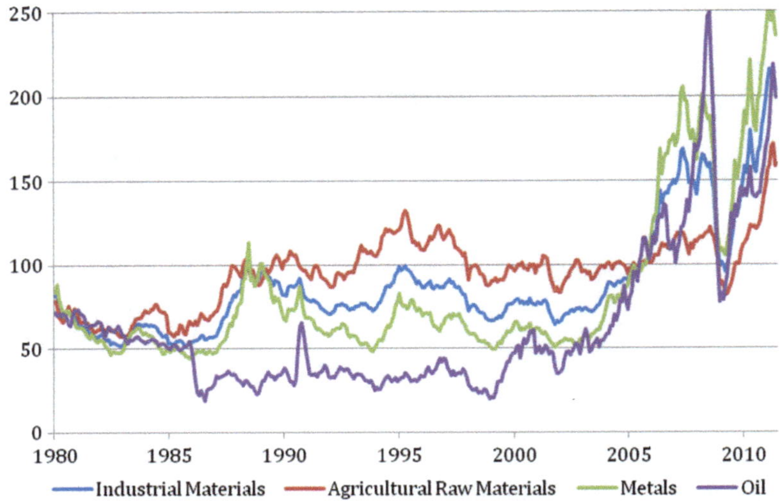

Graph 6.1 Price indices for oil metals, agricultural goods and industrial materials from 1980 to 2011. Base year 2005 = 100 (Source: International Monetary Fund 2011)

and India are now outside of this system. Although both are gradually building up strategic petroleum reserves and are in close contact with the IEA, they are not bound by its institutional rules and norms (Kohl 2010). Furthermore, emerging powers do not take all to serious the informal consensus not to invest in pariah states with appalling human rights records and undermines Western influence through granting unconditional development aid (Hurst 2006).

This brings up the next point, the changing rules of global resource flows. Western international oil companies (IOC), dubbed the "Seven Sisters," controlled world oil production until the 1970s when the OPEC cut into their market power (Deutch 2007: 7). The recent rise of state-owned companies including Russian Gazprom and Petróleos de Venezuela has cornered the IOCs. With the nationalization of the heavy oil deposits in the Orinoco basin, the Venezuelan government now controls the countries' oil sales to the U.S. (Pirog 2007). National Oil Companies (NOC) from emerging consumer states also joined the roulette of resources. By 2007, NOCs produced 52% of world oil supply and owned 88% of proven reserves (Energy Information Administration 2009). The Financial Times thus named the leading NOCs the "New Seven Sisters" (Hoyos 2007). On the other hand, private companies still dominate many raw material markets, such as Vale, Rio Tinto and BHP Billiton control 70% of seaborne iron ore trade. At the same time, however, first and foremost Russia, China, India, and Tanzania begun to impose varied forms of barriers on raw material exports (Korinek and Kim 2010). All this contributes to a lesser capability of Western consumers to dictate the directions and kinds of resource flows.

Even in liberal economies, the resource sector is a politically protected one. Chinese state companies, for example, failed a number of times to acquire or to purchase interests of the Australian mining companies Rio Tinto, OZ Minerals, and Lynas Corp due to government intervention. Among EU member states, the Spanish government opposed the bid of Germany's EON to overtake Endesa. The years ahead will show how the Europeans will deal with the expansion of Gazprom's businesses on the continent. European and American policy makers legitimate these protective measures and the stronger integration between resource policy and foreign policy with the "resource nationalism" of other actors (European Commission 2011; Kalicki and Goldwyn 2005; Youngs 2009: 42; Kirchner and Berk 2010).

The fourth element is the destabilization of exporting regions and political instability due to environmental degradation. Production of many critical resources is concentrated in instable or non-democratic countries, which potentially impacts the political leverage of consuming countries. Labor strikes in Venezuela, riots in Nigeria, and unrest in the Arab world undermine secure supply of oil. The civil war in Libya had only minor impacts and Saudi Arabia compensated for the loss with its remaining spare capacity. But if unrests would disrupt oil supply from Saudi Arabia, all major economies would feel the negative consequences (Morse 2011). The oil infrastructure of the country is far more vulnerable to terrorist attacks than is widely believed (Koknar 2009: 23).

The depletion of renewable resources, such as forests, land, and wild life due to climate change and unsustainable use, is another problem. Droughts, loss of fertile land, and water shortage were contributing factors to the Dafur conflict (United Nations Environmental Programme 2007: 77). The United Nations expects that "[a] s the global population continues to rise, and the demand for resources continues to grow, there is significant potential for conflicts over natural resources to intensify in the coming decades" (United Nations Environmental Programme 2009: 6). Poor countries will have to deal with the intensifying food crisis. The FAO estimates that the world would have to produce 70% more food to feed a population of 9.1 billion by 2050 (Food and Agriculture Organization 2009). The destabilization of states and failing states does not only threaten undisrupted supply of resources (Stewart 2007, 657), but resource-induced conflicts also undermine international security. But on many instances, not scarcity, but struggles over revenues from abundant resources drive conflicts (Collier and Anke 2000). However, empirical evidence shows that natural resources are seldom the cause of armed conflict and as in the case of water can more often than not be managed effectively (Delli Priscoli and Wolf 2009: 9).

Finally, sustainability alters consumption patterns of resources. Climate change mitigation, probably more than the coming scarcity, requires a change of energy structure. The emergence of renewable energies give signs of shifting power from oil-rich countries to the producers of electricity from water, wind, and sun. However, oil will still remain the most important fuel in a world with mainly fossil fuel based transport systems. Government subsidies for fossil fuels still are five times higher than those of renewable energies. By 2035, they will satisfy between 15% and 30% of energy demand by 2035 (International Energy Agency 2010: 80).

Renewable energies can replace fossil fuels as the material basis of comprehensive power. They make theoretically electricity available without overly reliance on imports. This undermines the strong position of OPEC countries (Jaffe 2009: 86). Because renewable resources generally allow non-rival use, consumption is less inclined to end in zero-sum games. While solving scarcity, "energy independence" will probably remain a dream (Nivola and Carter 2010). Clean technologies create new dependencies. States need to import the newest efficient technology to produce electricity, and they rely on important raw materials such as rare earth for permanent magnets in wind turbines (U.S. Department of Energy 2010). Large-scale projects require trans-boundary cooperation. The Desertec project, which is proposed to transport solar energy from the Sahara to Europe, depends on the cooperation and stability of Northern African countries. Furthermore, energy and resource efficiency and the circular economy are the new mechanisms to reduce vulnerability to supply disruptions. Efficiency of raw material consumption is also gaining ground. The European Union is pushing for an ambitious agenda of resource efficiency and China presented its first Circular Economy Law in 2009. The stronger focus on the environmental dimension of energy security raised also awareness for natural disasters as threats to undisrupted supply (Brown and Dworkin 2011). Huricane Katrina relentlessly demonstrated its disastrous impacts on the American oil industry.

In summary, geological scarcity and the ending age of low resource prices undermine comprehensive power of states. Although Western states at the moment do not face an absolute decline of resource supply, the shifting distribution of power implies a greater competition from emerging powers for resources as material foundations of national power. Because these are mostly outside of the institutional system, institutional power to influence behavior of the most important consumer states is limited. The changing rules of global supply towards more state intervention gradually constrain the power of Western states to direct resource flows. Different discourses of scarcity and supply risk claim for different views of the current resource system and further development, however, without a clear direction for the future. The following section explores possible future worlds that might emerge.

Three Worlds of Resource Supply in the 21st Century

With these tendencies in mind, how might resource supply and power develop in the 21st century?[3] Some observers, in particular in public discourse, argue that increasing resource scarcity and interdependence will inevitably cause local and

[3] In the literature, there are some thought experiments about possible futures of energy and politics. An interesting study by Friedrichs (2010) shows that there is no unilinear relation between "oil peak" and a particular policy outcome. However, he understands oil scarcity solely in material terms and does not refer to the shared ideas of the actors.

international conflicts. Optimists on the contrary think that people will finally learn how to cope with scarcity (Van der Linde et al. 2004). There is, of course, no direct causal link between scarcity and conflict. Instead, the common knowledge of actors, namely the structural/productive power mentioned above, determines the kind of future supply. They States and other actors share common ideas knowledge and practices about how the international system is organized and what anarchy, comprehensive and institutional power, and security actually mean. Depending on the common knowledge, states will either live in a Hobbesian, Kantian, or Lockean culture of anarchy (Wendt 1999: 257). Whilst the first envisions a dystopia of permanent conflict, the second is an ideal world of close friendship among states. The third is one of rivalry but not a "war of all against all." The current resource system best fits that of a Lockean world. Emerging and established powers see each other as rivals, however, do not try to block other's access to resources. Analysts described China's energy strategy as "hedging," a mix of cooperation and competition, and also understand US strategy in these terms (Tunsjø 2010; Tessmann and Wolfe 2011; Medeiros 2005). Political practice is oscillating between the two boundaries of the Lockean Worlds with the two other worlds. The following section shows how resource supply of the 21st century might look like under the three worlds, which are no more but scenarios.

Hobbesian World

In this world, natural resources and power closely link up in a fight for survival among enemies. Indirect means of institutional power are much less preferred than hard coercive means. The most "powerful" states are those which maximize their resource basis by coercion and successfully disrupt the supply of others. The grimmest Malthusian expectations prove true. Scarcity of resources and supply competition end in armed conflicts and resource wars (Klare 2001, 2009). States do not manage the turnaround of sustainability and still have oil-based economies and rebound effects leave achievements of resource efficiency without effect. Saudi Arabia's oil reserves disappointed expectations (Simmons 2005) and unconventional oil could not keep up with demand. The American gas shale miracle turns out to be nothing but hot air due to environmental concerns. Supply shortages shake economies around the globe. Because states strive for comprehensive power in terms of relative gains, they define supply of oil and central raw materials as a matter of survival. The quest for natural resources turns into a zero-sum game. On a "shrinking planet" with "rising powers" (Klare 2008), states engage in a race for resources and try to separate others from supply. The fierce competition leads to a deterioration of relations between emerging and established powers.

Knowing of the inelasticity of energy demand, producer countries exploit their resource richness to enforce their comprehensive power in the international system. As Russia frequently disrupts gas supply to blackmail European states and Sino-

Russian gas deals fail due to price rows, these have either to get their foreign policy in line with Russian claims or to face serious energy shortages. Thus, rising prices shift the power balance to net exporters of important metals and minerals (Harris 2010, 180). This however meets with strong rebalancing moves of importers, such as Europe positions its military forces against Russia. States further employ military control of sea lanes to disrupt supply of competitors. While the political use of resources strengthens power and national security in short terms, this also dries up global resource flows in general, harming national power and economic growth as well as the global security environment in the long term.

To secure their slice of the cake, great consumers are more willing to take greater risks (Moran and James 2009). They gradually draw on military means to protect investments abroad, supply routes and to not shy away from military intervention in resource rich countries to force resource access, especially in Africa. In a potpourri of arms-races and resource-races, the Middle East and Central Asia become highly militarized and the frontlines of conflict. The U.S. extends its military presence in the Middle East to protect its access to the remaining barrels on Saudi Arabian land. Meanwhile, other great powers, including European states, increase their troops in the region to balance the US and others. China deploys troops to Oman and Yemen and its new aircraft carriers are anchored in the Gulf of Oman. In Central Asia, China and European states regularly carry out missions to damage each other's pipelines.

Against previous expectations (Kostecka 2011), the "String of Pearls" turned out to be true as China is aggressively extending its military basis along its import routes and its naval projection power. In East Asian waters, regional conflicts for the Diaoyu/Senkaku Islands and the Chunxiao/Shirakaba Field and the Nansha Islands escalate in armed confrontations. In the Pacific Rim, countries deploy war ships to protect the development of manganese modules in the deep sea. Canada, Denmark, Norway, the U.S., and Russia have begun to militarize the Arctic (Blunden 2009). Moreover, a confrontation between China and Australia seems unavoidable since the former demands full control over Australia's nickel and copper reserves, while the latter denies such access.

At local levels, environmental degradation is causing severe and protracted conflicts (Homer-Dixon 1991; Kaplan 1994), in particular in Africa, Central Asia, and South East Asia. Food shortages in Africa create more failing states in the region and destabilize the regional security order. Massive flows of refugees move towards Europe, whose immigration policy comes under strain.

The quest for resources leads to the formation of new alliances. It drives a wedge between the long-standing allies of the NATO. The US and European states have major disagreements about the distribution of resources. Even within Europe, many states are on their own. States build occasionally ad-hoc alliances to outmaneuver other states, but these break apart as soon they have to decide upon distributing resources among them. Under this situation, with highly armed great powers and dwindling resources, the probability of great power wars is increasing.

Kantian World

In the Kantian world, power is not defined in national but global terms and so are natural resources. Political power is rarely linked to natural resources. If political actors seek to exert influence, they do so cautiously through indirect means. Thus, there are no "most powerful" states, as they define global order as a world society, resource wars do not happen. One is because buying oil from the market is cheaper and oil production would certainly suffer from the destabilizing effects of military intervention. The other is that states share a common interest in stable supply (Fettweis 2009). Actors recognize the win-win situation of power gains and the positive effects of interdependence. Because they see each other as friends, the supply of all resources becomes totally desecuritized and mostly a pure economic matter. Where governments cover up trade politically, they emphasize their common benefits. As consumers share a common interest in undisrupted supply at reasonable prices, they intensify and institutionalize international cooperation, including China and India (Grant 2006). Actors eventually agree on effective global regimes that encompass all major consumers and producers for energy and raw materials. Due to strong institutional norms that prohibit political use of resources, governments not even think of it. There are still different approaches to resource policy, including government-backed production and investments. However, due to full transparency of investments and reporting on prices, nobody considers that "nationalist" approaches would disrupt global markets but instead enhance economic competition.

Humanity Humankind deals effectively with scarcity. Where a resource is becoming scarce, increasing prices incite common research projects for alternatives and more efficient consumption (Adelman 1993). The oil peak turned out to be just another last century's myth. When oil prices further rise, actors compete with each other for the most efficient economy with the largest amount of renewable energies. The oil reserves are not close to being depleted, before economies nearly fully rely on renewable energies. Gas from Russia, Central Asia, and shale gas provide for sufficient base load capacity and extensive transnational electricity grids guarantee for the efficient use of energy. The transformed transport systems rely mainly on electricity and some gas. The "energy hubs" of the Arab Peninsula disappear and the global energy system becomes truly decentralized, but still interdependent. Where the market failed to stimulate change, governments, acknowledging the divisibility of resources, agreed on controlled depletion of a resource by assigning quotas.

The greatest project which states realized is the creation of a global circular economy. Because resource flows are trans-boundary and commodities cross many boundaries before used in the end-product, it is often difficult to identify inefficiency hot spots. But because state and private actors agree on full transparency of resource use along the value-added chain, actors can improve efficiency. International standards for product design, recycling content and resource efficiency guarantee a careful use of natural resources. Progress of recycling technologies and their distribution to developing countries enabled the world economy to satisfy the demand of most resources through recycling.

Finally, the "Kantian" world defines security not in terms of survival but risk. They comprehend threats to undisrupted supply not as a threat for national security but instead as a concern for the system as a whole. Common patrols secure major transport routes and critical choke points against piracy attacks, but sea routes are generally not very susceptible to supply disruption (Blair and Liebertbal 2007). Against the backdrop of fading U.S. military capacity, multinational forces effectively fill the lacuna left by U.S. hegemony.

Lockean World

In the Lockean world, states do see each other as rivals, but not enemies. Whereas they use control over natural resources to gain occasional advantages in foreign policy, they do not push this to an extreme. Resources and power are interrelated through diffuse market power and limited political intervention. The most "powerful" states are those which successfully realize a policy mix of giving enough freedom to resource companies, conduct appropriate intervention and promote renewable energies and a circular economy. Global resource supply experiences a prolonged situation of policy ambiguity. On the one hand, states engage in common resource exploration and development and conduct common projects to improve resource efficiency. On the other hand, resource access frequently creates international frictions. Especially American and Chinese competition for oil from Middle East, Nigeria, and Venezuela put a strain on bilateral relations. Due to the new financial power of China and India, the U.S. and Europe often get the short end of the stick. Although the visible hand of governments still guides the resource policy of many emerging powers, the real problem lies in competition for shrinking resources. As a consequence, trade conflicts over resource access are becoming more frequently. States do not wage conflict by means of military power. However, if general relations between states deteriorate and come into conflict over other issues, resources can become an instrument to gain decisive advantages (Yergin 2006: 77).

Apart from political intervention to inhibit resource exports on some occasion, national or international resource companies manage resource flows under normal conditions. Resource companies compete for control over resources mainly from an economic perspective to improve their competitive edge. States mostly rely on diffuse mechanisms of managing and manipulating market interdependencies through their national champions. They use market power to improve control over resources or they draw on "soft" political measures such as strategic stockpiling, subsidizing resource companies or enforcing rules of international regimes. Resource cartels such as OPEC for oil, a new gas-OPEC and national monopolies on rare earth and other materials limit supply in order to keep prices high, however, also ensure undisrupted supply.

Moments of conflicts are accompanied by phases of cooperation. Whilst oil is becoming scarcer and provokes some tensions, liquid natural gas, energy efficiency and renewable energies are central to a more harmonious atmosphere among great powers. Efforts for sustainability are often very sluggish, but each time oil and gas prices rise, a new wave of research and policy measures to realize more efficiency and more renewable energy are enough to avoid conflicts. However, many poor states which can neither keep up with the price increases nor build up renewable energy face state failure due to aggravating energy shortages (Elhefnawy 2008: 48).

Although formal global governance institutions of energy and resources are less successful, states find other ways of coordination. Although the IEA is still an important institution, it fails to integrate China and India and with Russia staying outside of the Energy Charta, it becomes irrelevant. The creation of a framework for raw materials and resource efficiency remains, besides the already established International Resource Panel, nothing but an attempt.

Instead, more informal and fragmented settings gain in importance (Florini 2010: 173). The G20 proves to be the central mechanism to discuss ad-hoc issues of energy and resource supply. Although it leaves many issues unmanaged, it is, at least, able to handle the most challenging questions. The most successful is that of an Energy Stability Board, which provides voluntary standards for coordinating overseas investments and green-energy investments. Private and government-owned companies found here an important platform to exchange views (Victor and Yueh 2010).

What Can We Learn?

There is neither an automatic link between natural resources and power nor between scarcity and conflict. This analysis suggests that the relevance of resources depends on the shared knowledge of the actors. The structural and productive power provide interpretation frameworks for how to comprehend comprehensive and institutional power in the international system. Whether international power is thought in terms of relative gains or in terms of absolute gains, also shapes the function of natural resources and how states will effectively deal with scarcity. Hence, three different future worlds, where resources act out differently, are possible. If humanity does not go down the worst-case scenario of a Hobbesian world, natural resources are unlikely to be causes for international conflicts. They could be contributing factors of existing conflicts at most. They can play a role in influencing power relations and might occasionally incite political frictions, but not more than that. It is also unlikely that a single resource strategy – market or state-based – nor a single resource will shape power in the 21st century. The political message is not to believe in the inevitable force of the material. Rather social actions can determine how humanity will deal with power under geological scarcity of natural resources.

This analysis overviewed possible effects of structural and productive power. But it did not consider their conditions of formation and the mechanisms which produce the linkage between natural resources and power. In addition to "securitization," other theoretical concepts can provide understanding these formation processes, such as discourse analysis, practice theory, or science and technology studies (Mayer and Wübbeke 2011). Further research should examine why and how specific natural resources are linked to power by what actors to reach which political goals.

References

Adelman, M. A. (1993). *The economics of petroleum supply*. Cambridge: MIT Press.

Agrawal, P. (2009). *China and India: A comparative analysis of approaches to energy security*. New Delhi: United Service Institution of India.

Auty, R. (1993). *Sustaining development in mineral economies: The resource curse thesis*. London: Routledge.

Barnett, M., & Duvall, R. (2005). Power in international politics. *International Organization, 59*(1), 39–75.

Bird, K. J., Charpentier, R. R., Gautier, D. L., Houseknecht, D. W., Klett, T. R., Pitman, J. K., Moore, T. E., Schenk, C. J., Tennyson, M. E., & Wandrey, C. J. (2008). *Circum-Arctic resource appraisal: Estimates of undiscovered oil and gas North of the Arctic circle*. Reston: U.S. Geological Survey.

Blair, D., & Liebertbal, K. (2007). Smooth sailing – The world's shipping lanes are safe. *Foreign Affairs, 86*(3), 7–13.

Blunden, Margaret. (2009). The New Problem of Arctic Stability. *Survival 51*(1), 121–142.

Brown, M. A., & Dworkin, M. (2011). The environmental dimension of energy security. In B. Sovacool (Ed.), *The Routledge handbook of energy security*. London: Routledge.

Buzan, B., Wæver, O., & De Wilde, J. (1998). *Security a new framework for analysis*. London: Boulder.

Castree, N. (2001). Socializing nature: theory, practice, and politics. In N. Castree & B. Braun (Eds.), Social nature: theory, practice, and politics. Malden: Blackwell Publishing, 1–21.

Cline, R. S. (1975). *World power assessment: A calculus of strategic drift*. Washington, DC: Center for Strategic and International Studies, Georgetown University.

Collier, Paul, & Anke, Hoeffler. (2000). Greed and grievance in civil war. In *The World Bank policy research working paper*. Washington, DC: World Bank.

Corden, W. M. (1984). Boom sector and Dutch disease economics: Survey and consolidation. *Oxford Economic Papers, 36*(3), 359–380.

Dahl, R. (1957). The concept of power. *Behavioral Science, 2*(3), 201–215.

Dalby, S. (2010). Exorcising Malthus's ghost: Resources and security in global politics. *Geopolitics, 9*(1), 242–254.

Davies, B., & Harré, R. (1990). Positioning: The discursive production of selves. *Journal for the Theory of Social Behaviour, 20*(1), 43–63.

Delli Priscoli, J., & Wolf, A. T. (2009). *Managing and transforming water conflicts, international hydrology series*. Cambridge/New York: Cambridge University Press.

Department of Defense (2009) Strategic and critical materials operations report to congress: Operations under the strategic and critical materials stock piling act during the period October 2008 through September 2009. Edited by Department of Defense, Washington, DC.

Deutch, J. (2007). Priority energy security issues. In J. Deutch, A. Lauvergeon, & W. Prawiraatmadja (Eds.), *Energy security and climate change*. Washington, DC/Paris/Tokyo: The Trilateral Commission.

Deutch, J. M., James, R. S., & David, G. V. (2006). *National security consequences of U.S. oil dependency: Report of an independent task force, independent task force report*. New York: Council on Foreign Relations.

Downs, Erica. (2007). China's quest for overseas oil. *Far Eastern Economic Review (September 2007), 170*, 52–56.

Downs, E. S. (2010). Who's afraid of China's oil companies? In C. Pascual & J. Elkind (Eds.), *Energy security. Economics, politics, strategies, and implications*. Washington, DC: Brookings Institution Press.

Ebel, R. E., Caruso, G., Nunn, S., & Schlesinger, J. R. (2000). *The geopolitics of energy into the 21st century. volume 1: An overview and policy considerations* (Vol. 1). *CSIC Panel Report*. Washington, DC: Center for Strategic and International Studies.

Elhefnawy, N. (2008). The impending oil shock. *Survival, 50*(2), 37–66.

Energy Information Administration. (2009). *Who are the major players supplying the world oil market? 2009*. www.eia.gov/energy_in_brief/world_oil_market.cfm. Accessed 29 July 2011.

European Commission. (2010). *Critical raw materials for the EU. Report of the Ad-hoc Working Group on defining critical raw materials*. Brussels: European Commission.

European Commission. (2011). *Tackling the challenges in commodity markets and on raw materials*. Brussels: European Commission.

Fettweis, C. J. (2009). No blood for oil: Why resource wars are obsolete. In G. Luft & A. Korin (Eds.), *Energy security challenges for the 21st century*. Santa Barbara: Praeger Security International.

Friedrichs, J. (2010). Global energy crunch: how different parts of the world would react to a peak oil scenario. *Energy Policy, 38*(8): 4562–4569.

Florini, A. (2010). Global governance and energy. In C. Pascual & J. Elkind (Eds.), *Energy security. Economics, politics, strategies, and implications*. Washington, DC: Brookings Institution Press.

Food and Agriculture Organization. (2009). *Global agriculture towards 2050*. Rome: High Level Expert Forum.

Grant, I. (2006). Geopolitics or petropolitics? China and the global oil regime. In A. Griffith (Ed.), *Global perspectives on oil and security*. Halifax: Dalhousie University Centre for Foreign Policy Studies.

Grover, V. I. (2007). *Water: A source of conflict or cooperation?* Enfield: Science Publishers.

Harris, Stuart. (2010). Global and regional orders and the changing geopolitics of energy. *Australian Journal of International Affairs 64*(2), 166–185.

Homer-Dixon, T. F. (1991). On the threshold – Environmental-changes as causes of acute conflict (Reprinted). *International Security, 16*(2), 76–116.

Hoyos, C. (2007). The new seven sisters: Oil and gas giants dwarf western rivals. *Financial Times*, 2007/3/11.

Hurst, Cindy (2006). China's Oil Rush in Africa (Washington, DC: Institute for the Analysis of Global Security) http://www.iags.org/chinainafrica.pdf

International Energy Agency. (2010). *World energy outlook 2010*. Paris: International Energy Agency.

International Monetary Fund. (2011). *IMF primary commodity prices, 2011/7/28 2011*. http://www.imf.org/external/np/res/commod/index.aspx. Accessed 3 Aug 2011.

Jaffe, A. M. (2009). OPEC: An anatomy of a cartel. In G. Luft & A. Korin (Eds.), *Energy security challenges for the 21st century*. Santa Barbara: Praeger Security International.

Kalicki, J. H., David, L. G., Kalicki, J. H., & David, L. G. (2005). Introduction: The need to integrate energy and foreign policy. In J. H. Kalicki & D. L. Goldwyn (Eds.), *Energy and security. Toward a new foreign policy strategy*. Washington, DC: Woodrow Wilson Center Press.

Kaplan, R. D. (1994). *The coming anarchy. How scarcity, crime, overpopulation, tribalism, and disease are rapidly destroying the social fabric of our planet*. Boston, Mass: The Atlantic.

Keohane, R. O. (1984). *After hegemony. Cooperation and discord in the world political economy*. Princeton: Princeton University Press.

Kirchner, E., & Berk, C. (2010). European energy security co-operation: Between amity and enmity. *Journal of Common Market Studies, 48*(4), 859–880.

Klare, M. (2001). *Resource wars*. New York: Owl Books.

Klare, M. (2008). *Rising powers, shrinking planet: The new geopolitics of energy* (1st ed.). New York: Metropolitan Books.

Klare, M. (2009). There will be blood: Political violence, regional warfare, and the risk of great-power conflict over contested energy resources. In G. Luft & A. Korin (Eds.), *Energy security challenges for the 21st century*. Santa Barbara: Praeger Security International.

Kohl, W. L. (2010). Consumer country energy cooperation: The international energy agency and the global energy order. In A. Goldthau & J. M. Witte (Eds.), *Global energy governance. The new rules of the game*. Washington, DC: Brookings Institution Press.

Koknar, A. M. (2009). The epidemic of energy terrorism. In G. Luft (Ed.), *Energy security challenges for the 21st century*. Santa Barbara: Praeger Security International.

Korinek, J., & Kim, J. (2010). Export restrictions on strategic raw materials and their impact on trade. In OECD (Ed.), *OECD Trade policy working papers*, Paris: OECD.

Kostecka, D. J. (2011). Places and bases. The Chinese Navy's emerging support network in the Indian Ocean. *Naval War College Review, 64*(1), 59–78.

Krasner, S. (1982). Structural causes and regime consequences: Regimes as intervening variables. *International Organization, 36*(2), 185–205.

Müller-Kraenner, S. (2008). *Energy security*. London: Earthscan.

Mayer, M., & Wübbeke, J. (2011) Explaining China's peaceful road to energy security: An eclectic approach (Conference Presentation). *Conference: Global resource conflicts. Political economy and transnational governance in the 20th century*, Humboldt University, Berlin.

Medeiros, E. S. (2005). Strategic hedging and the future of Asia-Pacific stability. *The Washington Quarterly, 29*(1), 145–167.

Moran, D., & James, A. R. (2009). Introduction. The militarization of energy security. In D. Moran, J. A. Russell, & J. A. Russell (Eds.), *Energy security and global politics. The militarization of resource management*. London: Routledge.

Moran, T. H. (2010). *China's strategy to secure natural resources: Risks, dangers, and opportunities*. Washington, DC: Peterson Institute for International Economics.

Morgenthau, H. J. (1948). *Politics among nations; the struggle for power and peace* (1st ed.). New York: A. A. Knopf.

Morse, E. L. (2011). Oil and unrest. *Foreign Affairs* March 2011: http://www.foreignaffairs.com/articles/67563/edward-l-morse/oil-and-unrest?page=show

National Research Council. (2007). Minerals, Critical Minerals, and the U.S. Economy. Washington, D.C.: National Academies Press.

Nivola, P., & Carter, E. E. R. (2010). Making sense of 'energy independence". In C. Pascual & J. Elkind (Eds.), *Energy security. Economics, politics, strategies, and implications*. Washington, DC: Brookings Institution Press.

Pirog, R. (2007). The role of national oil companies in the international oil market. In *CRS report for congress*, Washington, DC.

Selivanova, Y. (2010). Managing the patchwork of agreements in trade and investment. In A. Goldthau & J. M. Witte (Eds.), *Global energy governance. The new rules of the game*. Washington, DC: Brookings Institution Press.

Sieminski, A. E. (2005). World energy futures. In J. H. Kalicki & D. L. Goldwyn (Eds.), *Energy and security. Toward a new foreign policy strategy*. Washington, DC: Woodrow Wilson Center Press.

Simmons, M. R. (2005). *Twilight in the desert: The coming Saudi oil shock and the world economy*. Hoboken: Wiley.

Sovacool, B. (2011). Introduction. Defining, measuring, and exploring energy security. In B. Sovacool (Ed.), *The Routledge handbook of energy security*. London: Routledge.

Stewart, P. (2007). "Failed" states and global security: Empirical questions and policy dilemmas. *International Studies Review, 9*(4), 644–662.

Stokes, D., & Raphael, S. (2010). *Global energy security and American hegemony*. Baltimore: John Hopkins University Press.

Tessmann, B., & Wolfe, W. (2011). Great power and strategic hedging: The case of Chinese energy security strategy. *International Studies Review, 13*(2), 215–241.

The Economist. (2010). The difference engine: More precious than gold. 2010/09/17.

Tunsjø, Ø. (2010). Hedging against oil dependency: New perspectives on China's energy security policy. *International Relations, 24*(1), 25–45.

U.S.-China Economic and Security Review Commission. (2005). 2005 Report to Congress. Edited by U. S.-C. E. a. S. R. Commission, Washington, DC.

U.S. Department of Energy. (2010). Critical materials strategy. edited by U. S. D. o. Energy. Washington, DC.

United Nations Environmental Programme. (2007). *Sudan: Post-conflict environmental assessment*. Nairobi: United Nations Environmental Programme.

United Nations Environmental Programme. (2009). *From conflict to peacebuilding*. Nairobi: The role of natural resources and the environment.

United States Geographical Survey. (2011). *Commodity statistics and information 2011*. http://minerals.usgs.gov/minerals/pubs/commodity/. Accessed 7 Aug 2011.

Van der Linde, C., Mehdi Parvizi Amineh, Aad,C.,, & Dick De, S. (2004). Study on energy supply security and geopolitics. Clingendael International Energy Programme.

Victor, D. G., & Yueh, L. (2010). The new energy order managing insecurities in the twenty-first century. *Foreign Affairs, 89*(1), 61–73.

Wendt, A. (1999). *Social theory of international politics, Cambridge studies in international relations*. Cambridge, UK/New York: Cambridge University Press.

World Trade Organization. (2011). *China – Measures related to the exportation of various raw materials*.

Yergin, D. (2006). Ensuring energy security. *Foreign Affairs, 85*(2), 69–82.

Youngs, R. (2009). *Energy security. Europe's new foreign policy challenge*. London: Routledge.

Zimmermann, E. W. (1983). *World resources and industries, the world economy*. New York: Garland.

Chapter 7
The Military Balance in the Baltic Sea Region: Notes on a Defunct Concept

Magnus Christiansson

Power Politics? That Is So 1980s!

It is something of a general assumption that in the diverse field that we call International Relations the terminology associated with power politics has been closely associated with the realist approach. This is an understanding that creates a need for further clarification. As pointed out by Barry Buzan and Ole Waever in 2007, the security theory field is differentiated as European scholars have tended to be interested in a reflexive approach to the security concept, while American scholarship has focused on empirically validated cause-effect relationships relevant to policy issues (Buzan and Waever 2007). Buzan and Waever describe the social backdrop for these differences and make a contrast between "critical theory" and "problem-solving theory". Perhaps a premature conclusion would be that terms and concepts like military balance and power politics have disappeared from the discourse of both academia and politics in Europe. They sound like an anachronism from the Cold War that many are uncomfortable with.

In fact, what happened after the Cold War was that most European politicians came to cultivate the idea that something fundamental had happened in world politics. Not only was there an end to the confrontation between Superpowers, but the cooperative relations between states in Western Europe was now seen as extendable also to Eastern Europe. A process of enlargement of both the EU and NATO commenced. This was a New Europe. The fundamental idea of security among states was formulated in the 1990 *Charter of Paris for a New Europe*: "Security is indivisible and the security of every participating State is inseparably linked to that of all others" (CSCE 1990: 5). This is perhaps the clearest example of how power politics and spheres of influence were pushed aside in the discourse by treaty based cooperative politics. Furthermore, the idea of partnerships that blossomed in the 1990s was essentially a way to accommodate irregular security interests among the states in this New Europe.

Another driver of this development was the introduction of a term that successfully came to colonize the public discourse during the 1990s – globalization. This is

E. Fels et al. (eds.), *Power in the 21st Century*, Global Power Shift,
DOI 10.1007/978-3-642-25082-8_7, © Springer-Verlag Berlin Heidelberg 2012

not an argument that relates to the ongoing debate about how this phenomenon is, but rather that it became a concept that every successful politician in the 1990s had to be familiar with. Globalization was both cause and effect. It was a promise for many and a horrible prospect for others. Sometimes an ideological gesture, sometimes a depiction.

The principal loser in globalization is the state. The economic significance of the state is questionable in times when the global financial systems, or the electronic herd as Thomas Friedman would say, could overrun every country (Friedman 1999). Related to this, some would claim closely related, was the regionalization that in the European case was manifested by the accelerating integration process of the EU. This, often called "Europeanization", was expressed by the efforts to coordinate a number of policy areas – foreign policy, monetary policy, environmental policy, migration policy, to name just a few – via different degrees of EU institutionalization.

Consequently, a state-centric public debate on security faded away in many European countries during the 1990s. Since traditional power politics was absent from the agenda, attention turned to other problems. The focus of the *Council of the Baltic Sea States* (CBSS) is illustrative of this – environment, economic development, energy, education and culture. Not only is it common ground among its members, but it also reflects a diffusion of non-traditional security concerns. Security replaced strategy in the discourse.

This development was further accentuated after 9/11 and the US led Global War on Terrorism. Following the relative calm in the Balkans and the successful enlargement processes, an integrated Europe was now seen as normality and the major security concern was how much to support the remaining Superpower in its global endeavours. The NATO countries of the Baltic Sea region met this debate directly during 2003 when the "transatlantic rift" put loyalties to test. The EU countries of the Baltic Sea region met this debate indirectly as the common security and defence policy was gradually designed. Power politics was associated with the US. Europe equalled "effective multilateralism".

But then something happened. Geopolitics and power politics came back into the discourse. Actually, there had always been scholars and politicians of the old school that never believed in a "New Europe" (e.g. Mearsheimer 1990). However distinguished, during the 1990s they had a hard time finding any significant place in the debate or in the corridors of political power. Many experts on Eastern Europe and Russia pointed out early in the 1990s that the democracy developed under the Yeltsin regime was indeed "stillborn" and only vaguely similar to Western democracy (see for example Gill and Markwick 2000). But these experts, often critical to the "shock therapy" introduced by ingenuous Western economists, were marginalised and their warnings largely ignored (Hedlund 2005). The conclusions of these early observers put a question mark after the rhetoric on a whole, free and integrated Europe that most politicians were using. Furthermore, this question mark suggested that many of the policies associated with this "New Europe" were in fact dangerous and illusionary.

However, it took more than a decade for these thoughts to enter the mainstream of the debate. When Vladimir Putin came to power he seemed for many to belong to a new species in the post Cold War order: the elected autocrat (Zakaria 2003). His agenda was gradually revealed, as he openly contested the principles of an open society, centralized means of power and installed vassals from the old Soviet security apparatus. The military clash with Georgia in August 2008 was not a surprise for the experts, but proved to be an eye-opener for many in the Western European political circles. Over a sequence of a few days, it seemed for some, the Charter of Paris became an obsolete document from a previous era.

The British journalist Edward Lucas published an influential book called *The New Cold War: How the Kremlin Menaces both Russia and the West* in which he argues that the West underestimates the danger that Russia poses for the world (Lucas 2008). His message echoed what many Eastern European countries had warned of and feared as junior partners in the trans-atlantic integration process. Shifting attention to issues on a wider security agenda and military transformation based on a notion of a "New Europe" seemed risky if Russia's behaviour challenged the very cornerstones of the European security order. For example, when the Estonian President Toomas Ilves openly asked the question "Can Berlin be defended?" (Thielbeer 2008) he was not referring to a broad concept of societal security, but the idea of territorial defence abandoned after the Cold War. Quite suddenly terms like "history", "power politics" and "spheres of influence" entered the public debate in some countries. Admittedly, this shift in the debate was not paradigmatic, but it definitely represented a new diversity in the European debate (Valacek 2008).

Clearly, there had emerged a political agenda that reintroduced many of the concepts from the Cold War in the debate, and that this indeed made it an interesting subject from many perspectives. The discourse had shifted and this is, I would argue, a challenge for the International Relations dicipline in Europe. A great deal of the development of academia after the Cold War has been dedicated to revising and criticizing the traditional perspectives that had proved to be both misleading and hollow. The comeback of these very concepts, as used by key actors in European politics, provides a good opportunity to revisit theory in the light of an agenda set by the actors we are to study. This is the purpose of this chapter. It is a brief investigation of the state behaviour around the Baltic Sea, in order to assess the plausibility of military balance theory in the period 2008–2009 following the confrontation in Georgia.

The article will have four sections. In the first I will make my way into the conceptual jungle of the key concept of military balance. A central conclusion of this is to shift focus to military balancing. I will show in which ways it is possible to use this term, and what knowledge it could guide us to. In the second section I will describe the current military capabilities in the region. It will be a brief account that will represent fixed points that do not have theoretical or empirical importance in themselves. In the third section I will briefly describe and analyse the patterns of balancing behaviour among the states in the region using the theoretical toolbox introduced. Finally, I will discuss a few conclusions, both regarding military balancing in the Baltic Sea region as well as theory.

What Is Military Balance?

As hinted above it is far from obvious that there is academic support for a new agenda of power politics in Europe. Some would argue that revisiting obsolete theory would be to surrender to or even indirectly support politics that create a more unstable and conflict prone Europe. To use military balance is in fact using discursive power that will marginalise cooperative politics, and in the end become a self-fulfilling prophesy.

However, as pointed out by Alexander Wendt, the notion that international politics is shaped by power relations is not reserved for any specific strand in International Relations (Wendt 1999: 96–97). Applying it does not imply a specific agenda in itself. This means that the opposite argument could be made: after the clash in Georgia 2008 it would be to use discursive power to hide the importance of power politics in Europe. Instead, the theoretically important question is in what way power, including military power, matters. This is why so many of the studies of power politics seem misguided, not because it refers to a flawed (neo)realist heritage, but because they fail to address the importance of military power in a meaningful way.

Balance, whether military or other, is a metaphor. As Richard Little points out, this aspect of metaphor must be taken seriously "because the source of the metaphor (balance) has the ability to transform the accepted meaning of the target of the concept (power)" (2007: 19). Using it is an invitation to think of a scale where masses of military assets make the scale tip over to the advantage of the most powerful actor. Accordingly, when the *International Institute for Strategic Studies* (IISS) publishes its annual assessment of global military capabilities and defence economics, it is named *The Military Balance* (IISS 2010). However, an assessment of the Armed Forces around the Baltic Sea could tell us something about proportions of matter. But this in itself does not give any clue of the importance or impact of these proportions. An assessment could be used to find out patterns of defence spending and proportions of military equipment, but the label is misleading since it appears to provide an insight into which actors are more "powerful" than others in a specific region or conflict. To take but one contemporary example: one could argue that a country like Pakistan is just as important an actor in the Afghanistan conflict as the US, even if the latter ranks much higher on defence spending and military equipment.

One common way of describing this in theoretical terms is that power is a relation and not a resource. Whether defence spending of an actor results in this actor becoming "powerful" or not depends on the context. This relational approach to power underlines that any given power resource (like military resources) must be connected to a relation where power is to be exercised in order to assess its value.

Some kind of framework of assumptions of which actor is trying to get which other actor to do what needs to be established, before the importance of military capabilities could be determined. Some scholars call this a "policy-contingency framework". Not to use such a framework would be, in the words of David Baldwin, to discuss what constitutes a good card hand without knowing which card game to play (2006: 179–180).

However, I side with Olav Knudsen in that power as resource and power as relation do not necessarily rival each other. Power is on the one hand determined by the actor's own assessments where appearance of power becomes the guide to understanding relational action. At the same time the appearance interpreted by actors is the image of resources (2007: 11).[1] There are two crucial elements in this reasoning: the first concerns the constant process of resource assessments performed by governments, and secondly the subjective element of the actors, based on interpretation and role identities. Or in other words, the power of a government is, to a large extent, what other governments *think* it is (2007: 26).[2]

According to Knudsen it is this process of estimation and assessment that constitutes a researchable phenomenon. This defines balancing of power: "a tendency or a pattern of behaviour of compensatory reaction to perceived power differentials" (2007: 26). The lose term "compensatory reaction" opens the analysis for a wide range of state policies, and it makes analysis a bit more diverse than the two options provided by Stephen Walt: balancing defined as allying with other states or bandwagoning (1987: 17–21, 27–32). Furthermore, it is important to underline that Knudsen makes a major point that (neo)realists, like Kenneth Waltz, have been too focused on military capabilities, since the process is ubiquitous. Thus, the military balance is something distinct from the balance of power. An analyst can make a serious mistake by assuming that the study of military balancing does in fact give him a view of the balancing of power.

This angle provides the theoretical scope of this essay. In the following we will use the statistics of current patterns of defence spending and capabilities in the Baltic Sea region as the point of departure of this process of assessment. This part of the essay is simply a way to briefly sketch which (military) playing cards exist among the countries in the region. After that we will look closer at the different role conceptions, the (military) strategies that we find in the region. A meaningful use of military balance is thus a scholarly description of the cards while also covering the respective cardgames defined by the actors.

Finally this leaves us with a few limitations related to the scope of the study. From the chosen approach to military balance it is not entirely clear why there necessarily needs to be a regional limit. Indeed, as could be suspected, many factors and actors outside of the Baltic Sea region are likely to influence the strategies under study. International bodies like NATO are likely to have an impact and

[1] However, the ontological status of this image should not be linked to perception only.

[2] This applies if governments are the actors.

perhaps most importantly the policies of the US. It is quite likely that any process of balancing is not limited to the geography of the Baltic Sea. In other words: is there a Baltic Sea card game? We must keep in mind that balancing behaviour *in* the region might not necessarily be limited *by* the region.

While the process of balancing could describe the patterns of state actors in the region, it could simultaneously provide us with empirical input to evaluate the status of the Baltic Sea region as a "level of analysis" in international politics (see Buzan and Waever 2003). Theory could show us important dimensions in state behaviour, and state behaviours could in turn show in what sense there is a regional dimension. These are the caveats when the lexical definition of "Baltic Sea region" will be defined as the states in the CBSS, not counting Iceland which does not have an armed force.

Capabilities

Arguably the simples (and admittedly the roughest) way to measure military capabilities is to consult the military budget of a state.[3] While defence spending as percentage of GDP gives an idea of the priorities of a state, the defence spending is an indicator of the absolute size of a country's military toolbox. Depending on a number of factors, including geostrategic location, this toolbox includes tools adapted to mainly three elements: air-, land-, and sea warfare. The main components include brigades (ca. 5,000 troops), battalions (ca. 500–800 troops), squadrons (ca. 8–12 aircraft), as well as individual surface- and subsurface vessels (including cruisers, frigates, and submarines). However, it should be noted that from a balancing perspective, it is the budget *trends* following 2008 that are of greatest interest.

The 2009 ranking of the Baltic Sea region from the rough criteria of military spending in US$ gives the following list:

1. Germany 46.5 billion
2. Russia 41.05 billion
3. Poland 8.63 billion
4. Norway 5.94 billion
5. Sweden 5.61 billion
6. Denmark 4.58 billion
7. Finland 4.21 billion
8. Lithuania 501 million
9. Latvia 382 million
10. Estonia 358 million

[3] All figures are taken from IISS (2010). I would like to thank Carina Solmirano of SIPRI for valuable advice on defence statistics.

The Baltic States

The three Baltic countries have the smallest set of military playing cards. All three have decreased their defence budgets in 2009. For example Latvia cut down its defence budgets by 21%. Lithuania is by far the greatest spender in US$ with 501 million. Estonia and Latvia are close together with US$382 and US$358 million respectively. It is well worth noting that the total defence spending of the Baltic states (US$1.241 billion) is less than half of the second smallest spender in the region Finland.

The composition of the Armed Forces of the Baltic states are all shaped by the process of defence transformation leading up to the NATO membership. The Armies have invested heavily in expeditionary participation in US led missions like Afghanistan. They are all dependent on reservists, and active components vary from ca. 1,000 to 2,500 troops in each country. The Navies have set up a joint unit BALTRON with bases in Liepeda, Riga, Ventspils, Tallinn, and Klaipeda. The total surface capabilities include a couple of frigates, 19 patrol vessels of various specifications, and some 11 mine warfare ships. The Air Forces lack any fighter component and are limited to transport, a few helicopters, and support capabilities.

Denmark

The defence budget in Denmark was increased from US$4.46 billion in 2008 to US $4.58 billion in 2009. The plan was to gradually increase the budget until 2014. The style of the Armed Forces is that of an expeditionary corps with limited ability for self-reliance. Despite budget increases there will be cuts in the number of operational tanks, aircraft, and maritime response ships.

The core of the Army is a mechanized infantry brigade, supplemented by a training brigade. The training brigade consists of some nine training units that supply the mechanized brigade with expeditionary units. Besides this there are individual independent battalions and units in reconnaissance, special forces, engineers, and air defence. The ambition of the Army is to field 2,000 expeditionary troops.

The Navy has prioritized patrolling tasks and features some 49 ships for this purpose. Other than that there are 14 mine warfare ships and capabilities for flexible logistic support. There are two major bases at Korsøer and Fredrikshavn.

The Air Force is still depending largely on the F-16AM/F-16BM system. The political decision to purchase a replacement has been put on ice. The forces consist of 48 combat capable F-16s, and one squadron each of search and rescue and transport.

Norway

Norway has, perhaps a bit surprisingly, the largest defence budget among the Nordic countries. However, considering the near levelling of GDP figures when compared to neighboring country Sweden, it might seem more understandable. Norway spent US$5.94 billion in 2009 and that is a slight increase from the previous year.

The gist of the Army, based on conscription, is the *Northern Brigade*. One mechanized battalion in the brigade, (the *Telemark* battalion) is reserved for high readiness operations. Furthermore, assets include one special forces commando, one guards battalion, and one reconnaissance battalion.

The Navy has three major components: naval units, schools, and coast guard. The principal surface combatants are three frigates supported by six patrol ships and six mine warfare ships. It has six *Ula* submarines. The facilities include bases at Bergen, Ramsund, and Trondenes. The coast guard, with its base in Sortland, has some 13 patrol craft.

The Air Force has three squadrons of F-16s. In November 2008 Norway decided to procure *Joint Strike Fighter*. Complementing the fighter capability are individual squadrons of maritime reconnaissance, search and rescue helicopters, electronic warfare, as well as transport. The total of combat capable aircraft is 52.

Finland

The neighbouring country Finland has had a different development over the last years. Defence spending increased from US$3.455 billion in 2008 to US$4.21 billion in 2009. General conscription is maintained and thus the reserve forces still have an important function in the defence system. Thousands of reservists do refresher training every year.

Apart from the regimental size rapid reaction forces, the Army of Finland is based on mobilization of conscripts. The four military commands have a total strength of three Jaeger brigades, two air defence brigades, and one brigade each of armour, artillery, engineers, and signals. However, fully mobilized the Army has another 2 Jaeger brigades and some 6 infantry brigades, 29 infantry battalions, and no less than 170 companies in battle groups.

The Navy, with its headquarters in Turku, has maintained its focus on patrolling and coastal defence. It has 8 fast patrol craft and 19 mine warfare vessels, plus some 30 vessels for logistics and support. The amphibious forces are organized in a naval brigade. The Air Force is centered around the three fighter wings with F-18 *Hornets*. There is one fighter wing in each of the three air defence areas (West, East, and North) that Finland is divided into.

Sweden

The Swedish defence budgets have slightly decreased over the past few years and was US$5.61 billion in 2009. We can note the relatively high level of arms procurement, as well as the total of US$800 million that placed it as the world's eighth country in global arms deliveries in 2008. The non-socialist coalition government has had the dual policy of not adjusting defence spending, while maintaining the existing regiments and flotillas. Domestically this has led to a dual criticism: for creating under-financed defence budgets, and for hampering the rationalization and transformation of the Armed Forces. General conscription was *de facto* abandoned in July 2010.

The aim for the development of the Army is eight mechanized battalions, two artillery battalions, three air defence battalions, three engineer battalions and two logistics battalions. The Home Guard is to be organized into 60 multi purpose battalions. Recent development has created pressure to integrate armoured units as companies in the mechanised battalion structure.

The Navy organization has been restructured to include two surface flotillas, one surveillance battalion, one amphibious battalion, one submarine flotilla, and one logistics battalion. It has four submarines. The surface capabilities of the Navy are centered to the corvettes of *Visby*-class, with diverse operational qualities but with limited durability at sea. The Navy features some 22 vessels for mine warfare, but only one major cargo ship. The specialty of the amphibious battalion is combat in the archipilago ("brown waters").

The Swedish Air Force is dominated by the four squadrons with the fighter-ground attack plane JAS 39 *Gripen*. The original model with rather limited range is to be replaced with a long range version. Signals intelligence, airborne early warning, helicopters and air transport have one squadron each. Fighter control and air surveillance share one battalion, and there are two air base battalions.

Poland

Despite the initial plans for reductions of the Polish defence budget, resulting in the abandonment of the ambition to keep the goal of defence spending at 1.95% of GDP, the final decision came to an increase. The budget was US$8.63 billion in 2009.

The Army is centred around its mechanized corps (including the contribution to NATO's MNC NE Corps HQ). The corps consists of one armoured cavalry division, three mechanized divisions, one assault brigade, and one air cavalry brigade. The corps assets include two reconnaissance regiments, two artillery brigades, two engineer brigades and one engineer regiment, as well as chemical warfare components. The Polish have their two helicopter regiments as a part of the Army.

The Navy is divided into a surface combatant flotilla, a coastal defence flotilla, and a naval aviation brigade. The total of eight major surface combatant ships includes three frigates and five corvettes. It has five submarines. The mine warfare capability includes some 20 ships, and it has 8 light and medium landing ships. Naval bases are located in Kolobrzeg, Gdynia, Swinoujscie, Hel peninsula, and Gdynia-Babie-Doly.

The Air Force, with notable official individual flying hours for pilots at 160–200 h per year, has 128 combat capable aircraft. There is an interesting mix between old Warsaw Pact systems like MiG-29 and US platforms like F-16. The Polish have organized them into two tactical wings, and have also a transport air wing, a special air transport wing, as well as two rocket air defence brigades.

Germany

The development of the German defence budget over the last years is strongly linked to the financial crisis of 2008. However, unlike the Baltic states, the defence sector has been the target of the government's stimulus package. Thus, the Grand Coalition government raised the 2009 budget from US$41.6 billion in 2006 to US $46.5 billion in 2009. During 2010 the German debate has featured suggestions for substantial capability cuts as well as a highly controversial abandonment of conscription.

The German transformation of the Armed Forces will create units in three categories: response forces, stabilization forces and support forces. The Army consists of 12 brigades in total, commanded by 5 headquarters, of which 3 are deployable. The composition features an armoured division, a mechanized division, a special operations division, and an air mobile division.

The Navy has merged its Type Commands into two mixed flotillas: one with submarines, mine countermeasures, patrol boats, as well as special forces, and one with frigates and auxiliary squadrons. It has some 18 surface combatants, 37 mine countermeasure vessels, 12 submarines, 3 amphibious craft. The bases include Olpenitz, Wilhelmshaven, Glücksburg, Warnemünde, Eckenförde, and Kiel.

The air component consists of three main systems: Eurofighter, Phantom, and Tornado. The organization no longer has any Warsaw Pact systems. Germany has 303 combat capable aircraft. The Air Force also features a substantial transport command with 96 aircraft, and 83 helicopters.

Russia

The Russian defence system is perhaps the most difficult one to substantiate without major errors. A substantial part of the budget is classified. The Russian Armed Forces have been undergoing different forms of reform for more than one decade.

This is a process that is continuing. One estimate of defence expenditures approximates spending to US$41.05 billion in 2009, a slight increase on the year before.

Russia possesses a military playing card that none of the other countries in the region have: nuclear weapons. The Strategic Deterrent Forces, with personnel from the Navy and the Air Force, include 14 ballistic-missile submarines, 3 rocket armies, and 2 heavy bomber divisions. The doctrine still places great emphasis on these capabilities.

The Army consists of some 395,000 personnel, this is a figure that most likely will decrease over the coming years. It is organised into six military districts. The Leningrad Military District has two motor rifle brigades, a Spetsnaz brigade, one airborne division, plus various support elements.

The Navy consists of 142,000 personnel. It is organised into four major Fleet organisations: Northern Fleet, Pacific Fleet, Baltic Fleet, and Black Fleet (not counting the Caspian Sea Flotilla). The Baltic Fleet, with bases in Kronstadt and Baltiysk, has 2 submarines, 5 surface combatants, 22 patrol craft, and 11 mine warfare vessels. There is a substantial air component attached: fighters, ground attack, and helicopters. There is also one naval infantry brigade.

The Air Force consists of 160,000 personnel. The organisation will see significant restructuring over the coming years. The main components are the 37th Air Army with 2 heavy bomber divisions, 21 regiments of tactical bombers, 24 regiments of fighters, and 20 regiments of attack helicopters.

Summary Table

	BALT	DEN	NOR	FIN	SWE	POL	GER	RUS
Reg. army brigades	3	2	2	4	2	15	12	58
Surface combatants	2	0	3	0	5	8	18	42
Amph. landing craft	0	0	20	73	185	8	3	27
Combat capable air.	0	48	52	63	165	128	303	1859

The summary table is a highly rhapsodic way of portraying the "military costumes" in the Baltic Sea region – not counting nuclear capabilities, mobilization units and many other relevant capabilities. Strategists should object to its value, not just because its highly contestable value in relation to the notion of power, but to the fact that it says very little about the *qualitative* dimension. As an example: there is a difference between an amphibious landing craft that can transport a battalion (500–800 troops) and one that can carry a platoon (30–60 troops). Nevertheless, despite these objections it has some value since it hints at the bulk of military capabilities in the region. In the following we will study the impact and role of military capabilities in the behaviour of actors around the Baltic Sea.

Balancing Behaviour

Firstly, let us not assume that we should connect state behaviour to capabilities in themselves, but rather that identities, perceptions of history, and strategic culture could be just as useful for understanding these patterns. Hence, we should not group countries into "small", "medium" and "major" state categories after looking at the bulk of military hardware. Regardless of causal mechanism for behaviour: the point about the following section is to note the role of military balancing as discussed earlier. Very roughly we could then group the countries in the Baltic Sea region into three different types of strategic behaviour: assurance, avoidance and self-realization.

Strategies of Assurance

The typical characteristic for strategies of assurance is that reliance on foreign powers is relatively uncontroversial. Accordingly, the foreign policy behaviour of the US is relatively uncontroversial and there is often a great understanding for its pivotal role as strategic actor. In practice this means that NATO is the primary international security arena. The Baltic states, Denmark, Norway, and Poland all fall into this category.

One striking pattern of balancing is that all the proponents of a revitalisation of Article 5 within NATO could be found in this group of European countries. With the exception of Denmark, the other states have openly declared that the alliance should strengthen and uphold a credible deterrence in the region (Jonson 2010).

Perhaps the clearest example of balancing behaviour seems to be the strong foreign policy signals from the Baltic states after the Georgian crisis in 2008. However, this behaviour is more complex than one might assume. The Baltic states were hit by the financial crisis in 2008 and, as we have seen, their actual military capabilities were down during 2009. One could say that Lehman Brothers 2008 was just as important strategic factor as Georgia 2008.

Furthermore, as we noted above, the Baltic countries lack air force capabilities. This is definitely a "perceived power differential" that has led to intense policy initiatives. Not least since these countries decided to abstain from developing their own capabilities in the run up to membership in NATO. In this sense they all have rather extreme strategies of assurance. Note that Estonia has, apart from the symbolic representation in the Nordic Battle Group, some 150 men in Helmand province. Perhaps the signals about increased attention from the US, including the concept of "extended deterrence", will be sufficient for the needs of the Baltic states. The "wise man's group" report by former Latvian prime- and foreign minister Valdis Birkavs and former Danish defence minister Søren Gade, as well as the recent visit of US Chief of Naval Operations to the region, might be seen as further signs of increased attention (NB8 2010; US Navy 2010).

Though Denmark shares many of the traits of a rather pronounced strategy of assurance, it is difficult to notice any patterns of balancing behaviour. Quite contrary, capability differentials in the region are generally dismissed as a strategic factor. One telling fact is the almost total absence of naval capabilities adjusted to a Baltic agenda. The role of strategic assurance is firstly that it will give greater influence for a country with only 5.5 million inhabitants. It is in this light we should regard the relatively high casualty figures and the active role taken in Afghanistan and Iraq. Rather than "balancing" it is the unexpected costs in Afghanistan that was the major reason for the increased defence budget.

Norway has shifted its strategic attention to the North. Not only are some key military facilities relocated to signal this, but the strategic debate has pointed out the potentials of the Barents region as a major interest. However, the recent settlement with Russia on border disputes in this area has lowered the potential for any military confrontations considerably. Nevertheless, Norway has decided to purchase Joint Strike Fighter which fits with a strategy of assurance.

Poland has, like Denmark and the Baltic states, invested heavily in the transatlantic link. It has had nearly 2,000 troops as a contribution to ISAF. However, the country is also one of the "defencists" in NATO. Concerns over energy security has been on the top of the strategic agenda, but following the tragic plane crash incident in the Spring of 2010, that killed Lech Kaczynski and a great part of the military leadership, there was a short period of quite healthy relations between Poland and Russia.

Strategies of Avoidance

The defining trait of a strategy of avoidance is a traditional military self reliance. It is also marked with an ambiguous view of the US. Not surprisingly the EU constitutes the primary security arena. In the Baltic Sea region Sweden and Finland pursue this strategy.

However, there are some important differences between the two countries. They have made different choices between paths leading to a flexible operations defence or the maintenance of territorial defence. Sweden stumbles down the former path while Finland clings on to the latter.

In general Finland has kept its focus on territorial tasks for the Armed Forces. After the clash in Georgia in 2008, Sweden reintroduced a national perspective in its defence planning, reintroduced regional commands, national objectives and national exercises. The reactions in Finland rather confirmed the chosen path and reinforced existing arrangements. It is fair to say that the country, with its readiness brigades, mechanized battle groups, helicopter battalion, regional battle groups, as well as fighter squadrons, maintains a deterrence force. In terms of balancing behaviour it is clear that there were different reactions to Georgia: Finland raised its defence budget by 16% (IISS 2010: 117), while Sweden prolonged the analysis for its Defence Bill without any financial commitments.

However, there are also similarities. Both countries have great hopes for Nordic defence and security cooperation. Though this process arguably started in 2007 as a Swedish–Norwegian initiative, Finland soon became a part of it. A relatively successful project, at least from an organizational perspective, was the setting up of the Nordic Battle Group. However, this process was initiated before the clash in Georgia and was not motivated by balancing concerns.

More broadly, though, the whole project of Nordic defence and security cooperation is motivated by a concern for sustaining military capabilities over longer time. This includes both expeditionary as well as national systems. Connected with this is a gradual discursive move into solidarity, also in military terms, among the actors in the region. It is difficult not to regard this development without its implications for territorial integrity in the regional context. Regardless of the driving forces behind this declaratory solidarity, it certainly has created a discussion about its meaning for the Baltic states. Hence, the process behind the suggestions for declared solidarity in the EU-Nordic context might not have been an act of balancing, but it could produce patterns of balancing behaviour. If clarified, it becomes something to potentially act upon.

The historical track record of solidarity in Sweden and Finland, in military terms, is rather meagre. Sweden pursued a policy of condemning the Soviet aggression in the Winter War 1939 – but without officially sending any troops in support for Finland. After the fall of the Berlin Wall it was Denmark that first offered bilateral defence agreements with the Baltic states. Finland was the first to offer weapons, while Sweden waited to provide weapons until the Soviet troops had returned home. Accordingly, there has not been any official assurance from Sweden to provide military assistance in a case of turbulence in the Baltic states.

All together it is difficult to see the development as purely acts of military balancing. Though the Baltic Sea region is important for Sweden and Finland, it is not clear in what ways the military capability development is connected with this. In many respects Sweden has had a “deterritorialized” policy, and for Finland the policy has not changed too much, even if the compensatory tendencies at least could be registered after the Russian actions in Georgia.

Strategies of Self-Realization

A strategy of self-realization is a method of realizing the inherent possibilities as perceived by a state. In essence: to become something more. Perhaps the opposite strategy could be defined as bandwagoning; a strategy that is essentially an act of submission. The two countries in the region that pursue this strategy are Germany and Russia.

The post-Cold War order has put these two states in juxtaposition. This gradually became evident as there was no general EU mechanism for interaction with Russia. No doubt the bilateral dialogue is more important for the two. But this has also created a few question marks regarding the intentions and role of these countries in the Baltic Sea region.

Perhaps the strongest strategic bond between Russia and Germany is the energy issue. While Russia has an incentive to sell its gas and other energy products, Germany is dependent on deliveries of these products. Russia is Germany's leading energy supplier (German Foreign Ministry 2010). Germany has helped in exploiting gas fields in Russia, and the Nord Stream pipeline in the Baltic Sea is perhaps the most strategic joint venture up to date. One could of course speculate about the degree of interdependency, but it would be misleading not to note this common strategic interest.

However, there are also diplomatic signs of common strategic interests. Both countries ended up on the same side against the Americans in the events leading up to the 2003 Iraq war. On 4–5 June 2010 Russian President Medvedev met with Chancellor Merkel at Schloss Meseberg in Germany. The memorandum that followed the summit is interesting from many perspectives (German–Russian Foreign Ministries 2010). It suggests an EU–Russian Political and Security Committee on ministerial level, for diplomatic consultations. However, it also suggests the establishing of "ground rules for joint EU–Russia civil/military crisis management operations" (German–Russian Foreign Ministries 2010). An area for practical cooperation is defined as Transnistria where "EU–Russia engagement...would guarantee a smooth transition of the present situation to a final stage" (German–Russian Foreign Ministries 2010). It seems that the German course set to re-engage the Russians in a constructive dialogue that concerns the frozen conflict in Moldova, but it is not without risks. The signal of Germany and Russia making "suggestions" about the old Bessarabian question has many bad historical connotations.

The strategic juxtaposition is not the only trend. There are also many signs that Germany policy has been shifting. The Germany that once, in the words of Chancellor Kohl, was addicted to American power, has slowly drifted on to a new course. Germany is one of five NATO countries that have demanded withdrawal of US nuclear bombs from its soil. This is not only a German signal for disarmament and confidence building, since it is not coordinated with American interests. This does not necessarily raze the US pillar in its security policy, but it certainly weakens it.

Furthermore, there is also a German domestic factor to take into account. In late May 2010 President Horst Koehler resigned after a row over remarks where he linked the use of military forces to national interests. While it says something about the country's pacifist strategic culture it is also an interesting insight into the discourse of leading politicians. On the road to the upcoming military reform the almost sacred structure of conscription has been questioned. Not only does interaction shape a change of German policy, so is the domestic dimension.

In Russia, the general tendency since the late 1990s has been to give priority to rearmament. The planned procurement of *Mistral* class amphibious landing craft, for use in the Baltic setting, complicates things even further. A French–Russian bargain would put the Alliance coherence into question, since the Americans have been lukewarm and the Baltic states outright alarmist. In the summer of 2010 Russia deployed its non-strategic nuclear missile system Iskander in the Leningrad Military District, something that triggered protests from the Baltic countries (RiaNovosti 2010).

Apparently, one of the lessons drawn from the clash in Georgia in 2008 was that the Russians won most because of vast superiority. This, and other factors, has triggered a response for an ambitious military reform that is yet only in its initial stages. Also, the simulated nuclear assaults and the presidential authority to deploy forces outside the country without parliamentary permission, has created international attention. However, one must also consider its domestic background for the Medvedev-Putin duovirate and not only its function as balancing behaviour.

Military Balancing: Empirical Patterns and Theoretical Considerations

The point of departure for this article was that a new discourse on power politics has emerged in many European countries after Georgia 2008. The methodological considerations focused on the theoretical understanding of military balancing as a concept distinct from any meaningful understanding of power. We then considered the various military playing cards of the countries in the region, as well as the card games as they are defined by these actors. We noted that the countries in the Baltic Sea region used one of three strategies: assurance, avoidance or self-realization. We will now turn to an analysis of these patterns.

As we have seen concerning the countries that pursue strategies of avoidance and assurance, there are considerable differences in the strategic postures after Georgia 2008. We can conclude that the Baltic States, with small capabilities and a pronounced strategy of assurance, act very much in line with balancing theory. While cutting its defence spending because of the financial crisis, on the international arena they have actively tried to compensate for perceived power differentials towards Russia. Finland is an example of a country with compensatory behaviour, while pursuing a strategy of avoidance. Its initial reaction was to strengthen the traditional territorial defence. Countries like Denmark, Norway, and Poland have all relied on a strategy of assurance, but have not had a clear pattern of balancing. Sweden has neither balanced, nor sought security guarantees Table 7.1 illustrates this.

The patterns of military balancing between Germany and Russia are not evident. Though their interactions have been relatively intense on the economic and diplomatic levels, the general tendency to find common interests in world affairs makes it difficult to relate defence spending or even defence policy to this relationship. This is not to say that there is not a continuous process of estimation of each other, but rather that it could not easily be connected to an act of balancing. However, Russian armaments and increased defence spending could be related to a general

Table 7.1 Balancing and assurance in the Baltic Sea Region

		Assurance: Yes	Assurance: No
Balancing	Yes	Baltic states	Finland
	No	Denmark, Norway, Poland	Sweden

policy of regaining status in the international community after the Cold War. This seems to have been a recurring impulse that was stimulated already in the early Putin years as economic circumstances have become better. Neither Russia nor Germany base their strategies on assurance, and that is why it is difficult to place them in Table 7.1. The German policy comes closer to that of Denmark, Norway and Poland, and the Russian policy comes closer to that of Finland.

Do the findings of this article represent important dimensions of state behaviour, as promised by its theoretical point of departure? There are two dimensions to the answer of this question. The first relates to the policy implications of the balancing patterns. Arguably, the policies of assurance and avoidance are both dependent on faith in multilateral solutions and international regimes. Thus, no state expects to deal alone with major security problems in the region. But this also means that there will be major challenges in a situation when these institutions and regimes cannot function or provide functioning tools. Such a "bad case scenario", mirrored in a continued discourse on power politics in the Baltic Sea region, could be an interesting test of the value of any security policy pursued. The findings of this article are thus instrumental in a normative debate about the best course for stormy weather: balancing with assurance (the Baltic states), balancing without assurance (Finland), assurance without balancing (Denmark, Norway and Poland) or a policy without balancing or assurance (Sweden). So far, at least in the Nordic countries, the defence policy debate has rather been focused on how to transform the Armed Forces in a continued "good case scenario" in the Baltic Sea region.

The findings of this inquiry also reveal the challenge for Germany in a situation when the obligations of assurance in the region clashes with the national strategic interests. Just to take two examples: how will it act in a conflict that involves the Nord Stream-pipeline, and how will it act in a conflict that involves the Baltic countries? Will the air patrols of the Baltic states and the solidarity in the EU and NATO be determinant, or will the economic loyalties and interests be more important? Perhaps it is fair to assume that any development towards a "bad case scenario" will continue to reinforce Germany's impulse to act as a bridge builder between Russia and Europe, in order to avoid this strategic challenge.

Furthermore, the other dimension relating to the importance of military balancing in state behaviour is theoretical. A crucial aspect is if there are clear patterns of security dynamics among the nations in the Baltic, cooperation and conflict, as this would make it possible to regard it as a regional security complex (Buzan and Waever 2003: 44). Or in other words, are the threats located regionally, thus producing a Baltic Sea regional card game? The Baltic Sea region could then be compared to other subcomplex in Europe like the Balkans, or Magreb or the Levant in the Middle East.

However, the two actors Russia and Germany are too unconcerned with the region for this to be a plausible conclusion. Too much of the security policy dynamics of these actors is located outside of the region for this to happen. Furthermore, the frequent use of strategies of assurance makes it inevitable that the influence of outside powers have a crucial impact. Just to mention a few of these: the relationship to the US is a key factor and processes that take place within the EU and NATO. As hinted in studies of Nordic regional cooperation there always seems to be processes from the outside that set in when these become too independent (Sundelius 1982; Ring 2009).

Thus, it just seems to be impossible to fully understand and explain the foreign policy behaviour of any of the countries in the region from purely looking at regional factors. The major theoretical challenge seems to be the Eastern side of the region: Finland and the Baltic states. Are they (still) the insulator states that represent the borderlands towards the post-Soviet region, or are they part of Western European dynamics? However, the use of a balancing perspective has proved useful in the sense that it has revealed patterns of compensation among these states that could easily be forgotten if only using theories of governance or complex interdependence.

References

Baldwin, D. A. (2006). Power and international relations. In W. Carlsnaes, T. Risse, & B. A. Simmons (Eds.), *Handbook of international relations*. London: Sage.

Buzan, B., & Waever, O. (2003). *Regions and powers. The structure of international security*. Cambridge: Cambridge University Press.

Buzan, B., & Waever, O. (2007). After the return to theory. In A. Collins (Ed.), *Contemporary security studies*. Oxford: Oxford University Press.

CSCE. (1990). *Charter of Paris for a New Europe*.

Friedman, T. (1999). *The Lexus and the Olive Tree. Understanding globalization*. New York: Farrar, Straus and Giroux.

German and Russian Foreign Ministries. (2010). *Meseberg memorandum*.

German Foreign Ministry. (2010). http://www.aktion-europa.diplo.de/diplo/en/Aussenpolitik/RegionaleSchwerpunkte/Russland/Russland-Wirtschaft-Energie.html.

Gill, G., & Markwick, R. D. (2000). *Russia's stillborn democracy? From Gorbatchev to Yeltsin*. Oxford: Oxford University Press.

Hedlund, S. (2005). *Russian path dependence*. Oxon/New York: Routledge.

IISS. (2010). *The military balance 2010. The global assessment of global military capabilities and defence economics*. London: Routledge.
Jonson, P. (2010). The debate about Article 5 and its credibility. What is it all about? *NATO Defense College Research Paper* No. 58 May.
Knudsen, O. F. (2007). *Security strategies, power disparity and identity. The Baltic Sea region.* Aldershot/Burlingston: Ashgate.
Little, R. (2007). *The balance of power in international relations. Metaphors, myths and models.* Cambridge: Cambridge University Press.
Lucas, E. (2008). *The new Cold War. How the Kremlin Menaces both Russia and the West.* London: Bloomsbury.
Mearsheimer, J. (1990). Back to the future. Instability in Europe after the Cold War. *International Security, 15*(1), 5–56.
NB8. (2010). *NB8 wise men report.*
RiaNovosti. (2010). *Iskander missile deployment in northwestern Russia incomprehensible – Estonian defense minister.* http://en.rian.ru/mlitary_news/20100720/159873088.html
Ring, S. (red.) (2009). *Nordisk försvarstransformation – Militärstrategisk utveckling i Danmark, Finland och Norge efter det kalla kriget (FM Litt 922:2802)* Stockholm: FHS Ö166/2008:40.
Sundelius, B. (Ed.). (1982). *Foreign policies of Northern Europe*. Boulder: Westview.
Thielbeer, S. (2008). Baltische Befürchtungen: Das Verschenkte Georgien *Frankfurter Allgemine Zeitung* 26 August.
US Navy. (2010). CNO Visits Norway, Sweden. http://www.navy.mil/search/display.asp?story_id=55522.
Valacek, T. (2008). What does the war in Georgia mean for EU foreign policy? *Centre for European Reform briefing note*, August.
Walt, S. M. (1987). *The origins of alliances*. Ithaca: Cornell University Press.
Wendt, A. (1999). *Social theory of international politics*. Cambridge: Cambridge University Press.
Zakaria, F. (2003). *The future of freedom: Illiberal democracies of home and abroad.* New York: Barnes and Noble.

Chapter 8
The Monopoly of Violence in the Cyber Space: Challenges of Cyber Security

Roxana Georgiana Radu

> *"In the new politics, as in the new technology, the only constant is change."*
> Ball 1968: 5

Introduction

The conceptualization of cyber security is currently in the making. In the last decade, the frequent concerns with power and control in the cyber space, coupled with attempts at diminishing the risks posed by 'invisible actors' to critical infrastructure while ensuring free access, have represented real challenges to the adoption of national cyber security frameworks. In spite of the wide acknowledgement of cyber threats as a global problem, limited efforts to adopt a common approach towards reducing risks were undertaken till now at the international level. With more than 26% of world's population using the Internet as of 2009 (ITU 2010: ix), the cyber risks are growing. According to Libicki, only in the US, the "estimates of the damage from today's cyber attacks range from hundreds of billions of dollars to just a few billion dollars per year" (2009: xv).

The development of ICTs brought about a "powershift" (Toffler 1990), determining a major transfer of power from the "legitimate monopoly of violence"[1] to control over wealth and knowledge. The rise of the 'informational state'[2] challenges the status quo in international politics, allowing increased warfare capabilities for non-state actors in asymmetric conflictual settings. In particular, the Internet, as a borderless environment, became a space for distributed power

[1] In "Economy and Society", Max Weber provides the definition of the state as a political organization "upholding the claim to the monopoly on the legitimate use of physical violence in the enforcement of its orders" (1952b: 29).

[2] *See* Braman 2007.

E. Fels et al. (eds.), *Power in the 21st Century*, Global Power Shift,
DOI 10.1007/978-3-642-25082-8_8,

(Sassen 2000), with a new and much broader range of stakeholders challenging the idea of the nation state (McMahon 2002). Brian Loader refers to this as a "paradigmatic change in the constellation of power relations between individuals, governments and social institutions" (1997: 1), pointing to the transnational character of this transformation.

Apart from requiring less resources and being, to a large extent, risk-free endeavors for their initiators, cyber threats have tremendously reshaped the military, economic, social and political environment. The present study aims at investigating the global power shifts through the lenses of cyber security approaches and their outcomes globally. What are the political logics and the security mechanisms that dominate today's cyber space? Such exploration would be based on scrutinizing the theoretical understandings of cyber power and cyber security by identifying and analyzing the new risks, as well as the patterns of policy responses for three recent cyber attacks in Estonia, Georgia and South Korea. Different definitions and conceptualizations of *power* and *threat* give rise to opposed concepts. In the words of Myriam Dunn Cavelty, "the defining characteristic of the cyber-threats is their unsubstantiated nature: none of the worst-case scenarios have materialized, not even in part" (2010: 187). Nonetheless, these threats are currently placed at the top of the national security agendas around the world (Dunn Cavelty 2007). Recently, the United States has created its own Cyber Command, while the North Atlantic Treaty (NATO) became the first organization to implement a common cyber defense policy.

In the spring of 2007, Estonia was faced with a three-week denial of service attacks which disrupted the functioning of various governmental and bank websites, following the decision of the Estonian authorities to remove a Soviet monument for the Second World War. It represented the first case of cyber warfare (Traynor 2007; Tikk et al. 2008) and the responsibility for it was allegedly attributed to Russian authorities. The latter were also suspected of having launched the cyber attacks against Georgia in August 2008, prior to the start of the Russian–Georgian war over South Ossetia. Eleven months later, South Korea experienced a series of distributed denial of service attacks in July 2009 and this was believed to be an aggression coordinated by North Korea. Such politically motivated threats bring about the realization that the vulnerabilities of the Internet can no longer be controlled in a centralized manner, and as the risks are spread among end-users in different parts of the globe, more comprehensive strategies are required for addressing these.

This chapter is structured as follows. The first part deals with the changing conceptualizations of cyber security and power in a transnational environment, mediated by the use of information and communication technology (ICT) for protecting national assets. The second part draws on empirical cases of cyber attacks in Estonia, Georgia and South Korea to put into perspective the patterns of policy responses following major disruptions in the functioning of digital systems of state interest. The final section concludes and indicates directions for future research.

Changing Conceptualizations of Security and Power in the Cyber Space

Security and New Vulnerabilities in the Cyber Realm

Multiple definitions of cyber space[3] point at its dynamic character. By one comprehensive understanding, cyber space represents a "time-dependent set of interconnected information systems and the human users that interact with these systems" (Ottis and Lorents 2010). In this arena with high stakes, cyber conflicts appear as unavoidable. Indeed, the cyber world has been singled out as the "fourth battlefield" (Stone 2001) or the "battlespace" (Geers 2010: 16) shortly after its creation. While ubiquitous and instant connectivity is what makes cyber space so valuable, the same characteristics represent the greatest source of risk related to the virtual world (IBM 2010: 8). The growing dependence of individuals, groups, institutions and organizations – from local to international level – on computer-mediated systems has transformed the types of security threats over the years; initially, till the late 1960s, the incertitude revolved around technical failures, after which the danger of unauthorized access and fraud became more alarming. The first computer viruses were developed in mid-1980s (Nye 2010: 3), whereas the so-called "recreational hackers" (Sommer and Brown 2011: 16) appeared in the early 1990s; with the expansion of the World Wide Web in the early 1990s, both the functioning of economy and that of governments worldwide started to rely extensively on the provision of services mediated by information and communication technologies (ICTs), potentially challenged by a series of deliberate acts meant to affect the availability, integrity, authentication or confidentiality of information systems.

As the virtual realm remains a construct of human-embodied knowledge, its sources of power lie with its creators and users rather than with the programs themselves (Libicki 2007). A multitude of concepts refer to this digital transformation, employing phrases ranging from data-processing system to "information operations" (Everard 2000: 103). Placing information at the heart of the social transformation we are faced with today, Castells (1998) asserts the rise of the "informational mode of development" in the "network society". These differences in terminology have sector-specific origins and thus may differ in the day-to-day use of security analysts, military experts, policy-makers and academics (Billo and Chang 2004: 140). Following Galliers (2004), a distinction needs to be drawn between *data*, *information* and *knowledge*, in light of their context dependency and prerequisites for effective use. Though sometimes used as interchangeable

[3] *Cyberspace* is a term coined by William Gibson, who described it as "a consensual hallucination... A graphic representation of data abstracted from the back of every computer in the human system. Unthinkable complexity. Lines of light ranged in the nonspace of the mind, clusters and constellations of data. Like city lights receding" (Gibson 1985: 51).

concepts, "data" remain context-free and open to interpretation, whereas "information" is born in a particular setting and requires individuals' contribution to its understanding[4]; on the other hand, knowledge is "tacit and embedded" (Galliers 2004: 253), providing for beliefs that can inform and determine action. Jeffrey Hart and Singbae Kim proposed the term 'technoledge' (Hart and Kim 2000), a composite word from "technology" and "knowledge" to better capture the dominance of technology in the contemporary environment.

In the post-9/11 era,[5] the categorization of the different types of activities taking place in the cyberspace is often entrenched in the media hype depicting the constant threat posed by terrorists (Conway 2008). The perceived risks are often portrayed as threats, as imminent and direct actions rather than potential and indirect acts (Van Loon 2000). This does not only impart fear, but it furthers additional tensions over any kind of conflict in the virtual environment. Cyber attacks are now presented as the "high-tech Achilles heel" (Whitelaw 2007), having the potential for "catastrophic effects" (Technews 2011). One definition given to cyber attacks describes them as "deliberate disruption or corruption by one state of a system of interest to another state" (Libicki 2009: 23), emphasizing the strategic choice of the target. However, such a definition overlooks the intention driving cyber operations; a distinction introduced by Myriam Dunn between offensive activities (i.e., information warfare, cyber-crime, or cyber-terrorism) and defensive activities (such as information assurance or critical infrastructure protection[6]) helps in setting apart the attack and the deterrence sides. Yet, cyber deterrence represents just one part of the broader concept of cyber security as we know it today, since its scope is limited to "creating disincentives for starting or carrying out further hostile action" (Libicki 2009: 28). Evolving from the concept of 'computer security' in the late 1950s, and developing into a multi-dimensional concept employed frequently after 9/11, cyber security is still to be clearly defined (Cornish et al. 2009: 1). Recently, it is concerned not only with system integrity assurance, but also with "analyzing the risk to information networks of all sorts and then mitigating the identified risks by technical (and occasionally organizational) means" (Dunn Cavelty and Rolofs 2011).

As a priority for protecting against detrimental outcomes against citizens and against information systems, current security efforts require constant adaptation to a changing environment (British-North American Committee 2007). Cyber acts threatening state assets are transnational in their composition and effects (Hayashi 2007), which makes them more difficult to detect and contain. In the cyberspace, securing systems is of key importance, but it becomes extremely difficult to know what level of preparedness is needed, what types of preemptive actions should be pursued and against whom. What characterizes current debates on these issues is

[4] For a full overview of the taxonomy of definitions of *information, see* Braman (2007).

[5] 9/11 refers to the terrorist attacks on the World Trade Center in New York on 11 September 2001.

[6] Critical infrastructure protection does not refer only to preemptive actions, being "also about technology of control, constituting both a threat and a means of protection" (Dunn Cavelty and Kristensen 2008: 5).

the use of terminology traditionally belonging to security studies and conventional warfare. In fact, the study of the cyber phenomena has not departed considerably from the classical understanding of security issues around major historical events (Sulek and Moran 2009), but has rather transposed the existent concepts to the virtual space by expanding their meaning. Thus, the monopoly over control of violence remains the crucial check on power balance. In Krause's view, the "patterns of violence cannot be understood outside of the ways in which state power is mobilized and exercised as a part of the shifting balance between state and society, and between the state and military <technique>" (2009: 184). Yet, the post-Cold War era has seen the "privatization of intelligence capabilities" (Toffler 1990), which empowered non-governmental actors to a degree that no longer allows the state to be the single most authoritative source of power. The territorial sovereignty and physical control of borders, traditionally a primacy of state authorities, is now decreasing in importance. Simultaneously, a reverse movement can be identified: the "territorialisation of cyberspace", based on state efforts to exercise power over allocation of domain names, protection of physical infrastructure for information transfer and software limitations (Herrera: 2007). Governments thus became important users of the telecommunications services and key players in determining cyber regulation (Shahin 2007: 22).

However, beyond state confines, cyber operations grow out of a diverse range of interests and rely on different capabilities of materializing systems' disruption or corruption (data leakage, corporate espionage, etc.), causing breakdown of operations or inflicting panic on a global scale. For this reason, new players and new power centers need to be taken into account. A classification of those involved in cyber operations runs the risk of conceptual flaw, since the "users of the Internet do not fall into discrete camps, and least of all into a simple hierarchy of threats" (Cornish et al. 2009: 3). Focusing on the changing nature of conflicts, Kshetri's (2005) analytical framework of cyber attackers and their motivations differentiates between two types of cyber incidents: (a) targeted, having specific objectives identified; and (b) opportunistic, operationalized through the spread of viruses and worms Internet-wide. While the latter category is usually of lower priority and has no predefined target, the former poses major threats to national security and to the defense mechanisms in place. Khshetri observes that the "proportion of cyber attacks that are targeted is increasing over time" (2005: 553), and that the character of the cyber attackers has changed in the past few years. Furthermore, these alterations occur as part of a much broader socio–political transformation, in which the digitalization of values[7] plays an important role. Figure 8.1 provides an overview of the characteristics defining the profiles of particular cyber acts, with special emphasis on the way in which the underlying motivation of the attack defines its character.

[7] Digitalization of values refers to the sources of value existent in the online realm; high dependence on ICT for business profits or large digital networks increases the risk of targeted attacks (Kshetri 2005).

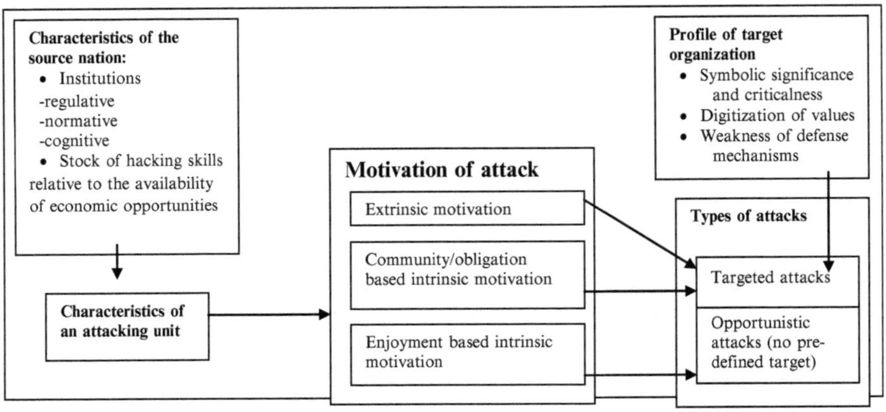

Fig. 8.1 Kshetri's framework for understanding the pattern of the global cyber attacks (Kshetri 2005: 545)

Power in the Cyber Space

The domain of power cannot be separated from the analysis of social structures and the manner in which different actors become powerful. In the cyber realm, power diffusion takes precedence over power transition. Drawing on analogies with seapower and airpower, the concept of cyber power has recently been used to capture the polymorphic character of force. Cyber power is "the ability to use cyber space to create advantage and influence events in other operational environments and across the instruments of power" (Kuehl 2009: 38). Among its specific features is the capacity to influence outcomes within the virtual realm and outside it (Nye 2010: 4), "intra" and "extra" cyber space power, affecting many connected domains. In this environment, both the physical (information infrastructure) and virtual (software, digital values, online assets) dimensions of power become critical for protection.

The fundamental challenges posed by the prominence of cyber space to the traditional functions the state are manifold: first, the contestation of the traditional state-organized force; second, the decrease in the importance of national territory and the cross-border character; and third, the reduced capacity of the state to control its citizens. Apart from that, every military conflict now comprises a virtual dimension (Geers 2010: 17), which considerably impacts international politics and power configurations.[8] What characterizes recent wars is "a disruption or loss of the state monopoly of violence" (Wulf 2004: 2). Apart from changing the setting and the nature of conflicts, the emergence of a parallel virtual space entails a new

[8] Back in 1990, in his book entitled *Powershift: knowledge, wealth and violence at the edge of the 21st century*, Toffler asserted that, in the age of new technology, "power, which to a large extent defines us as individuals and as nations, is itself being redefined" (Toffler 1990: 7).

positioning of state power. In the contemporary world, various forms of power are manifested simultaneously, remain interrelated and are often transnational. Braman (2007: 27) distinguishes between different phases: actual (as exercised), potential and virtual. The *potential* phase requires the possession of means for exercising power in the actual phase, whereas the *virtual* state refers to creating and using resources and techniques not yet in place. In these two phases, the role of technology cannot be separated. In the words of Hart and Kim, "power and technology are closely related to one another, so the assessment or measurement of power generally takes this interdependence into account" (2000: 35).

The instrumental definition of power comes from Weber, who understood it as "the chance of a man or of a number of men to realize their own will in a communal action even against the resistance of others who are participating in the action" (Weber 1952a: 180), thus manifesting itself only when resistance occurs. What is at stake is the "the probability that an actor in a social relationship can carry out his own will" (Nye 2010: 2). In Weber's view, patterned relations of power create systems of domination, which represent a special case of power structures. The main critique to this approach is that it neglects the context of power manifestation and it does not hold valid in the absence of a collective structure, which constitutes its basic assumption (Jordan 1999: 11). In line with the realist conception, sovereignty, as the "power of a state (or other accumulation of power) to make and enforce laws and to seek to have a monopoly of the use of force" (Price 2002: 25), has been perceived as immutable. With it, the contest over the control of violence was understood as a direct threat posed to the state. In the cyber realm, in which the states are no longer homogenous actors (Sperling 2010: 1), the control is limited.

Alongside state and non-state actor repositioning, multiple conceptions of power co-exist (Barnett and Duvall: 2005). A distinctive understanding comes from Foucault, who conceptualized power as "domination" and stressed the different positions of the powerful and the powerless.[9] Barnes interpreted it as social order,[10] based on the distribution of knowledge across society. Accordingly, this would be the "result of knowledge we all have of each other's knowledge" (Jordan 1999: 13), thus enhancing or restricting actors' capacity of action by the acknowledgement of sanctions. Observing the exercise of authority empirically, Hart (1976)

[9] Accordingly, "power applies to immediate everyday life which categorises the individual, marks him by his own individuality, attaches him to his own identity, imposes a law of truth on his which he must recognize and which others have to recognize in him. It is a form of power, which makes individuals subjects. There are two meanings of the word subject: subject to someone else by control and dependence, and ties to his own identity by a conscience or self-knowledge. Both meanings suggest a form of power which subjugates and makes subject to" (Foucault 1983: 212).

[10] Barnes (1988: 57) explains that "any specific distribution of knowledge confers a generalized capacity for action upon those individuals who carry and constitute it, and that capacity for action is their social power, the power of the society they constitute by bearing and sharing the knowledge in question. Social power is the added capacity for action that accrues to individuals through their constituting a distribution of knowledge and thereby a society".

distinguished between three different types of power: (a) as control over a resource[11]; (b) as control over actors, the result of coercion or persuasion that can be measured in terms of interactions between social actors; and (c) as control over events and outcomes, taking into account the interdependence among actors and the outcomes of collective action. However, these definitions are limited to analyzing power by the capacity of doing something or preventing others from doing a particular activity and do not go beyond taking actors' preferences and identities as given. For Singh, the concept of the concept of "meta-power" would capture better the type of power that is specific to the digital space, related to the role of interactive technologies in reshaping the preferences and identities, since "information networks change the very context – understood here as identities of issues and actors – within which interactions take place" (Singh 2007).

Investigating the balance of power and its foundations in cyberspace, Braman (2007) identified a new type of power – informational – complementing the other forms of power (instrumental, structural and symbolic) discussed in the literature. In her understanding, informational power "dominates power in other forms, changes how they are exercised, and alters the nature of their effects" (2007: 26) through the manipulation of their knowledge bases. Braman examines the transformation from bureaucratic to 'informational state', which uses control over information in three ways: (a) by making similar use of informational power as non-state actors and learning from them; (b) by extending the use of informational power in the interest of the state (private actors as regulatory bodies); and (c) by diversifying and multiplying the relations with other governments, expanding their own network. The aim of these strategies is to "produce and reproduce loci of power and to carve out areas of autonomous influence within the network environment" (2007: 36).

Politically-Motivated Cyber Attacks in Estonia, Georgia and South Korea

As ICT exponentially increases the planning capacity of individuals and organizations (Lenk 1997), attacks in the cyber space are less likely to be preceded by long deliberation periods or preparatory phases. On the contrary, with very low costs for their initiation, cyber strikes occur unexpectedly and are very difficult to identify, as they come from computers located in different countries and continents. The most utilized technique employed employed in recent cyber conflicts is the distributed denial-of-service attack (DDoS), which "overwhelms Internet-connected systems and their networks by sending large quantities of network traffic to a specific machine from multiple compromised machines" (Sommer and Brown 2011: 25–26). As such, DDoS attacks represent an exercise of hard power (Nye 2010), with the capacities of the physical infrastructure as the target.

[11] This understanding is similar to that of capabilities (Hart 1989).

Characteristics	Estonia	Georgia	South Korea
Main type of cyber attacks	DDoS	DDoS	DDoS
Timing	Removal of Bronze Soldier monument in Tallinn	Prior to the start of the Russian – Georgian war over South Osetia	"Testing of atomic devices"[a]
Timeframe	27 April – 18 May 2007	5 – 27 August 2008	July 2009
Targets	Websites of prime minister, president, banks, media outlets, television stations, schools[b]	Presidential website, governmental websites, news and media websites, financial institutions, other information websites[c]	Government, news media, and financial websites
Complementary actions	Neighboring Russia suspended the rail service	Start of a military offensive by Russian forces	US governmental websites attacked

a Following Kirk (2009)
b According to Myers (2007)
c Following Moses (2008) and Tikk et al (2008)

Fig. 8.2 Overview of major recent cyber attacks (2007–2009)

Such phenomena are not new. Chinese hackers have reportedly been involved in a number of cyber conflicts going back to August 1999, against Taiwanese, Indonesian, Japanese authorities (Denning 2000; de Kloet 2002), as well as against US targets (Bridis 2001). Very recently, attacks against two key Canadian government agencies have been attributed to Chinese hackers (Sabourin 2011). Figure 8.2 above offers an overview offers an overview of the main characteristics of the recent cyber attacks in Estonia, Georgia and South Korea. In all these cases, the cyber operations were coordinated and globally sourced. The damages remain unestimated in official reports. In the case of Estonia and Georgia, spamming through emails and defacement of websites also occurred, but these did not exceed the harm inflicted by the denial of service attacks. While the attackers remain unknown,[12] all these incidents have been linked to political motivations. The attacks on Estonia are believed to have been state-sponsored allegedly by Russia (Myers 2007; BBC News 2007) in the aftermath of the relocation of the statue of the Bronze Soldier of Tallinn, of symbolic importance both to the Russian minority in the country and to Russia itself.

Estonia and South Korea are almost entirely dependent on ICT. By 2007, 98% of all bank transactions in Estonia were done via electronic means and more than 80% of tax declarations were filed online. South Korea has one of the highest rates of

[12] Though attacks were sometimes claimed by individual hackers, a dominant state interest is not excluded.

Internet use in the world, and most of its governmental services are performed online. The state-level aggression in both countries targeted governmental websites, financial operations and media outlets portals, thus not only obstructing access to information, but also restricting or suspending the functioning of banking services. In South Korea, more than 20,000 computers were taken over and employed in the operation (Mills 2009). Even if the damage was smaller than in Estonia in 2007, the attacks against South Korean assets inflicted panic and emphasized new vulnerabilities. Though not attributed directly, these attacks have been publicly linked to North Korea's telecommunications ministry (Yonhap 2009).

In Georgia, the attacks were more intensive, but their time span was much shorter. Their effects, however, were long–lasting, as the cyber attacks preceded the start of the Russian–Georgian war over the independence status of South Ossetia and were blocking the channels of communication at a strategic moment. An average cyber attack lasted 2 hours and 15 minutes, and the longest one went on for 6 hours (Nazario 2008). Altogether, the functioning of 36 main websites was disrupted or suspended few days before the start of the war, but continued throughout the physical conflict as well. The temporary harm affected primarily the information flow before the war, limiting the ability of the state to communicate with its citizens. Employing cyber threats to supplement the means used in territorial conflicts does not represent a new practice. In September 2000, Israeli hackers targeted websites owned by Hezbollah and the Palestinian National Authority, triggering a series of responses from the Palestinian side in the so-called 'cyber holy war' (Cornish et al. 2009: 4).

Learning from these security challenges, different policy responses have been initiated all around the world. Estonia's cyber security strategy dates back to 2008 and UK launched its national cyber strategy in June 2009. The central influence of technology on defense planning, as a trend emerging in the aftermath of World War II (Granger 1978: 75), is now prominent in the adoption of action plans that refer to cyber war as one of the main threats. However, apart from the importance of national security cultures (Sperling 2010: 1), state-level strategies are influenced by many other factors, including the availability of new technology, power realignments, enforcement of international norms etc. The diffusion of technology transnationally creates additional difficulties for policy-making. As technology becomes more crucial in determining national warfare capabilities, there is a built-in risk of non-attribution and reduced or no accountability mechanisms. In the words of Sassen, "the greatest challenge comes from the lack of accountability built into many of the capabilities that can be deployed by powerful actors, be they private or governmental, in the pursuit of their interests" (2000: 29).

Conclusions

This chapter investigated the major transformation in the meaning of security and power in the virtual environment, by focusing on the risks posed by cyber attacks in a world dominated by technological advancements. The cyber operations targeted against state-level assets and their disruptive effects on the functioning of governmental and financial systems, as in the case of Estonia, Georgia and South Korea, demonstrate vulnerabilities that can no longer be tackled within the confines of the state. Back in 2004, Wulf observed that, in particular with regards to security challenges, "international policy remains decidedly state–centric" (2004: 12). For the power structures to properly address the transnational cyber security threats, a broad range of stakeholders needs to be empowered (IBM 2010: 9).

While the logic of competition and conflict still structures the monopoly over violence at all levels, there seems to be a "shift away from the singularly inward forms of state control to outward-looking, regional, or multilateral approaches, and away from law and regulation toward negotiation and agreement" (Price 2002: 3). This fundamental change results in initiatives for controlling against large-scale risks at different levels and outside the governmental sphere only. For global detrimental outcomes to be prevented, the implications of new security and power vulnerabilities need to be assessed. A paradigm shift towards multilateral agreements in cyberspace (Hughes 2010), while affecting the current status quo, might provide for alternatives modes of protecting basic social needs and values.

References

Ball, G. (1968). *The discipline of power: Essentials of a modern world structure*. Boston: Little, Brown and Company.

Barnes, B. (1988). *The nature of power*. Cambridge: Polity.

Barnett, M., & Duvall, R. (2005). Power in international politics. *International Organization, 59*, 39–75.

BBC News. (2007). Estonia hit by <Moscow cyber war>, 17 May 2007. http://news.bbc.co.uk/2/hi/europe/6665145.stm.

Billo, C., & Chang, W. (2004). *Cyber warfare: an analysis of the means and motivations of selected nation states*. Institute for Security Technology Study, Dartmouth College, report available at http://www.ists.dartmouth.edu/docs/cyberwarfare.pdf.

Braman, S. (2007). *Change of state: Information, policy, and power*. Cambridge: MIT Press.

Bridis, T. (2001). Net Espionage rekindles cold-war tensions – U.S. tries to identify hackers. *Wall Street Journal*, 27 June 2001. http://netwarfare.com/newcoldwar.htm.

British- North American Committee. (2007). Cyber attack: A risk management primer for CEOs and directors. http://www.acus.org/docs/071212_Cyber_Attack_Report.pdf.

Castells, M. (1998). *End of millennium, the information age: Economy, society and culture* (Vol. III). Oxford: Blackwell.

Conway, M. (2008). Media, fear and the Hyperreal: The construction of cyberterrorism as the ultimate threat to critical infrastructures. In M. Dunn Cavelty & K. S. Kristensen (Eds.), *Securing 'The Homeland': Critical infrastructure, risk and (In)security* (pp. 109–129). London: Ashgate.

Cornish, P., Hughes, R., & Livingstone, D. (2009). Cyberspace and the national security of the United Kingdom Chatham House Report. http://www.chathamhouse.org.uk/files/13679_r0309cyberspace.pdf.

De Kloet, J. (2002). Digitisation and its Asian discontents: The Internet, politics and hacking in China and Indonesia. *First Monday, 7*(9). http://firstmonday.org/htbin/cgiwrap/bin/ojs/index.php/fm/article/view/1789/1669.

Denning, D. (2000). Hacktivism: An emerging threat to diplomacy, American Foreign Service Association. http://www.fsjournal.org/sept00/Denning.cfm.

Dunn Cavelty, M. (2007). Critical information infrastructure: Vulnerabilities, threats and responses. *UNIDIR Disarmament Forum, 2007*(3), 15–22.

Dunn Cavelty, M. (2010). Cyber-threats. In M. Dunn Cavelty & V. Mauer (Eds.), *The Routledge handbook of security studies*. London/New York: Routledge.

Dunn Cavelty, M., & Kristensen, K. S. (2008). Securing the homeland: Critical infrastructure, risk and (in)security. In M. Dunn Cavelty & K. S. Kristensen (Eds.), *Securing 'the Homeland': Critical infrastructure, risk and (in)security*. London: Routledge.

Dunn Cavelty, M., & Rolofs, O. (2011). From cyberwar to cybersecurity: Proportionality of fear and countermeasures. Munich Security Conference, Munich, 3–4 Feb 2011. Paper available at http://www.securityconference.de/Article-Details.94.0.html?&no_cache=1&L=1&tx_ttnews[tt_news]=560&tx_ttnews[backPid]=92&cHash=55e618dc7b.

Everard, J. (2000). *Virtual states: The Internet and the boundaries of the nation–state*. London: Routledge.

Foucault, M. (1983). The subject and power. In H. Dreyfus & P. Rabinow (Eds.), *Michel Foucault: Beyond structuralism and hermeneutics* (2nd ed., pp. 208–226). Chicago: Chicago University Press.

Galliers, R. (2004). Reflections on information systems strategizing. In C. Avgerou, C. Ciborra, & F. Land (Eds.), *The social study of information and communication technology* (pp. 231–262). Oxford: Oxford University Press.

Geers, K. (2010). A brief introduction to cyber warfare, *Common Defense Quarterly* (Spring), 16–17

Gibson, W. (1985). *Neuromancer*. New York: Ace Books.

Granger, J. (1978). *Technology and international relations*. San Francisco: Freeman.

Hart, J. A. (1976). Three approaches to the measurement of power in international relations. *International Organization, 30*(2), 289–305.

Hart, J.A. (1989), ISDN and power, Discussion Paper 7, Center for Global Business, the Business School of Indiana University

Hart, J. A. & Kim, S. (2000). Power in the information age. In J. Ciprut (Ed.), *Of fears and foes: Security and insecurity in an evolving global political economy* (pp. 35–58). Westport: Praeger.

Hayashi, M. (2007). The information revolution and the rules of jurisdiction in public international law. In M. Dunn, S. F. Krishna-Hensel, & V. Mauer (Eds.), *The resurgence of the state: Trends and processes in cyberspace governance* (pp. 59–83). Aldershot/Hampshire: Ashgate.

Herrera, G. L. (2007). Cyberspace and Sovereignty: Thoughts on physical space and digital space. In M. Dunn Cavelty, V. Mauer, & S. F. Krishna-Hensel (Eds.), *Power and security in the information age: Investigating the role of the state in cyberspace* (pp. 67–94). Aldershot/Hampshire: Ashgate.

Hughes, R. (2010). A treaty for cyberspace. *International Affairs, 86*(2), 523–541.

IBM. (2010). *Meeting the cybersecurity challenge*: Empowering Stakeholders and. Ensuring Coordination. IBM U.S. Federal. White Paper. http://www-304.ibm.com/easyaccess3/fileserve?contentid=192188.

International Telecommunication Union. (2010). Measuring the Information Society. http://www.itu.int/ITU-D/ict/publications/idi/2010/Material/MIS_2010_without_annex_4-e.pdf.

Jordan, T. (1999). *Cyberpower: The culture and politics of cyberspace and the internet*. London: Routledge.

Kirk, D. (2009). What's behind cyber attacks on South Korea, US?. *CSMonitor*, 8 July 2009. http://www.csmonitor.com/World/Asia-Pacific/2009/0708/p06s24-woap.html.

Krause, K. (2009). War, violence and the state. In M. Brzoska & A. Krohn (Eds.), *Securing peace in a globalized world* (pp. 183–202). London: Palgrave Macmillan.

Kshetri, N. (2005). Pattern of global cyber war and crime: A conceptual framework. *Journal of International Management, 11*, 541–562.

Kuehl, D. (2009). From cyberspace to cyberpower: Defining the problem. In F. Kramer, S. Starr, & L. K. Wentz (Eds.), *Cyberpower and national security* (pp. 24–42). Washington, DC: National Defense University Press.

Lenk, K. (1997). The challenge of cyberspacial forms of human interaction to territorial governance and policing. In B. D. Loader (Ed.), *The governance of cyberspace: Politics, technology and global restructuring*. London: Routledge.

Libicki, M. (2007). *Conquest in cyberspace*. Cambridge: Cambridge University Press.

Libicki, M. (2009). *Cyberdeterrance and cyberwar*. Santa Monica: RAND.

Loader, B. D. (1997). The governance of cyberspace: Politics, technology and global restructuring. In B. D. Loader (Ed.), *The governance of cyberspace: Politics, technology and global restructuring*. London: Routledge.

McMahon, P. (2002). *Global control: Information technology and globalization since 1846*. Cheltenham: Northampton.

Mills, E. (2009). Botnet worm in DOS attacks could wipe data out on infected PCs, *CNet News*, 10 July 2009. http://news.cnet.com/8301-1009_3-10284281-83.html.

Moses, A. (2008). Georgian websites forces offline in <cyber war>, *Sunday Morning Herald*, 12 Aug 2008. http://www.smh.com.au/news/technology/georgian-websites-forced-offline-in-cyber-war/2008/08/12/1218306848654.html.

Myers, S. L. (2007). Cyberattack on Estonia stirs fear of <virtual war>. *New York Times*, 18 May 2007. http://www.nytimes.com/2007/05/18/world/europe/18iht-estonia.4.5774234.html.

Nazario, J. (2008). *Georgia DDoS attacks - a quick summary of observations, Arbor Networks*, 12 Aug 2008. http://asert.arbornetworks.com/2008/08/georgia-ddos-attacks-a-quick-summary-of-observations/.

Nye, J. (2010). *Cyber power*. Harvard Kennedy School, Belfer Center for Science and International Affairs. http://belfercenter.ksg.harvard.edu/files/cyber-power.pdf.

Ottis, R., & Lorents, P. (2010). *Cyberspace: Definition and implications*. Cooperative Cyber Defence Centre of Excellence, Tallinn, Estonia. http://www.ccdcoe.org/articles/2010/Ottis_Lorents_CyberspaceDefinition.pdf.

Price, M. (2002). *Media and sovereignty: The global information revolution and its challenge to state power*. Cambridge/London: MIT Press.

Sabourin, C. (2011). Chinese hackers behind cyber attack on Canada: Report, *Psysorg.com* (February 17). http://www.physorg.com/news/2011-02-china-hackers-cyber-canada.html.

Sassen, S. (2000). Digital networks and the state: Some governance questions. *Theory Culture & Society, 17*(4), 19–33.

Shahin, H. (2007). The reassersion of the state: Governance and the information revolution. In M. Dunn, S. F. Krishna-Hensel, & V. Mauer (Eds.), *The resurgence of the state: Trends and processes in cyberspace governance*. Aldershot/Hampshire: Ashgate.

Singh, J. P. (2007). Meta-power, networks, security and commerce. In M. Dunn Cavelty, V. Mauer, & S. F. Krishna-Hensel (Eds.), *Power and security in the information age: Investigating the role of the state in cyberspace* (pp. 45–66). Aldershot/Hampshire: Ashgate.

Sommer, P., & Brown, I. (2011). *Reducing systemic cybersecurity risk*. OECD report for Future Global Shocks Project. http://www.oecd.org/dataoecd/3/42/46894657.pdf.

Sperling, J. (2010). *The post-Westphalian state, national security cultures, and the global security governance*, EU-GRASP Working Paper no. 15. http://www.eugrasp.eu/uploads/media/WP15_final.pdf.

Stone, A. (2001). Cyberspace: The next battlefield. *USA Today*, 19 June 2001. http://www.usatoday.com/tech/news/2001-06-19-cyberwar-full.htm.

Sulek, D., & Moran, N. (2009). What analogies can tell us about the future of cybersecurity. In C. Czosseck & K. Geers (Eds.), *The virtual battlefield: Perspectives on cyber warfare* (pp. 118–131). Amsterdam: Ios Press.

Technews. (2011). Catastrophic effects that cyber-attacks may have. 28 Jan 2011. http://techweek.org/25041catastrophic-effects-that-cyber-attacks-may-have.html.

Tikk, E., Kaska, K., Rünnimeri, K., Kert, M., Talihärm, A.-M., & Vihul, L. (2008). *Cyber attacks against Georgia: Legal lessons identified*. Analysis document by the Cooperative Cyber Defense Center of Excellence (Tallinn, Estonia). http://www.carlisle.army.mil/DIME/documents/Georgia%201%200.pdf.

Toffler, A. (1990). *PowerShift: Knowledge, wealth, and violence at the edge of the 21st century*. New York: Bantam Books.

Traynor, I. (2007). Russia accused of unleashing cyberwar to disable Estonia. *The Guardian*, 17 May 2007.

van Loon, J. (2000). Virtual risks in an age of cybernetic reproduction. In B. Adam, U. Beck, & J. van Loon (Eds.), *The risk society and beyond: Critical issues for social theory* (pp. 165–182). London: Sage.

Weber, M. (1952a). Class, status, party. In H. Gerth & C. Wright Mills (Eds.), *From Max Weber* (pp. 180–195). London: Routledge.

Weber, M. (1952b). In G. Roth & W. Claus (Eds.), *Economy and society: An outline of interpretive sociology*. Berkeley: University of California Press.

Whitelaw, K. (2007). A high-tech Achilles heel: Washington plans stepped up defenses against cyberattacks. *U.S. News and World Report*, 26 Oct 2007. http://www.usnews.com/news/national/articles/2007/10/26/washington-plans-stepped-up-defenses-against-cyberattacks.

Wulf, H. (2004). *The bumpy road to re-establish a monopoly of violence*. Paper prepared for *Study Group on Europe's Security Challenges*, London School of Economics. http://www.lse.ac.uk/Depts/global/Publications/HumanSecurityReport/Wulfdraft.pdf.

Yonhap (2009). North Korean ministry behind July cyber attacks: Spy chief, 30 Oct 2009. http://english.yonhapnews.co.kr/northkorea/2009/10/30/0401000000AEN20091030002200315.HTML.

Chapter 9
Evaluating Maritime Power: The Example of China*

Sarah Kirchberger

The oldest and strongest emotion of mankind is fear,
and the oldest and strongest kind of fear is fear of the unknown.
H.P. Lovecraft (1927)

Introduction

China is often treated as a singular case. While sometimes useful, such an approach can have decided drawbacks. It is easy to lose sight of the fact that some developmental processes must pass through a series of stages that are universally observable and cannot easily be skipped. By adopting a broad comparative perspective China scholars can avoid this trap. Mapping China's developmental achievements against those of other rising powers – not only within the Asia Pacific region – using clearly defined criteria can yield a foothold not only for a fair evaluation of China's present status, but also of its potential for further progress.

The present paper will adopt such a perspective with regard to China's naval shipbuilding achievements. China's naval modernization has raised concerns in the US and across the whole Asia Pacific region. The discovery of a secret Chinese submarine base at Hainan in 2008 promptly lead to calls in Australia, Vietnam, and India to bolster submarine procurement programs.[1] In November 2007, a Chinese

*During 3 years as a naval analyst with Blohm + Voss the author had the chance to learn from numerous people in related industries, naval procurement agencies, and naval forces. She is indebted to all of them. Especial thanks are due to Jörg Möller for generously sharing his expert knowledge. She is also grateful to Hiroki Takeuchi, who commented on a first (and much more detailed) draft during the ISA Annual Convention 2011 at Montréal, Canada, March 16–19, 2011. Any errors remain the author's sole responsibility.

[1] For the discovery itself see Jane's Intelligence Review (2008). International reactions were widely covered in various news reports, i.e. *Daily Yomiuri,* 5 June 2008; *The Indian Express* online, 6 May 2008; *Times of India,* 3 May 2008.

E. Fels et al. (eds.), *Power in the 21st Century*, Global Power Shift,
DOI 10.1007/978-3-642-25082-8_9,

submarine remained undetected in the middle of a US Navy Pacific exercise area until it surfaced within torpedo range of the aircraft carrier USS Kitty Hawk (Hickley 2007). That even sophisticated surface ships can fall prey to diesel-electric submarines was painfully confirmed in 2010 when the South Korean corvette *Cheonan* was sunk, presumably by a North Korean torpedo.[2]

These incidents illustrate the fact that naval power cannot easily be assessed by counting vessels, or by comparing the technological sophistication levels of different countries' naval hardware. Navies are complex organisms, and there is also an asymmetric threat element involved. Conventional submarines are far more easily accessible to smaller navies than nuclear ones, but can evade detection and inflict high levels of damage to even the most powerful surface ships. With this "weapon of choice for the maritime underdog", a theoretically outgunned navy can make a military intervention scenario, say, for the defence of Taiwan against a Chinese attack, potentially too risky (Howarth 2006: 70).

It seems that there is no such thing as 'absolute' power with regard to navies. As Till (2009: 118) put it:

> The power of one navy is a relative thing, which can only be assessed in comparison with that of another navy, given the commitments they both face. A large navy faced with huge commitments may in fact prove surprisingly vulnerable to a much smaller navy with very limited commitments [...] The need to set the power of a navy against the size of its commitments is often overlooked.

It seems that overall naval capability is determined by several interrelated factors among which technology is only one. Others include logistics, training, maritime strategy, regular exercise experience, and not least the existence of an indigenous industrial base capable of sustaining the operational status of the fleet.

Given the above considerations, how can a rising naval power's actual level of sophistication be empirically evaluated? Regional threat perceptions, while important on a different level of analysis, are not necessarily very revealing. Especially in China's case, regional and Western threat perceptions can differ so widely as to pose more analytical difficulties than offering insights.

This paper therefore aims at establishing some basic guidelines for evaluating naval power derived from general principles before proceeding to an empirically based assessment of the Chinese case. It hopes to make a contribution towards a more multi-faceted understanding of China's naval build-up and its consequences for the Asia Pacific region. Questions to be addressed include:

- How can naval power be defined, measured and compared?
- What kind of countries usually emphasize the development of naval power, and why?
- How does China's naval power currently rank in international comparison, and how does China perform compared to geostrategically similar cases?
- And finally, what are the probable consequences of China's projected build-up for the naval balance of power in the Asia Pacific region?

[2] Cf. *The Economist,* May 20th 2010: "A guilty verdict for North Korea: Their number is up".

Some provisional answers will be attempted, but these will need to be further developed in more detailed research.

The Concept of 'Sea Power' and Its Meaning for China

The term 'sea power', first coined by Mahan in his 1890 classic, lacked a clear definition and was therefore understood by later authors in a wide variety of senses (cf. Mahan 1987 [1890]: 26–69; Till 2009: 20). If 'power' is defined in a Weberian sense, then sea power can be understood as "the capacity to influence the behavior of other people by what you do at or from sea" (Till 2009: 83). Two aspects of sea power are thus particularly important: one, that sea power is a relative rather than an absolute concept, or "something that some countries have more than others", but that most countries still possess to some degree (either through naval strength, shipbuilding capability, provision of services to seafarers, or through a combination of the above); and two, that sea power is "the product of an amalgam of interconnected constituents that are difficult to tease apart" (Till 2009: 22, 83). Such an understanding implies that it makes sense only to directly compare different countries' levels of sea power against each other, along certain explicit criteria, but that it will be difficult if not impossible to assign an absolute numerical value to this or that country's sea power. It also follows that sea power relations between states may be subject to change over time as the situation unfolds.

Sea power does not usually feature as a variable within the various formulae that Western as well as Chinese scholars have developed for measuring total national power.[3] Usually, some more generalized indicators of military strength (e.g. military manpower, defence budgets, nuclear weapons) are used in such computations. This may be due to the difficulty of quantifying a fuzzy, relative concept, and also to its somewhat limited applicability, because sea power is less relevant for landlocked countries even if some of those do maintain small inland waterway navies. And after all, navies typically constitute just one branch of any country's total armed forces.

However, for coastal countries with access to the high seas the existence or absence of sea power does play a role for determining overall national power. In the case of nuclear powers, ballistic missile submarines form an essential ingredient of a credible deterrence strategy. Apart from purely military functions that are mainly useful in times of conflict (and during maneuvers), navies also routinely contribute to their country's territorial integrity by safeguarding its maritime borders. Recently

[3] For an overview of various Western and Chinese approaches to measuring national power see Pfetsch (1994: 146–157) and Hu and Men (2004: 17–22). In his interesting 2008 study, Leonard comments on the recent proliferation of Chinese power indices in Chinese think tanks: "China must be the most self-aware rising power in history. [. . .] Measuring 'CNP' – short for Comprehensive National Power – has become a national obsession" (Leonard 2008: 84–85).

the protection of maritime resources and coastal installations against asymmetric threats such as terrorism, smuggling, illegal fishing, and waste dumping has become more relevant.[4] Another noteworthy duty of naval forces and coast guards is maritime search-and-rescue, as well as humanitarian aid during natural disasters or refugee crises, something well demonstrated in Asia during the tsunami catastrophe of 2004. On a more symbolic level, naval diplomacy and international maritime cooperation can further intraregional cooperation, or enhance any given state's international power perception.[5]

Even though it is hard to quantify the exact contribution of naval power to total national power, it is easy to realize the consequences should naval power be deficient or absent. Providing security from external threats is among the core functions of statehood as defined e.g. by Rice and Patrick (2008: 3) in their 'Index of State Weakness'. The protection of maritime borders against exterior threats and the maintenance of territorial integrity must accordingly be placed among the central duties of the state. It follows that coastal states with grave deficiencies in this area cannot be considered strong, regardless of how well they might perform in other areas.[6]

Like any coastal country China has several maritime security concerns to consider. The need for keeping up credible nuclear deterrence vis-à-vis the five nuclear-armed states in its vicinity (India, Pakistan, Russia, North Korea, and the USA) is one factor. Another is the safeguarding and policing of China's huge coastline and 200 nm Exclusive Economic Zone (EEZ) against maritime threats such as smuggling, illegal fishing, infiltration by spies, maritime terrorism, and piracy, to name just a few. China's close naval shipbuilding co-operation with Pakistan causes uneasiness in India. China furthermore has unresolved maritime claims that conflict with some of its neighbors in the South China Sea (i.e. the Spratly and Paracel Islands); and last but not least its unresolved conflict with Taiwan remains a geostrategic problem of prime importance due to the close proximity of the island to the Chinese coast and possible US and Japanese involvement in a military conflict.

As the map shows (Fig. 9.1), China's geostrategic situation is uncommonly complex. Several potentially hostile powers are located close to China's maritime border – in Taiwan's case the distance is only 185 km. The famous phrase ascribed to Douglas MacArthur of Taiwan being an "unsinkable aircraft carrier" located next

[4] Potgieter (2009) provides a good overview of these maritime challenges.

[5] Oddly illustrative of this were Northrop Grumman's full-page ads in various naval technology magazines during 2008 featuring Northrops's latest nuclear carrier design with a byline reading "Meet the world's most persuasive diplomat". On the current state of China's naval overseas missions cf. Yung and Rustici (2010), Li Mingjiang (2010).

[6] China's experience during the 'Opium Wars' in the nineteenth century is a good example of such a scenario. Oriented towards the Northwestern continental threat but weak in sea power, China easily fell prey to comparatively small forces of British and French gun boats with superior firing power.

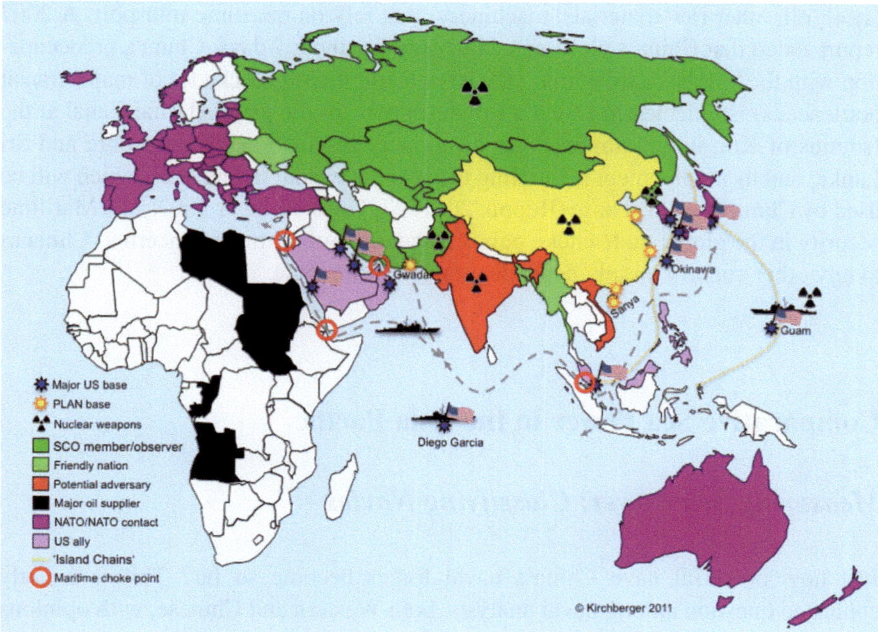

Fig. 9.1 China's geostrategic situation (Source: Map concept adapted from Le Monde, Atlas der Globalisierung (2006) using additional data from various news reports)

to vital sea lines has been widely echoed in Chinese strategic thinking and explains the near-obsessive quality of China's preoccupation with the Taiwan question.[7]

The prospects for the build-up and upkeep of a powerful navy however depend on China's steady economic development, which in turn rests on somewhat uncertain foundations. China is dependent on overseas export markets for its manufactured goods in the face of toughening competition from countries such as Vietnam that offer even lower labor costs to the world market. Financial or regional security crises on the other hand could slow down economic activities and therefore endanger China's development model. Moreover, as a veteran China watcher aptly expressed in her 2007 study of China's domestic and international constraints, China can be considered a 'fragile superpower' at best, because of the multitude of unresolved systemic problems (Shrik 2007: 269).[8]

Looking at the factors necessary for China's growth it is easy to see their relationship with naval power. China needs uninterrupted access to crucial materials

[7] According to Holmes and Yoshihara "the Chinese leadership almost certainly conceives of Taiwan not only in the nationalist terms that are the stock-in-trade of Western China watchers, but as a barrier to the nation's maritime destiny" (2008: 54–62; 56). Interviews conducted by me in 2001 with Chinese analysts in a Beijing think tank support this view.

[8] For a more detailed treatment of the interplay between domestic factors and China's naval development, see my earlier conference paper (Kirchberger 2011).

(steel, oil, other raw materials, machinery) that rely on maritime transport. A 2007 report stated that China's oil reserves last only for about 7 days. China's preoccupation with the "Malacca dilemma" (i.e. its vulnerability to blockades of major transit bottlenecks) is reflected in China's active support for the planned Thai Canal at the Isthmus of Kra; its investments into oil refinery installations in Singapore and Sri Lanka; and its involvement in building the port of Gwadar in Pakistan, which will be used by China as a naval base (Ruppik 2007: 27; Gu and Mayer 2007: 71). Maritime security in the global trade choke points is therefore of as much concern to China as to any other country largely dependent on maritime trade.

Comparative Sea Power in the Asia Pacific

Measuring Sea Power: Classifying Navies

Just how powerful have China's naval forces become so far? This is a hotly contested question among naval analysts, both Western and Chinese, with opinions ranging from very positive to very negative evaluations.

A major problem when trying to evaluate comparative naval power is which criteria to use. The easiest approach – counting vessels – is not very revealing, because it does not take into account the size of a navy's commitment nor its actual operational capability. Several scholars have therefore tried to come up with more or less compatible ranking systems for classifying navies. These systems try to use a combination of quantitative and qualitative factors for assigning overall capability rank. The key criteria used for such evaluations are *force structure* (i.e. type, age, and number of vessels); *sustainability* (i.e. the ability to keep naval forces on station), *function and capability* (the navy's primary task and geographic reach), *flexibility* (i.e. the variety and number of missions possible to undertake concurrently, which is determined by surplus forces or fleet redundancy), and *access to state-of-the-art technology* (cf. Till 2009: 115–116).

For the purpose of the present study, the classification system of ten naval ranks employed by Todd and Lindberg seemed most useful because their classification criteria are explicit and consistent, and because they have provided a complete ranking of all navies according to 1996 operational status (1996: 53–64, see Fig. 9.2 below). This allows for easy adjustments according to changed force levels, and allows for the upward or downward tracking of changing candidates such as China.[9]

[9] Till (2009: 114) employs a slightly different yet somewhat compatible classification system of nine ranks based on previous work by Eric Grove and Michael Morris. The main difference to Todd's and Lindberg's system consists in a further rank inserted between their ranks 1 and 2, while their ranks 7 and 8 are lumped together and their rank 9 is left out.

	Rank	Designation	Typical Inventory	Defining Capabilities	Current Examples[a]
'BLUE – WATER NAVIES'	1	Global-reach power-projection	All larger ship types in high numbers	Multiple, regular, and sustained power projection missions globally in addition to homeland defense	USA. (not more)
	2	Limited global-reach power-projection	CVN, other aviation-capable ships, many SSN/SSK, many support ships	At least one major power-projection operation globally in addition to homeland defense	France, UK (↓). (not more)
	3	Multi-regional power-projection	CVL, other aviation-capable ships, submarines, enough support ships	Power-projection missions in regions beyond own EEZ in addition to homeland defense	India, Russia, Italy, Spain, Brazil. (not more)
	4	Regional power-projection	Aviation-capable ships (DD, FF), submarines, some support ships	No at-sea fleet air support other than organic helicopters, therefore limited to area of land-based aircraft range for power-projection missions	China (↑), Japan (↑), Australia (↑), South Korea, Taiwan, Turkey, New Zealand, Pakistan (8 more)
'NON – BLUE WATER NAVIES'	5	Regional offshore coastal defense	Smaller ships (FF, Corvettes), no underway replenishment	Coastal-defense operations at least in own EEZ and slightly beyond	Thailand (↑), Malaysia, Indonesia, Bangladesh, Saudi Arabia, Norway, Singapore...(12 more)
	6	Inshore coastal defense	Only smaller ships (Corvettes, FAC)	Confined to inner reaches of own EEZ	Vietnam, Finland, the smaller Gulf States, North Korea...(21 in total)
	7	Regional offshore constabulary	Lightly armed OPV, PB and PC for coast guard – type duties	Geographic reach as in rank 5, but maritime policing instead of maritime defense	Iceland Coast Guard, Ireland, Mexico, Uruguay. (not more)
	8	Inshore constabulary	Only Patrol Boats and Patrol Craft	Confined to missions well within 200 nm zone (EEZ)	Myanmar, Philippines, Sri Lanka...(10 more)
	9	Inland waterway	Patrol Craft	Waterborne riverine defense of landlocked states	Azerbaijan, Bolivia, Paraguay, Laos...(ca. 14)
	10	Token navies	Often only 1 or 2 craft	Only very basic constabulary capabilities, if any	Ca. 58 navies

Fig. 9.2 World naval hierarchy according to the Todd/Lindberg classification system (Source: Criteria compiled from Todd and Lindberg (1996: 53-64) using current data)

As can be seen from Fig. 9.2, according to this system, China is currently ranked in level 4, or the lowest of the so-called 'blue-water'[10] ranks, regarding its current operational capability. The main reason for this is lack of fleet air support. Should China succeed in introducing a carrier capability into its fleet its rank would automatically rise to level 3.

[10] Note that Todd and Lindberg's definition of the term "blue-water navy" differs from commonplace usage, which often implies existing carrier capability.

Depending on the criteria used, about 25 navies, or roughly 16% of the world's ca. 150 navies, are currently categorized in ranks 1–4 and therefore constitute the most advanced "blue-water" navies. 41 navies (or ca. 27%) belong to the still relatively powerful categories five and six, designating respectable naval forces capable of effectively defending their maritime borders. An almost equal number of navies rank at 7–9, having effectively only coast guard-type capabilities, while 58, or ca. 37% of the world's navies, only belong to the 'token' category (rank 10), i.e. they have more symbolic than realistic capability. How can Asia's navies be classified according to those categories? An overview of an approximate ranking of the Asia Pacific navies was attempted with the result shown in Fig. 9.3.

According to the criteria of this ranking system China's overall naval capability is considered to be roughly on par with Japan, Australia, South Korea, Pakistan, and Taiwan, marked differences in their respective force structures (and downward tendencies in some cases) notwithstanding. This might seem rather surprising to some, yet it reflects the application of criteria as outlined in the earlier sections. India and Russia rank even higher due to their currently existing carrier capability, the defining criterion that separates ranks 3 and 4. While Malaysia, Singapore, Thailand, Indonesia and Bangladesh all wield respectable non-blue-water forces of rank 5, other regional navies fall behind.

Currently it seems clear that the most China could achieve within mid-term would be a rise to level 3, and that would mean having at least one operational carrier plus its air wing in place. In order to quickly compete with the sole remaining level 2 powers (the UK and France), China would either need access to Western high-tech weapons and sensor systems very fast, or its indigenous industry would have to make a 'great leap forward' of historically unprecedented magnitude. Neither scenario seems likely as long as the arms embargo persists and China is restricted to relatively less advanced Russian and Ukrainian technology.

Evaluating Relative Sea Power in the Asia Pacific

One way of looking at a country's naval force level is comparing its capability with the commitment the navy has to face. Since no two countries' geostrategic situations can be exactly the same, it is difficult to state *a priori* what would constitute a "reasonable" level of naval self-defence capability for any given country. Therefore it seems useful to tackle this question from an empirical rather than a normative angle, i.e., by observing the actual behavior of similar and typical cases and comparing this to China's behavior. The central assumption is that countries not currently involved in a war will typically be reluctant to invest more than the necessary minimum of resources into their naval forces. Usually they will be under pressure to consider which amount can be dedicated to maritime security without compromising other developmental priorities.

By looking at countries facing similar geostrategic situations and having roughly similar-sized economies as China, it should be possible to gain a rough

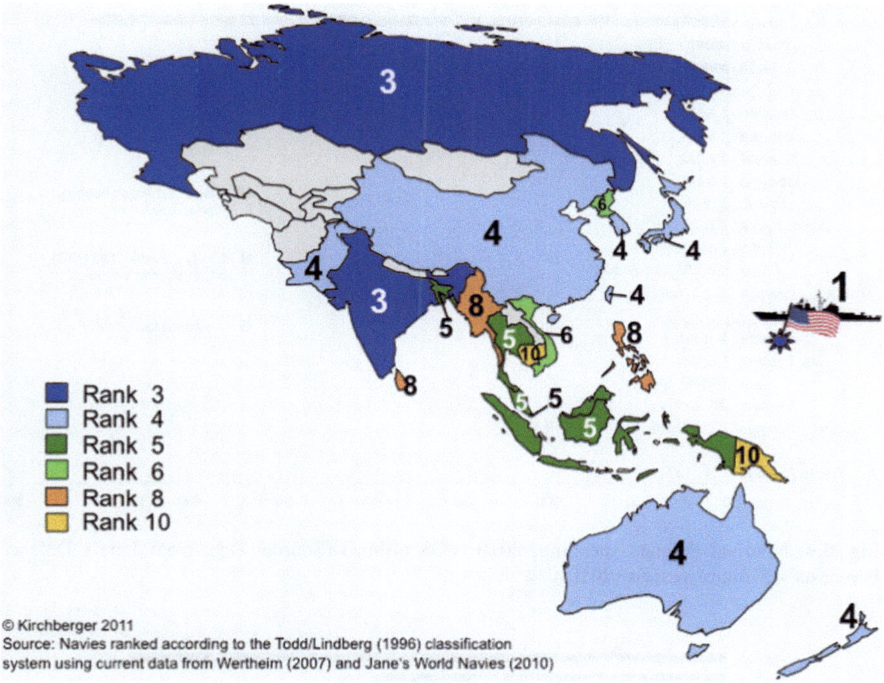

Fig. 9.3 Approximate ranking of Asia Pacific navies according to capability, 2010

understanding of what constitutes a "normal" naval force development level under such circumstances. This approach can then yield a means of identifying atypical cases by comparison with more typical ones. The other 'BRIC' countries – especially Brazil and India – seem appropriate choices for the following reasons: Both are countries with large populations and huge coastlines that aspire to play a dominant role in their respective world regions, and both are rapidly developing economies on a path similar to China's. They have similar strategic aims of becoming ever less dependent on outside assistance and influence (Fig. 9.4).

Looking at military spending – the most commonly used indicator of military prowess in national power indices,[11] both in nominal terms and as a GDP

[11] Using military expenditure as an indicator of national power is inherently problematic: "Military expenditure is not a measure of military capability. Nor is spending on personnel, equipment, R&D or operations and maintenance. As military expenditure data is a measure of the input of resources, it is best used for measuring the military's burden on the national economy, to assess the priorities of the government in the trade off between military and non-military activities, or as a measure of the cost of investing in the military. Very little extra information is actually revealed about a state's military strength or capability by making public its total military expenditure and its distribution on personnel, operations and maintenance, equipment and R&D..." (Stålenheim and Surry 2006: 2).

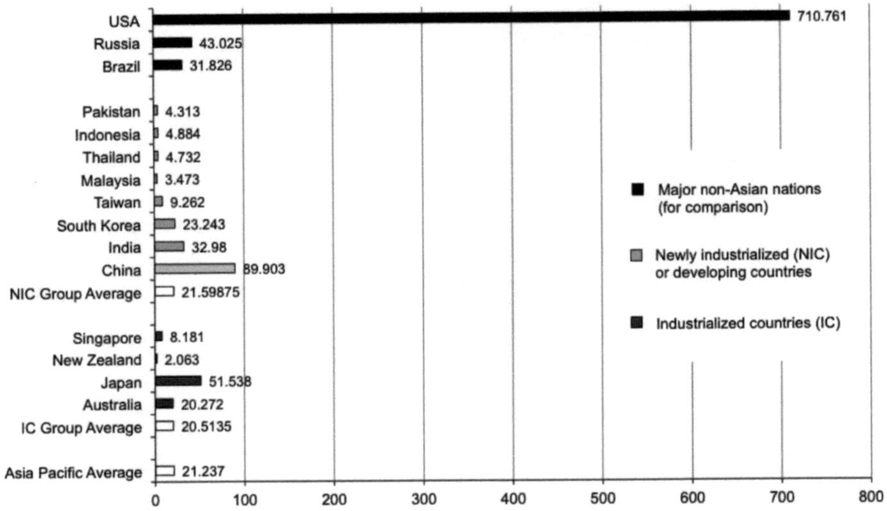

Fig. 9.4 Nominal defence spending, 2010 (US$ billion) (Source: Data from Jane's Defence Forecasts – Military vessels (2010))

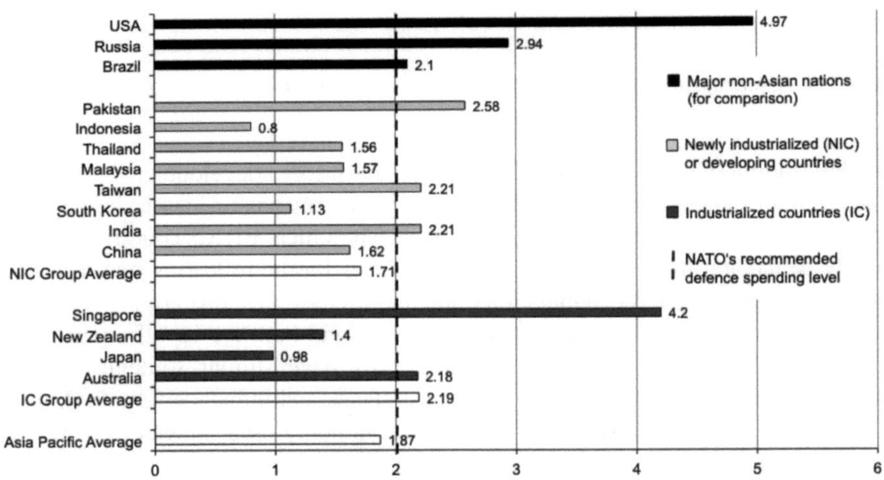

Fig. 9.5 Estimated GDP share of defence spending, 2010 (%) (Source: Data from Jane's Defence Forecasts – Military vessels (2010))

percentage, China does not seem to stand out. Even though real spending levels are probably higher than indicated by official figures, the same can be assumed to be true for some of the other countries, e.g. Russia and Japan (cf. Stålenheim and Surry 2006: 9) (Fig. 9.5).

Because governments need to protect both their land and maritime borders it could be expected that the relative size of a country's maritime border or the size of

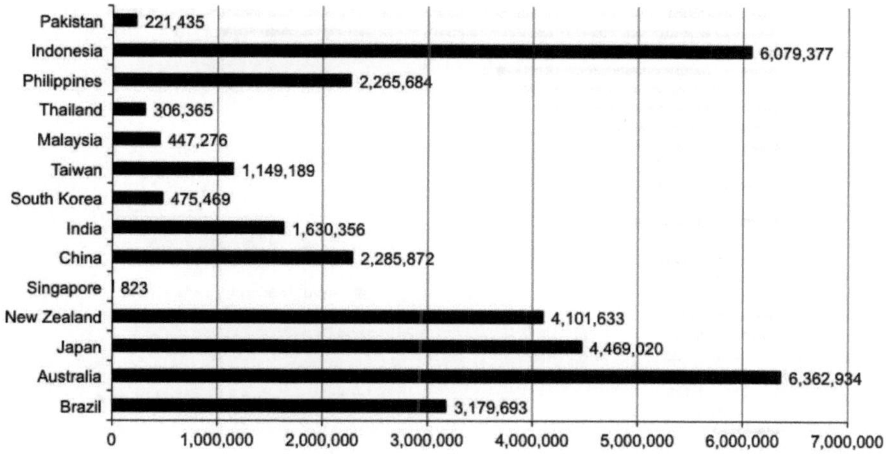

Fig. 9.6 Size of claimed exclusive economic zone (EEZ), km^2 (Source: Figures from the Sea Around Us project (www.seaaroundus.org) at the University of British Columbia, Canada)

its Exclusive Economic Zone (EEZ) could be a good indicator of willingness to finance sizeable naval forces. But empirically this does not seem to be the case. There are many countries especially in Sub-Saharan Africa with vast coastlines but negligible naval forces belonging to the 'token' category. And in Asia, some archipelagic countries – e.g. Indonesia and the Philippines – have the nominally largest coastlines and EEZs, but by far not the most capable navies or coast guards. However, the size of a country's claimed EEZ (usually the 200 nm zone adjacent to the country's coastline, therefore in most cases directly dependent on coast length) does give a rough indication of the area to be patrolled and therefore the size of a navy's commitment to homeland defence. It is clear that the larger the area, the larger the number of vessels needed to accomplish this. Therefore fleet size in itself is not a good indicator of overall capability, as was already stated, but has to be pitted against the navy's commitment to homeland defence as well as fleet age structure and operational state of the vessels (Fig. 9.6).

The Relation Between Trade Involvement and Ranking in the 'World Naval Hierarchy'

If China's overall financial commitment to defence so far does not seem out of proportion regarding the size of its economy, and its EEZ is among the larger ones in the region, what other factors serve to put China's naval modernization level in perspective? Figure 9.7 shows that there exists a fairly reliable correlation between 'blue-water navies' and their countries' levels of integration into world trade.

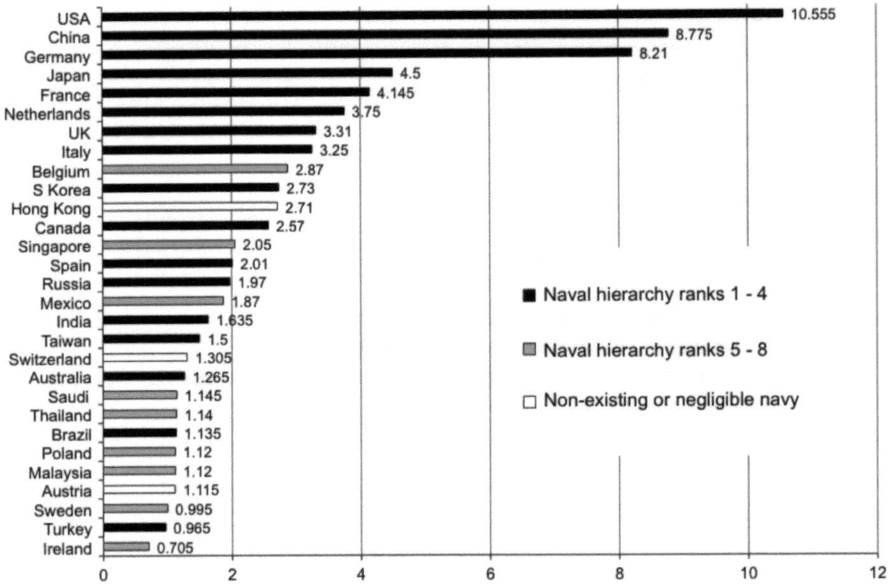

Fig. 9.7 2009 Percentage share of world trade and rank in the 'world naval hierarchy' (Source: World trade shares computed from WTO 2009 data. Navies ranked according to the Todd and Lindberg (1996) classification system using current data from Wertheim (2007) and Jane's World Navies (2010))

The shown 29 top trading nations constitute only ca. 15% of the world's 184 trading nations with WTO member or observer status. These 15% however control more than 80% of total world trade, with the remaining 155 (or 85%) of trading nations having only a share of less than 0.8% each. While all ca. 58 navies classified as 'token navies' belong to such less-integrated trading countries, the world's most capable navies (ranks 1–3) are all found within the group of top trading nations.

With the exception of Switzerland and Austria, the only landlocked countries appearing in the list, all 15% top traders maintain comparatively powerful naval forces. If the landlocked countries and Hong Kong are excluded, altogether 65% of them maintain navies of the 'blue-water' types (ranks 1–4). A further 27% still have quite powerful rank 5 navies. Only two, or 8% of these countries – Mexico and Ireland – have naval forces ranking below level 6 and must be considered anomalous cases.[12]

The correlation between naval power and trade share would not surprise Mahan, who already in 1894 observed that "the necessity of a navy [. . .] springs [. . .] from the existence of a peaceful shipping, and disappears with it, except in the case of a nation which has aggressive tendencies" (Mahan 1987 [1894]: 26). Active

[12] Ireland's navy has mainly coast guard-like duties, and Mexico relies heavily on the United States for maritime protection.

integration into world trade, it can be concluded, usually corresponds with relative wealth, which is a necessary condition for the maintenance of powerful naval forces, while overseas investments, large merchant marines, and dependence on trade routes usually associated with large trading countries require adequate and active maritime protection. Trade champions therefore have both the need as well as the means to afford powerful naval forces.

Based solely on the above observations, and given China's prominent share in the present world trade system – it is shown second after the USA only because Hong Kong's share is calculated separately – China's desire for a blue-water navy of rank 3 or 2, on par with such trading nations as France, the UK, Spain, Brazil, or Italy, seems not quite so unnatural.

Assessing China's Naval Build-Up: Achievements and Pitfalls

After evaluating China's overall naval power level comparatively from a macro perspective, the focus of the following analysis will now turn towards a more detailed review of China's fleet development in order to gain a better basis for future development projections.

China's Naval Modernization Strategy

When China embarked on naval modernization in the 1980s after the turmoil of the Mao era had ended, China followed a "two-track" approach. Its existing (but technologically outdated) Soviet-designed vessels were modified, while follow-up programs using new designs based on the old ones were simultaneously built. Mainly foreign-made weapon and sensor systems were integrated into these new ships. However, in addition to developing new designs, China also purchased newer Russian (or rather, ex-Soviet) ships – i.e. the Kilo class diesel submarines and Sovremenny class destroyers currently in service (Cole 2010: 86–95).

One incentive to rely on indigenous industries for naval shipbuilding, apart from autarchy considerations, is the fact that offensive power-projection weapons such as nuclear-powered submarines and aircraft carriers are generally unavailable on the export market. They have to be indigenously developed and built, even if sometimes with technical assistance of a more advanced country.[13] China is no exception to this rule. After the Sino-Soviet split, China developed the capacity to design nuclear-powered submarines and conventionally powered surface vessels of up to

[13] Brazil and India currently receive extensive assistance from France (Brazil) and Russia (India) for designing nuclear submarines, however, in each case short of actual nuclear propulsion technology transfers.

destroyer size. An aircraft carrier program is currently under way, for which China was able to purchase an empty hull from Ukraine, but support from there for actually finishing the ship will only go so far. China will have to restore the ship to full operational status largely on its own, and it is safe to assume that this will take considerable time yet, especially since China is restricted from technical assistance from Western countries that fellow BRIC countries Brazil and India can and do receive in their respective shipbuilding programs.[14]

Moreover, the quantitative success of China's commercial shipbuilding industries in recent years should not lead to the conclusion that large-scale spillover effects to China's naval shipbuilding facilities can automatically be expected. Recent studies of China's commercial shipbuilding note numerous persisting quality problems, a strong reliance on foreign technical support for all but the most simple commercial ship designs, and little chance of knowledge transfers due to the severe systemic differences between military and commercial shipbuilding (cf. Medeiros et al. 2005: 130–134, 152; Grubb and Collins 2008: 47).[15]

These systematic differences have several consequences. As is common knowledge in the naval shipbuilding community, the main challenge today lies not hull design, but in systems integration, because the task of integrating a large amount of highly sensitive electronic equipment within the crammed space of a warship is formidable. "Whereas a typical supertanker may have 200 major pieces of mechanical and electrical equipment between two dozen systems on the entire ship, a modern destroyer can have this level of complexity in its propulsion plant alone" (Grubb and Collins 2008: 46). Weapons and sensor systems pose even greater integration challenges than propulsion. These challenges multiply if components from different countries of origin have to be integrated within the same hull, as is usually the case in China due to its heavy reliance on Russian as well as French naval technology.

Given these beforehand considerations, how do these factors play out within the current fleet structure, and what trends can be expected to continue? The following figures give an approximate overview of China's current fleet age structure according to two major ship types, destroyers and submarines (Fig. 9.8).

[14] Even Russia has recently decided to break new ground in procuring a state-of-the-art French LHD design instead of developing its own. For an interesting discussion of technical issues awaiting China during the completion of its ex-Ukrainian carrier hull cf. Saw (2008: 33–35).

[15] The key areas of difference are technical complexity, vessel size, crew size, procurement cost, build time, and survivability requirements in a hostile environment. While commercial ships are "essentially [. . .] large steel boxes with relatively small engines and small crews, sufficient only to move the ship from port to port but nothing else", warships have to operate and survive long-term within a hostile environment, perform a variety of highly complex mission types, and give shelter and accommodation to large crews. They are "compact and outfitted with complex sensors, weapons, and communication and power distribution systems (often in duplicate). [. . .] Military ships have complex hotel systems to serve a crew that may number in the hundreds or thousands of people, and many have structural features to enhance performance and survivability" (Birkler et al. 2005: 30).

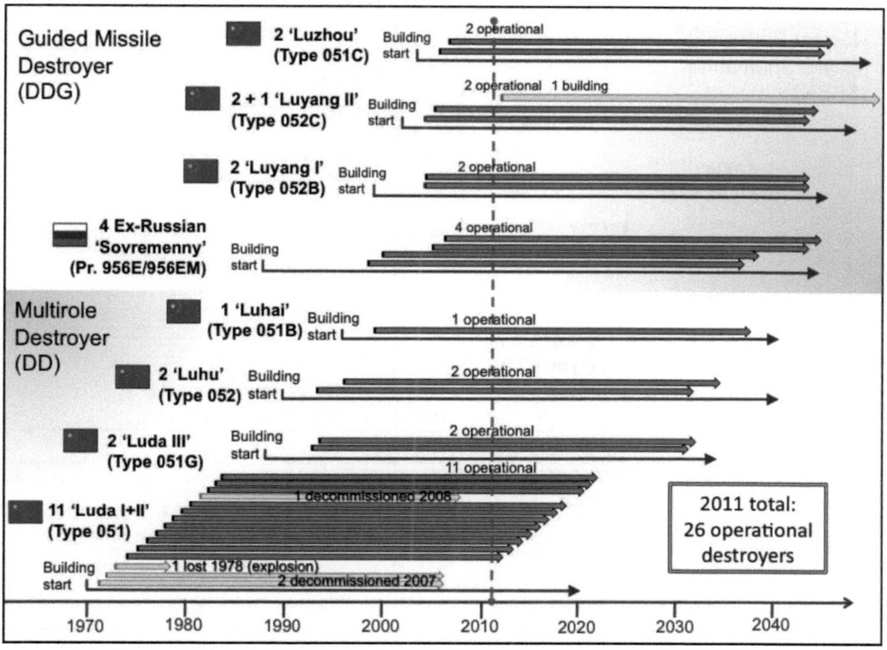

Fig. 9.8 Age structure of the PLA Navy destroyer fleet, 2011 (Source: Based on data from Wertheim (2007), Jane's Fighting Ships, and www.sinodefence.com)

Each arrow symbolizes one vessel, its length indicating approximate service life. As can be seen, China currently operates ca. 26 destroyers belonging to eight different ship classes, all – except the four Sovremenny-class – indigenously built. Assuming a maximum life span of ca. 40 years for steel surface vessels, the figure shows when newbuilding programs must be begun to offset retiring vessels. Half of China's currently operational destroyers still belong to the technically outdated 'Luda' I, II, and III classes (Types 051 and 051 G) that will see decommissioning during the next few years.[16] The old 'Luda' class destroyers still have steam propulsion, no organic helicopters, severely limiting their strategic value, and the earlier variant reportedly lacks the electrical power to operate all sensor and weapon systems simultaneously (Wertheim 2007: 118). Of the currently operational 26 Chinese destroyers, 50% still belong to this completely outdated class.

[16] Both the 'Luda' class destroyers and 'Jianghu' class frigates, which constitute the numerical backbone of the Chinese surface fleet, are badly constructed: "Both suffer from poor welding with signs of premature failure, inoperable machinery, and overall poor hull workmanship. These deficiencies, in turn, seriously degraded their war-fighting ability. Research has indicated that both the Luda and Jianghu are vulnerable to sinking from just one torpedo or missile hit." Among the further problems are lack of "both damage-control facilities and basic safety features (such as fire-retardant systems, automatic firefighting systems, or watertight doors)", as well as "basic design flaws in their weapon-control room that seriously degrade the vessel's warfighting capabilities [. . .] Many of these design flaws were further exacerbated by poor construction techniques used by China's shipyards in past years" (Medeiros et al. 2005: 143–144).

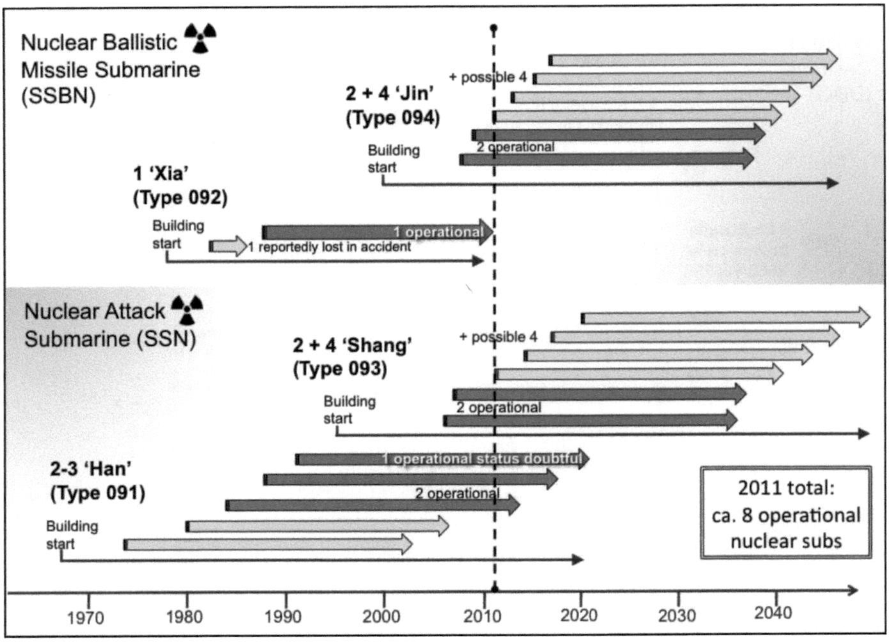

Fig. 9.9 Age structure of PLA Navy nuclear submarine fleet, 2011 (Source: Based on data from Wertheim (2007) and Jane's Fighting Ships (online version))

From an industry viewpoint it seems odd that China – in addition to purchasing the Russian Sovremennys – started building four different indigenous destroyer classes almost simultaneously, and at different shipyards. In one case (the Type 051B 'Luhai' class), only a prototype was built without follow-up vessels. Judging from near-universal experience of shipbuilding programs in Western countries as well as in the developing world, such a strategy seems highly unusual. Development cost for the first-of-class of any type is always disproportionally higher than the cost of follow-on vessels, which means the overall unit price can only be lowered if a sufficient number of units are built to one design. If shipbuilding programs are aborted after the first one or two ships, this usually indicates either sudden budgetary problems (i.e., extreme cost-overruns), or severe technical issues, or both. Moreover, producing several vessels of the same class not only offers economy of scale and learning curve effects, but also enhances interoperability within the fleet due to optimized training, logistics, and maintenance procedures. China's not acting in line with this rule, as well as the simultaneous purchase of the Russian Sovremennys, in all probability indicates severe and persisting problems with systems integration.

The Figs. 9.9 and 9.10 show fleet age structure of nuclear and conventional submarines assuming a shorter maximum age than for surface vessels of ca. 30 years.

China's nuclear submarine fleet is comprised of four different classes with 7–8 boats currently in operational status. The remaining boats of the oldest 'Han' (Type

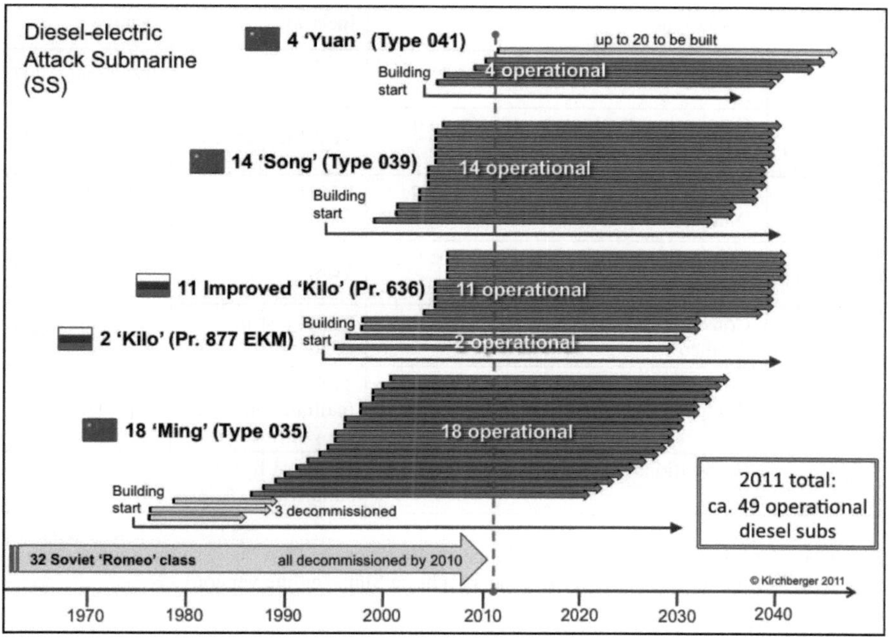

Fig. 9.10 Age structure of PLA Navy conventional submarine fleet, 2011 (Source: Based on data from Wertheim (2007), Jane's Fighting Ships, and www.sinodefence.com)

091) class have been dubbed "sharks without teeth", because apart from the usual Chinese problem of high internal radiation levels they suffer from an inability to fire missiles while submerged, something seriously impairing their strategic value. The single 'Xia' (Type 092) boat was also no success, while a second vessel of the same type seems to have been lost in an accident early on. The remaining boat has apparently never sailed beyond Chinese home waters, suffers from high levels of on-board noise, and is currently mainly used for missile trials, soon to reach the end of its service life. The newest class ('Jin'/Type 094) also encountered reactor problems at first. Two ships are operational but without ballistic missiles until trials of the JL-2 missile are complete. The 'Shang' (Type 093) class, designed to replace the ageing 'Han' boats, was designed with extensive Russian assistance and may be based on the Soviet Victor III class designed during the late 1970s (Shambaugh 2002: 272).

If building programs of the 'Jin' and 'Shang' classes progress as projected, with the older classes going out of service, China's nuclear submarine fleet could rise to 12 boats by 2020 from the eight currently in service as the chart shows.

As can be seen from Fig. 9.10, China currently operates ca. 49 diesel-electric submarines. This means that together with its nuclear boats the PLA Navy currently operates well over 55 submarines. This is a very high number in international comparison. In this China is roughly on par with Russia and second only to the USA, which operates 72 submarines (all of them nuclear-powered). The other two

Date	Vessel type	Incident	Source
1978	Destroyer (DD, Type 051, 'Luda')	Ship lost in explosion	Wertheim 2007
Ca. 1975 – 79	Conventional submarine (SS, Type 035, 'Ming')	Vessel lost in fire	Wertheim 2007
1985	Nuclear submarine (SSBN, Type 092, 'Xia')	Vessel lost in accident	Jane's fighting ships
1985	Conventional submarine (SS, Type 033, 'Romeo')	Vessel sunk	Wertheim 2007
1993/94	Conventional submarine (SS, Type 033, 'Romeo')	Vessel lost in accident	Wertheim 2007
2003	Conventional submarine (SS, Type 035, 'Ming')	Technical malfunction, entire crew suffocated	Various press reports
2005	Conventional submarine (SS, Type 035, 'Ming')	Onboard fire while submerged	Wertheim 2007

Fig. 9.11 Presumed accidents due to technical malfunctions of PLA Navy ships (Source: Assembled from Wertheim (2007: 110-118); Jane's Fighting Ships, online version)

BRIC countries – India and Brazil – only have 16 and 5 conventional submarines respectively, while Japan has 19 (Jane's World Navies 2009). Moreover, China's high number of boats cannot be expected to shrink in the near future due to the fact that the 13 Kilo class and 14 'Song' (Type 039) class boats were built almost simultaneously, and also at the same time as some of the 'Ming' and the newest 'Yuan' class boats, resulting in a fairly homogenous age structure of the fleet. However, one factor explaining this high ratio of submarines vis-à-vis surface ships, according to Howarth (2006: 13), "may simply be [organizational] inertia: since its foundation, the PLA Navy has always had a numerically strong submarine arm; it is therefore organizationally disposed to maintaining this capability". Given the fact that navies tend to be conservative in their outlook, this might explain the relative submarine preponderance.

The Chinese submarine fleet, despite its imposing size, loses some of its luster when technical limitations are taken into account. Accidents due to technical malfunctions have happened frequently in the past, including the widely publicized suffocation of a complete crew aboard a 'Ming' class submarine in 2003. This was only the worst in a series of problems with Ming class subs that have experienced fires and malfunctions on various occasions, showing that safety standards are still below state-of-the-art (Fig. 9.11).[17]

[17] While Howarth (2006: 18) correctly states that submarine operations are "naturally hazardous" and accidents are bound to happen to any navy, a cursory review conducted by me of publicized USN submarine accidents during the past 20 years showed that almost all USN submarine accidents were collisions, not technical malfunctions, and rarely resulted in casualties.

According to a recent study, China's mostly "old, noisy and slow" submarines are still outclassed by the fleets of most other submarine-operating navies in Northeast Asia at least in qualitative terms (Howarth 2006: 16). This is not quite true though with regard to the recently acquired Russian Kilo class boats because they are well armed, quiet, and capable. It seems however that precisely this advanced technology poses difficulties of its own: "Two of the four Kilos which the PLA Navy currently operates have been at sea only infrequently. [...] Crew training has also been problematic and the boats have had to be returned to Russia for battery repairs." Also, training levels of Chinese Kilo submarine crews are lower than Russian recommendations for this class. Moreover different training routines within the fleet mean that the Kilo crews cannot be exchanged with other submarine crews (Shambaugh 2002: 273). The still prevailing Leninist command structures within the PLA continue to gravely limit the submarine commander's leeway for decision-making, casting doubt on the operational value of China's submarine fleet in case of combat (Howarth 2006: 18–19).

Another limiting factor that continues to hamper China's naval modernization effort is a persistent dependence on foreign diesel propulsion plants as well as a limited ability to offset the negative effects of the arms embargo.[18]

In the realm of weapons and sensors, the most critical components of military ships in terms of combat capability, China is restricted from access to state-of-the-art components produced by the very few US and EU companies that effectively hold a quasi-oligopolistic market position. Consequently China relies on systems purchased from France or Italy before (or in spite of) the embargo, or on reverse-engineered developments of those systems; plus the proven, if not state-of-the-art, Russian and Ukrainian systems China has access to. The necessity of integrating systems of Russian, French, and indigenous origin within one and the same hull does prove problematic. This is a critical weakness that can only be alleviated by developing more indigenous systems, which is however an expensive and time-consuming task.[19]

This high degree of reliance on foreign goods, given the inconsistent availability of certain weapon systems, complicates serial production of some platforms. In particular, Chinese combatants lack long-range air-defense systems, modern anti–submarine warfare (ASW) weapons, and advanced electronic warfare capabilities needed to outfit its new ships (Medeiros 2005: 153–54).

With regard to the 'Luhu' class destroyers' mix of US, German, French, and Italian systems, Shambaugh concluded that this combination, and "the lack of spare parts and maintenance packages since 1989, has made operations and maintenance a nightmare" (2002: 268).

[18] For a more detailed treatment of technical issues see my earlier paper (Kirchberger 2011: 22–26).

[19] The systemic difficulties of becoming a "1st tier arms producer" capable of technological innovation are explained by Bitzinger (2003: 35–37). According to the five-rank classification of arms industries employed by Hoyt (2007: 13), China must still be considered a third tier producer facing a steep learning curve in the years to come.

China has managed to develop some systems based on reverse-engineered Russian and French technology, most famously the C-801 and C-802 sea-skimming cruise missiles and HQ-61, HQ-7, and LY-60 N air-defence missiles. However, these developments are still far behind the current industrial standard:

> . . .the capabilities of most of China's current naval SAM and SSM systems and much of its naval electronics are limited and not equivalent to U.S. capabilities or those of other Asian militaries. The limited range and accuracy of Chinese SSMs and SAMs create serious problems for air-defense and anti-submarine warfare. Many of these systems also do not operate with over-the-horizon targeting, further degrading their already-limited capabilities (Medeiros 2005: 139).

The most capable naval weapon systems in Chinese inventory are probably the imported Sovremenny class destroyers that came equipped with SS-N-22 'Sunburn' sea-skimming missiles. Developed specifically to target AEGIS carrier battle groups, only very limited countermeasures against them are currently available (Shambaugh 2002: 267). Figure 9.12 gives an overview of foreign weapon systems employed aboard PLA Navy ships.

Consequences for China's Carrier Program

What consequences do these limitations have for China's indigenous carrier aspirations? Analysts have differed widely regarding a plausible timetable for China's first Chinese-built carrier and its air wing entering service. Optimistic prognoses estimate this could be possible within the next 5 years, while others gravitate more towards 2020 and beyond (Scott 2007). The latter seems much more likely given China's past track record, and experience with similar programs in other countries. Not only is the business of carrier building from scratch a formidable task even for Western shipbuilders (cf. Todd and Lindberg 1996: 9; Birkler et al. 1998). Lately there have also been indications that the state of Russian support for China may be waning due to disagreements regarding widespread reverse engineering of Russian weapon systems.[20] So while China is currently engaged in refurbishing the 'Varyag' – a fairly antiquated Soviet era design – which was laid down already in 1988 and therefore has less than half of its life-span left upon completion, it will probably take some years yet until the completed vessel plus its air wing can be fully operational as a test and training vessel.[21] Moreover, one carrier will not be enough: according to a simple naval rule of thumb, in order to have one ship of any class readily deployable a navy actually needs three, because one will usually be docked for repairs while one will be engaged in training missions, leaving only one ship fully deployable (Holmes et al. 2009: 82–83).

[20] For several related articles giving lots of detail see *Kanwa's* December 2009 issue.

[21] The 'Varyag' was purchased from Ukraine as an empty hull already in 1998, and only recently began sea trials.

	No.	System	Year(s) of delivery	Vessels
France	2	100mm Naval Gun	1989	1 Jianghu II FFG
	14	Castor-2 Fire Control Radar	1994–2002	2x Luhu, 1x Luhai, 3x Luda I DDG, 8x Jiangwei II FFG
	6	DRBV-15 Sea Tiger Radars	1987–1999	2x Luhu, 2x Luhai, 2x Luda I DDG
	5	DUBV-23 Sonars	1991–1999	2x Luda, 1x Luhai, 2x Luhu DDG
	2	DUBV-43 Sonars	1994–1996	2x Luhu DDG
	336	R-440 Crotale SAM	1990–2002	2x Luhu, 1x Luhai, 3x Luda DDG
	28	AS-365/AS-565 Dauphin Helos	1987–1991	Various
Italy	17	RTN-20S Fire Control Radars	1991–2001	2x Luhu, 1x Luda III, 1x Luhai DDG, 6-7 Houjian PTG
Russia	10	K-27PL (Helix-A) Helos	1997–2000	Various
	4	Fregat/Top Plate Air Surv. Radars	2004	2x Luzhou, 2x Luyang I DDG
	8	MR-90/Front Dome FC Radars	2004	2x Luzhou, 2x Luyang I DDG
	144	48Ng/SA-10 Grumble SAM	2002-?	2x Luzhou DDG
	264	9M317/SA-17 Grizzly SAM	2005	2x Luyang I DDG
	Kilo-class SSK, Sovremenny-class DDG (as complete weapon systems)			

Fig. 9.12 Foreign weapon systems on PLA Navy vessels (A more complete list of non-Russian military transfers to China since 1989 is provided by Archick et al. (2005: 37–41)) (Source: SIPRI data cited by Grubb and Collins (2008: 48))

The building of a full-sized concrete mockup at Wuhan, supposedly for studying systems integration issues, is in itself indicative of a still severe lack of systems integration capability.[22] It is also important to note, as O'Rourke correctly states, that "none of these obstacles can be overcome swiftly, and none can be overcome merely by throwing more money at the problem" (2008: 21). It seems therefore hardly conceivable that China could simply leapfrog over its present difficulties.

[22] A December 2009 article in *Kanwa Asian Defence* titled "Structure of 'Wuhan aircraft carrier'", pp. 12–13, gives good photographs and insightful technical observations. *Kanwa* experts were able to inspect the structure and draw conclusions regarding the likely future carrier design.

While there can be no doubt that China could theoretically build a carrier hull, especially if provided with design blueprints from Ukraine, "China lacks the capability to build either large-capacity aircraft-lift elevators or steam catapults for the movement and launching of aircraft; so a Chinese carrier would have to rely on a ski-jump design. Thus, a Chinese carrier would not resemble in any way, shape, or form a U.S. "big-deck" carrier" (Medeiros et al. 2005: 150). Moreover, China, having solved all remaining systems integration challenges, would not only need an air wing, but also more large surface ships to engage in carrier protection in order to form a battle group.

The PLAN currently lacks enough modern multipurpose warships to adequately meet the needs of defending and replenishing a carrier. It is to this end that an expanding and improving shipbuilding infrastructure is a necessary condition for the development of modern, long-range naval capabilities (Medeiros et al. 2005: 150).

It appears that currently, in order to form just one carrier battle group, China's navy would need to deploy "virtually every advanced vessel in the fleet" (Shambaugh 2002: 271).

Concluding Remarks: Is China's Naval Build-Up Upsetting the Asian Balance of Power?

From the perspective adopted in this study, China's overall naval ambitions are judged to be comparable in scope to those of the other BRIC countries and therefore do not seem out of proportion for a country of China's size, trade interests, and geopolitical situation. However, China's high share of submarines in the fleet and its unresolved Taiwan issue will continue to raise concern among regional neighbors and the US nonetheless, and will require careful observation.

Judging from overall capability China's navy is still roughly on par with several other regional powers – e.g. Japan, South Korea, India, and Australia. Changing its status vis-à-vis the others would need significant progress not least with regard to China's carrier program and its indigenous electronics industry. This is not a short-time task, especially in the light of the arms embargo and increasingly strained relations with the Russian naval industry.

Taking into account China's dependence on uninterrupted maritime transport through critical bottlenecks such as the Strait of Malacca, it would even be possible to argue that it is not China's current naval strength, but rather China's comparative weakness that should be considered odd. Given its legitimate interests to protect maritime trade and its huge coastline and EEZ, China's further naval rise to a higher level of capability seems almost inevitable. Accepting this fact and understanding its implications will require much more detailed analyses of China's actual maritime behavior, technological progress, and possible strategic aims than are currently available, in order to avoid a "fear of the unknown" syndrome. However, the results of this study suggest that China's naval build-up, despite undeniable progress, seems to happen slower than suggested by some, leaving enough time for a cautious evaluation of all implications.

It seems that China's naval modernization will only result in a changed Asian power balance if other Asian nations fall behind while China continues to modernize. However, there is currently no evidence to support this view, since most Asian nations have also been modernizing their fleets these past few years. India, Japan, Australia, and South Korea all have powerful navies that can so far easily keep up with China given the fact that they have direct access to Western state-of-the-art technology while China has not. The US/EU arms embargo has left a definite mark on China's naval modernization despite some transgressions, slowing down the overall pace of China's technological progress. It has therefore proven to be an effective tool of cooling down a potential arms race in the Asia Pacific and should not be lifted as long as the original conditions for imposing it remain.

The greatest risk of China's naval build-up, in the opinion of this author, lies not primarily in additional or enhanced hardware, but in a possible misinterpretation of the situation and a misjudging of Chinese interests, strategies, and motivations, leading to hostile actions and reactions. As Susan Shirk correctly observes, "historically, rising powers cause war not necessarily because they are innately belligerent, but because the reigning powers mishandle those who challenge the status quo in one way or another" (2007: 261–262).

Judging from the ongoing inner-Chinese discussions of concepts such as the 'Peaceful Rise of China', 'Comprehensive National Power', or 'Soft Power', it may be true that China is indeed, as Leonard puts it, "the most self-aware rising power in history".[23] The goal of Chinese reformers, according to their concept of 'Comprehensive National Power' (CPN), is to develop a 'balanced power-profile' where military, economic, political and cultural power match harmoniously. When China's economic rise accelerated, Chinese officials became increasingly alert to the danger that "the rest of the world would see China's rise as a threat, and therefore gang up against it." Observes Leonard, "they hoped that if they refused to talk about their country's rise, the rest of the world might not notice it was happening" (2008: 86–88). However, the relative decline in Western economic power as a result of the 2008 financial crisis has made it increasingly difficult for China to hide its light.

All in all, it seems that precisely this kind of self-awareness on China's part, as well as China's dependence on peace and stability in the region for continued economic progress, may provide the rest of the world with options for engaging China constructively.

[23] Cf. Yan Xuetong's 2001 and 2006 articles, Hu's and Men's 2004 paper, and Lampton (2008: 20–36). A Chinese research project sponsored by former CCP Propaganda Chief and vice chair of the Central Party School Zheng Bijian examined the factors that contributed to success and failure of 40 historical 'rising powers'. The study concluded that rising powers that acted aggressively against the existing *status quo* usually came to grief, warning China against offensive courses of action (Leonard 2008: 84, 90).

References

Archick, K., Grimmett, R. F., & Kan, S. (2005). European union's arms embargo on China: Implications and options for U.S. policy, Updated May 27, 2005, CRS Report for Congress, Congressional Research Service, Washington, D.C.: The Library of Congress. http://www.fas.org/sgp/crs/row/RL32870.pdf. Accessed 1 Feb 2011.

Birkler et al. (1998). The U.S. aircraft carrier industrial base: Force structure, cost, schedule, and technology issues for CVN77. RAND corporation monograph reports, Santa Monica/Washington, D.C.: RAND. http://www.rand.org/pubs/monograph_reports/MR948.html. Accessed 15 Feb 2011.

Birkler, J., et al. (2005). *Differences between military and commercial shipbuilding: Implications for the United Kingdom's ministry of defense*. Santa Monica: RAND. http://www.rand.org/content/dam/rand/pubs/monographs/2005/RAND_MG236.pdf. Accessed 15 Feb 2011.

Bitzinger, R. A. (2003). *Towards a brave new arms industry?* Oxford: Oxford University Press.

Cole, B. D. (2010). *The great wall at sea. China's navy in the twenty-first century* (2nd ed.). Annapolis: Naval Institute Press.

Grubb, M. C., & Collins, G. (2008). Chinese shipbuilding: Growing fast, but how good is it?. *US Naval Institute Proceedings*, March 2008, 44–51.

Gu, X., & Mayer, M. (2007). *Chinas energiehunger: Mythos oder Realität?* München: Oldenbourg Verlag.

Hickley, M. (2007). The uninvited guest: Chinese sub pops up in middle of U.S. Navy exercise, leaving military chiefs red-faced. *Daily Mail Online* (www.dailymail.co.uk). 10 Nov 2007.

Holmes, J. R., Winner, A. C., & Yoshihara, T. (2009). *Indian naval strategy in the twenty-first century*. Oxon/New York: Routledge.

Holmes, J. R., & Yoshihara, T. (2008). *Chinese naval strategy in the 21st century. The turn to mahan*. London/New York: Routledge.

Howarth, P. (2006). *China's rising submarine power. The PLA Navy's submarine challenge*. New York: Routledge.

Hoyt, T. D. (2007). *Military industry and regional defense policy. India, Iraq, and Israel*. London/New York: Routledge.

Hu, A. & Men, H. (2004). The rising of modern China: Comprehensive national power and grand strategy. *Paper presented at the international conference of the Korea Institute of International Economic Policy (KIEP)*. Seoul, 19–20 Mar 2004. http://irchina.org/en/xueren/china/pdf/mhh3.pdf. Accessed 2 Mar 2011.

Jane's Fighting Ships, electronic version.

Jane's Intelligence Review. (2008). Secret Sanya – China's new nuclear naval base revealed. *Jane's Intelligence Review*, 21 Apr 2008.

Jane's World Navies. (2010). China. Jane's Information Group, electronic version.

Kanwa 12/2009. Frictions between Russia & China on imitation of Russian navy equipments. *Kanwa Asian Defence Monthly* 62 (Dec 2009), 15.

Kirchberger, S. (2011). China's rising naval power and its impact on global power shift. *Paper presented at the ISA Annual Convention 2011 at Montreal*, Quebec, 16–19 Mar 2011.

Lampton, D. M. (2008). *The three faces of Chinese power: Might, money, and minds*. Berkeley: University of California Press.

Leonard, M. (2008). *What does china think?* London: Fourth Estate.

Li, M. (2010). China and maritime cooperation in East Asia: Recent developments and future prospects. *Journal of Contemporary China (2010), 19*(64), 291–310.

Mahan, A. T. (1987). *The influence of sea power upon history 1660–1783* (5th ed.). New York: Dover Publications. reprint of 1894.

Medeiros, E. S., Cliff, R., Crane, K., & Mulvenon, J. C. (2005). A new direction for China's defense industry. RAND project air force. http://www.rand.org/pubs/monographs/MG334.html. Accessed 2 Mar 2011.

O'Rourke, R. (2008). *China naval modernization: Implications for U.S. Navy capabilities.* New York: Nova.

Pfetsch, F. R. (1994). *Internationale politik.* Stuttgart: Kohlhammer.

Potgieter, T. (2009). When maritime security is absent. In T. Potgieter & R. Pommerin (Eds.), *Maritime security in southern African waters* (pp. 5–22). Centre for Military Studies, Stellenbosch University, Stellenbosch: Sun Press.

Rice S. E., & Patrick, S. (2008). *Index of state weakness in the developing world.* Washington, D.C.: The Brookings Institution. http://www.brookings.edu/~/media/files/rc/reports/2008/02_weak_states_index/02_weak_states_index.pdf. Accessed 2 Mar 2011.

Ruppik, D. (2007). China unterstützt Umgehung der Straße von Malakka. *Schiff & Hafen*, Jan 2007, 27.

Saw, D. (2008). Evolution & revolution – Chinese naval developments. *Asian Defence & Diplomacy, 15*, 27–40.

Scott, R. (2007). China's naval ambitions: Congressional report details major warship programmes. *Jane's Navy International,* 1 July 2007.

Shambaugh, D. (2002). *Modernizing China's military. Progress, problems, and prospects.* Berkeley: University of California Press.

Shirk, S. L. (2007). *China: Fragile superpower.* Oxford: Oxford University Press.

Stålenheim, P., & Surry, E. (2006). Transparency in military expenditure and arms production. *Paper presented at the Xiangshan Forum 22–24 Oct 2006.* http://www.sipri.org/research/armaments/production/publications/unpubl_aprod/xiangshan. Accessed 13 Feb 2011.

Till, G. (2009). *Seapower: A guide for the twenty-first century* (2nd ed.). London/New York: Routledge.

Todd, D., & Lindberg, M. (1996). *Navies and shipbuilding industries: The strained symbiosis.* Westport: Praeger.

Wertheim, E. (2007). *The Naval institute guide to combat fleets of the world* (15th ed.). Annapolis/Maryland: Naval Institute Press.

WTO. (2010). Trade statistics database. http://stat.wto.org/CountryProfile/WSDBCountryPFHome.aspx?Language=E. Accessed 30 Jan 2011.

Yan, X. (2001). The rise of China in Chinese eyes. *Journal of Contemporary China (2001), 10*(26), 33–39.

Yan, X. (2006). The rise of China and its power status. *Chinese Journal of International Politics, 1* (2006), 5–33.

Yung, C. D., & Rustici, R. (2010). "*China's out of area naval operations: Case studies, Trajectories, Obstacles and potential solutions,*" with Isaac Kardon and Joshua Wiseman, Institute for National Strategic Studies China Strategic Perspectives 3, Washington, DC: National Defense University Press. http://www.ndu.edu/inss/docUploaded/ChinaStrategicPerspectives3.pdf. Accessed 25 Feb 2011.

Chapter 10
Drones as Future Air Power Assets: The Dawn of Aviation 2.0?

Louis-Marie Clouet

As the B-52 bomber and the ICBM were the symbols of the Cold War, the Unmanned Aerial Vehicle (UAV[1]) is often prensented as an icon of military power at the beginning of the 21st Century. It epitomises a new way to wage war, as current operations in Iraq, Afghanistan and Pakistan have put the spotlight on UAVs. Although largerly used by military forces – mainly U.S. and Israeli – since the Vietnam War, UAV acquired this renewed status very rapidly in the last decade, and is henceforth considered as a key asset for military and political leaders, a "force multiplier" and a deciding factor for a military, if not political, victory on the ground.

Futhermore, current UAVs only represent the first steps of a totally technological and industrial new territory, where technological innovations may profoundly transform the way to wage war, and lead the way to truly autonomous unmanned vehicles.

This article will try to explain in a first step the causes of this "drone moment", that came to age in the first decade of the 21st century as an heritage and renewal of mainly US military doctrine. If drones are to play a key role in the balance of military power, they are however deeply dependent of these doctrines of Revolution in Military Affairs and Air Power, and of all the technological "system of systems" that conditions their effectiveness.

At the end, the measure of their impact on military balance of power will result more from the capacity of nations to acquire, and develop technological innovations

---

[1] The most appropriate expression would be "drone system": the term UAV is currently changing into "Unmanned Air System" (UAS) as drones have initially been mainly air vehicles, but new systems are being developed as ground or naval vehicles. Furthermore, the core value for an UAS/V is increasingly the payload and less the platform. The term "drone", UAV or UAS used in this study will have the same acceptance, as this study will focus mainly on air vehicles: a precision will be used if the more exact term of the flying machine is employed – be it the platform itself or the onboard systems.

E. Fels et al. (eds.), *Power in the 21st Century*, Global Power Shift,
DOI 10.1007/978-3-642-25082-8_10, © Springer-Verlag Berlin Heidelberg 2012

connected to robotics, C4I,[2] articial intelligence, that are to be implemented into the military field. In that sense, they open a window of opportunity for new-entrants or re-entrants that could call into question traditional aeronautic nations' hierarchy.

The "Drone's Hour"

From intelligence and reconnaissance to hunter-killer

Without going back to the mongolfières of the eighteenth century, which were the first remoted-controlled sort of platforms designed to see "beyond the horizont" or "beyond the hill" – if not unmanned -, UAV already played an active role in the Vietnam war (3,435 sorties) and in the Persian Gulf War (over 520 sorties) (Curran et al. 2005: 64), essentially performing ISTAR[3] missions, which are still the main missions devoted to such systems. Soviet forces also used those systems, mainly for artillery targeting. But the major users of UAV had been the US armed forces during the Vietnam War, followed by Israel in the 1980s.

Recent advances in remote controlled flights and miniaturization have improved these non-piloted flying machines, capable of carrying out crucial missions for armed forces engaged on the ground: surveillance, reconnaissance, identification, targeting and fire-guidance, and anti-IED capacity.[4] Small tactical drones are still devoted to this "deported binoculars" role for ground forces. Micro-drones weigh less than 5 kg, for a 10 km range and 1 h autonomy; they fly between 100 and 250 m high. Tactical drones are operated by ground forces for reconnaissance missions and can fly over 5 h at around 5,000 m high.

Larger drones (Medium Altitude Long Endurance, MALE drones), through their superior payload of one metric ton and their communication liaison via satellite (SATCOM), can transmit data gathered in real time through the on-board radar and video captors over a wide territory and for an extended period of flight (over 20 h). High Altitude Long Endurance (HALE) UAVs such as the Global Hawk have a more strategic role and can fly over 30 h at more than 20,000 m high. New helicopter drones such as the MQ-5 Firescout are being developed, mainly to be deployed on ships and perform reconnaissance and strikes in a naval environement.

MALE UAVs such as the MQ-1 Predator and the MQ-9 Reaper have become an essential component of the modern armed forces because of their qualities on mission in comparison with a manned aircraft:

---

[2] C4I stands for Command, Control, Communications, Computers, Intelligence.

[3] A term used by the US Armed Forces, which stands for intelligence, surveillance, target acquisition and reconnaissance.

[4] IED: Improvised Explosive Device.

- Long endurance (24 h flying time), enabling a 'permanence' over the battlefield beyond the physiological limits of a human pilot;
- None-exposure of pilots to danger, reducing the risks to pilot's life and the political risk when pilots are killed or captured,
- Lower costs and extended disposable payload, enabled by eliminating all the systems needed for a human pilot.

Besides these qualities of endurance and none-exposure of pilots to danger, the value of the drone in assisting decision and command is intrinsically linked to the onboard sensors and, to a lesser extent, to the platform. Indeed, the sensors[5] condition the precision and the performance of the information collected and the rapid transmission of this information to theatre commanders, or even to units engaged on the ground. These sensors could quite literally be loaded onto a completely different platform to the remote-controlled motorised glider, if the criteria of the cost of flying a helicopter or a plane for an equivalent mission were not been taken into account.

However, drones have to conserve their advantage in cost and quality of usage compared with other aerial vehicles: drones should therefore not be seen simply as planes without pilots to be given the same missions as combat planes. Instead the focus of their design should concentrate on their advantage in relation to piloted planes, as Edward Luttwak underlines (2007: 782):

- Small planes (. . .) still too small to carry a human, equipped in various ways for observation, communication transmission, light strikes, etc.;
- Very long flying times, which would require special installations onboard a manned aircraft; and
- Extremely long range, just like the ultra-long flight length, and for the same reasons.

A heritage at the convergence of RAM, Air Power and COIN

UAVs encountered such a success because they appeared as the answer that came both from a conceptual reassessment of previous doctrines, namely the Revolution in Military Affairs (RAM) and the "Air Power" doctrines, and from the military requirements in Counter-Insurgency (COIN) operations in Iraq and Afghanistan, that partly contradicted the effectiveness of 'Air Power'.

Since the First World War, and particularly since the Second World War, Air Power doctrine has been closely linked to the US Air Force (USAF), and as a whole, to the doctrine of the US Armed Forces. Both as an ideology and a reality, Air Power is a US specificity – to the point that "modern military aviation history and USAF history are indissolubly linked" (de Durand 2004: 20). Air power has a

[5] Radar detection of moving targets (Synthetic Aperture Radar (SAR)/Ground Moving Targets Indication (GMTI)), infrared video, coupled with a satellite link for real time transmission of images, laser designator, etc.

profound resonance with American strategic culture, offering the promises of short, decisive wars, without – or with few – human losses.[6] Lessons learned from the tactical and strategic failures of the Vietnam War led to a review of USAF military doctrine, that took account of the failure of strategic and tactical bombing in North-Vietnam and underlined the importance of missions such as penetration of a hostile airspace and suppression of enemy air defences (SEAD) by destroying radars or by electronic counter-measures. This also led to the development of the first precision ammunition laser-guided bombs. In that sense, the lessons learned by the USAF were clearly demonstrated in the 1991 Gulf War: it was the operational maturity of technological innovations (miniaturization, cost reduction and power growth of electronic systems). Operation "Desert Storm" took advantage of the progress in three fields: precision, detection and communication, which can be considered as the three main founding elements of the RAM. The RAM was conceptualized at the beginning of the 1990s, formalizing the lessons and results of the First Gulf War.[7]

Two main developments of the RAM, detection and communication, enabled to create networks combining sensors (observation means) and "shooters" (arms systems) in real time. According to supporters of the RAM, "seeing everything enables to reach everything, which means destroy everything on a battlefield. It is therefore essential in the RAM logic to acquire and retain 'information dominance'" (de Durand 2003: 61). The advent of the Global Positioning System (GPS) – allowing effective navigation – and broadband SATCOM – allowing to transmit surveillance pictures and videos – were the two major innovations that conferred a military value to UAVs (Weiner 2009: 113). Although Air Power was the core of USAF doctrine, and so far, of its supremacy over the other services, it did not seem interested at first in UAVs, until the other services, particularly the US Army, began to show such interest during the 1990s with the development of own UAV programs (Weiner 2009: 113).

Precision was the other main revolution that gave a military value to UAVs: the creation of precisely guided ammunition enabled the reduction of the Circular Error Probability to a few meters.[8] This allowed substituting fire precision to zone saturation (like the "carpet bombing" of the Second World War) with two consequences: it allowed to considerably reducing the "collateral damages" and henceforth, armed forces could operate from a secure range and limit own exposure to enemy fire. Precision-guided munitions have amounted to 7–8% of the tonnage of bombs dropped in 1991, 35% during operation Allied Force in Kosovo in 1999, and 65% in operation Enduring Freedom in 2001. The extreme doctrinal development lead to strikes

[6] A propos the closely relation between Air Power and American strategic culture, see Cohen 1994.

[7] On the 1991 Gulf War Air operations and their assessment, see Keeney and Cohen 1993.

[8] During the First Gulf War, ca. 17,000 Precision Guided-Munitions were used in action, of which 9,342 were Laser-guided versions. By comparison, approximately 210,000 unguided bombs were dropped in the same war (Keeney and Cohen 1993: 226). Of the coalition forces' total weapons expenditures (guided bombs, antiradiation missiles, and air-to-surface missiles), US expenditures amounted from 89% to 99% (Keeney and Cohen 1993: 203).

conducted not only at a security range on a theatre of operation, but from intercontinental range, completed by the insertion on the theatre of human and robot scouts, the use of ground forces (particularly special forces) being a last option. For instance, pilots of MQ9-Reaper UAVs are located in Creech Air Force Base in Nevada, watching and striking in Afghanistan in real-time 7,500 miles away (Zucchino 2010).

Asymmetric and Symmetric Counter-Measures to Air Power and RAM

UAV are therefore the inheritors of the RAM: they are perfectly inserted in this network centric warfare, connected by SATCOM in real-time with operative commanders and troops on the ground, remotely piloted, and capable to strike precisely with guided missiles and bombs. They are also subject to the limits of RAM and Air Power.

First, they are highly dependent (for larger UAVs) on bandwidth and satellite communication. If the liaison with the drones is lost, they are out of control,[9] particularly in mountain environments. They also prove to use an ever-growing bandwidth capacity in order to transmit real-time videos. This technology path chosen by the American armed forces carries the seeds of its own limitations: the American drones accumulate thousands of hours of video images, to the point that military leaders acknowledge difficulties in analysing this mass of information in order to extract useful information from it for the forces engaged on the ground (Conference on "MALE drones: challenges and European perspectives" 2010[10]). Moreover, projects for future American drones increase the number of onboard sensors, their capability for *de facto* following a growing number of potential targets simultaneously, data to be transmitted in real time and processed as quickly as possible.

RAM developments have also faced counter-measures, for instance in Kosovo in 1999, where Serbians armed forces preferred to play an asymmetric game against the proven American air superiority. Using deceit and camouflage, they dispersed their forces: precision and real-time intelligence reach limits when there is no target (de Durand 2003: 66). Serbian forces also used their radars only by intermittence, not permitting the US aircraft to target them; Serbian air-defence was not totally destroyed in the first days of the allied air operations, and it prevented the allied aircraft to fly below 15,000 ft – and to have the capacity to better identify and destroy potential ground targets. Human shields have also been used against air strikes, be it in Iraq or in the Palestinian Territories. Because of the high level of dependency of modern armed forces on the cyberspace, this could also prove to be a

[9] This problem may be solved by using UAVs in networks: one UAV allows to maintain the liaison with others drones.

[10] Conference on "MALE drones: challenges and European perspectives", 7 April 2010 at Ifri Paris. See also Drew 2010.

new Achilles' heel: US Predator UAVs have already been hacked by Iraqi insurgent in recent years (Gorman et al. 2009). In a clear 'bypass strategy' the insurgents used a commercial software for downloading movies and mp3 files (estimated price : 26 USD) in order to collect the data transmitted by the drone to ground stations – only because the data was not encrypted in order to accelerate its transmission. According to Boutherin, "air power is particularly affected [from such technical bypass strategies] because its functioning and mission accomplishment are closely linked to information and communication systems and to networking" (Boutherin 2010: 11–12).

RAM and 'traditional' Air Power have also shown limits when they were confronted with counter-insurgency and with war "among the people", as Rupert Smith put it (Smith 2007). It is very difficult for a pilot in a fighter/bomber jet to identify precisely and discriminate a target in a few seconds; in the past, this led to tragic errors by inflicting 'collateral damages'. In this regard, UAVs have been a solution in such difficult contexts as Afghanistan. UAV have "become an essential component of modern aeroterrestrial operations" (Paloméros and Joly 2009: 67). They have the unique advantage to keep flying in a definite zone, an essential quality that allows them to catch ephemeral phenomenon such as the launching of a rocket. Additionally, they give a unique reactivity in terms of intelligence and information control, particularly in order to target and treat time sensitive targets.

Symmetric threats to Western dominance can also emerge as increasingly sophisticated surface-to-air threats take shape (Boutherin 2010: 13–14). As Brustlein points out, "Western armed forces have gotten used to enjoying air superiority above theatres of operations and taking full advantage of this asset by constantly observing the battlefield and the adversary posture" (2011: 22), a task particularly dedicated to UAVs because of their qualities outlined above. Opposition forces are currently trying to procure equipment in order to intervene in the third dimension for offensive (cruise missiles, ballistic missiles, and UAVs) and defensive purposes (integrated and multi-layered air defence systems) (Bolkcom 2006: 2). There is therefore a growing demand on the international market for radars, SAM systems capable of intercepting stealth aircraft, cruise missiles, and also UAVs. Non-Western countries – particularly Russia and China – play a major role in selling these capacities to states that are neither able nor willing to buy such armaments from Western countries (Clouet 2011). The wide distribution of S-300 missiles presents a serious challenge to Western air superiority: this type of long range anti-aircraft and anti-cruise missiles has already been sold to China, India and a dozen of other countries. Iran and Syria have expressed their desire to acquire such systems as well as other modern SAM systems with shorter range.

That is why SEAD missions still represent a major task for Western/American armed forces. During operation "Desert Storm", Allied air forces destroyed the air defence system Kari that was protecting Iraq, by combining modern aircraft, platforms and arms systems, among them stealth F-117 aircraft, USMC F/A-18, USAF F-G4G protected by electronic warfare aircraft (EF-111, EC-130 and EA-6B). Drones played also a role as a feinted air offensive that inducted Iraqis air defence teams to use their radars, and to expose them to American anti-radar missiles. After 7 days of air strikes, radar emissions by Kari air defence systems had been reduced by 95% (Lambeth 2000: 111–13).

Israel also used drones to overcome air defence systems. After the dramatic experience of the Kippur War in 1973, when 77 Israeli aircraft were shot down by Syrian air defence – particularly by soviet-made SA-6 or SA-7 – Israel's armed forces had fundamentally upgraded their SEAD doctrine and put it into action during Operation "Cast Lead",[11] combining reconnaissance and electronic warfare drones, fighters/bombers, unguided and precision guided bombs and missiles, reconnaissance, alert, control and command aircraft, diverse electronic warfare systems and artillery with guided ammunition.

A Useful Remedy for Counter-Insurgency and Close-Air Support Missions

Lessons about air doctrine learned from Afghanistan are, firstly, that a distinction between strategic and tactical bombing tends to blur, because of the extension of the range of weapons. Air Power has come back with greater utility as a close-air support for ground forces engaged in counter-insurgency operations in Afghanistan: in this regard UAVs play a crucial role, giving the ground forces a permanent intelligence reconnaissance and surveillance knowledge of the battlefield.

UAVs therefore play a central role for commanders and troops on the ground, enabling them to "see first, understand first and then finish decisively" (Curran 2005: 64). UAVs provide the crucial information for line-of-sight and beyond-line-of-sight reconnaissance, rapid movement, target identification and engagement, and eventually, battle damage assessment. Drones operators can gather a fine knowledge of the zone they fly over, because they can stay for hours and for months scrutinising the same zone (see Quintana 2011),[12] in contrast to a jet pilot who just flies over in a few seconds; moreover, drone operators are assisted by analysts and can have direct communication with other soldiers on the ground. Drones thus have become critical force multipliers, as a division commander in Iraq has put it: "My #1 irritant as a division commander is *not* having UAV assets to execute my mission" (Curran 2005: 64, own emphasis).

The dominant UAV user is currently the US Department of Defense, which has more than 6,000 unmanned aircraft in its inventory and is continuing to acquire

[11] UAVs accounted to 70% of mobilised aircraft during Operation "Cast Lead", and were responsible for one third of air mission realized by Tzahal (see Vandewalle and Viollet 2009: 27).

[12] This enables drone operators to know the habits of the inhabitants, and to distinguish a "normal" behavior of a civilian inhabitant from the behavior of an insurgent. This quality is particularly useful in the context of "war among the people" and COIN operations. Drones are also useful tools against Improvised Explosive Devices (IED) as they watch the roads that are used by allied forces in Afghanistan.

more, from short-range reconnaissance systems to less numerous, but more expensive, medium-sized and large unmanned aircraft systems (Congressional Budget Office 2011: 51[13]). MQ-9 Predator B/Reaper drones are currently widely used by the American forces in their strike campaign against Al-Qaida leaders in Yemen, Afghanistan and Pakistan. Drones have also been used as "hunter-killers" in Afghanistan and Pakistan in order to disrupt Al-Qaida's organisation, both under the Bush and the Obama administration: in July 2010, a senior US official revealed that about 650 "extremists" had been killed by drone strikes in Pakistan's Federally Administered Tribal Areas since Obama took office (53 strikes in 2009, 850 until October 2010). This new kind of missions has led to a debate of the legality and ethics of such killings, reinforced by the inadvertent dead of civilians and subsequent negative images of drones within the population (International Institute for Strategic Studies 2009).

Future Evolutions: The Dawn of Aviation 2.0

In a frequent comparison, the UAVs appear to follow a similar path to the beginning of aviation in the twentieth Century. We may indeed be at the dawn of Aviation 2.0, as unmanned aircraft offer increasingly large perspectives of development in the next century, that are only partially envisioned today.

Armed forces – although quite cautious regarding the real impact of future UAS on military affairs – henceforth integrate UAV in their development and procurement schemes. Two main constraints will be the budget available for R&D and procurement in the next decades and the technological challenges that have to be overcome.

An Central Military Tool with Increasingly Expanding Missions

UAV – as well as ground and naval unmanned vehicles – are foreseen to take an increasing place among military arsenal in the next decades, depending however on technological innovations. The existing deep "capacity gap" between the US Air Force (and the US Navy) and other nations' air forces regarding manned aircraft

[13] According to this report, the US Air Force plans to purchase 288 Reapers (48 per year from 2011 through 2016) and 28 Global Hawks from 2011 through 2018. In 2002, the US Army had only three deployed systems, over 200 in 2005 and has roughly 490 medium-sized unmanned aircraft in its inventory in 2011. Through 2016, the US Army plans to purchase 20 Shadows to replace losses, upgrade the existing Shadows, and purchase 107 more of the medium-altitude Grey Eagles.

The US Navy plans to purchase 36 BAMS aircraft at a cost of about $9.4 billion by 2020 (a Global Hawk warrant optimized for naval operations) and 61 MQ-8B Firescout unmanned helicopters, and, through 2026, the Navy's plans call for purchasing a total of 65 BAMS and 168 Firescout.

may become deeper with the introduction of UAS. The US armed forces already reflect the growing importance of UAS. A recent benchmark frequently cited is the Fiscal Year 11' DoD acquisitions, which is the first time UAVs outnumbered manned airplanes (Kimmey 2010). In the 2009 Unmanned Systems Integrated Roadmap (USIR) (see U.S. Department of Defense 2009), the DoD envisions that UAS will be able to cooperate on the ground, on water as well as in the sky. In the 2030s, UAS will operate increasingly autonomously and will be able to flight for months at a time without the need for refuelling. They may be able to fly in squadrons – with or without manned aircraft.

If UAVs follow the same path as heavier-than-air aircraft, Unmanned Combat Air Systems (UCAS) will be the next predictable major development in the field of UAS. For the moment and in the next years, UAS will retain mainly ISR missions and will therefore predominantly see their sensors upgraded. Armed UAVs will have the same platform on which an armed payload will be fitted, but UAS will not be able to compete with fighter or bomber aircraft in terms of payload, reactivity to combat situation or survivability.[14] However, as the USIR envisioned already in 2005, missions devoted to UAS may expand quickly when UAS have an advantage over manned systems, in particular for the "three jobs best left to UAS: the dull (long dwell), the dirty (sampling for hazardous materials), and the dangerous (extreme exposure to hostile action)" (U.S. Department of Defense 2009: 43).[15] UAVs may also be able to refuel manned and other unmanned aircraft and replace Airborne Warning and Control Systems (AWACS) (Hoffmann and Weisberger 2011).

Nations, which already possess drones and the essential intelligence they bring, can also have a greater say and a more pivotal role in military decision-making, particularly in the framework of a coalition. Drones will therefore not only be a force multiplier, but will also confer a military-political weight for those countries that can control intelligence, comparable to the use of observation satellites on a strategic and operative level.

UAS will more and more become the central military tool, in air, but also on the ground and at sea, leaving man presence out of any danger area. These developments are already envisioned and prepared: UCAS demonstrators are being developed in America and in Europe. This will likely only be the beginning as manned aircraft see their costs rising to extreme heights. Additionally (and related to this), no new combat aircrafts are foreseen in the Western world beyond the Joint

---

[14] For the time being, UAVs cannot compete with manned aircraft: Seven Georgian drones were reportedly shot down by Russian fighter aircrafts in April and May 2008. This shows that UAVs are not appropriate if air dominance is not achieved (see International Institute for Strategic Studies 2009, Boutherin 2010: 17–18).

[15] This may include reconnaissance, signals intelligence, mine detection and counter-measures, precision target location and designation, battle management, chemical/biological reconnaissance, counter cam/con/deception, electronic warfare, Combat Search and Rescue (SAR), communications/ data relay, information warfare, digital mapping, littoral undersea warfare, SOF team resupply, weaponization/strike, act as GPS pseudolites or insert covert sensors.

Strike fighter in the US and the Eurofighter, the Dassault Rafale and the Saab Gripen in Europe, which will stay in service for the next 40 years – their successor may indeed be combat drones. The emergence of such combat drones will therefore be gradual and will result in mixed fleets of manned and unmanned combat aircrafts (Grozel and Moulard 2008). This may pose some technological problems and human presence may still be needed as the ultimate capacity to abort or adapt a strike according to the specific circumstances or to react to an unforeseen offensive action – a capabilities a UAS does not possess at the moment.

In European military technology circles there is a debate of the necessity to follow American "technologism" (Desportes 2009). It may not be in the European armed forces interest to return to a vicious circle imposed by American capabilities and technological choices. The Americans themselves are also unprepared to the types of adversaries and the kinds of conflicts they face, leading to equipment reductions and financially unsustainable armies. Even the US army has to make difficult choices in its various programs for R&D and acquisition as it is confronted with rising public debts and unable to avoid the increasing costs of its arms programs (e.g. the Joint Strike Fighter or the F-22 amongst others). The increasing use of drones has also encountered limits, i.e. the difficulty to cope with the ever-growing demand of bandwidth and capacities for analysing of the rocketing quantity of in real-time data collected. To avoid falling into the same trap, European countries must rebalance their weapon choices with a more just and optimised ratio of "technology/force volume" (Desportes 2009: 417).

Capability choices are at the heart of the rationale for competition. This is especially true in times when a state's budgetary capabilities are constrained and weigh on the equipment choices of the national armed forces. However, short-term constraints, as pressing as the needs are to support the armed forces capabilities, should not weigh unduly and hinder long-term investments with debt. As Philippe Coquet underlines, "the danger of being tempted by reducing financial costs in the short-term compared with operational capacity is doubtless not the slightest" (Coquet 2008: 34).

A Global Race for Drones

Because of the recent efficiency of US UAVs in operations in Afghanistan and Pakistan, UAVs are increasingly seen as a key asset that modern armed forces need to have in their arsenals. Currently, more than 50 countries have purchased surveillance drones. Many have also started to develop indigenous programs in light of procurement problems on the international market. The US is currently the main innovator in this field (followed by Israel, which is also a major producer and user of drones) and is not willing to lose its existing advantage of being the leading producer and user of drones.[16] Furthermore, UAS are still covered by the Missile Technology Control Regime (MTCR).[17] In this sense, drones also follow the same pattern as other high-technology military systems. Many countries that cannot buy American equipment have to buy from other suppliers. Israel may be an important alternative source for UAV procurement, although it also has to overcome Washington's opposition. Recent sales of Israeli drones to Russia were cautiously observed by the US. The delivered Israeli UAVs were explicitly ordered for studying them in order to develop Russian-made drones (RIA Novosti 2010). India announced in 2011 the development of an armed UAV that could fire missiles and flies at 30,000 ft; Pakistan has declared that it should acquire drones from China, Iran has unveiled a drone called "ambassador of death" by President Mahmoud Ahmadinejad. China has exposed a new model of its armed jet-propelled WJ-600 drone. China is set to sell UAVs to its long-term partner Pakistan (Wan and Finn 2011).

Considering the increasing military necessity to deploy UAS, and the difficulty to acquire drones from other sources than the US and her allies, the major incentive for a country is to take the opportunity of this new kind of military equipment to get into the race for military and aeronautic industry. The newly expanding drone market is therefore an opportunity for countries to enter the aeronautic industry, as "the UAS revolution implies a return to faster cycles of design, development and production. (..) The UAS industry supply-chain demands flexibility and low-cost solutions combined with the highest technical specifications" (Heyward 2010: 65). Drones are easier to develop in comparison with a highly complex and costly fighter jet, which only a few countries manage to manufacture – and at growing costs: a MQ9-Reaper is said to cost about $10,5 million, in comparison with a $150 million F-22 fighter jet. General Atomics, which manufactures the Predator and the Reaper, was not a traditional aeronautic firm, and Boeing for instance had to adapt to this new challenger and created a special branch dedicated solely to UAVs. Northrop-Grumman seems to have finished developing manned aircrafts and instead concentrates to become a drone manufacturer.

Budget cuts in European defence systems since the end of the Cold War and the growing costs of weapons have rendered it increasingly difficult for European countries to develop and produce their own systems. This situation has remained unchanged until today and is likely going to continue. In the past, some analysts have defended the political and economic interest of the U.S. monopoly on production and sales of weapons by arguing that "from a purely economic point of view, the U.S. obviously has an advantage in terms of arms production. They have a large

[16] With regards to arms procurements this also poses a problem of independence for those close allies, which (like France) have an own aeronautic industry and want to keep a relative autonomy for the procurement of equipments for own armed forces.

[17] The MTCR is an informal and voluntary political agreement among 33 countries to control the proliferation of unmanned rocket and aerodynamic systems capable of delivering weapons of mass destruction (see U.S. Department of Defense 2009: 39).

domestic market for weapons, and their research capacity in terms of development and production cannot be equalled" (Kapstein 1994: 16). European countries would therefore have every interest in "abandoning their inefficient arms industry, freeing up resources for more productive needs" (Ibid. 1994: 18). "[E]ven protected under the cover of national security, [these inefficient industries] are often supported thanks to a special interest argument" (Ibid.).

The relevance of developing and producing weapons on a national basis is now again called into question, while the resources allocated for defence are once more the target of likely budgetary cuts. However, the "value for money" argument brandished by the British authorities to justify their choice of arms purchases tends sometimes to view purchases of equipment as purely off the shelf – American, but not only. In economically tough times "Made in the UK" or "Made in France" equipment purchases are perceived as support for costly industries, while equipment, much needed by soldiers committed in Afghanistan and Iraq, is sorely lacking (Page 2009).

In economic terms, the maximisation of security production for a state comes from acquisition choices between the national production of weapons necessary for national security, and the import of these weapons from allies or friendly countries. Most often, the arms policy derives from a mixture of these two extremes. This choice also arises from a defence posture, in particular the coalition policy held by the country in question. Applied to the case of NATO and European arms producing countries, the basic issue remains the reliability of the transatlantic relationship and particularly American engagement vis-à-vis Europe: A "risk of abandonment on the one hand and entrapment on the other" (Kapstein 2002: 142).

Drones are shuffling the cards: admittedly, the US is far ahead of its competitors. But Israel is already the second major UAV manufacturer, because of its experience in this field since the 1980s. European countries have lost time with their slow understanding that they need to participate in the race. France for instance has tried to develop an indigenous UAV, based on the Israeli Heron-TP, but the program suffered a 5-year delay. French Minister of Defense Gérard Longuet just decided, after 3 years of procrastination, that Dassault's project in cooperation with BAe Systems would be French choice, and not an off-the-shelf procurement of American MALE UAVs (which was the choice favoured by the French Air Force) or the other EADS-led European Talarion (Trévidic 2011). Many European countries are striving to develop their own indigenous UAV program: for Germany, drones are clearly identified as the future of the aeronautic industry – a development that could allow Germany to retake a leading position lost after the Second World War and leave "Aviation 1.0" to other European countries (Grozel and Moulard 2008: 397). In fact, it could be far easier for a new contender to begin with drones, as the core value of UAVs is not primarily the platform, something quite simple to develop (particularly in the case of tactical drones), but its payload. And as this payload consists mainly of electronic devices (sensors), R&D may focus on dual-use developments that allow are already in use in civilian electronics.

European countries in particular must determine those crucial weapons for which a high technological level must be retained, from those which do not need an "excess of technology" which would be harmful to their hardiness and the optimisation of their use. Without a doubt, drones belong in the first category, because their added value is contained in their on-board sensors and data transmission capabilities. It would be inadvisable for European countries to stand apart from innovations coming from drones (Ranquet 2009/10: 65–70).

Conclusion: A Question of Long-Term Autonomy for European Countries

Drones will be at the heart of military developments (including updated doctrines) in the next decades on the condition of parallel technological innovations in the field of robotics. They will also be at the heart of doctrinal debates about Air Power – reflecting the learned lessons in Afghanistan and Iraq for the preparation of potential future conflicts.

Developing indigenous drones and trying to match US capabilities is a difficult path to follow, even for European countries, who strive to maintain their technological level in order to follow the technological course of their major ally. European countries will also be confronted with a growing competition from other new entrants on the drones market: at the beginning this will be limited mainly to smaller tactical drones, but later also account for larger and more technology-intensive drones.

Growth in the European aviation industry has been achieved with support from those European countries most engaged in supporting national – and more recently European – military capabilities and manufacturers. The political will of European countries has been a deciding factor in the achievements of the last 20 years, such as the emergence of an autonomous space industry, the creation of a civil aviation company (Airbus, which was able to break up the American domination of the aircraft market) and the creation of national and transnational European industry groups such as EADS, Thales, BAe Systems and Finmeccanica, which are positioned with sufficient spread to challenge US domination of the defence industry (Clouet and Nardon 2010).

All European industry actors in the sector have grasped the importance of drones for the future of the aviation industry. They are now looking to position themselves in the drones market.[18] There are, however, three risks:

[18] Considering only MALE UAVs and UCAVs in Europe: Dassault, partnered with Saab and other European manufacturers, is developing a UCAV demonstrator called Neuron and is also looking to position itself in the MALE drones market with the SDM (System of MALE drone): the sensor was developed in cooperation with Thales and Indra, on a Heron platform offered by IAI. BAE Systems has its own MALE drone programme Mantis and is now beginning to develop a Franco-British MALE UAV on this basis. Finmeccanica is developing an Italian drone Molynx. EADS is developing the "Advanced UAV" drone Talarion, working with Thales and Indra for the on-board radar; this drone has been the subject of a €60 million risk assessment study financed in tripartite by Germany, France and Spain.

- European efforts may lead to competing national programmes;
- The European market for drones could remain fragmented, leading to micro-series of drones with similar characteristics, but with an exorbitant cost per unit when compared with American or Israeli products; and
- Developments may lead to intra-European fratricide competition for export markets.

The long-term industrial challenge is the survival of European R&D offices and other related sections of the European defence and aeronautic industry, because the development programmes of military drones condition the development of connected industrial technology capabilities[19] (standardization and spare parts logistics, C4I, robotics, artificial intelligence[20]). If Europe misses the train, "it will lose contact with one of the most dynamic defence and aerospace markets of the 21st century" (Heyward 2010: 67) and other military and industrial powers like China and India will not wait.

Whatever choices European countries may make on the future of their drone systems, the European dimension must be central, not only on a symbolic level, but also for avoiding duplication and a scattering of efforts, and for strengthening R&D and production capabilities in defence and aviation on a European scale. These decisions will be tantamount to Europe's role as an influential military and industrial power in the competitions of the 21st century.

References

Bolkcom, C. (2006, June 5). Military suppression of enemy air defenses (SEAD): Assessing future needs. Congressional Research Service, RS21141.

Boutherin, G. (2010). Puissance aérospatiale et multidimensionnalité du champ de bataille. Quelques éléments sur les engagements de demain. *Air and Space Power Journal Afrique & Francophonie, 1*(4), 4–28. Winter 2010.

Brustlein, C. (2011, July). Toward the end of force projection? I. The anti-access threat. *Focus stratégique*, 20 bis.

Center for Strategic and International Studies, Defense-Industrial Initiatives Group. (2009, October 15). Unmanned aircraft systems, 2010–2050: Implications for the industrial base. *CSIS Current Issues, 14*.

Clouet, L.-M. (2011). La prolifération des technologies aérospatiales russes et chinoises: Enjeux militaires, technologiques et industriels. In G. Boutherin & C. Grand (Eds.), *Envol vers 2025: Réflexions prospectives sur la puissance aérospatiale*. Paris: La documentation française.

Clouet, L.-M., & Nardon, L. MALE drones: Europe's options?. Note de l'Ifri, http://ifri.org/downloads/notecerfaespacedronesgb.pdf. Accessed July 2010.

Cohen, E. (1994). The US Mystique of air power. *Foreign Affairs, 73*(1), 109–124.

[19] See notably Center for Strategic and International Studies 2009.

[20] The integration of drones into air space presupposes the development of powerful artificial intelligence capacities, in particular for the "sense and avoid" "systems" intended to avoid in flight collisions. Such systems are currently on the agenda of the European Defense Agency.

Conference on "MALE drones: Challenges and European perspectives", 7 April 2010 at Paris: Ifri.
Congressional Budget Office. (2011, June). Policy options for unmanned aircraft systems. Washington, DC.
Coquet, P. (2008, June). La notion de partage capacitaire en question. *Focus stratégique*, 8, Ifri.
Curran, M. (Summer 2005). UAVs: A critical multiplier of current and future forces. RUSI Defence Systems, Royal United Services Institute.
de Durand, E. (2003/2). "Révolution dans les affaires militaires" "Révolution"ou "transformation"?. *Hérodote, 109*, 57–70.
de Durand, E. (2004/3). Le retour de la puissance aérienne. *Hérodote, 114*, 17–34.
Desportes, V. (2009). Armées: 'Technologisme' ou 'juste technologie'? ["Armies: 'technologism' or 'just technology'?"]. *Politique étrangère, 74*(2), 403–418.
Drew, C. (2010, January 11). Military is awash in data from drones. *New York Times.*
Gorman, S., Dreazen, Y. J., & Cole, A. (2009, December 17). Insurgents Hack U.S. Drones. *Wall Street Journal.* http://online.wsj.com/article/SB126102247889095011.html (consulted 17 July 2011).
Grozel, M., & Moulard, G. (2008). *Drones, mystérieux robots volants. Les yeux et le feu du XXIe siècle.* Paris: Lavauzelle.
Heyward, K. (2010, June). Unmanned aerial systems: A challenge to European industry?. *RUSI Defence Systems*, Royal United Services Institute.
Hoffmann, M., & Weisberger, M. (2011, May 16). New UAV roles in DoD 30-year air plan. *DefenseNews, 26*(19).
International Institute for Strategic Studies. (2009, May). The drones of war, *IISS Strategic Comments*, 15(04).
Kapstein, E. B. (1994). America's arms-trade monopoly: Lagging sales will starve lesser suppliers. *Foreign Affairs, 73*(3), 13–19. May–June.
Kapstein, E. B. (2002). Allies and armaments. *Survival, 44*(2), 141–155. Summer.
Keeney, T., & Cohen E. (Ed.). (1993). Gulf war air power survey (GWAPS) Summary Report. Washington, DC: Government Printing Office.
Kimmey, P. (2010, February 18). Ravens, reapers, and robots: Unmanned vehicles and the military. Center for Strategic and International Studies (consulted 7 June 2011).
Lambeth, B. S. (2000). *The transformation of American air power.* Ithaca: Cornel University Press.
Luttwak, E. N. (2007). Les armements peuvent-ils devenir abordables? ["Can armaments become affordable?"]. *Politique étrangère, 72*(4), 773.
Page, L. (2009, February). Today's question: What is value-for-money in defense acquisition?". In *The meaning of value for money, RUSI Defence Systems*, London: RUSI.
Paloméros, J.-P., & Joly, F. (2009, June 9). Drones en Afghanistan, la nécessaire complémentarité des vecteurs, Défense nationale et sécurité collective. 720.
Quintana, E. Unmanned systems: Confusing ethics. RUSI commentary. http://www.rusi.org/analysis/commentary/ref:C4DAEB5DD10A7F/ (consulted July 15 2011).
Ranquet, B. (2009). Défense de la technologie: Rendre à la technologie son importance dans le domaine militaire ["Defence of technology: Give the technology back its importance in military field"]. *Revue internationale et stratégique, 76*, 65–70. winter 2009–2010.
Smith, R. (2007). *The utility of force: The art of war in modern world.* New York: Knopf.
Trévidic, B. (juillet 2011). Drones: la France choisit Dassault au détriment d'EADS. *Les échos,* 22–23.
U.S. Department of Defense. (2009). FY2009–2034 Unmanned Systems Integrated Roadmap, Washington, D.C, www.acq.osd.mil/psa/docs/UMSIntegratedRoadmap2009.pdf
Vandewalle, Y., & Viollet, J.-C. (2009, December). Rapport d'information par la Commission de la Défense nationale et des Forces armées sur les drones, [Parliamentary report on UAVs by the National Defence and Armed Forces Commission]. 2127, Paris: Assemblée nationale.
Wan, W., & Finn, P. (2011, July 4). Global race on to match U.S. drone capabilities. *The Washington Post.*

Weiner, S. L. (2009). Evolution in the post-cold war air force: Technology, doctrine, and bureaucratic politics. In H. M. Sapolsky, B. H. Friedman, & B. R. Green (Eds.), *US military innovation since the cold war*. London/New York: Routledge.

Zucchino, D. (2010, February 21). Drone pilots have a front-row seat on war, from half a world away. *Los Angeles Times*.

Part III
Power and International Political Economy

Chapter 11
The International Monetary System: Diffusion and Ambiguity

Benjamin J. Cohen

Ample evidence exists to suggest that the distribution of power in international monetary affairs is changing. But where does monetary power now reside, and what are the implications for governance of the international monetary system? On these questions, uncertainty reigns. The aim of this essay is to shed some new light on the dynamics of power and rule setting in global finance today.

I will begin with a brief discussion of the meaning of power in international monetary relations, distinguishing between two critical dimensions of monetary power, autonomy and influence. The evolution of international monetary power in recent decades will then be examined. Major developments have dramatically shifted the distribution of power in the system. Many have noted that power is now more widely diffused, both among states and between states and societal actors. Finance is no longer dominated by a few national governments at the apex of the global order. Less frequently remarked is the fact that the diffusion of power has been mainly in the dimension of autonomy, rather than influence – a point of critical importance. While more actors have gained a degree of insulation from outside pressures, few as yet are able to exercise greater authority to shape events or outcomes. Leadership in the system thus has been dispersed rather than relocated – a pattern of change in the geopolitics of finance that might be called *leaderless* diffusion.

A pattern of leaderless diffusion generates greater ambiguity in prevailing governance structures. Rule setting in monetary relations increasingly relies not on negotiations among a few powerful states but, rather, on the evolution of custom and usage among growing numbers of autonomous agents – regular patterns of behavior that develop from long-standing practice. Impacts on governance structures can be seen at two levels: the individual state and the global system. At the state level, the dispersion of power compels governments to rethink their commitment to national monetary sovereignty. At the systemic level, it compounds

This paper first appeared in: *International Affairs:* Vol. 84, No. 3 (2008).

E. Fels et al. (eds.), *Power in the 21st Century*, Global Power Shift,
DOI 10.1007/978-3-642-25082-8_11, © Springer-Verlag Berlin Heidelberg 2012

the difficulties of bargaining on monetary issues. More and more, formal rules are being superceded by informal norms that emerge, like common law, not from legislation or statutes but from everyday conduct and social convention.

Monetary Power

For the purposes of this essay, the international monetary system may be understood to encompass all the main features of monetary relations across national frontiers – the processes and institutions of financial intermediation (mobilization of savings and allocation of credit) as well as the creation and management of money itself. As Susan Strange once wrote: 'The financial structure really has two inseparable aspects. It comprises not just the structures of the political economy through which credit is created but also the monetary system or systems which determine the relative values of the different moneys in which credit is denominated' (Strange 1994:90). Both aspects are influenced by the distribution of power among actors.

And what do we mean by power in monetary relations? Briefly summarizing an argument that I have developed at greater length elsewhere (Cohen 2006), I suggest that international monetary power may be understood to comprise two critical dimensions, autonomy and influence. More familiar is the dimension of *influence*, defined as the ability to shape events or outcomes. In operational terms, this dimension naturally equates with a capacity to control the behavior of actors – 'letting others have your way,' as diplomacy has jokingly been defined. An actor, in this sense, is powerful to the extent that it can effectively pressure or coerce others; in short, to the extent that it can exercise leverage or managerial authority. As a dimension of power, influence is the essential *sine qua non* of systemic leadership.

The second dimension, autonomy, corresponds to the dictionary definition of power as a capacity for action. An actor is also powerful to the extent that it is able to exercise operational independence – to act freely, insulated from outside pressure. In this sense, power does not mean influencing others; rather, it means not allowing others to influence you – others letting *you* have your way.

The distinction between the two dimensions of power is critical. Both are based in social relationships and can be observed in behavioral terms; the two are also unavoidably interrelated. But they are not of equal importance. Logically, power begins with autonomy. Influence is best thought of as functionally derivative – inconceivable in practical terms without first attaining and sustaining a relatively high degree of operational independence. First and foremost, actors must be free to pursue their goals without outside constraint. Only then will an actor be in a position, *in addition*, to exercise authority elsewhere. Autonomy may not be *sufficient* to ensure a degree of influence, but it is manifestly *necessary*. It is possible to think of autonomy without influence; it is impossible to think of influence without autonomy.

For state actors in the monetary system, the key to autonomy lies in the uncertain distribution of the burden of adjustment to external imbalances. National economies are inescapably linked through the balance of payments – the flows of money generated by international trade and investment. One country's surplus is another country's deficit. The risk of unsustainable disequilibrium represents a persistent threat to policy independence. Excessive imbalances generate mutual pressures to adjust, which can be costly in both economic and political terms. Deficit economies may be forced to curtail domestic spending or devalue their currencies, at the expense of growth and jobs; surplus economies may experience unwanted inflation or an upward push on their exchange rates, which can threaten international competitiveness. No government likes being compelled to compromise key policy goals for the sake of restoring external balance. All, if given a choice, would prefer instead to see others make the necessary sacrifices. For states, therefore, the foundation of monetary power is the capacity to avoid the burden of adjustment required by payments imbalance.

The capacity to avoid the burden of adjustment is fundamentally dual in nature, subdividing into what I have characterized as the two 'hands' of monetary power (Cohen 2006). These are the power to delay and the power to deflect, each corresponding to one of two different kinds of adjustment burden. One burden is the continuing cost of adjustment, defined as the cost of the new payments equilibrium prevailing after all change has occurred. The power to delay is the capacity to avoid the continuing cost of adjustment by *postponing* the process of adjustment. The other burden is the transitional cost of adjustment, defined as the cost of the change itself. Where the process of adjustment cannot be put off, the power to deflect represents the capacity to avoid the transitional cost of adjustment by *diverting* as much as possible of that cost to others. The power to delay is largely a function of a country's international liquidity position relative to others, comprising both owned reserves and borrowing capacity. Especially advantaged are the issuers of currencies that are widely used by others as a reserve asset, since issuers can thus finance deficits simply by printing up more of their own money. The power to deflect, by contrast, has its source in more fundamental structural variables that determine an economy's relative degree of openness and adaptability.

For societal actors in the monetary system, the key to autonomy lies in the uncertain relationship between relevant market domains and legal jurisdictions. In an increasingly globalized world, the reach of financial markets is persistently growing. Yet political authority remains rooted in individual states, each in principle sovereign within its own territorial frontiers. Hence a disjuncture prevails between market domains and legal jurisdictions that creates ample room for opportunistic behavior by enterprises or private individuals. The very policy independence that is so prized by governments tends to create differences in market constraints and incentives that may well be exploited to advantage. For societal actors, the foundation of monetary power is the ability to navigate successfully in these interstices between political regimes.

Autonomy, in turn, is the key to influence. Because monetary relations are inherently reciprocal, a potential for leverage is automatically created whenever operational independence is attained. The question is: Will that potential be actualized? Two modes are possible in the exercise of monetary influence: passive and active. Autonomy translates into influence in the accepted sense of the term – a dimension of power aiming to shape the actions of others – only when the capacity for control is deliberately activated.

The requirement of actualization is often overlooked. The potential for leverage that derives automatically from autonomy – the passive mode of influence – is another way of describing what economists call externalities. At best, it represents a contingent aspect of power, exerted without design and with impacts that tend to be dispersed and undirected. Only when the potential for leverage is put to use with self-conscious intent do we approach the more common understanding of influence: the active mode, involving sharper focus in terms of who is targeted and toward what end. Unlike the passive mode, the active mode implies a 'purposeful act.' Both modes begin with monetary autonomy as a basic and necessary condition, and in both cases other actors may feel compelled to comply. But in the passive mode externalities are incidental and unpremeditated, whereas in the active mode pressure is applied directly and deliberately. The active mode, in effect, politicizes relationships, aiming to translate passive influence into practical control through the instrumental use of power. From a political economy point of view, as we shall see, the difference between the two modes is critical.

Diffusion

For both states and societal actors, the distribution of monetary power has shifted dramatically in recent decades. Not long ago the global system was dominated by a small handful of national governments, led first and foremost by the United States. Most countries felt they had little choice but to play by rules laid down by America and, to a lesser extent, its partners in the Group of Seven (G7); markets operated within strict limits established and maintained by states. Today, by contrast, power has become more widely diffused, both among governments and between governments and market agents. The diffusion of power, however, has been mainly in the dimension of autonomy, rather than influence – a pattern of leaderless diffusion in financial geopolitics. The days of concentrated power in a largely state-centric system are now over.

Principally responsible are three major developments: (1) the creation of the euro; (2) the widening of global payments imbalances; and (3) the globalization of financial markets. Each of these developments has effectively added to the population of actors with a significant degree of autonomy in monetary affairs.

The Euro

Most obvious is the creation of the euro, dating from 1999, which was always expected to have a major impact on the geopolitics of finance. Even without the participation of Britain and some other European Union (EU) members, Europe's Economic and Monetary Union (EMU) was destined to become one of the largest economic units in the world, rivaling even the United States in terms of output and share of foreign trade. A shift in the balance of power across the Atlantic thus seemed inevitable. Europe's new money, building on the widespread popularity of Germany's old Deutschmark (DM), would pose a serious threat to the predominance of America's greenback as an international currency. The euro area – Euroland, as some call it – was bound to become a major player on the monetary stage. Typical was the view of Robert Mundell, a Nobel laureate in economics, who expressed no doubt that EMU would 'challenge the status of the dollar and alter the power configuration of the system (Mundell 2000:57).

To a significant degree, those early expectations have been realized. A decade on, Europe's monetary power clearly has been enhanced. The euro has smoothly taken over the DM's place as the second most widely used currency in the world. Euroland itself has grown from 11 members to 15, with as many as a dozen or more countries set to join in future years. Some measure of power has indeed shifted across the Atlantic.

Europe's gains, however, have been mainly in the dimension of autonomy, rather than influence. Currency union has manifestly reduced the area's vulnerability to foreign-exchange shocks. With a single joint money replacing a plethora of national currencies, participants no longer have to fear the risk of exchange-rate disturbances inside Europe and, in combination, are now are better insulated against turmoil elsewhere. For a continent long plagued by currency instability, that is no small accomplishment. Moreover, with the widespread acceptability of the euro, EMU countries now enjoy a much improved international liquidity position. Deficits that previously required foreign currency may now be financed with Europe's own money, thus enhancing the group's power to delay. Operational independence plainly is greater now than it was before.

So far, though, Europe has conspicuously failed to convert its enhanced autonomy into a greater capacity for control in monetary affairs (Cohen 2008). Contrary to the predictions of many, the euro has yet to establish itself as a truly global currency, thus depriving participants of an instrument that might have been used to help shape behavior or outcomes. Nor has membership in EMU yet enabled European governments to play a more assertive role in world monetary forums such as the International Monetary Fund (IMF) or G7. Though freer now to pursue internal objectives without external constraint, Euroland has yet to actualize the potential for overt leverage that monetary union has created.

The euro's weaknesses as an international currency are by now familiar. The new money did start with many of the attributes necessary for competitive success, including a large economic base, unquestioned political stability, and an enviably low rate of inflation, all backed by a joint monetary authority, the European Central Bank (ECB), that is fully committed to preserving confidence in the currency's value. But as I have argued previously (Cohen 2003: 575–595), the euro is also hampered by several critical deficiencies, all structural in character, that dim its attractiveness as a rival to the greenback. These include limited cost-effectiveness, a serious anti-growth bias, and, most importantly, ambiguities at the heart of the monetary union's governance structure. Not surprisingly, therefore, experience to date has been underwhelming. Only in the EU's immediate neighborhood, where trade and financial ties are especially close, has the euro come to enjoy any special advantages as the natural heir to the DM. That is EMU's natural hinterland – 'the euro's turf,' as economist Charles Wyplosz (1999: 89) calls it. Elsewhere, Europe's money remains at a distinct disadvantage in trying to overcome the incumbency advantages of the already well established dollar.

Likewise, Euroland's weaknesses as a political actor are by now obvious. Joined together in EMU, one would have thought, European states would surely have more bargaining power than if each acted on its own. Europe's voice would be amplified on a broad range of macroeconomic issues, from policy coordination to crisis management. Yet here too experience to date has been underwhelming. In practice, membership in EMU has not enabled EU governments to play a more influential role in the IMF or other global forums, mainly because no one knows who, precisely, speaks for the group. Since no single body is formally designated to represent EMU in international discussions, the euro area's ability to project power on monetary matters is inherently constrained. Laments Fred Bergsten, a euro enthusiast, EMU 'still speaks with a multiplicity, even a cacophony, of voices... Hence it dissipates much of the potential for realizing a key international role' (Bergsten 2005: 33).

Overall, therefore, the power configuration of the system has been altered far less than Mundell or others had anticipated. The Europeans clearly are now better placed to resist external pressures. Their collective autonomy has been enhanced. But Europe is still a long way from exercising the kind of leverage that monetary union might have been expected to give it. Influence has not been effectively actualized. Monetary power, on balance, has been dispersed rather than relocated from one side of the Atlantic to the other.

Global Imbalances

A second major development in recent years has been the emergence of unprecedented global imbalances – most particularly, a wide gap in the balance of payments of the United States, matched by counterpart surpluses elsewhere, particularly in East Asia and among energy-exporting nations. (Notably missing is Euroland, which has maintained a rough balance in its external accounts.) In 2006 America's deficit swelled past $850 billion, equivalent to some 6.5% of U.S. gross domestic product (GDP). Although now shrinking a bit, the shortfall continues to add to an already record level of foreign debt. Net of assets abroad, US liabilities reached $2.6 at end-2006, equal to roughly a fifth of GDP. Correspondingly, reserve holdings of dollars in surplus countries have soared, rising above $3 trillion by 2006. For many, imbalances on this scale seem certain to alter the balance of monetary power between the United States and the larger surplus countries. The only question is: How much?

In terms of the autonomy dimension of power, the impact is obvious. With their vastly improved international liquidity positions, surplus countries are now much better placed to postpone the process of adjustment when they wish. Their power to delay is clearly enhanced. A decade ago, when financial crisis hit East Asia, governments in the region – under intense pressure from the United States and the IMF – felt they had little choice but to initiate radical economic reforms, backed by tight monetary and fiscal policies. Resentful of being forced to pay such a high transitional cost of adjustment, they were determined to insulate themselves as much as possible against similar pressures in the future. The result today is a greatly heightened capacity for operational independence.

Most notable is China, whose currency reserves have now passed the $1.4 trillion mark and continue to grow by as much as $20 billion each month. The Chinese have been the target of a determined campaign by the United States and others to allow a significant revaluation of their currency, the yuan, also known as the renminbi. Beijing, however, has stood firm, resisting all pleas. Since a well publicized switch from a dollar peg to a basket peg in mid-2005, the yuan has appreciated in small steps by little more than 15% – far short of what most observers think is needed to make a real dent in China's trade surplus. Plainly, the world's largest stockpile of reserves gives China more room for maneuver than it might otherwise enjoy.

But does enhanced autonomy translate into greater influence? Certainly there is an increase of influence in the passive mode. Simply by exercising their power to delay, surplus countries have placed more pressure on the United States to do something – or, at least, to *think* about doing something – about its deficits. But are we witnessing an increase of influence in the active, purposive mode? About that, the outlook is more ambiguous.

Indirectly, influence might be increased through the operations of the newly fashionable sovereign wealth funds that many surplus countries have created to earn better earnings on a portion of their reserves. Already there are more than 30 such funds controlling assets in excess of $2.5 trillion, a figure that could grow to as much as $15 trillion over the next decade. In principle, it is possible to imagine that at least some of these funds might be deployed strategically to gain a degree of leverage in recipient states. Investments might be carefully aimed toward institutions that are known to have privileged access to the corridors of governmental power – institutions like Citibank and Merrill Lynch in the United States, which in the midst of the recent credit crunch together attracted more than $20 billion from wealth funds in Asia and the Middle East. In practice, however, potential target states are not without means to monitor or limit politically risky investments within their borders. The balance of power has by no means tipped as much as it might appear.

Alternatively, influence might be increased directly through the use of newly acquired reserve stockpiles to threaten manipulation of the value or stability of a key currency like the dollar. There is nothing complicated about the option. Indeed, as Jonathan Kirshner reminds us, 'currency manipulation is the simplest instrument of monetary power and... can be used with varying degrees of intensity, ranging from mild signaling to the destabilization of national regimes' (1995:8). Yet the results could be devastating for a key-currency issuer like the United States. If any nation is in a position to use its newly acquired influence in this manner, it is China. At any time, Beijing could undermine America's money by dumping greenbacks on the world's currency exchanges or even simply by declining to add dollars to China's reserves in the future. Such threats would take little effort on China's part and could be carefully calibrated for maximum effect. The advantages for China are enormous.

But there are also disadvantages, as the Chinese themselves well understand. Beijing's dollar hoard could hardly be sold all at once. Hence any depreciation of the greenback would impose costs on China as well, in the form of capital losses on its remaining holdings. Dollar reserves today are equal to about one-third of China's GDP. For every 10% depreciation of the greenback, therefore, China would lose something in excess of 3% of GDP – no small amount. In addition, dollar depreciation would greatly erode the competitiveness of the exports that are so vital to China's economic growth. In reality, currency manipulation is a two-edged sword that could end up doing China far more harm than good – a kind of 'nuclear option,' to be used only *in extremis*.

Hence here too it is not at all clear that the balance of monetary power has tipped as much in favor of China and other surplus countries as it might appear. Indeed, now that dollar holdings have grown so large, it actually makes more sense for China and others to support – rather than threaten – the greenback, whether they like it or not, in order to avert a doomsday scenario. Some see this as nothing more than enlightened self-interest. Others see it as more akin to the notorious balance of terror that existed between the nuclear powers during the Cold War – a 'balance of financial terror,' as former US Treasury Secretary Lawrence Summers (Summers 2004) has described it. Neither side wants to risk a MAD (mutually assured destruction) outcome.

In short, global imbalances too have caused a shift in the balance of monetary power, but as in the case of EMU, mainly in the dimension of autonomy. Reserve accumulations have not clearly amplified the influence, whether direct or indirect, of the large surplus countries. Here too, power has been largely dispersed rather than relocated.

Financial Globalization

Finally, there is the change in the international monetary environment that has been wrought by the globalization of financial markets. The story is familiar. Where once most financial markets were firmly controlled at the national level and insulated from one another, today across much of the globe barriers to the movement of money have been greatly reduced or effectively eliminated, resulting in a scale of financial flows unequaled since the glory days of the nineteenth-century gold standard. One consequence, observers agree, is a distinct shift in the balance of power between states and societal actors. By promoting capital mobility, financial globalization enhances the authority of market agents at the expense of sovereign governments.

Key to the shift is the wider range of options that comes to privileged elements of the private sector with the integration of financial markets: a marked increase of autonomy for societal actors in a position to take advantage of the opportunities now afforded them. In effect, financial globalization means more degrees of freedom for selected individuals and enterprises – more room for maneuver in response to actual or potential decisions of governments. Higher taxes or regulation may be evaded by moving investment funds offshore; tighter monetary policies may be circumvented by accessing external sources of finance. Ultimately, it means a fading of the strict dividing lines between separate national moneys, as weaker domestic currencies are traded in for more attractive foreign moneys like the dollar or euro – a phenomenon that I have referred to previously as the new geography of money (Cohen 1998). No longer, in many places, are societal actors restricted to a single currency, their own domestic money, as they go about their business. Now they have a choice in what amounts to a growing competition among currencies. The functional domain of each money no longer corresponds precisely with the formal jurisdiction of its issuing authority. Currencies have become increasingly *deterritorialized*, their circulation determined not by law or politics but by the preferences of market agents.

Mirroring the increased autonomy of societal actors, in turn, is a loss of some measure of operational independence by states. Financial globalization has forced governments into a trade-off between exchange-rate stability and monetary-policy autonomy. Some still prioritize the external value of their currency, resigning themselves to a loss of control over domestic monetary aggregates and interest rates. Many others have moved toward some form of inflation targeting, replacing exchange-rate targeting as a monetary rule. Either way, state authority is compromised. The essence of the challenge has been captured by David Andrews in what he calls the capital mobility hypothesis: 'The degree of international capital mobility systematically constrains state behavior by rewarding some actions and punishing others... Consequently, the nature of the choice set available to states... becomes more constricted' (Andrews 1994). Governments are compelled to tailor their policies, at least in part, to what is needed to avoid provoking massive or sudden financial movements. Market agents gain leverage in relation to public officials.

Here again, though, we must note that the influence gained is largely passive rather than active. Few knowledgeable observers of the decentralized decision processes of the marketplace would argue that the pressures now exerted on governments are somehow designed with conscious political intent. An informal kind of veto over state behavior has emerged. But it is a power that is exercised incidentally, through market processes, rather than directly in pursuit of a formal policy agenda. State autonomy is threatened, but not from a design that is purposive or hostile. Here too the pattern is essentially one of a leaderless diffusion of power.

Ambiguity

All these developments, in turn, are having a profound impact on governance structures in the monetary system. The greater the population of actors with a significant degree of autonomy in monetary affairs, the harder it is to reach any sort of consensus on critical questions. By definition, autonomous agents can more easily resist pressures to conform. Hence a greater degree of ambiguity is introduced into the way the system is run. Increasingly, structures of governance are being remolded in an evolutionary fashion through the gradual cumulation of custom and usage. Formal rules (specific prescriptions or proscriptions for behavior) are being superceded by more informal norms (broad standards of behavior defined in terms of rights and obligations), in a manner not unlike that of English common law – unwritten law (*lex non scripta*) in lieu of written or statute law (*lex scripta*).

The impact on governance structures can be seen at two levels: the individual state and the global system. At the state level, the dispersion of power compels governments to rethink their historical commitment to national monetary sovereignty. At the systemic level, it compounds the difficulties of bargaining on international monetary issues.

National Sovereignty

Tradition has long assigned the primary role in monetary governance to the sovereign state. As a matter of practice, governments have been assumed to enjoy a natural right of monopoly control over the issue and management of money within their borders. Ever since the seventeenth-century Peace of Westphalia, the conventions of standard political geography have celebrated the role of the nation-state, absolutely supreme within its own territory, as the basic unit of world politics. By the nineteenth century, the norm of national monetary sovereignty had become an integral part of the global governance structure. Just as political space was conceived in terms of those fixed and mutually exclusive entities we call states, currency spaces came to be identified with the separate sovereign jurisdictions where each money originated. With few exceptions, each state was expected to maintain its own exclusive territorial currency. I have labeled this the Westphalian model of monetary geography (Cohen 1998).

Though never written down anywhere, the norm of monetary sovereignty was of such long standing that by the mid-to-late twentieth century it had taken on the legitimacy of a formal rule. Today, however, that old tradition has been shaken by the new growth of competition among currencies across national borders, resulting from financial globalization. As currencies become increasingly deterritorialized, governments find themselves driven to reconsider their historical attachment to the

Westphalian model. The monetary sovereignty norm is gradually being eroded by changes of practice and circumstance.

National monetary sovereignty clearly does have its advantages, including the privilege of seigniorage (the ability to finance public spending via money creation) and the power to manage monetary conditions. But in a world where growing numbers of societal actors can now exercise choice among diverse currencies, there are also distinct disadvantages. Most notable is the need to prioritize the goal of preserving market confidence in the value and usability of the nation's money – the 'confidence game,' to recall Paul Krugman's (Krugman 1998) name for it. The label is ironic because, as in any con game, the effort to play may prove an exercise in futility.

The dilemma is simple. To preserve confidence in its currency, a government must above all make a credible commitment to 'sound' macroeconomic management, meaning a strong emphasis on low inflation and financial stability. Monetary policy must not appear to be overused for expansionary purposes; fiscal policy must not be allowed to finance deficits via the printing press. Such policy discipline – what Krugman (Krugman 2001) calls 'root-canal economics' – is of course by no means undesirable, as any victim of past government excesses can attest. High inflation and financial instability can destroy savings, distort incentives, and suppress productive investment. Conversely, if sustained, 'sound' management policies may indeed successfully enhance a currency's reputation. However, there is also a distinct downside. Root-canal economics can be extremely costly in terms of lost output or higher unemployment, owing to structural deficiencies that may inhibit an economy's ability to adjust to a constrained policy environment. Experience demonstrates that tight monetary and fiscal policies can in fact turn into dismal austerity policies, depressing growth for a prolonged period of time.

Faced with this dilemma, governments have three choices. One is to continue playing the confidence game, whatever the cost. The other two choices would replace a country's national currency with a *regional* money of some kind (Cohen 2004). Currency regionalization occurs when two or more states formally share a single money or equivalent. In one variant of regionalization, countries can agree to merge their separate currencies into a new joint money, as members of EMU have done with the euro. This is *currency unification*, a strategy of 'horizontal' regionalization. Alternatively, any single country may unilaterally or by agreement replace its own currency with an already existing money of another, an approach typically described as full or formal *dollarization* ('vertical' regionalization). Both variants involve a delegation of traditional powers away from the individual state. Monetary sovereignty is either *pooled* in a partnership of some sort, shifting authority to a joint institution like the ECB, or else *surrendered* wholly or in part to a dominant foreign power such as the United States.

Already, under the pressure of currency competition, a number of governments have opted to abandon their traditional monetary sovereignty. In 2000, Ecuador adopted America's greenback as its exclusive legal tender, followed a year later by El Salvador. In effect, both chose to become monetary dependencies of the United States rather than fight on to sustain a money of their own. Others have established currency boards – a more limited form of vertical regionalization – or have talked seriously about a monetary union of some kind. Tentative plans have already been drawn up for currency unification in West Africa and in the Gulf region of the Middle East and are under discussion elsewhere. In the opinion of many informed observers, it is only a matter of time before the universe of moneys will be radically shrunk (Beddoes 1999).

In reality, of course, it is easier to talk about currency regionalization than actually to do something about it. Giving up a national currency is not easy. As I have argued elsewhere (Cohen 2004), attachments to the tradition of monetary sovereignty remain strong in most parts of the world however costly the confidence game may be. But there is no question that for many governments, the stark choice must now be faced. The shift in the balance of power between states and societal actors has unquestionably undermined the foundations of the traditional Westphalian model. As a result, a previously clear norm is now increasingly clouded with uncertainty.

International Bargaining

Much the same is happening at the systemic level, where prevailing governance structures have also been brought into question by ongoing shifts in the distribution of power. As a corollary of the traditional norm of monetary sovereignty at the state level, governments have long relied on formal or informal negotiations among themselves to lay down the rules of the game at the systemic level. As far back as the Genoa conference of 1922, the dynamics of rule setting have centered on hard-won bargains struck among a few leading states with the capacity to cajole or coerce others into agreement. That was the scenario at the Bretton Woods conference of 1944, which was dominated by the United States and Britain. The pattern could also be seen in the negotiations that led up to the earliest amendments of the charter of the IMF, providing for the creation of special drawing rights (negotiated in the 1960s by the Group of Ten) and ratifying a new system of flexible exchange rates (mainly the product of a 1975 agreement between France and the United States). In this respect, the geopolitics of finance were no different from other issues in geopolitics, where power has always played a pivotal role.

But that was before so many more states gained a degree of autonomy in monetary affairs. The more governments feel insulated from outside pressure, the less likely it is that they will meekly accept the *diktat* of an inner circle of self-appointed leaders. Bargains at the top will not be treated with the same respect as in the past. Existing or proposed new rules will no longer enjoy the same degree of legitimacy among states further down the hierarchy, unless these states too are made part of the decision process.

A diffusion of monetary power is nothing new, of course. The 1960s and 1970s, when US hegemony seemed to be in decline, also saw the emergence of new powers in monetary affairs. Then too there was an increase of ambiguity in governance structures, especially after the breakdown of the Bretton-Woods par value system in 1971–1973. But even after those troubled decades the inner circle remained remarkably small, limited essentially to the United States and its partners in the G7 – as evident, for example, in the celebrated Plaza and Louvre accords of the 1980s and the management of financial crises in Mexico and East Asia in the 1990s. What is distinctive about today, by contrast, is the sheer number of states that now feel entitled to a seat at the high table.

That, of course, explains why recent years have seen a proliferation of new forums designed to widen participation in global discussions. A turning point came after the Asian crisis, when broad new interest was sparked in reform of what soon came to be called the 'international financial architecture.' One result was the Group of 20 finance ministers' and central-bank governors' forum (G20), which was created in 1999 and now meets annually to discuss a range of economic and monetary issues. In addition to representatives of the G7 and European Union, the G20 brings to the table some dozen 'systemically significant economies,' including Argentina, Australia, Brazil, China, India, Indonesia, Korea, Mexico, Russia, Saudi Arabia, South Africa, and Turkey. A second initiative was the Financial Stability Forum (FSF), also dating from 1999, which is charged with improving the functioning of financial markets and a reduction of systemic risk. Convened twice a year, the FSF includes some 43 members representing 26 states and a variety of international financial institutions and supervisory bodies. Forums like the G20 and FSF are obviously intended to enhance the legitimacy of current reform efforts.

The same concerns also explain why so much attention is now being paid to the allocation of quotas at the IMF, which *inter alia* determine the distribution of voting power among the Fund's members. Many advanced economies – including especially the members of the European Union – appear to be over-represented in the Fund's voting system, while some of the larger emerging-market economies are clearly under-represented. Past quota adjustments, it is generally agreed, simply have not kept up with the transformation of the world economy. In 2006, IMF governors agreed it was time to implement a new 'simpler and more transparent' formula to guide adjustments in the future, generating a plethora of competing proposals (Cooper and Truman 2007). To date, consensus on any single approach has proved elusive – not at all surprising given the zero-sum nature of the game. Any gain of voting shares for some countries must necessarily come at the expense of others. But some reallocation of quotas clearly does seem to be in the cards.

Wider participation, however, will not make rule setting any easier. Quite the contrary, in fact. The efficiency of decision making obviously suffers as more actors are given a part in the process. According to standard organization theory, the difficulties of negotiation actually increase exponentially, not just in proportion, with the number of parties involved. The more voices there are at the table, the greater is the temptation to smooth over unresolved differences with artful compromises and the deliberate obfuscations of classic diplomatic language. Clarity is sacrificed for the sake of avoiding the appearance of discord. Much room is left for creative interpretation.

Worse, even when some measure of agreement is achieved, little can be done about it. Apart from the IMF, none of the existing forums have any powers of direct enforcement. Bodies like the G7, G20, and FSF are essentially regularized procedures for consultation – little more than talking shops. Some advantage may be gained from the exchange of information and viewpoints that is facilitated. But wider participation, per se, does nothing to ensure that newly autonomous actors will feel obliged to compromise some part of their operational independence if it does not suit their interests. And even the enforcement powers of the IMF are limited today to just the poorest countries in the system, which remain the organization's only regular clients. The Fund's leverage rests largely on the conditions it may attach to its lending. But richer states, with their access to the global financial markets, no longer need the IMF for financing. Hence many are free to ignore Fund pronouncements, whatever the allocation of member quotas.

A case in point is provided by the Fund's recent effort to tighten up its rules for the management of exchange rates by member governments – the first revision since 1977 of the principles for what is called bilateral surveillance of currency practices (International Monetary Fund 2007). Central to the revision is a new injunction urging states to avoid practices that cause 'external instability.' But there is little that the Fund can do if nations choose to resist. Some countries, like China (the obvious target of the new injunction), continue to maintain formal pegs that generate large trade imbalances. Others that have ostensibly abandoned pegging in favor of inflation targeting nonetheless intervene massively to manage their exchange rates, whatever the external consequences – a pattern of behavior known as "dirty" floating. The high reserve holdings generated by today's global imbalances make dirty floating feasible for many. Only governments that lack the requisite liquidity are susceptible to IMF blandishments.

Overall, therefore, the prospect is for growing ambiguity in the system's governance structures. Whether they are part of the bargaining process or not, newly autonomous states now have more leeway to follow their own instincts. Some will undoubtedly continue to play the confidence game, at whatever cost in terms of 'external stability.' Others may well prefer to pool or surrender their monetary sovereignty in some degree. In effect, many governments have been freed to make up their own rules as they go along through practice and the gradual cumulation of experience.

In time, of course, patterns of behavior that originate in self-interest may lead to shared expectations (inter-subjective understandings) and can eventually even become infused with normative significance. Often, what starts from a logic of consequences (a concern with material impacts) comes ultimately to rest on a logic of appropriateness (a concern with what is 'right'). That kind of evolutionary process, relying on the development of informal norms rather than formal rules, is a hallmark of English common law. Increasingly, it is becoming central to international monetary governance as well.

Conclusion

The dynamics of power and governance in global finance today are indeed changing. A leaderless diffusion of power is generating greater uncertainty about the underlying rules of the game. At the state level, governments increasingly question the need for a strictly national currency. At the systemic level, governance now relies more on custom and usage, rather than inter-governmental negotiation, to define standards of behavior.

Greater ambiguity is not necessarily a bad thing, especially if it allows states and societal actors to get along without undue friction. But it does also have distinct disadvantages that cannot be ignored. Governance plainly is less tidy when effectuated through social conventions rather than formal agreements. *Lex non scripta* is inherently more opaque than *lex scripta*. Hence a wider latitude is afforded actors for strategic maneuvers that could come at the expense of others. Outcomes may be neither as stable nor as equitable as we might prefer. Crises could become more frequent or difficult to manage if more governments feel free to do their own thing, discounting disruptive externalities. Burdens of adjustment could fall disproportionately on the weakest members of the system that have benefitted least from the leaderless diffusion of power.

Can anything be done to lessen such risks? Since states remain the basic unit of world politics, responsibility continues to reside with governments, which still have little choice but to try to resolve their differences through negotiation. What is needed, however, is a change of bargaining strategy to conform more comfortably to the new distribution of power. With autonomy spread more widely among actors, it is becoming increasingly fruitless to aim for specific prescriptions for behavior – what in biblical language might be called "thou-shalt" types of rules. More governments are now in a position simply to ignore detailed injunctions when they wish. But it is not impractical to aim for the reverse – general "thou-shalt-not" types of rules that set outer limits to what might be considered acceptable. Even the most insular governments are apt to recognize that there is a common interest in keeping potential externalities within bounds. If prevailing governance structures are to retain any practical influence at all, that is the direction in which the dynamics of rule setting must now move.

References

Andrews, D. M. (1994). Capital mobility and state autonomy: Toward a structural theory of international relations. *International Studies Quarterly, 38*(2), 193–218.

Beddoes, Z. M. (1999). From EMU to AMU? The case for regional currencies. *Foreign Affairs, 78* (4), 8–13.

Bergsten, C. F. (2005). The euro and the dollar: Toward a "finance G-2"? In A. Posen (Ed.), *The euro at five: Ready for a global role?* Washington, DC: Institute for International Economics.

Cohen, B. J. (1998). *The geography of money*. Ithaca: Cornell University Press.

Cohen, B. J. (2003). Global currency rivalry: Can the euro ever challenge the dollar? *Journal of Common Market Studies, 41*(4), 575–595.
Cohen, B. J. (2004). *The future of money*. Princeton: Princeton University Press.
Cohen, B. J. (2006). The macrofoundations of monetary power. In D. M. Andrews (Ed.), *International monetary power* (pp. 31–50). Ithaca: Cornell University Press.
Cohen, B. J. (2008). The euro in a global context: Challenges and capacities. In K. Dyson (Ed.), *The euro at ten*. Oxford: Oxford University Press.
Cooper, R. N., & Edwin, M. T. (2007). *The IMF quota formula: Linchpin of fund reform* (Policy brief in international economics, Vol. PB07-1). Washington, DC: Peterson Institute for International Economics.
International Monetary Fund. (2007). IMF surveillance – the 2007 decision on bilateral surveillance. Fact sheet.
Kirshner, J. (1995). *Currency and coercion: The political economy of international monetary power*. Princeton: Princeton University Press.
Krugman, P. R. (1998). The confidence game. *New Republic*, 5 Oct. 1998.
Krugman, P. R. (2001). Other people's money. *New York Times*, 18 July 2001.
Mundell, R. (2000). The euro and the stability of the international monetary system. In R. Mundell & A. Cleese (Eds.), *The euro as a stabilizer in the international economic system*. Boston: Kluwer.
Strange, S. (1994). *States and markets* (2nd ed.). London: Pinter.
Summers, L. H. (2004). *The US current account deficit and the global economy*. Washington, DC: Per Jacobsson Foundation.
Wyplosz, C. (1999). An international role for the euro? In J. Dermine & P. Hillion (Eds.), *European capital markets with a single currency*. New York: Oxford University Press.

Chapter 12
Leaders in Need of Followers: Emerging Powers in Global Governance

Stefan A. Schirm

Introduction

In the last decade, policy-makers, the media and academic research have been increasingly discussing the new role of emerging powers in the world economy and in global governance. Countries such as Brazil, China, India and South Africa as well as Germany, Japan and Russia have been assigned a greater influence in economic as well as political matters in their regions and in world politics. Often labelled as 'regional powers', 'middle powers' or 'would-be great powers' (Hurrell 2006; Nolte 2006), 'uncertain powers' (Maull 2006: 281), and 'new titans' (*The Economist* 2006), these countries are today widely perceived as pivotal states in international relations. The reasons for the assignment of a new role and often of increased power to these states are their demographic and geographic size, their economic and military capacities and their political aspirations. The countries defined here under the rubric of 'emerging powers' dominate their neighbours in terms of power over resources, that is, population, territory, military capacity and gross domestic product. In addition, they articulate a wish to change the distribution of power in the international system and to assume leadership roles in global governance.

This increased ambition became visible, for instance, with the bid made by Brazil, India, Germany and Japan for permanent seats on the United Nations Security Council (UNSC) as well as in the first two countries' leading role in the founding of the Group of 20 (G20) at the Cancùn meeting of the World Trade Organization (WTO). The trade G20 spoke for many developing and newly industrializing countries in confronting the industrialized world and in letting the Cancùn talks fail. Thus, these emerging powers are often seen as 'new influentials' (Lima and Hirst 2006: 27) in multipolar world politics and as countries challenging

This chapter first appeared in: *European Journal of International Relations*: Vol. 16, No. 2.

E. Fels et al. (eds.), *Power in the 21st Century*, Global Power Shift,
DOI 10.1007/978-3-642-25082-8_12, © Springer-Verlag Berlin Heidelberg 2012

the lead of the industrialized countries, especially of the US, in shaping international relations (Decker 2003; Hurrell and Narlikar 2005). Industrialized emerging powers such as Japan and Germany also challenged the existing distribution of power, for example, with their attempts to gain more influence in the UN and with Germany's striving to attain the position of managing director at the International Monetary Fund (IMF).

However, the performance of emerging powers shows a considerable gap between their aspirations and their ability to reach their goals. Brazil, India, Germany and Japan did not succeed in their aim to attain permanent seats in the UNSC despite a well-organized diplomatic campaign. Likewise, the trade G20 did not succeed in liberalizing industrialized countries' markets for agricultural products despite confrontational negotiating strategies at the WTO meeting in Cancún in 2003 and a more cooperative stance at the meeting in Geneva in 2004. Thus, the underlying question is: why do emerging powers sometimes fail to reach their goals?

Analytical Approach: Inclusive Leadership

Research on emerging powers in world politics has been conducted mainly in the form of case studies on individual countries (for example Ganguly 2002; Hakim 2004; Katada et al. 2004; Lima and Hirst 2006; Schirm 2005; Schoeman 2000). These studies examine the growing power over resources, varying institutional settings, the relationship towards established powers and the driving forces behind the new impetus in emerging powers' international activities, but they do not offer convincing explanations for the ambivalent performance of emerging powers or for their partial failure to achieve their goals. The gap between the aspiration for power and actual 'power over outcomes' (Russett 1985: 208) has not yet been sufficiently explored. In addition, only very seldom are emerging powers analysed in a comparative perspective. A comparison between an industrialized country like Germany and a newly industrializing country like Brazil has not yet been undertaken, even though both show a considerable gap between aspiration and actual influence. Hence, current research lacks a comparative, comprehensive analysis of the reasons for failure and success in emerging powers' strategies.

The underlying question behind the causes for emerging powers' performance is a question of the basic conditions for leadership. In the literature on leadership in international politics (see Ikenberry 1989, 2001; Kindleberger 1981; Pedersen 2002) and in other social sciences such as in international business (Bennis 2006; Sashkin 2006) it is widely acknowledged that successful leadership depends not only on resources and ambition but also crucially upon the support of followers. In this regard, research on emerging powers has been focusing too much on great powers, on the material capabilities and on the activism of emerging powers, and too little on followership. Factors such as resources, ambition, institutions and great power policies certainly influence emerging power performance, but they have to be complemented by the additional explanatory variable 'followership'. I argue that it is essentially the lack of support by neighbouring countries which precluded emerging powers from successfully pursuing their goals in several instances. In order to perform successfully, their leadership must be accepted by followers, especially by neighbouring countries since gains in power affect the respective region directly. Followership by neighbouring countries is a necessary condition to give these countries the power base for both regional and global power projection. The necessity of support by neighbours or more distant followers depends on whether a regional dimension is at stake (as in the UNSC reform) or not (as in the WTO negotiations). Thus, the specific question to be addressed in this article is: *under which conditions do potential followers support emerging powers' bids for leadership?*

In order to proceed deductively from the argument that emerging powers' leadership crucially depends on followership, it is necessary to specify possible reasons for support. For this purpose I develop a hypothesis which suggests two conditions for the acceptance of emerging power leadership. The hypothesis is based on the premise that emerging powers cannot coerce other countries' support and therefore need to deliver incentives to ensure acceptance for their leadership: *the inclusion of the interests and/or ideas dominant in another country into an emerging power's leadership project is a necessary condition for this other country to accept the policy positions, shift in power and/or status desired by the emerging power and to follow its lead.* Thus, the basic argument is that the incorporation of potential followers' interests and/or ideas into an emerging power's leadership project is necessary in order to neutralize potential resistance and stimulate support for this project.

This argument is based on the idea of non-coercive, benign leadership which is 'organized around more reciprocal, consensual, and institutionalized relations. The order is still organized around asymmetrical power relations, but the most overtly malign character of domination is muted' (Ikenberry 2001: 28). A capacity of self-restraint through common ideas, rules and institutions for 'power sharing vis-a-vis smaller states in a region' is crucial for benign leadership (Pedersen 2002: 684). The hypothesis outlined above implies that emerging powers have to offer potential followers material incentives and/or shared ideas which are perceived as superior to the option of not following the emerging power or to that of following other leaders. A consequence of the latter would be that followers reject or withdraw from emerging powers' initiatives or that they choose to cooperate with established powers, such as the United States. Also, as the literature on hegemonic stability argues, benevolent leaders must be able to accept a certain degree of free-riding by the followers to secure the cooperative system (Kindleberger 1981: 247).

In sum, this article addresses the conditions under which potential followers support emerging power leadership by looking at the components of their leadership projects and by identifying those components necessary to achieve followership. This approach intends to complement other explanations and sees followership as a necessary but not sufficient condition for the successful performance of emerging powers.

The cases presented were selected to provide a range of different situations and thereby variation on the independent (interests/ideas in leadership project) as well as on the dependent (followership) variable.

Leadership is defined as the ability to make others follow goals and positions which these others did not previously share and/or to make others support an increase in status and power of the emerging power. This definition includes influence through material incentives and the ability to exert 'soft power' through shared ideas and agenda setting, that is, 'getting others to want what you want....It co-opts people rather than coerces them' (Nye 2003: 9). Variation on the independent variable 'leadership project' comprises different forms of leadership with regard to global governance *structures* (UNSC), *directorship* (IMF and WTO) and *policy positions* (on trade in the WTO). These leadership projects differ in scope, content and institutional setting. Therefore, they can be expected to also afford different degrees and forms of inclusion of potential followers' interests and ideas. Interests and ideas with regard to global *economic* governance may plausibly encompass trade policy (liberalization vs. protectionism), investment and aid, as well as promoting a common cause and sharing general views on how international relations and the world economy should be organized. Leadership in global *security* governance requires the inclusion of security interests, ranging from sharing specific positions (e.g. on the regional distribution of power) over the provision of safety guarantees to a credible message from the power seeker to potential followers that it will not dominate them. Thus, committing to common positions, building coalitions and refraining from acting unilaterally belong to the core elements of non-coercive leadership.

Followership is defined, mirroring leadership, as supporting the goals and positions of another country which were not shared previously and/or as accepting a relative loss of status and power vis-a-vis the emerging power. Variation on the dependent variable 'followership' includes, first, the geographic dimension, looking both at individual neighbours (UNSC and directorship cases) and at geographically more distant followership (WTO case). By including both individual neighbours and a broader group of potential followers it is possible to assess whether the change in policy positions, power and/or status has an accentuated effect in the immediate region. Second, variation on the dependent variable is also achieved by examining different policy areas such as security and trade as well as considering a mixture of status and specific issues (finance and trade).

Interests are defined here as societal *material considerations*, for example, about tariffs and subsidies, and access to international decision-making. *Ideas* are defined as societal *expectations and beliefs* about national, regional and international identities or about how to organize the international system. Interests and ideas are considered to be crucial influences on governmental preference formation in foreign (economic) policy (see Schirm 2009).

The empirical exemplification of the hypothesis comprises two emerging powers in three case studies. Brazil and Germany are both considered to be emerging powers, to possess power over resources as well as ambition to change the status quo, and to have both failed in some of their endeavours and succeeded in others. Through the inclusion of an industrialized and a newly industrializing power in the analysis, this article investigates whether the hypothesis holds through different degrees of economic development and through different forms of embeddedness in geopolitical coalitions, institutional settings and historical legacies. Brazil's and Germany's leadership will be analysed with regard to: (1) their aspiration for new governance *structures* (permanent membership in the UNSC); (2) their bid for *directorship* in international organizations (WTO, IMF); and (3) their performance in influencing global trade *policy* (WTO). The potential followers to be examined will be Argentina (for Brazil) and Italy (for Germany) in the first two cases and the respective groups the emerging powers wanted to lead, namely the trade G20 (for Brazil) and the EU (for Germany), during the WTO Doha Round in the third case.

The case studies are organized systematically following the same structural pattern. First, a short account of the development is given. Second, the leadership project of the emerging power is analysed with regard to its components: does it include the material interests and/or ideas of the potential follower? Third, the followership or non-followership will be analysed with regard to its motives.

In investigating the leadership project and the motives for (non-) followership, this article will refer first to documents (press releases, speeches by governmental decision-makers), and second to research by academic experts and to well-renowned newspapers. In order to assess the question whether the leadership project offered enough shared ideas and/or interests to induce followership it is crucial to look at the communication between the governments of potential leaders and followers as well as between the governments and their electorates as conducted through public statements. Public statements of democratically accountable politicians are the best way to trace what a society considers legitimate in terms of collectively shared ideas and/or dominant interests. Obviously, exemplifying hypotheses via the statements of politicians can provide only plausibility, not proof. A public statement by the government underlining its positions with regard to material interests or ideas does not necessarily provide the real reasoning behind the government's preference. For example, when governments publicly underline their preferences with ideas and values, they can create a rhetorical picture in order to promote hidden material interests such as protectionism or market access. However, public statements do provide evidence for what the government considers acceptable and legitimate to the voters. Thus, I assume that governmental preferences will in principle reflect attitudes grounded on real endogenous patterns of legitimate ideas and interests. In order to secure this link between governmental preferences and societal ideas and interests, the empirical evidence on the dependent variable – governmental preferences in favour or against followership – focuses on quotes of decision-makers, of the politically responsible ministries and of heads of government who, based on the standard assumption of self-interest to remain in office, will base their positions on patterns considered legitimate by voters.

Structure: Emerging Powers' Bids for Permanent Membership in the UNSC

Prior to the negotiations on a general reform of the United Nations in 2005, Brazil and Germany orchestrated a diplomatic initiative together with India and Japan (the G4) in order for these countries to obtain permanent seats on the UNSC as part of the general reform. The G4 countries' central claim was that the existing composition of the UNSC permanent members, the P5 (USA, Russia, UK, France, China), did not represent the distribution of power in today's international order and that, rather, it should reflect the rise of emerging powers. All four countries based their aspirations on the idea that their membership would give the UNSC increased representativity and legitimacy. In the end, the initiative failed and none of the G4 countries gained a permanent seat. The most overt resistance came from countries neighbouring the G4: Argentina and Mexico opposed Brazil, Italy rejected Germany's aspiration, Pakistan opposed India and several Asian countries rejected Japan's bid. Although the P5 countries might not have been happy about the idea of sharing their exclusive veto power with new members, it was the UN General Assembly, where the principle of 'one country–one vote' rules, which ultimately did not provide the qualified majority necessary for the G4 to obtain the changes. Why did this diplomatic initiative of northern and southern emerging powers fail?

Brazilian Leadership Project

Evidence suggests that Brazil's and Germany's definition of their bid – that their permanent membership would raise the legitimacy and representativity of the UNSC – was not shared by their neighbours. Brazilian President Lula (2003) articulated the Brazilian definition in a speech before the UN General Assembly:

> The security council must be fully empowered to deal with crises and threats to peace.... Above all, its decisions must be seen as legitimate by the Community of Nations as a whole. Its composition – in particular as concerns permanent membership – cannot remain unaltered almost 60 years on. It can no longer ignore the changing world. More specifically, it must take into account the emergence in the international scene of developing countries.... Brazil believes that it has a useful contribution to make.

In his State of the Union address before the Brazilian Congress, Lula (2005a: 233) emphasized the need for a higher 'representativity and legitimacy' of the UNSC through the inclusion of emerging powers. In his speech at the 61st General Assembly of the UN, Lula (2006) again stressed the democracy and legitimacy argument: 'Along with the G4 countries, Brazil holds that the expansion of the Security Council must envisage the entry of developing countries as permanent members. This would make that body more democratic, legitimate and representative.' In addition to these ideational arguments for permanent membership, Brazil has also stressed two material reasons: its contributions to UN peacekeeping operations and to the UN budget (Ministério de Relações Exteriores 1998/2005; *The Economist* 2004: 50–51).

Argentinian Followership

In the 1990s then President of Argentina, Carlos Menem, had already rejected a Brazilian bid for a permanent seat on the grounds that it would distort the regional distribution of power: 'Then Mr Menem openly attacked the idea of giving Brazil a permanent seat on the UN Security Council, saying this would upset the regional balance of power' (*The Economist* 1997). In 2005 Argentina's President Nestor Kirchner diverged considerably from the Brazilian definition of the UNSC by stressing that such a reform would 'perpetuate' inequality: 'That is why we consider that any reform of the United Nations must provide the Organization with more transparency and democracy, without creating new situations of privilege that would perpetuate the inequality between its members' (Kirchner 2005a). As its own alternative reform proposal, Argentina, together with Italy and others, founded the Uniting for Consensus group and promoted the idea of enlarging the UNSC by non-permanent members. The Argentinian Minister of Foreign Affairs, Rafael Bielsa (2005), argued:

> With 'Uniting for Consensus', Argentina will push for a Security Council with new members, but only 'non-permanent ones'. We believe that we should not create new privileges that would go against the democratic spirit of the United Nations. Council members should be accountable for their actions, and this can be attained through periodic elections.

The Argentinian Ambassador to the UN, César Mayoral (2004), also promoted the idea of a regional Latin American seat as an alternative to an upgrading of Brazil.

German Leadership Project

The German Foreign Minister Joschka Fischer stated in a speech before the UN General Assembly in 2004 that Germany is willing to assume more responsibility by entering the UNSC as a permanent member and that this would make the UNSC more representative by adapting it to today's 'geopolitical realities' (Fischer 2004a). Chancellor Gerhard Schröder also emphasized the role of Germany as one of the largest contributors to the UN budget and to UN peacekeeping operations as a reason for the legitimacy of its candidature for a permanent seat (Hellmann and Roos 2007: 22–25, Schröder 2004). Even though a permanent regional European seat in the UNSC was widely discussed in Europe and Germany, the German government treated that possibility as something impossible to achieve and did not make any effort to promote it. In this regard Fischer declared (2004b): 'If an enlargement of the UNSC occurs, Germany is a candidate for a permanent seat.... A European seat ... is not attainable in the next few years. Therefore we stick to our candidature.' It is telling, that although the possibility of a common European seat figured prominently (1) in statements by the EU High Representative for Foreign Policy, Javier Solana, (2) in speeches by representatives of other EU member states (such as Italy, see below), and (3) even in the coalition agreement of the governing parties (Social Democrats and Greens) in Germany 2002, no official German statement before the UN actually mentioned the possibility of a European seat (Hellmann and Roos 2007: 16).

Italian Followership

Italian Foreign Minister Franco Frattini (2004a) declared in an interview with the *Corriere de la Sera*:

> I would turn the question to my friend Fischer. Why doesn't Germany follow the example of Alcide de Gasperi and Konrad Adenauer, of the Europe of 50 years ago, and work with us toward a European seat?... Adding new permanent seats now would bury the idea of a unified European participation.

In a speech to the 59th UN General Assembly, Frattini (2004b) emphasized:

> Italy is in favour of a Security Council reform inspired by the principles of greater inclusiveness, effectiveness, democratic participation, and geographic representation, starting with the developing countries. We are firmly convinced that the best way to pursue such a reform is to establish new non-permanent seats. Since the states occupying these seats would have to be periodically elected, they would be accountable to the general membership.

Thus, Italy rejected the German leadership project and proposed an alternative which stressed democratic accountability.

In sum, the two emerging powers failed to convince potential followers with their ideational definition of the leadership project. An enlargement of the P5 to a P9 would have essentially extended the veto privileges to another four of the 192 UN member countries, without giving the remaining 183 UN members an increased voice. The option of regional seats, for example a Latin American and a European seat, was also not pursued by the G4. In order to make the other countries follow, Germany and Brazil could have modified their leadership project, for example, in the direction of rotating regional seats which would be more often held by the larger countries than by the smaller ones. In addition, the two emerging powers could have refrained from pursuing the veto rights possessed by the P5. Neither Germany nor Brazil, however, was able or willing to include the ideas and interests of potential followers in their leadership project.

The two potential followers consequently founded a group of likeminded countries that opposed the attempt of the G4 and advocated higher representativity and legitimacy of the UNSC through more non-permanent members and a watering down of veto powers. The 12 founding members of this anti-G4 Uniting for Consensus group included the immediate neighbours of the G4: Argentina, Italy, Pakistan and Korea. The group grew to nearly 40 members and actively opposed the G4 plan by promoting their alternative reform. The motivation was a different definition of the ideas of representativity and legitimacy in the UN from that proposed by the G4 in conjunction with the attempt at balancing the G4's desire for increased power (see quotes earlier and Dinger 2006: 117).

Brazil and Germany also failed to convince on the basis of their material contributions to the UN budget and to peacekeeping missions because other member states contributed more than they did. Mexico, for example, contributed 1.9% to the UN budget compared to Brazil's 1.5% in 2004–2006 (United Nations 2003), and Italy ranked ninth on the official list of contributors to peacekeeping operations, where Germany only ranked 18th (United Nations 2007). In sum, Brazil and Germany in no way included the interests of potential followers in their leadership project and even competed with these states to gain UN member support, especially in Africa, for their respective reform plans. Thus, the potential followers rejected the ambitions of the emerging powers and successfully orchestrated resistance.

Directorship: Emerging Powers' Bids for Top Jobs in International Organizations

Apart from their ambition to change the structure of the international distribution of power by obtaining permanent membership in the UNSC, Brazil and Germany also tried to attain more influence by occupying the directorship in international organizations: Brazil unsuccessfully in the World Trade Organization (WTO), Germany successfully in the International Monetary Fund (IMF). Because the bids for directorship occurred in different organizations, a short account of the development in the respective cases will be given at the beginning of the section on each leadership project.

Brazilian Leadership Project

In 2005, the Brazilian government under President Lula da Silva campaigned for a Brazilian candidate, Luiz Felipe de Seixas Corrêa, for the position of the Director-General of the WTO, the organization's top job. Seixas Corrêa had been Brazil's Ambassador to the WTO and was a key architect of the developing countries' G20 at the WTO conference in Cancùn in 2003 (see next case study). President Lula

(2005a: 236–237) presented this candidacy in his yearly Message to the Congress as a key issue of his foreign policy, namely, as part of the 'sovereign integration' of his country into world politics and as a 'candidacy of a representative of Brazil' ('candidatura de um representante do Brasil').

While the President framed the leadership project by stressing Brazil's sovereignty and national representation in international organizations, the candidate, Seixas Corrêa (2005), tried to be more diplomatic, for example, before a meeting of the Economic Association of Carribbean States (CARICOM):

> It is essential to ensure wider participation of developing countries in decision-making in the WTO. . ..The next Director-General of the WTO must be fully prepared to facilitate the harmonious integration of developing countries in decision-making in the WTO.. . . He must be able to fully represent the collective will of the members.

In the same speech he also criticized his main competitor for the WTO job, the EU's Trade Commissioner Pascal Lamy (who actually got the job), by stating: 'It is hard to accept that, having control of the World Bank and of the IMF, developed countries should also be at the helm of the WTO' (Seixas Corrêa 2005). Despite Seixas Corrêa's presentation of the project as something benefiting all developing countries and directed against a 'common evil' (the dominance of developed countries), Brazil's candidate failed to be elected in the 'one country–one vote' electoral process of the WTO in which the developing countries possess the majority. Seixas Corrêa's multilateralist appeal apparently did not outweigh the President's nationalistic stance.

Argentinian Followership

Brazil not only failed to win the majority of WTO member states but also failed to win the support of its closest regional ally in the Common Market of the South (Mercosur), Argentina. Argentina supported the candidate from Uruguay (another Mercosur member) for the position and stressed that it had committed itself to the Uruguayan candidate prior to the candidacy of Seixas Corrêa and therefore could support the Brazilian candidate only as a second choice, 'segunda preferencia' (Ministerio de Relaciones Exteriores 2005). In the same press release, the Argentinian Foreign Ministry complained of failed coalition-building: 'Argentina made a great effort with the Brazilian and the Uruguayan governments in order to reach a single regional candidature' (Ministerio de Relaciones Exteriores 2005).

Why did Argentina not follow Brazil's leadership project? The first and more banal answer would be that it had indeed committed to the Uruguayan candidate before Brazil had launched its own and could therefore not step back now. In this case, Brazil was too late in claiming leadership and ignored pre-existing commitments of potential followers. Thus, the leadership attempt was amateurish. This answer is not convincing since Brazilian foreign policy is traditionally considered to be very professional and Brazil had just successfully orchestrated the creation of the trade G20 in 2003, proving its political and diplomatic skills (see next case study). Furthermore, Brazil could have tried to persuade Argentina and Uruguay to drop the Uruguayan candidate in favour of its own – as Germany did vis-a-vis Italy.

The lack of explanatory power of the first answer (amateurism) leads to a second, more complex interpretation involving the recent history of relations between Argentina and Brazil and considering international relations as a series of cooperative situations in which present behaviour is influenced by past experiences. Under this perspective, Argentina might not have trusted Brazil's commitment to multilateral rules since economic interest groups had had to suffer several times under Brazilian unilateral action and under the breaking of commercial agreements in Mercosur by Brazil in the years prior to the WTO candidacy (Malamud 2005; Rodrik 2003: 17–18). Brazilian–Argentinian relations had been shaped by 'bitter disagreements' (Lima and Hirst 2006: 31) in the years 1999–2005. In addition, Brazil had not proven a good multilateralist on the regional scale because it had been reluctant to strengthen regional institutions in Mercosur in order not to weaken its own national sovereignty, that is, in order not to let common rules restrict its room for manoeuvre as the most influential member of the regional grouping (Schirm 2005: 122). Valladão (2006: 10) concludes:

> Despite frequent statements in favour of Mercosur, the Lula government is showing itself rather reluctant to accept a deeper integration in a regional bloc that would share institutions which would give other member countries some tools capable of influencing Brazilian policy.

Thus, Brazil's attempt to define a leadership project in terms of potential followers' ideas and interests, such as strengthening the developing world against the developed nations, might not have achieved the necessary credibility due to Brazil's behaviour in regional multilateralism. Nor did the framing of Brazil's candidacy by the President as a national project help convince followers that their ideas and interests would be included. Finally, Brazil's participation and performance in the G5 preparatory group of the WTO meeting in Geneva 2004 (see next section) probably raised doubts about its commitment to multilateralism and plausibly contributed to the Argentinian refusal to back Brazil's candidate. The Argentinian President Nestor Kirchner (2005b) expressed his general dissatisfaction with Brazil's unilateral power-seeking:

> If there is a job open at the World Trade Organization, Brazil wants it. If there is a space at the United Nations, Brazil wants it. If there is a job at the United Nations Food and Agriculture Organization, Brazil wants it. They even wanted to have a Brazilian pope.

German Leadership Project

The IMF managing director traditionally comes from a European country, while the World Bank boss is usually American. Germany had never occupied this position before 2000. The first German candidate was Caio Koch-Weser, Deputy Finance

Minister, in 1999. After strong US opposition, German Chancellor Gerhard Schröder nominated Horst Köhler, boss of the European Bank for Reconstruction and Development (EBRD), in March 2000 as Germany's new candidate.

Germany fulfilled the task of convincing the other European member states essentially by promoting Köhler consistently not as a national candidate, but as the European candidate to be implemented against the resistance of the US. Thus the German project was defined as a common European project against the global hegemon, encompassing both a balance of power notion and a shared European identity. After receiving the backing of all EU partners in a test vote in the IMF, Chancellor Schröder (2000a) emphasized that the unanimous support of EU member states for the German candidate:

> ... is the result of European solidarity as a basis for its ability to act. With this result, Europe has underlined its determination to occupy the position of the managing director of the International Monetary Fund.... I assume, that an agreement with the US and Japan is achievable now.

With this statement, Schröder clearly framed the leadership project as a common European cause to be carried through vis-a-vis the US. During the process of gaining support from the other EU countries for their candidates Koch-Weser and Köhler, the spokesman of the federal government, Bela Anda, and Chancellor Schröder frequently pointed to the European nature of this candidature, German consultations with other EU governments, and the rising number of supporters (see Press Conferences 14.1., 1.3., 9.3. 2000, Federal Press Office [BPA], Berlin). Bela Anda declared: 'This is not only about a German candidate, but about a European candidate, who is German' (BPA 1.3. 2000b). Schröder (2000b) explicitly emphasized the aim of achieving a 'European consensus' in favour of the German candidate, mentioning the support of the Netherlands, Poland, the Czech Republic and Great Britain for Köhler. In addition to stressing the common European idea, Schröder placed pressure on Italy with this detailed specification of the supportive countries and his encompassing consultations within the EU.

Italian Followership

The German definition of its candidacy as a European project was apparently accepted by other countries insofar as the European Council of Finance Ministers (ECOFIN) supported the German candidate unanimously. Italy had actually had its own candidate for the IMF job since 1999, but ultimately supported the German candidate. The public debate in Italy and the statements of the Italian government changed from an initial rejection of the German candidate and attempts to promote its own candidate, towards a labelling of the Italian candidate as a 'reserve candidate' (*La Repubblica*, 15 February 2000: 37) and support for the German candidate 'fully and without conditions' ('pieno e incondizionato', Foreign Minister Lamberto Dini, quoted in *Corriere della Sera* 14 March 2000: 23).

According to statements of key Italian decision-makers in the weeks of negotiations over the position of the IMF managing director, Italian support for the German candidate was essentially due to three factors. First, Germany always presented its candidate as a European candidate, thus giving ideational incentives to other EU members by framing the leadership project as a common cause. Second, the firm American rejection of the first German candidate triggered European solidarity and the EU closed ranks. Third, Germany drove a skilfully orchestrated campaign by constantly involving other EU governments in its plan to occupy the position. Thus, Germany managed to achieve the support of followers without their own candidates in order to put pressure on the difficult follower which did have its own candidate. Pressure was put on Italy also by framing the leadership project as a European project and thus defining any resistance as anti-European.

Evidence for these three factors can be found in public statements and in influential media. For example, US behaviour towards Germany's first candidate, Caio Koch-Weser, was seen in Italy as an 'American veto' ('veto americano'), while the support for the second German candidate, Horst Köhler, was then described as a 'European candidacy' ('candidatura europea'; *Corriere della Sera* 14 March 2000: 23). In the end, the shared definition of the situation and shared underlying ideas – European integration and solidarity – induced Italy to follow the German leadership project. The final blow to the Italian candidacy came when, after most EU countries had already expressed support for the German candidate, the British Prime Minister Tony Blair officially endorsed Köhler. The leading Italian daily *Corriere della Sera* (Ferraino 2000: 23) proclaimed: 'After France and the Netherlands, now the United Kingdom gives its support to the German candidate. Blair paves the way for Köhler', and writes, '[Prime Minister] Massimo D'Alema has declared that he expressed directly to the German Chancellor the Italian determination to support a strong European position.'

Policy: Emerging Powers' Performance in WTO Negotiations

Analysing the Brazilian and the German performance in the course of the multilateral negotiations on trade liberalization within the Doha Round of the WTO allows for an understanding of their leadership with regard to policy. The following analysis will not focus on the potential followership of a single neighbouring country, but will instead consider the respective group of countries which the emerging powers intended to lead, namely, the trade G20 for Brazil and the EU for Germany.

The Doha Round of the WTO started in 2001 and was labelled the Development Round, emphasizing not only the general aim of any WTO activity, that is, liberalization of trade, but acknowledging that the needs of developing countries were to be especially considered. The negotiations proceeded in WTO meetings in Cancùn 2003, Geneva 2004 and Hong Kong 2005 and were suspended in 2006 by the WTO Director General, Pascal Lamy, due to a stalemate between the parties. The most important negotiators were the US, the EU and the trade G20. The latter was founded at the meeting in Cancùn by an initial group of 20 developing and newly industrializing countries led by Brazil and India in order to strengthen the negotiating power of the developing world vis-a-vis the developed countries. The summit in Geneva in 2004 was prepared by a Group of five (Australia, Brazil, EU, India, US), which agreed on a framework for negotiations and thus overcame the stalemate of Cancùn through mutual concessions. The ministerial meeting in Hong Kong once again ran into a stalemate which remains unresolved today (2008). At the Hong Kong meeting, the G20 showed diverging interests and did not reach the unified stance achieved in Cancùn. The issues at stake were trade liberalization and elimination of export subsidies for agricultural products (core aim of developing and newly industrializing countries), liberalization of trade for industrial products and services (a core aim of the industrialized countries) and the 'Singapore Issues' on investment, public procurement, competition and trade facilitation (another core goal of the industrialized countries).

Brazilian Leadership Project

While Brazil has traditionally striven for leadership and reform of the international economic system, its position became more aggressive towards the developed world after the socialist Lula da Silva became President in 2002. Brazil's leadership project in founding the G20 at the WTO Meeting in Cancùn started as a reaction to the EU–US common agricultural proposal and was subsequently legitimized as an attempt to give the developing world more influence in the WTO by making the trade system 'less autocratic' and promoting specific trade interests of the developing world more efficiently vis-a-vis the industrialized countries. Thus, Brazil framed its leadership as including both the ideas and the material interests of a heterogeneous group of countries. This conceptualization of the Brazilian leadership project can be found in statements of decision-makers. Foreign Minister Celso Amorim (2003), whose ministry is responsible for trade, stated: 'Trade must be a tool not only to create wealth but also to distribute it in a more equitable way', and he criticized the present order as an 'autocratic international trade system'. President Lula (2005b) stressed the Brazilian ambition to fundamentally change international politics: 'Our great challenge is to design a new international trade and economic geography.'

Underlining the participation of the developing countries in the negotiations, the Brazilian Ambassador to the WTO, Seixas Corrêa (2005), declared:

> I firmly believe it would be detrimental to developing countries if we were to apply to the WTO decision-making models such as the ones followed in the World Bank and in the IMF. Member-driven negotiations based on consensus building are the sole and unique path to equitable and fair results.

With regard to the integration of material interests of potential followers, Minister Amorim (2004a) emphasized:

> ... we have been coordinating a Group of 20 ... as a voice in favour of freer trade in agriculture ... and against the billions spent on trade-distorting agricultural subsidies. It is not an exaggeration to say that the G-20 for the first time in trade negotiations brought home a twin message on trade liberalization and social justice.

In order to gain acceptance of its leadership, Brazil modified its position with the aim of including the interests of potential followers which reached from net food exporters (Cairns Group) over net food importers (Cuba, Venezuela) to protectionists on agriculture (China, India). In 2003, before the Cancùn Ministerial meeting, Brazilian trade specialists researched how much an approximation of the Brazilian position (focusing on market access as a competitive exporter of agricultural products) to the position of other developing countries, especially India's (focusing more on reduction of export subsidies and on preferential treatment for some products), would cost the Brazilian agricultural sector and concluded that it would not be substantially affected (Delgado and Soares 2005: 14–15; Narlikar and Tussie 2004: 953–962; Veiga 2005). Thus, Brazil changed its position and included the material interests of potential followers: the national goal of improving access to developed countries' agricultural markets was subordinated to the common goal of reducing export subsidies of developed countries.

In 2004 Brazil deviated from this inclusive position when negotiating in the G5 group with the US, the EU, Australia and India: equal priority was now given to the national preference for market access and to other G20 interests, whereas export subsidies had been dominant in 2003. At the Joint Press Conference of the G5 in June 2004, Foreign Minister Amorim (2004c) declared: 'We agreed that we have to proceed on analyzing the three pillars and supporting them in parallel.' Thus, export subsidies were now dealt with by Brazil 'in parallel' with market access and domestic support, though the G20 had agreed in Cancùn to give priority to export subsidies. The framework agreement from July 2004 and the membership of Brazil (and India) in the G5 was hailed in the annual message of President Lula (2005a: 236–237) to Congress as a major achievement: 'Brazil and India now belong to a group of five ... which exerts a preponderant function.... Thus, the developing countries were integrated, for the first time, into the center of the decision making process.' The statement shows that Brazil did not necessarily want to change the official decision-making process of the WTO, but instead aimed at *upgrading* its own position by joining a small informal club. The US confirmed this impression with United States Trade Representative (USTR), Robert Zoellick, declaring that Brazil's role in the G5 'fits the role that Brazil plays in the world economy and trading system' (WTO 2004: 2). Foreign Minister Amorim (2004b) attributed Brazil's influence in the G5 in July 2004 to its role as leader of the trade G20, declaring, 'the framework agreed last weekend would not have seen daylight without the active participation of the G20'.

G20 Followership

The case of the Brazilian leadership of the trade G20 from Cancùn to Hong Kong offers variation within one case because it includes moments of strength (Cancùn 2003) as well as weakness (Geneva 2004/Hong Kong 2005) with regard to gaining followership. While Brazil managed to convince a broad, heterogeneous group of followers in 2003 via inclusiveness on material interests and by credibly promoting common ideas, it lost support from followers when it damaged its credibility on both points in 2004 with its performance in the G5. First, some G20 developing countries felt that their trade interests were not adequately represented in the G5 package and criticized Brazil for having promoted its own trade interests too strongly (Delgado and Soares 2005: 29–31). Compared to the joint position of the G20 in Cancùn 2003, the G5 negotiating package of 2004 placed slightly more emphasis on market access (the core Brazilian interest) and less emphasis on reduction of export subsidies (the G20's collective goal). Second, Brazil was criticized for joining an exclusive, opaque decision making body, and having thus undermined the goal of the G20 to make the international trade system less autocratic. The Brazilian behaviour in the G5 was especially disappointing for some G20 followers because Brazilian officials had publicly stated that they would represent trade interests broadly and enhance an inclusive decision-making process (see statements above).

Criticism of the Brazilian performance in the G5 was articulated in the official G20 Ministerial Declaration of New Delhi in March 2005 (G20 2005: 5) which stressed the necessity for:

> . . . a participative negotiating process . . . [as] an essential element for securing a legitimate outcome to these negotiations to the benefit of the whole membership. Ministers acknowledged that the Geneva process may need to be supported by other forms of engagement provided they are conducted in a transparent and inclusive manner.

With remarkable clarity, this joint statement of G20 ministers expressed the dissatisfaction of followers with their leaders' performance in Geneva 2004. In their view, Brazilian leadership lacked legitimacy (that is: shared ideas) as well as the benefit of all (that is: inclusive interests). Consequently, at the WTO meeting in Hong Kong in December 2005, the G20 showed fissures. The issues were not aggregated to the same degree achieved in Cancùn 2003. Hong Kong also showed divergence between the G20 leaders: contrary to India's position, Brazil was hesitant towards an opening of services markets; China, in contrast to Brazil, did not want to open markets for agricultural products; and Brazil remained defensive about liberalization of its market for industrial goods, a move favoured by China. Even though Brazil and India still performed as spokes-countries for the G20, their ability to lead the common cause was weaker than it had been in Cancùn. The meeting in Hong Kong ended without result ('World Trade: Hard Truths', in *The Economist* 20 December 2005; Delgado and Soares 2005: 32–37; Meier 2005: 1).

Summing up, the shared idea of a south–south coalition vis-a-vis the industrialized countries necessary for leadership acceptance was apparently jeopardized by the *upgrading* of Brazil into the G5. This process was accompanied by the partial mismatch of specific trade interests of G20 countries with those of Brazil. The criticism of Brazil's leadership in the New Delhi Declaration of the G20 pointed more towards the procedural aspects of G5 negotiations than the material results. In sum, Brazilian performance in the WTO presents an ambivalent picture. On one hand, it can partially be seen as a success because Brazil managed to bring together the G20 at Cancùn (by offering shared ideas and integrating interests) and to gain concessions from the EU on export subsidies in 2004. On the other hand, followership was weakened by Brazil's participation in the G5 and its reduced ability to integrate positions for the Hong Kong meeting to the degree that it had in Cancùn. The development of the followership in the G20 from Cancùn 2003 to Hong Kong 2005 also sheds light on the question of the lack of support for the Brazilian candidacy for the WTO top job. While followership among the G20 was strong in 2003, it decreased after Geneva 2004 and eroded further with the New Delhi Declaration before the election of the WTO Director-General in 2005.

German Leadership Project

German leadership attempts in international trade negotiations were low profile. Had they not been, Germany would have had difficulty finding followership among European neighbours since EU members had agreed upon trade policy as a common policy. Nevertheless, the German performance with regard to the WTO negotiations will be investigated here for systematic reasons to maintain the comparative approach of this article and because it is worthwhile examining how the largest economy and trading country in the EU acted in a policy area in which it had committed itself to decide together with others. Germany does not sit directly at the WTO negotiating table – that function is reserved for the EU Trade Commissioner – but it does join other member states in giving a mandate to the Commission. In shaping this mandate, Germany has great influence because it possesses one of the largest voting quotas in the European Council. However, the consensual decision-making culture in the EU remains a limiting factor for Germany's use of its influence. Thus, the core question in this case study is: can there be leadership in a communitarized policy area, or does the delegation of agenda-setting and executive powers as well as the need for consensus inhibit leadership as well as followership?

As the EU's leading trading nation, with roughly one-third of its GDP dependent on exports, Germany has traditionally been an advocate of trade liberalization. This traditional role was softened during the Red–Green Coalition (1998–2005) of Chancellor Gerhard Schröder with the inclusion of environmental and social standards in Germany's trade agenda (Falke 2006). However, even under the tenure of the last Red–Green Minister of the Economy, Wolfgang Clement (his Ministry being responsible for trade policy), Germany had returned slowly to its traditional position. This trend has continued since 2005 under Chancellor Angela Merkel's government. In order to promote a compromise between its interest in accessing developing countries' markets for industrial products and developing countries' interest in accessing the European market for agricultural products, Germany pressed the EU for reform of the Common Agricultural Policy (CAP) and especially for a reduction of agricultural export subsidies as a bargaining chip in the WTO. Though Schröder had given in to the French reluctance for substantial reforms of the CAP in 2002, since the tenure of Minister Clement and especially after the failed WTO meeting in Cancùn in 2003, Germany (and Schröder himself) pressed with more energy and success to achieve its position despite French resistance (Falke 2006: 192–197). Thus, the bigger reform impetus on agriculture, which has provided the EU with a greater ability to broker compromises vis-a-vis the developing world, was also a result of German influence. The Deputy Minister for the Economy, Bernd Pfaffenbach (2005) confirmed this point when stating:

> ... with its offer to eliminate all subsidies for agricultural products, the EU has – by the way also because of the strong demands of the Chancellor [Schröder] – set the long awaited signal of compromise towards the interests of the developing countries.

Germany's leadership project rested not only on its material interest in accessing markets, but also on two ideas. First, German politicians traditionally portray their country's role as that of a *moderator* which subordinates its national interests to the common weal of the European cause. This attitude was confirmed in a statement made by the Minister of the Economy, Michael Glos (2006): 'Vis-a-vis its European partners Germany will continue to play the role of a moderator in order to strengthen the negotiation position of the EU also externally'. Second, German decision-makers regularly underlined the increasing *interdependence* between developed countries and developing countries as a core characteristic of international trade relations (Pfaffenbach 2005). In this regard, German politicians have emphasized the special needs of developing countries and introduced the Everything But Arms (EBA) initiative, which allows exports from the Least Developed Countries (LDCs) into the EU without any tariffs or quotas.

EU Followership

Like the German leadership project itself, its followership is also only partially visible. An assessment of the exact influence of Germany compared to the possible influence of other EU members or the EU Commission on the common position is hard to make due to the communitarized character of European trade policy. Evidence for followership can be found in the EU's common position representing more German than French demands in Geneva 2004 (Agence France Presse 31 July 2004; Clement 2004; *EuroNews* 26 July 2004). As France and Germany are considered the most important EU members with regard to trade policy (Falke 2005), the Geneva position seems to underline a certain preponderance of German influence. German leadership in the EU is confirmed by experts. *The Economist* concluded regarding Chancellor Merkel: 'If her influence keeps growing, this summit may have marked the start of Germany's emergence as the central power in an EU of 25' ('The European Union Summit: Cries and Gestures', in *The Economist* 20 December 2005). Hulsman and Techau (2007: 17) write: 'Germany is viewed as the decisive catalyzing force for European decision making.... Berlin is perceived as the most altruistic of the "Three Big" in Europe.' This impression of German leadership qualities stands in contrast to the first Schröder administration (1998–2002) before the failed WTO meeting in Cancùn, in which France and Germany had annoyed potential European followers by presenting bilateral agreements as *faits accompli* (Guérot 2007: 40).

Since the Cancùn meeting, Germany has integrated the interests (access to developing countries' markets for industrial products) and ideas (moderator of common goals, international interdependence) of potential followers to the degree necessary to make the common European trade policy lean more to the German side than to the French side, which is traditionally more protectionist on agriculture and less interested in market access for industrial products. Evidence for followership of German leadership can also be found with regard to the EBA. The German Minister for the Economy, Michael Glos (2005), stated, 'The "Everything But Arms" initiative which was introduced by Germany ... has grown to be a model for other industrialized countries', and the Italian Minister for Productive Activities, Antonio Marzano (2003), declared on behalf of his country's EU Presidency:

> It is a path on which the EU is already embarked, attaching great attention to the issue of... opening our markets to the LDCs without reservation.... We are confident that initiatives such as Everything But Arms (EBA) could be followed by others.

On the other hand, one can also argue with regard to the suspension of the Doha Round in 2006 that Germany was not able to gain enough followership – especially with France – for a substantial reform of the CAP. This, in turn, would have been the precondition for a convincing offer to the trade G20 in order to make the latter open their markets for industrial products and services – the primary German goal. However, if this same logic is applied to the case of Brazil or to the US, then no country had sufficient power over outcomes, because none of these countries has managed to reach a successful result in the Doha Round. In sum, the question at the beginning of this section on German leadership is to be answered as follows: yes, there can be leadership and followership in a communitarized policy area, but both are less coherent and less visible than in the other cases.

Conclusion

The case studies presented in this article have demonstrated that the degree to which the leadership projects of emerging powers included the interests and/or ideas of other (neighbouring) countries correlated clearly with the latter's support for the emerging powers' leadership projects. Including the interests and ideas of other countries in the leadership project triggered followership, whereas neglecting them resulted in criticism or opposition. Therefore, the hypothesis is plausibly confirmed: *the inclusion of the interests and/or ideas dominant in another country into an emerging power's leadership project is a necessary condition for this other country to accept the policy positions, shift in power and/or status desired by the emerging power and to follow its lead.* Uneasiness amongst or even resistance by the non-emerging powers to the changes expected from a successful pursuit of leadership was only neutralized and transformed into followership when the leadership project incorporated the interests and/or ideas of the potential follower(s). These ingredients for successful leadership did not differ according to whether neighbours or more distant countries were the ones to follow: leading a group of countries apparently requires the same strategies independent of geography. However, resistance to a shift in power in favour of emerging powers was especially visible amongst neighbouring countries. In addition, the necessity of support by neighbours or distant followers depends on whether a regional dimension is at stake (UNSC) or is not at stake (WTO negotiations). Comparing the cases shows that the correlation between inclusiveness of leadership projects and followership did in fact hold throughout the variation in the cases, issues and countries examined.

In the case study on emerging powers' attempts to change the *structure* of global governance, both countries examined here performed in parallel. Brazil's and Germany's bids for permanent seats on the UN Security Council are clear cases for missing inclusiveness. Both emerging powers strived for a national *upgrading* of their respective positions in the international system and defined this goal as an improvement of the UNSC's representativity and legitimacy. The potential followers examined, Argentina and Italy, did share the impression that the UNSC's legitimacy and representativity needed to be improved, but proposed regional seats and/or more non-permanent seats as the best way to achieve these goals. The emerging powers not only ignored the alternative model offered by their potential followers, but even antagonized potential followers further by rhetorically supporting the ideas of regional seats and enhanced multilateralism without actively pursuing them. The potential followers criticized the emerging powers and built a coalition in order to prevent the empowerment of individual countries desired by Brazil and Germany. The emerging powers did not include interests and ideas of potential followers in their project. The leadership attempt failed. No reform of the UNSC occurred.

The emerging powers' bid for *directorship* in international organizations shows an interesting variation as Brazil failed while Germany succeeded. Brazil did not credibly include the interests and ideas of the potential follower Argentina in its leadership project. Inconsistency led to a lack of credibility. While the Brazilian candidate for the WTO top job framed his bid as a common cause of the developing countries and stressed an antagonism vis-a-vis the industrialized world, the Brazilian President made clear that the project was a 'candidacy of a representative of Brazil' and not of the developing world. In addition, Brazil's plea for multilateralism suffered a lack of credibility from the Argentinian point of view because of Brazil's previous unilateral behaviour in Mercosur. The latter might indicate a spillover effect from regional to global governance. Unlike the Brazilian case, Germany successfully framed its candidacy for the position of the managing director of the IMF as a European cause. Germany involved its neighbours continuously in consultations over its project and always stressed that its candidate was a representative of Europe. Open US opposition helped Germany close the European ranks behind its candidate. In the end, Italy supported the German candidate and downgraded its own candidate to a 'reserve candidate'. Emphasizing the common European cause and denying the pursuit of national empowerment formed the recipe for Germany's success.

The emerging powers' leadership projects with regard to *policy* positions on global trade governance constituted the largest case study in this article. Brazil started with the successful founding and leading of the trade G20 at the WTO meeting in Cancùn 2003. For that leadership purpose, Brazil underlined its desire to represent the developing world vis-a-vis the industrialized countries and to make the international system less 'autocratic'. In addition to this incorporation of shared ideas into its leadership project, Brazil also modified its material position on trade in order to better integrate the interests of potential followers. This inclusiveness of interests and ideas resulted in wide spread followership of Brazil's leadership. Correspondingly Brazil lost some of the backing of the G20 in 2004 when it participated in an exclusive preparatory group, the G5, and when it slightly weakened the inclusion of followers' interests in its negotiating position. The G20 countries criticized the Brazilian performance in the G5 in March 2005 and were less united at the WTO meeting in Hong Kong in December 2005 than they had been in Cancùn. The initial success and the later weakening of Brazil's leadership in the G20 correlates with changes in Brazil's procedural (how were the negotiations conducted?) and material (with which positions were they conducted?) credibility in promoting the G20's common cause.

Germany's performance with regard to global trade policy was the hardest case study in that it represented an example of more diffuse leadership due to the nature of trade policy as a common EU policy. Evidence suggests that Germany was successful in shaping some EU trade positions, including the elimination of export subsidies and the Everything But Arms initiative. Just as in the case of the candidacy for the IMF directorship, Germany framed its activities as a European endeavour in pursuit of a common cause, thus emphasizing shared ideas and interests. The Minister of the Economy even denied German leadership altogether by describing the country's role in EU trade policy as one of a 'moderator'. In addition, Germany avoided antagonism with regard to specific trade interests of other EU countries. Only after the failure of Cancùn did Germany press France to reform agricultural policy in order for the EU to be able to make a more attractive offer within the WTO negotiations. In sum, Germany did not perform as a clear leader, but did influence EU initiatives by attaining followership through moderating the European cause.

The case studies reflect the different degrees of obstacles hindering the emerging powers from achieving their goals. The reform of international structure (UNSC) proved to be the most difficult. Also, distinct regional institutional settings and power-sharing mechanisms became evident with Germany embedding its strategy in the European context with more ease than Brazil could integrate its policy in the context of Mercosur. All case studies evidenced the correlation between the inclusiveness of leadership projects and the degree of support by others. Only when the emerging power actively tried to include the interests and/or ideas of potential followers in its project was it able to obtain support. An interesting question for further research on emerging powers is why they did not make more effort to achieve followership, for example in pursuing membership in the UNSC.

In sum, the evidence shows that leadership by emerging powers gains followership only if it is credibly framed as a project also representing the goals of others even to the point of changing one's own goals and thus blurring the distinction between the goals of the emerging power and those of followers. Thus, emerging powers can reach their aims and lead others only if they credibly perform as multilateralists who accept downgrading or merging of their own interests in favour of a common denominator and who are willing to subordinate their national sovereignty to a collective purpose. In order to lead others and shape global governance, an emerging power has to credibly behave as the first among equals.

Acknowledgements An earlier version of this article was presented at the ECPR Joint Session Workshop on 'The Rise of (New) Regional Powers in Global and Regional Politics', European Consortium for Political Research, Helsinki, 7–12 May 2007. I am grateful to Hanns Maull, Alfredo Valladão, Laura Carsten, the participants of the ECPR workshop and to the anonymous reviewers for valuable comments.

References

Agence France Presse. (2004). WTO-Kompromiss über Abbau von Handelshemmnissen rückt näher, 31 July.

Amorim, C. (2003). The real Cancún. *The Wall Street Journal*, 25 September. www.mre.gov.br/portugues/imprensa/artigos/twsj250903

Amorim, C. (2004a). The foreign policy of the Lula government. Lecture by the Minister of Foreign Affairs of Brazil at the London School of Economics (LSE), London, 17 March. www.mre.gov.br/ingles/politica_externa/discursos/discurso_detalhe.asp?ID_DISCURSO=2332

Amorim, C. (2004b). The new dynamic in world trade is multipolar. Article by the Minister published in *The Financial Times*. www.mre.gov.br/ingles/politica_externa/discursos/discurso_detalhe.asp?id_discurso=2436

Amorim, C. (2004c). Statement of the Brazilian Foreign Minister at the *Joint Press Conference of the WTO Meeting* of Brazil, India (Trade Minister Nath), USA (USTR Robert Zoellick), Australia (Trade Minister Mark Vaile), and the EU (Trade Commissioner Pascal Lamy). Transcript of the Joint Press Conference, 13 June, Sao Paulo. http://trade-info.cec.eu.int/doclib/docs/2004/june/tradoc_117738.pdf

Bennis, W. (2006). The end of leadership: Exemplary leadership is impossible without full inclusion, initiatives, and cooperation of followers. In W. E. Rosenbach & R. L. Taylor (Eds.), *Contemporary issues in leadership* (pp. 129–142). Boulder: Westview Press.

Bielsa, R. (2005). Statement of the Argentine Minister of Foreign Affairs. United Nations General Assembly – General Debate, 18 September. www.un.int/argentina/english/statements/miscelaneous/Bielsa2005.htm

Bundespresseamt (BPA). (2000a). Press conference of the federal government. Press Secretary Bela Anda, 14 January, Federal Press Office, Berlin.

Bundespresseamt (BPA). (2000b). Press conference of the federal government. Press Secretary Bela Anda, 1 March, Federal Press Office, Berlin.
Bundespresseamt (BPA). (2000c). Press conference of the federal government. Chancellor Gerhard Schröder, 9 March, Federal Press Office, Berlin.
Clement, W. (2004). Clement begrüßt erfolgreiche WTO-Verhandlungen. Statement of the German Minister of the Economy, press release by the Ministry, 2 August. www.bmwa.bund.de/Navigation/Presse/pressemitteilungen,did=38690.html
Corriere, D. S. (2000). Fmi, l'Europa sceglie Koehler, 14 March, p. 23.
de Lima, M. R. S., & Hirst, M. (2006). Brazil as an intermediate state and regional power: Action, choice and responsibilities. *International Affairs, 82*(1), 21–40.
Decker, C. (2003). Wo war der Wille in Cancún? Der Fehlschlag der WTO Ministerkonferenz. *Internationale Politik, 58*(10), 57–60.
Delgado, N. G., & de Soares, A. C. O. (2005). *The G-20: Its origins, evolution, meaning and prospects* (Global Issue Papers, Vol. 25). Berlin/Rio de Janeiro: Heinrich- Böll-Stiftung.
Dinger, D. (2006). *Zwischen Furcht und Bewunderung? Italienische Haltungen zur neuen deutschen Außenpolitik.* Frankfurt/Main: Peter Lang Verlag.
EuroNews. (2004). EU findet gemeinsame Linie für WTO-Verhandlungen in der Doha-Runde. 26 July.
Falke, A. (2005). EU–USA trade relations in the Doha Development Round: Market access versus a post-modern trade policy agenda. *European Foreign Affairs Review, 10*(3), 339–357.
Falke, A. (2006). German trade policy: The decline of liberal leadership. In H. W. Maull (Ed.), *Germany's uncertain power. Foreign policy of the Berlin Republic* (pp. 185–198). Basingstoke: Palgrave.
Ferraino, G. (2000). Dopo Francia e Olanda, anche il Regno Unito dà il suo appoggio al candidato tedesco. Fmi, Blair spiana la strada a Koehler. Corriere della Sera, 11 March, p. 23.
Fischer, J. (2004a). Für eine Reform der Vereinten Nationen. Speech at the *49th General Assembly of the UN*, 23 April, New York. http://auswaertiges-amt.de/diplo/de/infoservice/presse/reden/archiv/2004/040923-reformvn.html
Fischer, J. (2004b). Unser Einfluss in Brüssel wird eher unterschätzt. Interview with the German Foreign Minister in *Stuttgarter Zeitung*, 22 October. www.auswaertiges-amt.de/diplo/de/infoservice/presse/interviews/archiv/2004/041022-fischerdtrolleeu.html
Frattini, F. (2004a). Italy does not want nationalist challenges. *Corriere de la Sera*, 27 September. Interview with the Italian Foreign Minister, in Maurizio Caprara. www.esteri.it/eng/6_38_227_01.asp?id=1398&mod=2&min=1
Frattini, F. (2004b). Speech before the *59th General Assembly of the UN.* www.esteri.it/eng/6_38_90_01.asp?id=1389&mod=3&min=3
Ganguly, S. (2002). Introduction: India as an emerging power. *The Journal of Strategic Studies, 25*(4), 1–5.
Glos, M. (2005). Bundespressekonferenz zur WTO-Ministerkonferenz in Hongkong. Statement of the German Minister of Economy, Press Release of the Ministry (BMWi), 19 December. www.bmwi.de/BMWi/Navigation/Presse/reden-und-statements,did=87586.html
Glos, M. (2006). Statement of the German Minister of Economy, Press Release of the Ministry (BMWi), 1 January. www.bmwi.de/BMWi/Navigation/Presse/pressemitteilungen,did = 1060000.html
Group of 20 (G20) (2005). G-20 ministerial declaration, New Dehli, 19 March 2005. In: G-20 two years of activities of the G-20: Moving forward the Doha Round. www.g-20.mre.gov.br/conteudo/19082005_Breviario.pdf
Guérot, U. (2007). Alors viens, Marianne! Deutschland muss Frankreich europapolitisch aus der Schmollecke holen. *Internationale Politik, 62*(1), 39–45.
Hakim, P. (2004). The reluctant partner. *Foreign Affairs, 83*(1), 114–124.
Hellmann, G., & Roos, U. (2007). *Das deutsche Streben nach einem ständigen Sitz im UN-Sicherheitsrat* (Institut für Entwicklung und Frieden INEFReport, Report No. 92). Duisburg: INEF.

Hulsman, J. C., & Techau, J. (2007). Zu hohe Erwartungen? EU-Präsidentschaft und G-8-Vorsitz. 2007 verspricht ein Schlüsseljahr für die deutsche Außenpolitik zu warden. *Internationale Politik, 62*(1), 16–25.
Hurrell, A. (2006). Hegemony, liberalism and global order: What space for would-be great powers? *International Affairs, 82*(1), 1–20.
Hurrell, A., & Narlikar, A. (2005). *A new politics of confrontation? Developing countries at Cancún and beyond*. UK: Mimeo, Oxford University/Cambridge University.
Ikenberry, J. G. (1989). Rethinking the origins of American hegemony. *Political Science Quarterly, 104*(3), 375–400.
Ikenberry, J. G. (2001). *After victory: Institutions, strategic restraint, and the rebuilding of order after major wars*. Princeton: Princeton University Press.
Katada, S. N., Maull, H. W., & Inoguchi, T. (Eds.). (2004). *Global governance: Germany and Japan in the international system*. Aldershot: Ashgate Publishers.
Kindleberger, C. P. (1981). Dominance and leadership in the international economy: Exploitation, public goods, and free rides. *International Studies Quarterly, 25*(2), 242–254.
Kirchner, N. (2005a). Statement by His Excellency Dr Nestor Kirchner, President of the Argentine Republic. UN general assembly – plenary meeting. www.un.int/argentina/english/statements/miscelaneous/President2005.htm
Kirchner, N. (2005b). Statement of the Argentine President quoted in *Buenos Aires Herald* 11 May, p. 3. http://prensa.cancilleria.gov.ar/parche.php?file=11389783.htm
La Repubblica. (2000). Fmi, accordo su Koch-Weser cade il veto opposto dai Francesi, 15 February, p. 37.
Lula da Silva, L. I., Inacio, L. (2003). Speech of the Brazilian President before the *58th General Assembly of the UN*, 23 September, New York. www.mre.gov.br/ingles/politica_externa/discursos/discurso_detalhe.asp?ID_DISCURSO=2162
Lula da Silva, L. I., & Inacio, L. (2005a). *Mensagem ao Congresso Nacional [State of the Union Address to the Congress]*. Brasilia: Presidência da República do Brasil.
Lula da Silva, L. I., Inacio, L. (2005b). Statement of the Brazilian President before the South America–Arab Summit in Brasilia, Buenos Aires Herald, 11 May, p. 7. http://prensa.cancilleria.gov.ar/parche.php?file=11389787.htm
Lula da Silva, L. I., Inacio, L. (2006). Statement by HE Mr Luiza Inacio Lula da Silva, President of the Federative Republic of Brazil at the General Debate of the 61st Session of the United Nations General Assembly, 19 September, New York. www.un.org/webcast/ga/61/pdfs/brasil-e.pdf
Malamud, C. (2005). The increase in bilateral conflicts in Latin America: Its consequences in and outside the region. Real Instituto Elcano, Madrid. www.realinstitutoelcano.org/analisis/755.asp
Marzano, A. (2003). Statement of the Italian Minister for Productive Activities (Italy on Behalf of the Presidency of the European Union) at the *V Session of the WTO Ministerial Conference* in Cancun, 11 September, WTO Document WT/MIN(03)/ST/6, Geneva. http://www.wto.org/english/thewto_e/minist_e/min03_e/statements_e/st6.pdf
Maull, H. W. (2006). Conclusion: Uncertain power – German foreign policy into the twenty-first century. In H. W. Maull (Ed.), *Germany's uncertain power. Foreign policy of the Berlin republic* (pp. 273–286). Basingstoke: Palgrave.
Mayoral, C. (2004). La Argentina y el Consejo de Seguridad de la ONU. Article by the Argentinian Embassador to the UN in *La Nacion*, 19 July. www.mre.gov.br/portugues/noticiario/internacional/selecao_detalhe.asp?ID_RESENHA=64329&Imprime=on
Meier, K. (2005). Brasilianische Außenpolitik im Jahr 2005: Welchen Preis zahlt die Regierung Lula für einen 'Multilateralismus des Südens'? Friedrich Ebert Stiftung, Bonn. www.fes.de/international/lateinamerika/kurzberichte/kurzbericht_brasilien_sep2005.pdf
Ministerio de Relaciones Exteriores. (2005). Sobre el proceso de selección del Director General de la OMC. Informe para la Prensa No 127/05, 19 April. www.mrecic.gov.ar/portal/prensa/comunicado.php?buscar=1623&fecha=19/04/2005&numero=127/05&titulo=Sobre%20el%20proceso%20de%20selecci%F3n%20del%20Director%20General%20de%20la%20OMC

Ministério de Relações Exteriores. (1998/2005). O Brasil no Conselho de Segurança. www.mre.gov.br/portugues/politica_externa/grupos/onu/obrasil_cons.asp?imprime=on

Narlikar, A., & Tussie, D. (2004). The G20 at the Cancun Ministerial: Developing countries and their evolving coalitions in the WTO. *The World Economy, 27*(7), 947–966.

Nolte, D. (2006). *Macht und Machthierarchien in den internationalen Beziehungen: Ein Analysekonzept für die Forschung über regionale Führungsmächte* (German Institute of Global and Area Studies, GIGA Working Paper, Vol. 29). Hamburg: GIGA.

Nye, J. S. (2003). *The paradox of American power: Why the world's only superpower can't go it alone*. New York: Oxford University Press.

Pedersen, T. (2002). Cooperative hegemony: Power, ideas and institutions in regional integration. *Review of International Studies, 28*, 677–696.

Pfaffenbach, B. (2005). Wird die Doha-Runde ihrer Zielsetzung als Entwicklungsrunde gerecht? Speech of the Deputy Minister of the Economy, 7 June. www.bmwi.de/BMWi/Navigation/Presse/reden-und-statements,did=67944.html

Rodrik, D. (2003). Argentina: A case of globalisation gone too far or not far enough? In J. J. Teunissen & A. Akkerman (Eds.), *The crisis that was not prevented: Argentina, the IMF, and globalisation*. The Hague: Forum on Debt and Development. www.fondad.org/product_books/pdf_download/9/Fondad-Argentina-BookComplete.pdf.

Russett, B. (1985). The mysterious case of vanishing hegemony; or, is Mark Twain really dead? *International Organization, 39*(2), 207–231.

Sashkin, M. (2006). Leadership that matters: A new vision of leadership. In W. E. Rosenbach & R. L. Taylor (Eds.), *Contemporary issues in leadership* (pp. 7–20). Boulder: Westview Press.

Schirm, S. A. (2005). Führungsindikatoren und Erklärungsvariablen für die neue internationale Politik Brasiliens. *Lateinamerika Analysen, 4*(11), 107–130.

Schirm, S. A. (2009). Ideas and interests in global financial governance: Comparing German and US preference formation. *Cambridge Review of International Affairs, 22*(3), 501–521.

Schoeman, M. (2000). South Africa as an emerging middle power. *African Security Review, 9*(3), 47–58. www.iss.co.za/Pubs/ASR/9No3/SAMiddlePower.html.

Schröder, G. (2000a). Statement by the German Chancellor. Press Release No. 88/00, Bundespresseamt, 3 March, Berlin.

Schröder, G. (2000b). Presseunterrichtung durch Bundeskanzler Schröder und den Premier-minister des Königreichs Niederlande, Wim Kok, am 9. März 2000 im Bundeskanzleramt. Bundespresseamt BPA, 9 March, Berlin.

Schröder, G. (2004). Speech at the German–Japan Economic Meeting, Tokio 9.12.04. www.tokyo.diplo.de/vertretung/tokyo/de/03/bilaterale_beziehungen/bk_20besuch_20dezember_2004/seite_rede_20-wirtschaftsforum.html

Seixas Corrêa, L. F. de. (2005). Statement by Ambassador Luiz Felipe de Seixas Corrêa at the*V Special Meeting of the Council for Trade and Economic Development (COTED) of CARICOM*, Georgetown, Guyana, 06/01/2005. www.mre.gov.br/ingles/politica_externa/discursos/discurso_detalhe.asp?ID_DISCURSO=2544

The Economist. (1997). Argentina and Brazil: Sweet nothings? 18 September.

The Economist. (2004). Brazil's foreign policy: A giant stirs, 12 June, pp. 50–51.

The Economist. (2005). World trade: Hard truths, 20 December.

The Economist. (2006). The new titans. A survey of the world economy, 16 September.

United Nations (UN) (2003). Resolutionen 58/1 A und B: Beitragsschlüssel fü die Aufteilung der Ausgabenlast der Vereinten Nationen 16.10.03/23.12.03. www.auswaertiges-amt.de/www/de/aussenpolitik/vn/vereinte_nationen/finanzen_html

United Nations (UN) (2007). Ranking of military and political contributions to UN operations, 31 July, New York. www.un.org/Depts/dpko/dpko/contributors/2007/jul07_2.pdf

Valladão, A. (2006). Brazil: An ambiguous leader. Paper prepared for the GIGA Conference on *Regional Powers in Asia, Africa, Latin America and the Middle East*, 11–12 December, Hamburg.

Veiga, P. da. M. (2005). Brazil and the G-20 group of developing countries, managing the challenges of WTO participation case study 7. www.wto.org/english/res_e/booksp_e/casestudies_e/case7_e.htm#fntext1

World Trade Organization (WTO). (2004). WTO meeting US, EU, Brazil, India, and Australia, Joint Press Conference (C. Amorim, P. Lamy, R. Zoellick, M. Vaile, Nath). 13 June, Sao Paulo. trade-info.cec.eu.int/doclib/docs/2004/june/tradoc_117738.pdf

Chapter 13
A Power Through Trade? The European Union and Democracy Promotion in ACP States

Dennis Nottebaum

Introduction

Economic integration has been at the heart of the European integration process and part of the raison d'être of the European Union (EU). Thanks to the development of the internal market the EU has become the largest economic unit on the planet and a formidable power in trade. At the same time, the EU is increasingly becoming a power through trade (Meunier and Nicolaidis 2005, 2006): It uses access to its vast internal market as a bargaining chip to induce changes in its trading partners' internal affairs. The size of the European single market combined with an increasingly supranational decision-making process in external economic relations renders the European Union a powerful actor in international trade negotiations. Whoever wants to do business with Europe has to play by the rules the Union establishes, including areas ranging from human rights to democracy, from development policies to good governance.

Promoting democratic governance is one of the declared ends in EU trade negotiations. Most agreements with developing countries only have limited economic consequences for the EU, but they do offer policy incentives and opportunities for political influence abroad. Moreover, the economic gains for partner countries are considerable in most cases given the size of the European market, which ensures strong incentives for them to play by the rules the agreement establishes.

Ultimately, EU trade power is used to achieve two goals. First, it seeks to secure access to new markets and hence both uses and maximizes its power in trade. Second, the EU also uses its trade power as a tool to achieve secondary objectives such as the promotion of social and political norms and standards, especially in developing countries. This latter form is what Meunier and Nicolaidis (2005) term 'power through trade', a strategy of realizing non-trade objectives through trade relations. Meunier and Nicolaidis (2005, 2006) argue that this strategy may be used as a potential instrument for the EU to exert geopolitical power (Table 13.1).

E. Fels et al. (eds.), *Power in the 21st Century*, Global Power Shift,
DOI 10.1007/978-3-642-25082-8_13, © Springer-Verlag Berlin Heidelberg 2012

Table 13.1 Forms of EU trade power (Source: Meunier and Nicolaidis (2006: 910))

Nature of trading relations	Power *in* trade: exporting goods, services and capital	Power *through* trade: exporting standards and norms
Bilateral	Symmetric and asymmetric bargaining power over market access	Democratization, development, governance and adoption of standards
Regional	Reciprocal market access	Exporting EU single market rules and broader governance tools to other regions
Global	Multilateral bargaining, specific and diffuse reciprocity	Shaping the multilateral system through deep trade agenda

This paper analyzes whether the EU's trade power translates into a factor that stimulates democratization and may therefore be a key component in efforts of democracy promotion vis-à-vis the group of African, Caribbean and Pacific (ACP) states. Based on the premise that (economic) power is fungible, meaning that it can become power in another area (in this case the domestic realm of the trading partner), this paper assesses to what extent trade with the European Union has induced and stimulated democratization processes in partner countries. The basic question here is how successful the EU has been in promoting its democratic values alongside its trade relations in order to assess whether trade power is a viable tool for the EU to exert geopolitical influence.

Methodology

The analysis is based on a large-*n* study of a panel dataset including data on trade flows and democratic development, as well as several control factors. The panel covers the years from 1991 to 2008. 1991 has deliberately been chosen as a starting point since the ratification of the Lomé IV convention in the previous year had been the first time that a clause on democratic principles became a central aspect of a preferential trade agreement between the EU and the group of ACP states.[1] The study analyzes the impact of trade relations with the European Union, operationalized as trade openness, on the development of democracy in ACP states using a two-stage least-squares model (2SLS): In order to preempt potential endogeneity and simultaneity biases a gravity model is constructed to create an instrumental variable (IV) for trade openness in a first stage. This is followed by a regression of

[1] Although these clauses were not officially established as conditionalities before the revision of the Lomé IV convention in 1995, the case of Togo in 1993 was the first instance in which development aid was suspended on the grounds of democratic deficits in relation with election fraud and arbitrary arrests. Although these sanctions did not directly relate to preferential trade relations, the EU has always linked trade and aid vis-à-vis ACP states. Thus, the case of Togo serves as a powerful illustration of the tool of conditionality even before it had formally been established.

the constructed instrument on indicators of democratic development. We account for other factors that have been identified as important for the development or demise of democracy by including relevant control variables.

Large-*n* studies have become a popular method for the analysis of developments of democracy. This is due to the fact that they provide a relatively high statistical significance when analyzing the general impact of one or more factors on a dependent variable, in this case the level and quality of democracy. It is therefore the ideal way of assessing a rather specific effect. The downside of large-*n* studies is that their results face limitations (as all research methodologies do) because highly specialized analyses may lead to erroneous conclusions when they are not performed in the context of all relevant controls of cross-sectional and over-time interference. It may be "predicated on a mountain of precarious homogenizing assumptions about cases, populations, variables and causation" (Ragin 2005: 93). A strong system of controls will therefore be imperative for the quality of this project; a fact that will be satisfied by incorporating a number of relevant control variables in order to check for influential factors such as individual status of (economic) development, regional particularities, or external pressures.

The analysis of data on a relatively large number of countries will offer general insights into the effect of trade relations on processes of democratization. This will enable us to assess the 'power through trade'-hypothesis as to its validity. Large-*n* studies generate findings that may be generalized in order to test theories. This comes at the expense of applicability: The more abstract the analysis the larger the probability that specific factors of influence and contextual evidence are left unaccounted for (Coppedge 1999). Thus, the findings of this study remain sensitive to the particularities of individual contexts, especially on the country level. We will return to this limitation in the final part of this paper.

Moreover, this study explicitly deals with EU trade relations with less and least-developed countries for the simple reason that the effects of trade on the state of democracy are expected to be most pronounced in these cases. We believe that this reduction in scope may benefit the results without calling them into question. Although trade relations with other partners would possibly generate further or even different findings, we do think it necessary to eliminate the disturbing effects that the inclusion of states like Russia or China that are in a distinctly different situation than those countries of interest here would cause. We will elaborate on the theoretical foundations of our focus on developing countries later in this article.

Significance

Does democracy go hand in hand with international trade? Or can democratic change be induced by way of trade relations? These questions seem relevant on at least two grounds. First, a democratic political system is widely believed to be conducive to the process of development and essential for understanding and fulfilling economic needs. Other authors have shown that democracy can have a positive effect on economic growth, and vice versa (for example Barro 1996, 1997; Bussmann 2001). Promoting trade openness and economic development may hence be a prime tool for the promotion of democracy around the world. Second, the common perception among policymakers and researchers alike that there is a positive link between trade openness, growth, and democratic governance has been an important rationale for deepening trade liberalization at global and regional levels. To the extent that trade fosters democracy, the implications are crucial for future negotiations of EU trade agreements.

However important and timely the topic, the academic debate on links between trade and democracy is far from settled. Systematic empirical research remains scarce, and those studies that are available arrive at different conclusions. To name just a few, Margit Bussmann (2001), using data on the late twentieth century, finds only little evidence that trade openness affects democratic development, while Li and Reuveny (2002) report a negative relationship. López-Córdova and Meissner (2008) conduct a long-run analysis of the phenomenon and report a positive relationship between international trade and democracy. Furthermore, there are numerous publications analyzing the relationship between democratic governance and other economic indicators, such as growth, equality, or foreign direct investments, the results of which are overall inconclusive.

This study seeks to contribute to this ongoing debate. To our best knowledge, it will encompass the first systematic assessment of EU democracy promotion efforts through trade. The EU has used trade agreements for the advancement of democratic principles and liberal values for two decades. Nevertheless, apart from specific case studies a comprehensive analysis of this method has yet to be conducted (Jünemann and Knodt 2007). The relevance of this study is therefore rooted in the need for an assessment of democracy promotion efforts through trade in order to understand the mechanisms at work and develop the tools. Ideally, this study will both contribute to the debate on whether trade relations and economic openness boost democratization and to the assessment of the tools the EU uses to promote its values and norms via trade agreements.

Theoretical Considerations

Much has been said about the EU as an international power and its position in global affairs. Its distinct difference to the classical Westphalian nation state in particular has to be considered when assessing its role in international relations. Despite its growth in capabilities and competences, the EU will remain a composite construction made up of sovereign nations who voluntarily choose to pool some of their powers and sovereignty rights. Especially in the realm of foreign policy, which lies at the core of a state's exclusive competences, the transfer of responsibilities proves difficult (Smith 2000). This will continue to impose serious constraints on the capabilities of the European Union, particularly when it comes to the external projection of power. It therefore seems highly unlikely for the EU to become a traditional power with a notable capacity to project hard power any time soon, neither in terms of capabilities, nor in its political will.

The question then is, if Europe is unlikely to become a power in the traditional sense, what kind of actor is it and in which direction is the Union heading? Influential theories have been put forth that regard Europe as a 'transformational', 'civilian' (Telò 2006) or 'normative power' (Laïdi 2008; Manners 2002).[2] Whichever term is employed and however the concept is defined, trade is identified as a key source of influence in all theorizations. The European Union has signed trade agreements with more than a 100 countries mostly granting some sort of access to the European market. Starting in the early 1990s, these agreements have included references to the protection of human rights, individual freedoms and other democratic values. Most of these rules are enforceable through a repeal of preferential access to the European market and other penalties.

What this tells us is that the EU certainly is a power in international trade relations, given the scope of its activities and the pull-factor of the common market. A central part of its *raison d'être* is precisely the economic integration that has rendered the EU one of the most influential actors in international economic affairs. Economic power therefore is a key mechanism whereby the Union exerts influence internationally and promotes its interests. The promotion of democratic ideals and principles of good governance -core values on which the EU is built -through trade thus seems to be a logical consequence of the debate on the EU's role as an international power.

On Democratization

Given the complexity of the subject matter, the study of democratization processes has been a hotly debated issue in the social sciences at least from the mid twentieth century until today. The questions of how democracy comes into being, which factors influence its persistence or disappearance, and how this process may be influenced both from the outside and from within a given state or region have been intensely analyzed over the years. The field has produced a large amount of theories and hypotheses attempting to find answers to these questions. Theories of democratization can at a very basic level be subsumed under four rather broad paradigms (following Teorell 2010). These shall be examined in more detail in this part. Table 13.2 offers a summary at a glance.

[2] For a detailed discussion of the character of the EU's power, see Stivachtis 2007.

Table 13.2 Overview of democratization paradigms (Adapted from Teorell (2010), Chap. 1)

Paradigm	Trigger for democratization	Strengths and weaknesses
Structural	Structural factors, e.g. social, economic, institutional developments	+ Claims testable with statistical techniques + analysis of longterm, structural developments – lack of micro foundations – neglect of human agents
Strategic decision-making	Strategic decision-making by political elites and human agents	+ Emphasis on transition and role of actors – narrow set of actors – focus on short-term developments – danger of tautological explanations
Social forces	Relationships among social classes	+ Integration of structural and individual elements – neglect of non-class actors – lack of empirical testing
Economic	Structural and individual factors; material resources and rational behavior	+ Integrated approach + empirical rigor and formal modelling – lack of empirical corroboration

The Structural Paradigm

The structural paradigm is based on the idea that political change results from underlying social, economic and cultural characteristics of a society. Thus, structural theorists focus on a rather mechanical procedural view of democratization that largely disregards individual and collective action. This is not to say that agency is entirely irrelevant for this paradigm, but it is rather treated as a "black box". Structural developments lead to political change, while the role of social actors does not enter the concept as an explanatory variable.

The first and arguably most influential structural approach to democratization to appear related democratic to economic development.[3] Lipset's seminal work in 1959 established the basic claim that democracies tend to be more socio-economically developed than non-democracies; a finding that has remained largely unchallenged to the day (Lipset et al. 1993; Lipset 1994; Moore 1995; Geddes 1999; Epstein et al. 2006; Barro 1999; Boix and Stokes 2003; Boix 2003 provide econometric evidence). Lipset credits the idea to Aristotle:

> From Aristotle down to the present, men have argued that only in a wealthy society in which relatively few citizens lived in real poverty could a situation exist in which the mass of the population could intelligently participate in politics and could develop the self-restraint necessary to avoid succumbing to the appeals of irresponsible demagogues. (Lipset 1959: 75)

[3] This theory of democratization has become widely known under the name of *modernization theory* (Przeworski and Limongi 1997). Wucherpfennig and Deutsch (2009) provide a useful overview of the state of the debate.

Although other studies (as well as common sense) suggest that economic development is by far not the only factor in democratic transitions (dix 1994; stepan 1986),[4] it is unmistakably among the most important (Milner and Kubota 2005). Hence, modernization theory has been one of the hotly debated ideas in the study of democracy over the last decades. In a groundbreaking article Przeworski and Limongi (1997) reject the endogenous hypothesis that economic development brings about democracy. According to their findings, democracies come into being almost randomly, with similar chances at all levels of development. Thus, "[d]evelopment makes democracies endure, but it does not make them more likely to emerge" (Wucherpfennig and Deutsch 2009: 3). Although their arguments were extremely influential on verbal grounds, their analysis was subject to a number of methodological and interpretive shortcomings (Boix and Stokes 2003; Inglehart and Welzel 2005; Epstein et al. 2006). "In sum, the statistical evidence we have to date strongly suggests that both exogenous and endogenous democratization are systematically associated with socio-economic development." (Wucherpfennig and Deutsch 2009: 4)

> Economic development is, indeed, strongly linked to pervasive shifts in people's beliefs and motivations, and these shifts in turn change the role of religion, job motivations, human fertility rates, gender roles, and sexual norms. And they also bring growing mass demands for democratic institutions and for more responsive behavior on the part of elites. These changes together make democracy increasingly likely to emerge, while also making war less acceptable to publics (Inglehart and Welzel 2009: 39).

Additionally, further research has shown that the relationship between democracy and economic development is not necessarily linear. The probability of democratic governance does not increase automatically with the level of economic prosperity (Jackman 1973; Arat 1988). Rather, the importance of a middle income range has been highlighted in several studies suggesting that for countries within this range the probability of regime change towards a democratic mode of governance is highest (Huntington 1984; Diamond 1992; Vanhanen 1997). Acemoglu and Robinson (2006), drawing on this model, put the distribution of income and assets at the center of a theory of political transitions. They find that better distributions of income prop efforts to democratize. Moreover, they underline the impact of capital abundance as a factor that stabilizes democracy.

Economic development affects a society in several ways that in most instances prove beneficial for the advent of democratic culture, including the rise of democratic values, a decrease in class tensions and inequality, and growth of a middle class and structures of civil society (see Gill 2000: 3; Diamond 1992: 475 for more

---

[4] Lipset (1959) himself argued in favor of a large number of socio-economic conditions for democracy, not -as is often claimed -for a simplistic relation between income and democracy.

detailed accounts). Economic openness and trade provide a counterweight to governmental power. Economic theory and evidence suggest that in most cases open economies tend to generate more wealth than closed ones (Sachs et al. 1995; Edwards 1998; Frankel and Romer 1999; Dollar and Kraay 2004). This is often accompanied by the growth of a politically aware middle class. The dispersion of economic power enables a large number of actors to participate in decision-making. The process spills over from the economic into other societal and political realms. Economic development and openness towards international trade have hence been identified as key enabling factors for democratic transition.

Thus, the central observation on which modernization theory foots -a positive correlation between economic development and democracy -is nowadays hardly disputed. As Boix (2003: 1–2) fittingly points out "[e]xcluding Duverger's law on the effect of single-member districts on party systems, it may be the strongest empirical generalization we have in comparative politics to date". Based on Lipset's hypothesis a vast amount of research has been conducted into more specific structural factors accounting for democratic development. This includes, but is not limited to, economic freedom (Burkhart 2000), economic crises (Gasiorowski 1995), natural resources (Dunning 2008; also Sachs and Warner 1995), income distribution (Acemoglu and Robinson 2000b; Acemoglu et al. 2008; Reuveny and Li 2003), social spending (Rudra 2005) and -in a more general fashion -economic growth (Helliwell 1994; Barro 1996).

Other structural approaches linked democratic development to a certain type of culture in a country. Some scholars highlighted individualist cultural elements (discussed in Huntington 1991), others polyarchy (Dahl 1971) or civic culture (Almond and Verba 1965) as central enabling factors for democratic systems. Although the cultural paradigm helped explain why democracy persisted (exogenous democratization) in some contexts and not in others, it is not a particularly powerful explanation for the emergence of democracy (endogenous democratization) as such.

The Strategic Decision Making Paradigm

Dankwart Rustow (1970) was among the first to criticize Lipset's approach for neglecting the question of how democracy comes into being. He developed a model of phases explaining how democratization takes place. This includes three distinct phases -the preparatory, decision and habituation phases which all transitions from authoritarianism to democracy consist of. Rustow's model received only limited academic attention for the ensuing years until O'Donnell and Schmitter (1986) published their groundbreaking study on what has now become known as the "transition paradigm". They reasserted Rustow's phase model and posited that virtually no structural prerequisites were needed for the initiation of a democratization process. Rather, strategic decision making and the role of political elites were seen as crucial elements of the transition process.

Rustow's initial terminology has since been amended while the overall core of his argument remains a central aspect of the strategic decision making paradigm. Thus, democratic transitions undergo the three phases of liberalization, democratization and consolidation which are heavily influenced by political elites that bargain about strategic choices. Democratization in this sense is seen as a top-down process that critically depends on diversions within the authoritarian leadership -a strong opposition is deemed insufficient as a democratizing force in cases where the leadership is cohesive and undivided. While O'Donnell and Schmitter (1986) acknowledge the potential impact of long-run structural developments, they retain Rustow's emphasis on short-term dynamics and human agency as key factors in democratic transitions. It is therefore unsurprising that the strategic decision making paradigm has not lead to any further generalizations of the process of democratization. Prerequisites of democratic transitions are based on micro-level developments as well as country- and situation-specific factors, a view that has been reasserted forcefully in more recent studies (Przeworski 2000).

Against the rather deterministic stance of the structural paradigm the strategic decision making approach evolved from individual actors and human agency. This fundamental shift has had a profound impact on the academic debate and was indeed influential for the development and design of democracy promotion policies that aimed to directly support certain democratic activists in authoritarian contexts. The obvious downside of the paradigm is its insistence on short-term factors at the expense of longterm, structural developments. This is especially controversial given that actors take on a central position in the transition model, but the circumstances in which these actors have developed their preferences and political agendas remains beyond the analysis. This leads to a situation where the explanatory factors within the model are very close to the outcome they seek to explain. This, as Teorell (2010: 21) rightly points out, "borders on tautology".

The Social Forces Paradigm

The third paradigm is informed by a Marxist approach centered around the role of social classes in the development of democracy. Barrington Moore published the seminal work on which this approach rests in 1966. His argument foots on the role of the landed upper class and the peasantry in the development of agrarian into industrial societies and his analysis of why some countries developed into democracies and others into dictatorships as a result. His focus on the material interests of actors that are differentiated in terms of their class has resonated with much of the successive literature. Unlike in the strategic decision making paradigm, democracy is here seen as a result of a development from below and thus a bottom-up struggle between actors with different economic interests.

Moore's approach was prominently advanced by Rueschemeyer et al. (1992), who argue that the working rather than the middle class is the decisive actor in a model of relative class power: the development of democracy thus hinges on the expansion in size and power of the working class as well as the relative weakening of the landowners. Thus, the approach presents an early synthesis of the two previous mentioned paradigms by incorporating the role of (social) actors and human agency into a democratization model based on structural factors. However, the theoretical fundamentals remain largely untested. Research has so far primarily been based on selective case studies that allow for relatively context-specific insights but do not provide any empirical evidence. Moreover, the approach has been criticized for its deterministic explanations for democratization and its neglect of non-class actors, such as human rights activists or religious organizations (Teorell 2010).

The Economic Synthesis

The most recent paradigm to emerge has been based on an economic approach towards studying democratization (see for example Acemoglu and Robinson 2006; Boix 2003). Since it incorporates aspects of all previously mentioned paradigms it can be regarded as a synthetic approach, although it also introduces new aspects. This particularly pertains to the analytical methods used, which are derived – as the name of the paradigm suggests – from economics. Formal modeling and the employment of econometrics have resulted in a push towards more rigorous ways to analyze increasingly sophisticated sets of data and derive predictions based on economic theory.

The economic model primarily foots on structural conditions that impact both individual and collective decision making as well as rational choice. Game theoretical elements are often used to analyze these processes. Moreover, the group of relevant actors wielding influence is expanded to its maximum, now including the whole population regardless of (though not unaffected by) social status.

These studies have put forth two crucial factors favoring democratization (Teorell 2010). First, certain supply-side conditions have to be met. Democratization is more likely the lower the costs of redistribution and the higher the costs of repression for the elite.

Second, demand-side conditions have to be satisfied. A certain degree of social pressure based on grievances directed against the elite needs to be present in order to establish some degree of protest. This protest has to be to be organized in order to be effective (Apolte 2012). A collective identity among an existing and rather stable demos is another prerequisite for the coherence of the protest movement.

Trade and Democratization: A Digression

Given the focus of this study on the impact of trade flows on democratization, literature that particularly focuses on the interrelation of these two factors is of special importance here.[5] Despite the fact that older accounts would broadly fit with the structural approach highlighted previously, more recent accounts consider a larger set of explanatory paths, providing analyses based on economic syntheses.

Li and Reuveny (2002) report a negative relationship between trade and democracy. However, their method of dealing with endogeneity by lagging the independent variable has been criticized as inadequate (Eichengreen and Leblang 2008). Rigobon and Rodrik (2005) use identification through heteroskedasticity and also report a negative relationship, while Bussmann (2001) and Giavazzi and Tabellini (2005) find no relationship at all.

One of the most extensive studies so far has been conducted by López-Córdova and Meissner (2008). Similar to the approach employed here, the authors use a gravity model to derive an instrumental variable for trade openness. Using data from 1870 to 2000 they report a positive impact of trade on democracy; a result that has been confirmed for a smaller sample by Yu (2005). Eichengreen and Leblang (2008) analyze the possibility of bidirectionality and find – with some exceptions – evidence for the existence of positive feedback effects running into both directions.

A Simple Economic Theory of Democratization

At the most basic level, a model of democratization starts with the observation that in terms of preferences for different types of regimes there usually is a conflict between an elite (mostly well endowed with capital) and the larger part of the population, the citizens. Since democracies tend to cater more to the needs of the latter while autocratic systems are usually more mindful of the elite, we can state that citizens have a stronger preference for democracy. "So if there is going to be a conflict about what types of political institutions a society should have, we will have the majority of citizens on the side of democracy and the elite on the side of nondemocracy." (Acemoglu and Robinson 2006: 21) In a simple model, the distribution of *de facto* political power between the two factions will likely decide the mode of governance of the country: the more de facto power the citizens have, the more democratic the country will be, *ceteris paribus*, and vice versa.[6]

As intuitively appealing as this model may be, it certainly is oversimplified and underestimates dynamic effects and the importance of *de jure* power, i.e. institutions. In a more realistic setting, citizens are likely to seek to transform their de facto power (which may be short-lived) into *de jure* power, whose purpose it is to guarantee their de facto power in the future. Thus, political institutions are

[5] It should be noted that some of the subsequently mentioned studies use broader definitions of economic globalization than just "trade flows".

[6] The theoretical framework presented here is primarily a verbalized, non-formal version of a more comprehensive theory developed by Acemoglu and Robinson (2000a, b, 2001, 2002). See also Apolte (2012) for a critique and extension.

needed in order to manifest the transitory nature of de facto power. In an autocratic setting, the elite controls *de jure* power while the citizens may or may not have de facto power. In the event of a political transition the citizens will want to gain more permanent power -*de jure* -, hence their demand for institutionalization.

In this model de facto power of the citizens is the game changer, the force behind democratization. Once citizens accumulate de facto power and pose a credible revolutionary threat, the elite will be forced to make concessions, which can only be credible in the form of institutional changes (the citizens otherwise won't believe that promises made today would be kept in the future under a potentially different allocation of power). Thereby, changes in the distribution of de facto power result in the demand for *de jure* power, or in other words democratization.[7]

Now, the question is how trade can contribute to this process. Determinants of democracy and democratization are manifold. Every move to democracy is a unique process based on a diverse set of factors. As stated above, no single cause is sufficient to bring this change about. Still, some factors can be identified that stimulate change in de facto power and promote democratization. The degree of organization within civil society certainly is an important factor when it comes to the question of how to use de facto power strategically. Shocks and crises may foster or undermine the processes in multiple ways, as do interventions from the outside. Arguably one of the most important factors is economic openness and the evolution of a middle class (Acemoglu and Robinson 2000b).

> This is because both a financially independent middle class and the integration of the domestic economy with the world economy are at the same time both necessary conditions for and natural effects of economic success in the modern world. As a result, democratic ideology of [developed countries] may penetrate the middle class and undermine the legitimacy of the regime. (Lin and Nugent 1995)

Several different models have been proposed to predict patterns of trade and to analyze the effects of trade policies. This paper essentially draws on two theoretical constructs and combines them to create a theory of how democracy promotion via trade relations works. This backdrop consists of the Heckscher-Ohlin and Stolper-Samuelson theorems, both widely accepted and regarded as robust, and of elements of game theory.[8]

The Heckscher-Ohlin model (originally: Ohlin 1933) builds on Ricardo's theory of comparative advantage by predicting patterns of commerce and production based on the factor endowments of a trading region. A Heckscher-Ohlin world consists of two countries that produce two goods with one country being relatively labor abundant and the other being relatively capital abundant. Relative endowments of the factors of production (labor and capital) determine a country's comparative

[7] An alternative strategy for the elite may of course be the use of force and repression to reduce the de facto power of the citizens.

[8] Other influential trade theories (New Trade Theory, specific factors model, etc.) are disregarded as they are all less compatible with the research question at stake here and the specifications of the study.

advantage. Countries have comparative advantages in the production of those goods for which the required factors of production are relatively abundant locally. This is because the prices of goods are ultimately determined by the prices of their inputs. Goods that require inputs that are locally abundant will be cheaper to produce than those goods that require inputs that are locally scarce. Evidence strongly suggests that a capital-abundant country is usually more developed than a labor-abundant one. When these two countries now start to trade with one another each will specialize in that good in whose production the production factor that the country possesses in relative abundance is used more intensively. Hence the labor abundant country will produce and trade the labor intensive good while the capital abundant state specializes in the capital intensive one. As a result both countries will gain from trading with one another while the abundant factor of production will benefit most, *ceteris paribus*.[9]

The Stolper-Samuelson theorem (originally: Stolper and Samuelson 1941) is an extension of the Heckscher-Ohlin model. It describes a relation between the relative prices of output goods and relative factor rewards, specifically, real wages and real returns to capital. The theorem states that a rise in the relative price of a good will lead to a rise in the return to that factor which is used most intensively in the production of the good, and conversely, to a fall in the return to the other factor. Applied to the context of trade between a developing, labor-abundant country and a developed, capital-abundant country we can expect trade to induce a rise in average wages in the developing country and a rise in returns to capital in the developed country. Socially the rise of a working and middle class in the developing country will be a result. This has been identified as one of the key factors in democratization processes (e.g. Diamond 1992; Gill 2000).

A game theoretical approach now suggests that a wealthier middle class will simultaneously call for more political rights (as explained previously). The society, having changed from being pyramid shaped (few rich, many poor) to being diamond-shaped (dominant middle class), will on economic grounds be more likely to democratize. Findings strongly support the claim that democratic governance is closely related to and rises alongside median income levels (Acemoglu and Robinson 2006).

Hence, by combining trade theory with game theoretic basics we can expect trade between developed countries -in this case the European Union -and less developed ones -ACP states -to foster democratization in the latter. The respective parts of this theoretical construct have been tested in numerous studies analyzing different countries over time and found to be robust in their claims.

[9] Due to limited space the Heckscher-Ohlin model can only be paraphrazed in its basic structure here. See Leamer (1995) for a more in-depth account. Overviews may also be found in virtually any textbook on trade theory and international economics.

EU Democracy Promotion By Trade: A Framework

EU policies on democracy promotion, human rights and good governance have developed significantly since 1990. Initially set in a context of development policy the theme of aiding democratic development abroad has increasingly become a priority in itself in external relations of Western states, including the European Union. Democracy, the rule of law, respect for human rights and other fundamental freedoms have become a central objective within the Common Foreign and Security Policy (CFSP) and external trade policy. Agreements with third countries have included provisions for the respect of these norms and values. More specifically, democratization elements have become pivotal aspects of EU trade agreements starting with the fourth Lomé Convention signed between the EU and 71 ACP countries in 1989/1990. Most recently, the Treaty of Lisbon emphasized that the EU would act in international affairs according to the values upon which it was founded, including democracy, human rights and the rule of law.

The Treaty on the European Union (TEU -commonly referred to as the Treaty of Maastricht) was the first legal framework in which the EU adopted democracy promotion as a central objective. In article 11 the member states commit themselves "to develop and consolidate democracy and the rule of law, and respect for human rights and fundamental freedoms". Article 181 extends this provision to economic, financial and technical cooperation with third countries: "Community policy in this area shall contribute to the general objective of developing and consolidating democracy and the rule of law, and to the objective of respecting human rights and fundamental freedoms."

As a consequence, the European Union has started to insert human rights and democracy clauses in all its agreements with non-industrialized countries. Since then, democratization and human rights issues have been mainstreamed into all aspects of EU policy making. Partly for this reason, the EU is often described as a 'value-driven' actor, which constitutes a rationale for the promotion of its own value system (Knodt and Jünemann 2007). Although conflicts persist within the EU, democracy 'European-style' certainly is a success story in that it has created sustainable peace and prosperity under the maximization of individual freedoms throughout the better part of the continent. The EU therefore seeks to promote its own value system beyond its borders. The scholarly literature offers two main models of how this kind of external democracy promotion may work. The first model sees democratization mainly as a conditionality-induced process (Ethier 2003; Schimmelfennig et al. 2003; Haughton 2007), in which conditionality can be both positive and negative. Positive conditionality refers to the case in which one party offers a benefit to the other in exchange for compliance with a given set of rules. On the contrary, negative conditionality entails punishment in a case where an actor violates a norm, the most prominent case being that of sanctions. Accordingly, positive trade conditionality is a type of intergovernmental bargaining in which an external actor – the EU – offers market access and preferential, in the past often non-reciprocal treatment to a third country in exchange for compliance with a given set of democratic norms and procedures. The government of the target state makes a decision on whether or not to comply on the basis of cost-benefit calculations – i.e. whether the promised rewards outweigh expected adoption costs.

The second model of external democracy promotion is somewhat based on modernization theory as described above and focuses on socioeconomic development. This idea of 'social learning' (Tocci 2007) maintains that democratization is a multi-step process in which economic development leads to societal pluralism and the emergence of a strong middle class that, in turn, demands political participation and accountability of the government (Lipset et al. 1993; Lipset 1994; Moore 1995). At the same time, "(t)hrough participation in, or close contact with, the EU institutional framework, parties may come to alter their substantive beliefs, visions and purposes (e.g. changing views on human rights, identity, sovereignty or democracy). They may also alter their preferred strategies (i.e. negotiation, compromise and international law over unilateralism, brinkmanship and political violence)" (Tocci 2007: 15).

Both models are present in the EU's strategy of promoting democracy through trade. It combines the modernizing effects of economic openness and interaction (social learning) with the conditionality of agreements on labor rights, human rights and the rule of law (carrots and sticks).

Conceptual Analysis

Based on the existing literature on the relationship between trade openness and democracy and especially the findings of the most recent publications by López-Córdova and Meissner (2008) and Eichengreen and Leblang (2008) one would expect that trade between the EU and ACP states has had a positive impact on democracy in the latter. Accordingly, the central hypothesis of this study is formulated as follows:

H1: Increasing levels of trade openness of ACP states towards the European Union in the period from 1991 to 2008 have had a positive impact on levels of democracy in ACP states.

The variables we employ in order to test this hypothesis are described in the following. The appendix features a more detailed account on data sources of all variables.

Measuring Democracy

Democracy is a notoriously hard concept to measure quantitatively. Questions regarding definitions (what is democracy, how can it be defined, or even quantified?) and doubts concerning the quality of data gathered in less-developed countries (LDCs) – among other factors – may call results into question. Arguably the most established and frequently used indices of democracy today are the Polity IV dataset and Freedom House surveys, both of which will be employed for the dependent variable.[10] While the primary dependent variable "democracy" is derived from the Polity IV dataset (Marshall and Jaggers 2010), a combined measure of Polity IV and Freedom House data is used to check the robustness of the results.

Polity IV

The Polity IV measure of democracy is based on three major dimensions. The **competitiveness of political participation** measures the degree of institutionalization of political participation and competition, e.g. via the existence of competing political parties or government control over political liberties. **Competitiveness and openness of executive recruitment** measures the way in which a head of government is selected, for instance through free and fair elections or through hereditary succession. **Constraints on the chief executive** reflects the degree to which a head of government has to take into consideration the views of others (e.g. a legislative body) in the decision-making process.

The Polity score captures these dimensions on a 21-point scale ranging from −10 (hereditary monarchy) to +10 (consolidated democracy). It should be noted that countries are only included in the Polity IV data set if they achieved independence by 1998 and had a population of 500,000 or more that year. For the analysis this means that some of the smaller island states in the Caribbean and Pacific region had to be excluded.[11]

Freedom House

The Freedom House index is based on surveys on political rights (including free, fair, and competitive elections) and individual liberties (including freedom of information, organization, and religion). It scores each country on a scale from

[10] Thus, I implicitly adopt the (limited) definition of democracy that each indicator follows.

[11] Additionally, a handful of countries had to be excluded due to incomplete or subquality data. Thus, the final sample consists of the following 47 ACP states: Angola, Benin, Botswana, Burkina Faso, Burundi, Cameroon, Central African Republic, Chad, Comoros, Congo, Congo (Democratic Republic), Cote d'Ivoire, Djibouti, Equatorial Guinea, Ethiopia, Fiji, Gabon, Gambia, Ghana, Guinea, Guinea-Bissau, Guyana, Jamaica, Kenya, Lesotho, Madagascar, Malawi, Mali, Mauritania, Mauritius, Mozambique, Namibia, Niger, Nigeria, Papua New Guinea, Rwanda, Senegal, Sierra Leone, Solomon Islands, South Africa, Sudan, Swaziland, Tanzania, Togo, Trinidad and Tobago, Uganda, Zambia.

1 to 7, with 1 being the best value. It must be noted that while Freedom House has undertaken some efforts to objectify its criteria and coding rules, the scores still result from a largely subjective measure based on an elaborate checklist. The reliability of the coding procedure and the data used thus remains beyond the control of outsiders. Difficulties with both indices mainly arise from the quality of data and information used and the fact that they take the coded features at face value without being able assess the substances and nuances (Berg-Schlosser 2007). Moreover, both measure only selected dimensions of democracy, which is the primary reason for employing both indices here. This suggests that empirical democratic research is inevitably biased in some way or another; a fact that needs to be kept in mind when using indicators of democracy in quantitative analyses (Munck and Verkuilen 2002; Müller and Pickel 2007).

Operationalizing Trade Openness

Following the existing literature, we operationalize the variable "trade openness" as the natural logarithm of the product of exports and imports divided by GDP. Trade flows are usually reported by both trading partners since country A's exports to country B should equal country B's imports from country A. Nevertheless, the figures that are actually reported often differ, especially in cases of North-South trade. Hence, we follow the suggestions of Baldwin and Taglioni (2006) and apply the following formula in order to derive average bilateral trade figures:

$$\ln\{(A_{od}{}^{*}A_{do}{}^{*}B_{od}{}^{*}B_{do})^{1/4}\} \qquad (13.1)$$

where A and B are the two trading partners and o stands for origin and d for destination, representing the trade flows.

Descriptives

A first illustration using simple, unweighted means of the democracy indicator and trade openness over time is presented in Fig. 13.1. The graph suggests a mildly positive correlation between trade openness and the measure of democracy.[12]

[12] This observation is confirmed by a correlation coefficient of .61 (significant at the.01 level).

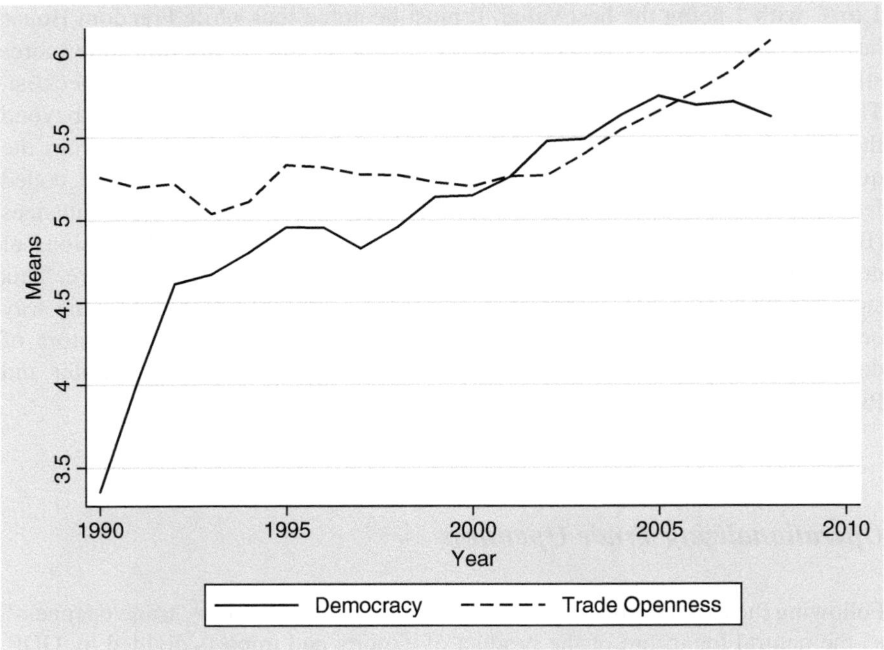

Fig. 13.1 Annual means of democracy scores (ln) and trade openness (ln) of ACP states

Endogeneity

Before conducting more elaborate econometric tests, a major issue that research on the relationship between democracy and economic development data often suffers from needs to be addressed. The challenge is that in most likelihood a two-way causal relationship between trade and democracy is present. Thus, while this study focuses on the impact of trade on democracy, Mansfield et al. (2000) argue that democracies are more likely to promote trade openness, while Grossman and Helpman (1994) follow the contrary argument that powerful industries may find it easier to lobby for protectionism in democratic states. Consequently, as Eichengreen and Leblang (2008) point out, the quality of this kind of research is contingent upon the strategy of identification that is employed. This is based on the insight that using observed data on trade flows as a variable in a regression on democracy scores suffers from serious issues of endogeneity and simultaneity and leads to biased estimation results. Thus, in the following we are going to elaborate on the instrumental variable strategy employed here to avoid this problem.

Meanwhile, it should also be noted that while trade openness is the explanatory variable of interest here several other explanatory factors that are employed as control variables here potentially also suffer from endogeneity biases. To forestall this, all independent variables will be included in lagged form, although this is a notably weaker instrumental strategy than the one used for trade openness.

Identification

Most recent studies on the relationship between trade openness and democracy have used a gravity model to identify the exogenous component of trade (see for example Eichengreen and Leblang 2008; Li and Reuveny 2002; Lim and Decker 2007; López-Córdova and Meissner 2008). The gravity model looks to country size as a measure of output and (potential) benefits from trade and distance between trading partners as a proxy for transportation costs. The literature has shown that both factors are robustly related to trade. The gravity model has hence become a widely accepted tool for the creation of an instrument for trade openness that is arguably apt to avoid endogeneity and simultaneity biases (see also Frankel and Romer 1999). We therefore conduct a two-stage least-squares model in which the first step consists of a gravity model to create this instrument, which in a second stage is regressed on democracy scores, controlling for several intervening variables.

Gravity Model

The gravity model goes back to Newton's *Law of Universal Gravitation*, developed in 1687. The law stated that the attractive force between two objects i and j is determined by

$$F_{ij} = G\frac{M_i M_j}{D_{ij}^2}$$

where

- F_{ij} is the attractive force,
- M_i and M_j are the masses of the two objects i and j,
- D_{ij} is the distance between the two objects, and
- G is a gravitational constant depending on the units of measurement for mass and force.

The concept's introduction into economic research is credited to Jan Tinbergen (1962). He proposed that a formula similar to the one originally formulated by Newton could be applied to international trade flows. It has since become a widely used concept that has been applied to a whole range of what we might call "social interactions" including migration, tourism, and foreign direct investment. Following Tinbergen, a general gravity law for trade between two entities may be expressed in roughly the same notation as Newton's original model:

$$T_{ijt} = G\frac{GDP_{it}GDP_{jt}}{D_{ij}}$$

- T_{ijt} represents the total volume of trade between the two entities i and j at time t,
- GDP_{it} and GDP_{jt} are the economic sizes of i and j at time t,

- D_{jt} is the distance between the locations i and j, and
- G is a gravitational constant.

However, predicted levels of openness based on this standard gravity model of trade would again face an endogeneity bias as they use GDP as a variable. GDP is robustly related to the development of democracy, and vice versa. Hence, we need to find a model which only uses exogenous factors to predict trade openness, similar to Newton's model. Frankel and Romer (1999) suggest a gravity equation that mostly uses geographic -and hence arguably exogenous -variables to predict trade openness. We utilize a similar model here. Based on this, the augmented (log-linear) gravity equation takes the following form:

$$\ln\left(T_{ijt}/GDP_{jt}\right) = \beta_0 + \beta_1 \ln(Area_{it} * Area_{jt}) + \beta_2 \ln(Pop_{it}) + \beta_3 \ln\left(Pop_{jt}\right) - \beta_4 \ln\left(D_{ij}\right) + \beta_5\left(LL_j\right) + \beta_6\left(Island_j\right) + \varepsilon_{ijt}$$

where the notation is defined as follows

- T_{ijt}/GDP_{jt} represents trade openness in country j (an ACP state) at time t
- $Area_{ijt}$ is the landmass of the two entities i and j, respectively, at time t
- Pop_{ijt} is the population of the two entities i and j, respectively, at time t
- D_{ij} is the distance between the locations i and j
- LL_j is a dummy that takes the value of 1 if country j is landlocked and 0 if not
- $Island_j$ is a dummy that takes the value of 1 if country j is an island state and 0 if not
- β_0 is a constant
- ε_{ijt} is an error term

The now standard gravity model of trade in IV estimations (see Frankel and Rose 2000) uses several other dummy variables to account for further cultural and geographic factors. However, given the fact that we are looking at the European Union as a whole, there is no point in the inclusion of other dummy variables on common language and colonial heritage in this model. The diversity of languages in the EU and the fact that virtually all ACP states used to be colonized by one (or more) EU member states renders these dummies ineffective and therefore obsolete. Similarly, none of the ACP states shares a common border with the EU, the corresponding dummy variable can therefore be excluded as well.

Subsequently, the estimated values for all β-coefficients are used to predict the logarithm of trade openness for each ACP state in relation to the EU. This leaves us with the desired instrument for trade openness, which in the following step is entered (with a 1 year lag) into the regression equation as a predictor for the level of democracy.[13]

[13] In practice, the 2SLS model is carried out by Stata in one model. The two stages are described separately here for reasons of clarity and illustration.

Regression

The creation of an instrument for trade openness allows us now to assess its impact on democratization without running the risk of biased results due to endogeneity. We take a simple regression in the following form as a starting point:

$$Y = a + bX + e$$

where Y is the dependent variable (democracy), X is the independent variable of interest (trade openness), a is the Y intercept, b is the slope and e an error term that is larger than zero. Since democracy -obviously -is influenced by other variables than trade openness, we consult the literature on the interrelationship between economic indicators and political development to identify a number of variables that need to be included in the regression as independent control variables. However, including any other variable that has been proven to influence democracy would again pose the risk of endogeneity. Thus, the control variables need to be chosen carefully. As an example,

> [i]t may [...] be compelling to think that the level of democracy is positively related to human capital accumulation. However, schooling and other indicators of human capital are likely to be influenced by past and anticipated changes in the political regime, which also creates an endogeneity problem. [...] Similarly, including a measure of the level of democracy in neighboring countries could lead to endogeneity problems as well as the identification problems highlighted in the literature on neighborhood effects. (López-Córdova and Meissner 2008: 549)

Inserting the control variables that we identify as both relevant and exogenous yields the following equation:

$$\begin{aligned}\mathrm{Democ}_{jt} = {} & \beta_0 + \beta_1 \ln(\mathrm{Open}_{jt-1}) + \beta_2 \mathrm{Muslim}_{jt-1} + \beta_3 \mathrm{LifeExp}_{jt-1} + \beta_4 \mathrm{OilDep}_j \\ & + \beta_5 \mathrm{Island}_j + \beta_6 \mathrm{BritCol}_j + \beta_7 \mathrm{IMF}_{jt-1} + \varepsilon_{jt}\end{aligned}$$

where the notation is defined as follows

- Democ_{jt} is the level of democracy in country j (an ACP state) at time t
- Open_{jt-1} is the instrument for the level of trade openness of country j at time $t-1$ (as described previously)
- Muslim_{jt-1} is the share of Muslim population in country j at time $t-1$
- $\mathrm{LifeExp}_{jt-1}$ is the life expectancy in country j at time $t-1$
- OilDep_j is a dummy that takes the value of 1 if country j depends on oil exports and 0 if not
- Island_j is a dummy that takes the value of 1 if country j is an island and 0 if not
- $\mathrm{BritCol}_j$ is a dummy that takes the value of 1 if country j has been a British colony and 0 if not

- IMF_{jt-1} is a dummy that takes the value of 1 if country j has outstanding IMF loans at time t−1 and 0 if not
- β_0 is a constant
- ε_{ijt} is an error term

Findings

We use a two-stage least-squares model to carry out our instrumental variable regression. The results are summed up in Table 13.3. The findings confirm a positive relationship between trade openness and democracy in ACP states. The coefficients are significant at the .001 level, both in a model including random and fixed effects (results of a Hausman test suggest that the fixed effects model delivers slightly better estimates).

There's a rather long tradition of studies seeking to explain a propensity to democratize in different national contexts by reference to their colonial origin. The basic idea behind this is that colonialism left countries with defunct and underdeveloped socio-economic structures and therefore more unlikely to develop stable structures of government, especially democratic ones. A couple of studies put forth that British colonial heritage -as an exception and in contrast to French and Spanish - left former colonies with stronger structures of self-government and therefore planted the seed for democratic evolution (Acemoglu et al. 2001; Bernhard et al. 2004).

Table 13.3 Regression results

	(1) Random effects	(2) Fixed effects
Trade openness	1.052***	1.522***
	(0.182)	(0.262)
IMF dummy	1.570*	1.826**
	(0.742)	(0.826)
British colony	−0.0338	
	(1.354)	
Island	6.980***	
	(1.916)	
Muslim population	−0.0146	
	(0.0194)	
Life expectancy	0.0967*	0.159***
	(0.0426)	(0.0480)
Oil dependency	−8.922***	
	(2.074)	
Constant	−16.34***	−25.80***
	(3.145)	(4.224)
N	721	721

Standard errors in parentheses; dependent variable: democracy (polity IV); trade openness is instrumented as described in the text

*$p < 0.05$, **$p < 0.01$, ***$p < 0.001$

In order to account for this we include the "British colony"-dummy in our model. However, our results confirm Barro's (1999) and Teorell's (2010) findings that former British colonies did in fact not enjoy a significantly more democratic development than other countries included in the sample. On the contrary we find that British colonial origin has no statistically significant effect on democratic development.

In terms of religious heritage, it has often been argued that countries with a predominantly Muslim population are less likely to democratize than others (Fish 2003). We don't find empirical support for this assertion in this framework. The results show a tiny negative association between the Muslim dummy and democratization, which however is statistically insignificant across all models employed here.

We do find a positive, statistically significant and rather large correlation between the IMF dummy and democratic development. This could be interpreted as a confirmation that economic distress and crises may function as catalysts in movements towards more democracy. It suggests that economic turmoil alongside outside intervention by the IMF and structural adjustments associated with it foster democratic development.

Our findings in terms of oil dependency once again lend support to the so called "resource curse" (Ardani and Jacques 2010). The effect of a dependency on oil exports on democratic development in the sample is negative and quite large, suggesting that countries that fundamentally depend on fuel exports see their chances for democratization severely diminished. However, the indicator is omitted from the model with fixed effects. This can arguably be ascribed to the fact that our model only includes a small number of countries that are defined as oil dependent. At the same time the dummy is not time-variant across the period of observation.

For similar reasons the island dummy is excluded from the fixed effects model. Nonetheless, based on the model we employ as a robustness test (see Table 13.4) we can state that island status seems to be highly positively correlated with democratic development. Teorell (2010), crediting Almond (1989), provides a possible explanation for this, the Seeley-Hintze Law. The law "holds that the greater the insulation of a nation-state from outside influence, the less political power would be centralized within the state." (Teorell 2010: 5) This insulation is maximized in an island state, which may be seen as an explanation for the fact that island states fared markedly better in terms of democratization in our model than non-island states. Additionally, island states, especially small ones, tend to be relatively dependent on international trade for the simple reason that resources and production possibilities are often limited and strategies focusing on exports are their primary way to generate growth (Armstrong and Read 2002). This openness may feed back into their democratic development.

Life expectancy, used as a proxy for the state of development of the country is significantly positively associated with democratic development. This indirectly lends support to the central claim of our theoretical model. It underlines the importance of socio-economic development ("modernization") for democratization.

Table 13.4 Robustness checks

	(1) Random effects	(2) Fixed effects
Trade openness	0.482***	0.552***
	(0.0791)	(0.0974)
IMF dummy	0.749*	0.851**
	(0.309)	(0.327)
British colony	0.342	
	(0.613)	
Island	2.902***	
	(0.861)	
Muslim population	−0.00767	
	(0.00879)	
Life expectancy	0.0448*	0.0602**
	(0.0175)	(0.0187)
Oil dependency	−4.386***	
	(0.920)	
Constant	−3.048*	−5.019**
	(1.343)	(1.595)
N	787	787

Standard errors in parentheses; dependent variable: democracy (polity IV & FH); trade openness is instrumented as described in the text

$*p < 0.05$, $**p < 0.01$, $***p < 0.001$

Let us now turn to the explanatory variable of interest in this analysis. The empirical findings confirm that trade openness towards the European Union has been associated with a positive democratic development in ACP states. The effect is statistically significant and robust. Although the coefficient is somewhat lower when using an alternative measure of democracy (see Table 13.4), the effect itself is retained and remains statistically significant at the .001 level. Albeit the fact that the possibility of the omission of (yet undiscovered) variables that might be responsible for the effect on democratization cannot entirely be ruled out, we can conclude that exerting influence through trade seems to be a viable tool in this context.

The results counter the policy dilemma argument put forward by some analysts (e.g. Li and Reuveny 2002). Based on findings that globalization tends to erode prospects for democracy they argue that policy makers face a dilemma in choosing between economic growth and openness on the one side and democratic reforms and good governance on the other. This argument feeds into the debate on whether autocratic developing states face better outlooks in terms of economic development than democratic ones. With particular focus on a large number of developing countries our results suggest that this trade-off does not exist (at least not in cases that are covered by the scope of this paper). We can rather conclude that trade openness/economic development and democracy/good governance are two sides of the same coin and thus goals that cannot only be followed simultaneously, but that are even mutually reinforcing. “We believe there is adequate information available to argue that international trade or, at the very least, fundamental factors that drive openness to trade can help increase the process of building and consolidating democracy." (López-Córdova and Meissner 2005: 28)

In order to test the robustness of these results, we employ an alternative measure of democracy on the left-hand side of our model and run the same estimation as previously described. The alternative measure consists of a combined index of democracy based on both Polity IV and Freedom House data (Teorell et al. 2010b).[14] The index was developed by Axel Hadenius and Jan Teorell and has been shown to outperform its constituent indexes in terms of validity and reliability (Hadenius and Teorell 2005).

The results we obtain are summed up in Table 13.4. Although the coefficients themselves are somewhat smaller than the ones observed previously, the robustness test confirms the findings. Once again we report both a random and fixed effects model. Although the Hausman test this time suggests that the random effects model is more accurate, this does not jeopardize our results. We still find a robust positive effect of trade openness on democratization in ACP states.

Concluding Remarks

In 2005, Meunier and Nicolaidis concluded that "[o]ne of the most interesting questions about European trade policy today is how far the EU will be [. . .] able to transform its structural power into effective influence. In particular, can the EU become an important foreign policy actor through the back door, by using trade instead of more traditional diplomatic or military means?" The answer that this article gives is that the EU is indeed able to transform its structural economic power into actual political influence on the ground. Our model provides firm evidence that -from the view of ACP states -involvement in trade relations with the European Union can foster processes of democratization. Although the effect itself is smaller than that of some domestic factors the empirical findings suggest that trade between the European Union and the group of ACP states by and large goes hand in hand with democratization in the latter. This effect holds even when controlling for a number of intervening factors and across different variables and thus diverging definitions of democracy. What can we infer from this with regards to the EU's capabilities to wield influence and thus exert power by way of trade relations vis-à-vis the ACP states (and -possibly -by extension to similar regions in the world)?

[14] The "(s)cale (of this index) ranges from 0 to 10 where 0 is least democratic and 10 most democratic. Average of Freedom House (. . .) is transformed to a scale 0–10 and Polity (. . .) is transformed to a scale 0–10. These variables are averaged into fh_polity2. The imputed version has imputed values for countries where data on Polity is missing by regressing Polity on the average Freedom House measure."(Teorell et al. 2010a: 45) This also explains why the robustness test includes a larger N than the original test.

The findings add to the existing literature on international and external determinants of democratization. International influences on transition processes remain understudied and have so far largely fared as one factor among many in rather specific case studies (Pevehouse 2005). Broader links in the international system thereby remain external to transition studies, although they are paramount for policy making and strategic orientation on part of international actors. Knowledge of international aspects of democratization is therefore a key prerequisite for the design of successful policies of democracy promotion and assistance from abroad.

'Power through trade' theory as noted above regards trade as a vehicle for the exertion of power and – in our applied form – the support of democratic governance mechanisms. The results obtained here confirm this central claim of the theory, suggesting the presence of a positive link between trade and democracy. Arguing within our theoretical construct of democratization processes induced by trade openness, we can therefore conclude that economic interaction with the European Union seems to be working in the way of benefitting laborers in ACP states, empowering them with de facto power and inducing a process of institutionalizing *de jure* power. Trade works as a transmission channel here, underlining that the EU's economic power may indeed serve its political interests as a tool of power projection.

What we can infer from this is that using its economic power for the exertion of influence could be a primary tool for the EU as an actor in international affairs. Given that the Union (still) largely lacks more traditional means of power the use of trade and economic interaction as transmission channels can be regarded as a viable alternative to other strategies of power projection.

It should also be noted that trade relations function as a means of wielding soft power, primarily through social interaction and learning. Intercultural exchange is a major component of economic and business relations that is apt to impact sociocultural development in the trading partners' realms. In this sense, it does not only matter that ACP states interact with the outside world, fostering their economic development, but also with whom they interact. Values, rules and norms are transmitted and exchanged in interpersonal relations. And it does indeed play a role which value system the two trading partners adhere to when it comes to the diffusion of democratic and good governance principles (Gokcekus and Knörich 2006; Nottebaum and Gokcekus 2011).

Nonetheless, at this stage the 'power through trade' strategy should be taken with a grain of salt. Promoting liberal democratic values is not necessarily a source of peace and stability but can indeed be a conflict driver.

> [T]he EU tends to assume that the liberal recipe of 'peace through commerce' which has worked so well in its own case applies uniformly elsewhere. Yet, we also know that trade can fuel conflict when conducted within a context of unfair rules, deep social inequalities and corrupt governance, and without sufficient attention paid to its destructive byproducts such as adjustment costs, export dependence, price volatility or illegal trafficking. In order to bring its external action into line with its internal philosophy, the EU needs to develop trade policies that are sensitive to such potential conflicts (Meunier and Nicolaidis 2006: 920).

Europe needs to bear this in mind if it wants to develop in the direction of a normative power. The possibility is certainly there, as we have shown. But in order to minimize the risk of undermining local developments, fuelling conflicts and invoking neocolonialist traits the EU needs to develop a strategy that is sensitive to local particularities. And this is precisely where the past strategy of lumping together trading partners and signing agreements that largely fail to address country-specific factors faces limitations.

Consequently, what remains to be analyzed is the way in which trade openness influences democracy in individual contexts. While we can state that based on this assessment there is in fact a positive impact we cannot conclude how exactly this influence works in any specific country and what its specific effects really are. In this sense the analysis performed here is an essential step in the attempt to assess the 'power through trade' hypothesis. Nonetheless, a comprehensive analysis of the specific effects of factors such as conditionality clauses, social learning, etc. on the development of democratic norms and practices in partner countries is a necessary next step in the analysis of the EU as a power through trade vis-à-vis ACP states. This would then allow us to establish whether the EU's influence is directional and intended, or rather a byproduct of trade relations regardless of preferential trade agreements with conditionality clauses and socialization effects. This subsequent analysis could consist of in-depth comparative case studies of the interactions between trade openness and democracy in specific contexts (i.e. countries). This paper is therefore to be seen as a part in a larger effort to assess the EU's practice of promoting its core norms and values abroad via trade. To borrow a mathematical analogy, these findings provide the necessary condition for the argument, while the sufficient condition remains to be satisfied.

Acknowledgements The author wishes to thank Thomas Apolte, Omer Gokcekus, Nathalie Tocci, Britta Weiffen, Martin Welz, Wichard Woyke, the members of the EU research group at the Münster Graduate School of Politics and participants at the ECPR-SGIR 2010 summer school in Tübingen and the 7th ECPR-SGIR conference 2010 in Stockholm for helpful comments and suggestions. The author retains full responsibility for all remaining errors and shortcomings.

References

Acemoglu, D., & Robinson, J. (2000a). Inequality, growth and development: Democratization or repression? *European Economic Review, 44*(4–6), 683–693.

Acemoglu, D., & Robinson, J. (2000b). Why did the west extend the franchise? Growth, inequality and democracy in historical perspective. *Quarterly Journal of Economics, 115*, 1167–1199.

Acemoglu, D., & Robinson, J. (2001). A theory of political transitions. *American Economic Review, 91*(4), 938–963.

Acemoglu, D., & Robinson, J. (2002). The political economy of the Kuznets curve. *Review of Development Economics, 6*(2), 183–203.

Acemoglu, D., & Robinson, J. (2006). *Economic origins of dictatorship and democracy*. Cambridge: Cambridge University Press.

Acemoglu, D., Johnson, S., & Robinson, J. (2001). The colonial origins of comparative development: An empirical investigation. *American Economic Review, 91*(5), 1369–1401.
Acemoglu, D., Johnson, S., Robinson, J., & Yared, P. (2008). Income and democracy. *American Economic Review, 98*(3), 808–842.
Almond, G. (1989). The international–national connection. *British Journal of Political Science, 19*(02), 237–259.
Almond, G., & Verba, S. (1965). *The civic culture: Political attitudes and democracy in five nations, an analytic study*. Boston: Little, Brown.
Apolte, T. (2012). Why is there no revolution in North Korea? The political economy of revolution revisited. *Public Choice*, 150(3–4), 561–578.
Arat, Z. (1988). Democracy and economic development: Modernization theory revisited. *Comparative Politics, 21*(1), 21–36.
Ardani, K., & Jacques, B. (2010). Petro-dictators: Does the price of oil impact freedom? A reexamination of the political dimension of the resource curse. *Journal of International Policy Solutions, 12*, 31–39.
Armstrong, H., & Read, R. (2002). The phantom of liberty? Economic growth and the vulnerability of small states. *Journal of International Development, 14*(4), 435–458.
Baldwin, R., & Taglioni, D. (2006). *Gravity for dummies and dummies for gravity equations*. (NBER Working Paper 12516). Cambridge: National Bureau of Economic Research.
Barro, R. (1996). Democracy and growth. *Journal of Economic Growth, 1*(1), 1–27.
Barro, R. (1997). *Determinants of economic growth: A cross-country empirical study*. Cambridge: MIT Press.
Barro, R. (1999). Determinants of democracy. *Journal of Political Economy, 107*(S6), 158–183.
Berg-Schlosser, D. (2007). *Democratization: The state of the art* (2 rev. ed.). Opladen: B. Budrich.
Bernhard, M., Reenock, C., & Nordstrom, T. (2004). The legacy of western overseas colonialism on democratic survival. *International Studies Quarterly, 48*(1), 225–250.
Boix, C. (2003). *Democracy and redistribution*. Cambridge: Cambridge University Press.
Boix, C., & Stokes, S. (2003). Endogenous democratization. *World Politics, 55*(4), 517–549.
Burkhart, R. (2000). Economic freedom and democracy: Post-cold war tests. *European Journal of Political Research, 37*(2), 237–253.
Bussmann, M. (2001). Examining causality among conflict, democracy, openness, and economic growth. Unpublished paper, University of Alabama.
Coppedge, M. (1999). Thickening thin concepts and theories: Combining large N and small in comparative politics. *Comparative Politics, 31*(4), 465–476.
Dahl, R. A. (1971). *Polyarchy: Participation and opposition*. New Haven: Yale University Press.
Diamond, L. (1992). Economic development and democracy reconsidered. *American Behavioral Scientist, 35*(4/5), 450–499.
Dix, R. (1994). History and democracy revisited. *Comparative Politics, 27*(1), 91–105.
Dollar, D., & Kraay, A. (2004). Trade, growth, and poverty. *The Economic Journal, 114*(493), 22–49.
Dunning, T. (2008). *Crude democracy: Natural resource wealth and political regimes*. Cambridge: Cambridge University Press.
Edwards, S. (1998). Openness, productivity and growth: What do we really know? *The Economic Journal, 109*(447), 383–398.
Eichengreen, B., & Leblang, D. (2008). Democracy and globalization. *Economics and Politics, 20*(3), 289–334.
Epstein, D., Bates, R., Goldstone, J., Kristensen, I., & O'Halloran, S. (2006). Democratic transitions. *American Journal of Political Science, 50*(3), 551–569.
Ethier, D. (2003). Is democracy promotion effective? Comparing conditionality and incentives. *Democratization, 10*(1), 99–120.
Fish, M. (2003). Islam and authoritarianism. *World Politics, 55*(1), 4–37.
Frankel, J., & Romer, D. (1999). Does trade cause growth? *American Economic Review, 89*(3), 379–399.

Frankel, J., & Rose, A. (2000). An estimate of the effects of currency unions on trade and growth. *Quarterly Journal of Economics, 2*, 437–466.
Gasiorowski, M. (1995). Economic crisis and political regime change: An event history analysis. *American Political Science Review, 89*(4), 882–897.
Geddes, B. (1999). What do we know about democratization after twenty years? *Annual Review of Political Science, 2*(1), 115–144.
Giavazzi, F., & Tabellini, G. (2005). Economic and political liberalizations. *Journal of Monetary Economics, 52*(7), 1297–1330.
Gill, G. J. (2000). *The dynamics of democratization: Elites, civil society, and the transition process*. New York: St. Martin's Press.
Gokcekus, O., & Knörich, J. (2006). Does quality of openness affect corruption? *Economics Letters, 91*(2), 190–196.
Grossman, G., & Helpman, E. (1994). Protection for sale. *The American Economic Review, 84*(4), 833–850.
Hadenius, A., & Teorell, J. (2005). Assessing alternative indices of democracy. Committee on Concepts and Methods Working Paper Series (August 2005).
Haughton, T. (2007). When does the EU make a difference? Conditionality and the accession process in Central and Eastern Europe. *Political Studies Review, 5*(2), 233–246.
Helliwell, J. (1994). Empirical linkages between democracy and economic growth. *British Journal of Political Science, 24*(2), 225–248.
Huntington, S. (1984). Will more countries become democratic? *Political Science Quarterly, 99*(2), 193–218.
Huntington, S. (1991). *The third wave: Democratization in the late twentieth century*. Norman: University of Oklahoma Press.
Inglehart, R., & Welzel, C. (2009). How development leads to democracy-what we know about modernization. *Foreign Affairs*, March/April 2009, 33–48.
Inglehart, R., & Welzel, C. (2005). *Modernization, cultural change, and democracy: The human development sequence*. Cambridge: Cambridge University Press.
Jackman, R. (1973). On the relation of economic development to democratic performance. *American Journal of Political Science, 17*(3), 611–621.
Jünemann, A., & Knodt, M. (2007). *Externe Demokratieförderung durch die Europäische Union – European external democracy promotion*. Baden-Baden: Nomos.
Knodt, M., & Jünemann, A. (2007). Introduction: Conceptionalizing the EU's promotion of democracy. In A. Jünemann & M. Knodt (Eds.), *Externe Demokratieförderung durch die Europäische Union-European external democracy promotion* (pp. 9–32). Baden-Baden: Nomos.
La Porta, R., Lopez-de Silanes, F., Shleifer, A., & Vishny, R. (1999). The quality of government. *Journal of Law, Economics, and Organization, 15*(1), 222–279.
Laïdi, Z. (2008). *EU foreign policy in a globalized world: Normative power and social preferences*. New York: Routledge.
Leamer, E. (1995). *The Heckscher-Ohlin model in theory and practice* (Princeton studies in international economics, 77). Princeton: International Finance Section, Department of Economics, Princeton University
Li, Q., & Reuveny, R. (2002). Economic globalization and democracy: An empirical analysis. *British Journal of Political Science, 33*(1), 29–54.
Lim, J., & Decker, J. (2007). Democracy and trade: An empirical study. *MPRA Paper*.
Lin, J. Y., & Nugent, J. B. (1995). Institutions and economic development. In T. N. Srinivasan (Ed.), *Handbook of development economics*. Amsterdam: Elsevier. 2301–2370
Lipset, S. (1959). Some social requisites of democracy: Economic development and political legitimacy. *The American Political Science Review, 53*(1), 69–105.
Lipset, S. (1994). The social requisites of democracy revisited. *American Sociological Review, 59*(1), 1–22.

Lipset, S., Seong, K., & Torres, J. (1993). A comparative analysis of the social requisites of democracy. *International Social Science Journal, 45*(2), 155–173.
López-Córdova, J. E., & Meissner, C. M. (2005). *The globalization of trade and democracy: 1870–2000* (NBER Working Paper, Vol. 1117). Cambridge: National Bureau of Economic Research.
López-Córdova, J. E., & Meissner, C. M. (2008). The impact of international trade on democracy: A long-run perspective. *World Politics, 60*, 539–575.
Manners, I. (2002). Normative power Europe: A contradiction in terms? *Journal of Common Market Studies, 40*, 235–258.
Mansfield, E., Milner, H., & Rosendorff, B. (2000). Free to trade: Democracies, autocracies, and international trade. *The American Political Science Review, 94*(2), 305–321.
Marshall, M., & Jaggers, K. (2010). *Polity IV project: Political regime characteristics and transitions, 1800–2009*. Fairfax: Center for Systemic Peace, George Mason University.
Meunier, S., & Nicolaidis, K. (2005). The European Union as a trade power. In C. Hill & M. Smith (Eds.), *International relations and the European Union* (4th ed.). Oxford: Oxford University Press.
Meunier, S., & Nicolaidis, K. (2006). The European Union as a conflicted trade power. *Journal of European Public Policy, 13*(6), 906–925.
Milner, H., & Kubota, K. (2005). Why the move to free trade? Democracy and trade policy in the developing countries. *International Organization, 59*(01), 107–143.
Moore, B. (1966). *Social origins of dictatorship and democracy: Lord and peasant in the making of the modern world*. Boston: Beacon.
Moore, M. (1995). Democracy and development in cross-national perspective: A new look at the statistics. *Democratization, 2*(2), 1–19.
Müller, T., & Pickel, S. (2007). Wie lässt sich Demokratie am besten messen? Zur Konzeptqualität von Demokratie-Indizes. *Politische Vierteljahresschrift, 48*(3), 511–539.
Munck, G., & Verkuilen, J. (2002). Conceptualizing and measuring democracy: Evaluating alternative indices. *Comparative Political Studies, 35*(1), 5–34.
Nottebaum, D., & Gokcekus, O. (2011). Corruption and EU enlargement: Race to bottom or top? Unpublished paper.
O'Donnell, G., & Schmitter, P. (1986). *Transitions from authoritarian rule: Tentative conclusions about uncertain democracies*. Baltimore: John Hopkins University Press.
Ohlin, B. (1933). *Interregional and international trade*. Cambridge: Harvard University Press.
Pevehouse, J. (2005). *Democracy from above: Regional organizations and democratization*. Cambridge: Cambridge University Press.
Przeworski, A. (2000). *Democracy and development: Political institutions and well-being in the world, 1950–1990*. Cambridge: Cambridge University Press.
Przeworski, A., & Limongi, F. (1997). Modernization: Theory and facts. *World Politics, 49*(2), 155–183.
Ragin, C. (2005). Case-oriented research and the study of social action. In N. Kersting & L. Cronqvist (Eds.), *Democratization and political culture in comparative perspective* (pp. 91–102). Wiesbaden: VS Verlag.
Reuveny, R., & Li, Q. (2003). Economic openness, democracy, and income inequality. *Comparative Political Studies, 36*(5), 575–601.
Rigobon, R., & Rodrik, D. (2005). Rule of law, democracy, openness, and income: Estimating the interrelationships. *Economics of Transition, 13*(3), 533–564.
Rudra, N. (2005). Globalization and the strengthening of democracy in the developing world. *American Journal of Political Science, 49*(4), 704–730.
Rueschemeyer, D., Huber, E., & Stephens, J. D. (1992). *Capitalist development and democracy*. Chicago: University of Chicago Press.
Rustow, D. (1970). Transitions to democracy: Toward a dynamic model. *Comparative Politics, 2*(3), 337–363.

Sachs, J., & Warner, A. (1995). *Natural resource abundance and economic growth* (NBER Working Paper, 5398). Cambridge: National Bureau of Economic Research.
Sachs, J., Warner, A., Åslund, A., & Fischer, S. (1995). Economic reform and the process of global integration. *Brookings Papers on Economic Activity, 1*(1995), 1–18.
Schimmelfennig, F., Engert, S., & Knobel, H. (2003). Costs, commitment and compliance: The impact of EU democratic conditionality on Latvia, Slovakia and Turkey. *Journal of Common Market Studies, 41*(3), 495–518.
Smith, M. (2000). Conforming to Europe: The domestic impact of EU foreign policy co-operation. *Journal of European Public Policy, 7*(4), 613–631.
Stepan, A. (1986). Paths toward redemocratization: Theoretical and comparative perspectives. In G. O'Donnell, P. C. Schmitter, & L. Whitehead (Eds.), *Transitions from authoritarian rule: Comparative perspectives*. Baltimore: Johns Hopkins University Press.
Stivachtis, Y. A. (2007). *The state of European integration*. Aldershot: Ashgate.
Stolper, W., & Samuelson, P. (1941). Protection and real wages. *The Review of Economic Studies, 9*(1), 58–73.
Telò, M. (2006). *Europe, a civilian power?: European Union, global governance, world order*. Houndmills/Basingstoke/Hampshire: Palgrave Macmillan.
Teorell, J. (2010). *Determinants of democratization: Explaining regime change in the world*. Cambridge: Cambridge University Press.
Teorell, J., Charron, N., Samanni, M., Holmberg, S., Rothstein, B. (2010a). The quality of government codebook, version 27 May 2010. University of Gothenburg, The Quality of Government Institute.
Teorell, J., Charron, N., Samanni, M., Holmberg, S., Rothstein, B. (2010b). The quality of government dataset, version 27 May 2010. University of Gothenburg, The Quality of Government Institute.
Tinbergen, J. (1962). *Shaping the world economy: Suggestions for an international economic policy*. New York: Twentieth Century Fund.
Tocci, N. (2007). *The EU and conflict resolution. Promoting peace in the backyard*. London: Routledge.
Vanhanen, T. (1997). *Prospects of democracy: A study of 172 countries*. New York: Routledge.
Wucherpfennig, J., & Deutsch, F. (2009). Modernization and democracy: Theories and evidence revisited. *Living Reviews in Democracy, 1*, 1–9.
Yu, M. (2005). Trade globalization and political liberalization: A gravity approach, Unpublished paper, University of California, Davis.

Data Appendix

Data	Definition and source
Trade flows/trade openness	Data on trade flows has been compiled from the IMF *Directions of Trade* database and is denominated in US$ at current prices
GDP	GDP data in US$ comes from the IMF World Economic Outlook database
Democracy	*Polity IV:* The Polity score captures three dimensions (competitiveness of political participation, competitiveness and openness of executive recruitment, constraints on the chief executive) on a 21-point scale ranging from −10 (hereditary monarchy) to +10 (consolidated democracy). Data source is Marshall and Jaggers (2010)

(continued)

Data	Definition and source
	CoG Index (Combination of Freedom House and Polity IV): The Freedom House index is based on surveys on political rights (including free, fair, and competitive elections) and individual liberties (including freedom of information, organization, and religion). It scores each country on a scale from 1 to 7, with one being the best value. It must be noted that while Freedom House has undertaken some efforts to objectify its criteria and coding rules, the scores still result from a largely subjective measure based on an elaborate checklist. The reliability of the coding procedure and the data used thus remains beyond the control of outsiders. Hadenius and Teorell (2005) combine Polity IV and Freedom House scores into one index. The "(s)cale [of the CoG index, DN] ranges from 0 to 10 where 0 is least democratic and 10 most democratic. Average of Freedom House [including both the civil liberties and the political representation measure, DN] is transformed to a scale 0–10 and Polity is transformed to a scale 0–10. These variables are averaged into fh_polity2. The imputed version has imputed values for countries where data on Polity is missing by regressing Polity on the average Freedom House measure."(Teorell et al. 2010a: 45) Data source is Teorell et al. (2010b)
Population	Population data for ACP states comes from the IMF World Economic Outlook database. EU population figures were obtained from Eurostat, augmented with data from the World Bank and Statistisches Jahrbuch where Eurostat data was incomplete
Distance	Distance is measured as great circle distance between the capital city of the respective ACP state and Brussels. Data comes from Jon Haveman's website[15]
Landlockedness	Data source is Eichengreen and Leblang (2008)
Island	Data source is Eichengreen and Leblang (2008)
Muslim population	Share of Muslim population in 1980. Data source is La Porta et al. (1999), via Teorell et al. (2010b)
Oil dependency	Dummy that identifies a country as dependent on oil exports when more than 30% of its exports were fuel products in 2007. Self-created dummy following the methodology of Ardani and Jacques (2010) based on data from the World Bank's World Development Indicators
Life expectancy	Data source is Teorell et al. (2010b)
British colony	Data source is Eichengreen and Leblang (2008)

[15] See http://www.macalester.edu/research/economics/page/haveman/trade.resources/tradedata.html (accessed 20 July 2010).

Chapter 14
Power Shift: Economic Realism and Economic Diplomacy on the Rise

Maaike Okano-Heijmans

Introduction

Latecomer countries – including Asian, post-colonial and transition states – are strengthening their role and influence in global politics and economics in a system that has long been dominated by Western countries. Confronted with the viscosity of global governance and international political and financial institutions, the governments of these emerging countries primarily use economic tools and commercial relations to strengthen their position.[1] This makes for paradoxical responses of established powers, with European 'old money' being haughty against and at the same time afraid of Asian 'new money' that is needed to save several European countries from bankruptcy. The unfolding reality raises important but complex questions about the role that economic factors play in the way power is conceived by governments of both industrialized and emerging countries, and how economic power is projected and exercised on the international stage.

This chapter aims to contribute to a better conceptualization of the economic dimension of power in (International Relations) theory, and to improve understanding of its application in practice. This requires consideration of the political philosophy and economic systems of countries – and of how the many variations in this configuration operate in relation to each other. Aside from this normative and organizational context, the (evolving) position of a country in international politics

This chapter owes much to earlier collaboration and joint publication with Frans-Paul van der Putten, a colleague at the 'Clingendael' Institute. The author wishes to thank him for his creative inspiration then and now, and for his (in)direct support for this writing. The author is furthermore grateful to other colleagues for useful comments on an earlier draft.

[1] Throughout this chapter, the term 'emerging countries' is used interchangeably with 'emerging economies' and 'advanced developing economies' – all of which can be found in scholarly and newspaper articles on related topics. The focus in this chapter is on emerging countries in Asia, with a particular emphasis on China.

E. Fels et al. (eds.), *Power in the 21st Century*, Global Power Shift,
DOI 10.1007/978-3-642-25082-8_14, © Springer-Verlag Berlin Heidelberg 2012

needs to be considered. A dichotomy of 'systems' in 'the West and the rest' is tempting, but while this distinction may be useful for certain purposes, government interventions during and in the aftermath of the global financial crisis of the late 2000s in regions and countries as diverse as Europe, the United States (US), China, and South Korea, show that differences in capitalism, public-private cooperation, and international economics cannot be captured by this simple bifurcation alone.[2] This is why – if the aim is to delineate the workings, purposes and consequences of the economic dimension of power – a meaningful analysis should include a historical, organizational and ideological perspective.

A starting point of this chapter is the assertion that the governments of emerging economies are *relatively* more willing than their counterparts in the US and Europe to intervene extensively in the domestic economy and in international economic relations in order to achieve political goals that directly serve their own strategic interests.[3] It deserves emphasis that this is *not* to say that the US and European countries do not intervene at all in their economies – now or at earlier stages of their development; the difference is relative.[4] A second point is that these emerging countries are prepared to use political instruments to further economic and commercial goals to relatively greater extents than their Western counterparts. Influence attempts are facilitated, amongst others, by direct links between government and the private sector – including through state-owned enterprises and sovereign wealth funds. Examples include China's economic cooperation/development aid to gain support of foreign governments for its 'one-China' policy and its unofficial ban on exports of raw earths to Japan in the midst of a political and territorial dispute between the two countries in 2010.

In the aftermath of the Asian Financial Crisis of the late 1990s, Karel van Wolferen argued that:

> As Asia regains its role as the fastest-growing region in the world and holds an ever more important place in the global political economy, the conceptual challenge posed by the 1997–1998 crisis will acquire increased relevance in creating a prosperous and peaceful world. (van Wolferen (2003: 57–58)

The conceptual challenge he referred to is even bigger and more relevant now than it was then. Signs are increasing that, just as Europe exported its own (Westphalian) state system of power in international relations to the rest of the world, so too do the emerging countries, especially in Asia, increasingly shape and reconfigure the international system (Okano-Heijmans and van der Putten 2009a). The novelty is less structural – although it does involve the abandonment or postponement of what might have been a post-statal society – and more procedural

[2] For a useful analysis of how capitalism within the United States and European countries evolved since 1815, see Kaletsky (2010).

[3] Established powers have followed a similar path that emphasised economic tools and purposes in an early stage of development, see also Chang (2003).

[4] Recent examples of state intervention in Western countries include bailouts of private companies and quantitative easing in the late 2000s.

and ideological, it entails a move beyond the emphasis on the military-economic linkage that transformed European states into established powers,[5] and acts as an impediment to the exportation of democracy by Western countries. The most important characteristic that Asian countries share is a relatively extensive state influence in the economy and a comprehensive approach to shaping and practicing economic diplomacy. Improved understanding of both theory and practice of the economic dimension of international relations – here referred to as economic realism and economic diplomacy respectively – thus grows in importance due to shifting power balances.

The central argument here is that as advanced developing countries, led by China, emerge as influential players, they are changing the rules of the game in international relations to the advantage of large countries where the state has greater influence over economic activity. Small countries and countries with open economies and a relatively strict separation of the public and private spheres have (even) more difficulty getting their voices heard. The rise of big Asian countries with a strong state is subsequently accelerated, while European countries lose influence. To substantiate this argument, this chapter addresses two main questions. First, what theoretical assumptions underlie the function of economic power in international relations and how can the correlated use of economic and political instruments and goals be conceptualized? Second, how is economic diplomacy practiced in the strategic competition for global power and influence? The theoretical underpinnings and the practical application are introduced, respectively, in the first and second main sections. The second question is addressed in a case study on China, the main challenger of the 'old' power configuration and thereby the prime example of the evolving use of the economic dimension of power.

Theorizing the Economic Dimension of Power

Linkages between economics and politics in practice have existed since ancient times. Reference to the use of sanctions can be found in the history of the Peloponnesian War by Thucydides, who mentions a trade boycott imposed by Athens against Sparta's ally Megara. Moreover, Ancient Greece already knew so-called *proxenoi*: Citizens who promoted policies of friendship or alliance with the city they voluntarily represented, in return for honorary titles from the state. Centuries later, in the wake of expanding international trade in Europe in medieval times, the number of representatives of merchants in the main harbour cities in Southern Europe vastly increased and the *Lex Mercatoria* regulated commercial dealings.

[5] Tilly argues that the expansion of military force drove the processes of state formation in Europe (1990: 122–126).

Scholarly inquiries came much later, with Jacob Viner, Albert O. Hirschman and Quincy Wright acting as frontrunners in the field. Essentially, they took on Hans Morgenthau's argument that 'it is necessary to distinguish between (...) economic policies that are undertaken for their own sake and economic policies (...) whose economic purpose is but the means to the end of controlling the policies of another nation' (Morgenthau 1968/1948: 28–29). Thinking on the interlinkages between politics and economics continued in the 1970s, with studies on, for example, the employment of economic tools – including bilateral trade flows – for political purposes.[6]

The mode of conducting international politics wherein politics and economics are pragmatically linked and readily employed in a country's international dealings with other countries, is referred to here as 'economic realism'.[7] As alluded to above, this is not a new phenomenon. Today, however, China and other emerging countries practice economic realism to an unprecedented extent and in more varieties than ever. In the words of former US national security advisor Zbigniew Brzezinski: 'We are dealing with something qualitatively different from what has gone before. It is a general awakening of the far east' (quoted in Pilling 2010).

The main challenge is how to (re)conceptualize the economic dimension of power in a way that does justice to current realities and contemporary debates. Because, while most actors in the international system attempt to wield economic power, realities may differ widely between countries in different regions and at varying stages of development. China's economic and political systems, for example, are so completely different from others, that one cannot easily expect that country to be able to follow or imitate other examples – not Japan, for example, and much less so European ones. Yet if similarities are discerned, the question arises what methods should be used to analyze the origins of common features.[8] A first step is, thus, to clearly delineate the assumptions underpinning economic realism.

Theoretical Assumptions

The underlying argument for economic realism rests on several theoretical understandings about power and the state. Individually, these are hardly new – but as a whole, they point to an evolving use of power, characterized by a growing role of economic instruments and purposes. The first assumption concerns the continued importance of the role of the state, which is regarded as the *primary* actor, amid a growing number of actors. This is not to say that the state is regarded as a unified unit; instead the state is seen 'as a set of fragmented and often not easily

[6] See for example Strange (1992: 1–15), Baldwin (1985), Keohane and Nye (1977).

[7] This phenomenon has also been referred to as 'mercantile realism': mobilizing potential power while carefully hedging against possible threats (Heginbotham and Samuels 1998).

[8] For more on this argument see Radtke (2008).

defined institutions with a variable impact on social outcomes.' Power, in turn, is regarded as a multi-dimensional concept, the nature of which depends on where it is exercised, who is involved in the power relations and who is the subject of power (both quotes in this paragraph from Smith 2009; see also Allison 1999/1971).

Secondly, economic realist thinking recognizes David Baldwin's distinction between the *targets* or domain of an influence attempt (who is to be influenced) and the *objectives* or scope of an attempt (in what ways does one actor try to influence another) (Baldwin 1985: 15–18). This distinction facilitates differentiation between the primary, secondary, and perhaps even tertiary goals and targets of a given influence attempt – an indication of the relative importance attached to any particular policy goal. Notwithstanding the (sometimes disappointing) outcomes of policies, instruments are often used for a variety of reasons. That is to say, by resorting to economic power, 'governments seek to gain or preserve military, political, ideological, economic, and even emotional values' (Knorr 1975: 134). To enhance commercial profit, strengthen one's image or leadership role, or secure global goods are but a few examples of what these goals may entail.

Furthermore, while targets and the scope of policies are defined one-sidedly by the state that is utilizing economic diplomacy, the effectiveness of a policy needs to be measured with reference to others. This derives from the *relational* nature of the concept of power[9] – an approach also inherent in Joseph Nye's argument for soft power, which emphasises that power always depends on the context in which the relationship exists (Nye 2004: 2). As an illustration, consider instruments with a clear economic dimension (withholding official development aid, imposing bilateral sanctions) that are employed by the Japanese government as attempts to influence North Korea. The employment itself says little about whether or not Japan is successful in changing the regime in Pyongyang in the way it desires (see Okano-Heijmans 2010.

The importance of recognizing power, including economic power, as a relational concept becomes more obvious when considering the *bases* of national economic power.[10] In absolute terms, the main bases of national economic power are the volume, structure and organization of a state's foreign economic transactions. However, the volume of trade and capital exports relative to the market value of the output of goods and services (GNP) needs to be considered as well. After all, when these volumes are relatively large, a country is more susceptible to economic pressure from the outside. Put differently, while sheer magnitude may provide levers for pressure on other states, it also tends to enhance a country's vulnerability to external pressure. This points to what Klaus Knorr referred to as the two sides of national economic power: the *active* side, being concerned with what a country can do to others, and the *passive* side, constituting a country's ability to limit what other countries do to it. Seen in this way, although China's active influencing power

[9] This contrasts with the noncontextual definition of power typically adopted by realists, who argue that capabilities as such make for power. See for example Gilpin (1981: 13).

[10] This paragraph follows Knorr (1975: 79, 84).

grows with the steady rise of its economy, its dependency on trade and foreign investment in the country acts as an impediment. Relatively recent efforts to strengthen domestic demand will enhance Beijing's passive economic power. Considering the rivalry between the US and China it is in a sense ironic that Washington in particular pushes Beijing to embark on this structural reform.

The fourth assumption of economic realist thought is that, while analysis of actual policies and actions is of importance, it is equally important to recognize and study *inaction* – instances where one would have expected action – as well as *deliberate avoidance* of positive steps. These occurrences need to be interpreted as a way of projecting power since, in the words of Stephen Lukes, 'there is no good reason for excluding failures to act from the scope of power on principle' (Lukes 2005: 480). This is to take serious the fact that economic levers may also be used to *prevent* certain things from happening, and that negotiations may be deliberately postponed or blocked for the same purpose. The concept 'negative economic diplomacy' is useful to refer to (a combination of) such punitive, conditional, postponing and obstructionist behaviour. Rising displeasure of BRIC-counties in the G20 as this forum failed to make substantial progress with co-operation in the lead-up to the 2010 Seoul Summit , is one example of this.

Last but not least, it needs to be recognized that ways of practicing economic realism – that is, the uses of particular strands of economic diplomacy – shift along a *continuum* of economic/financial and political tools and objectives.[11] Countries at varying stages of development and in different regions tend to employ certain strands more than others; that is, they are inclined to employ a particular set of tools for particular purposes. This completes the circle by bringing the discussion back to its starting point: that economic realism is practiced differently between countries.

While ideological underpinnings evolve only very slowly in any particular country, changing economic and politico-strategic realities make for a shift in the 'theatres' (international organizations and other fora for negotiation) wherein and countries between which the fiercest confrontations arise. It is thus no surprise that the growing tensions on trade issues between the US and China in 2010 are reminiscent of the trade disputes between the US and Japan of the 1970–1980s. Back then – as concerns rose of an East Asian challenge to American hegemony – it was the Japanese automobile industry that triggered protectionism in the US, whose industry was losing its competitive edge. Today it is the green industry of China, in particular, that creates a vastly more competitive landscape in sectors wherein the US has failed to innovate substantially. While the industries and the countries differ, both the challenger and the established power display similar behaviour to secure their interests, with the former depending on innovative economic capabilities and the latter on its established (political) position.

[11] More on this in the next section.

Politics, Economics and the State

The scope and modes of state intervention in (domestic) economic life determine the capacities and, thereby, the extent to which a state can endeavour to exercise economic power. These may be structured through typologies that discern differences between countries – between industrialized and emerging countries, and within these groups. Earlier research by Kent Calder drew this distinction on the basis of two national characteristics: the degree of state intervention and the propensity to allocate strategic resources toward priority sectors through directive means (see Fig. 14.1 – I) (Calder 1993: esp. 6). A typology is thereby exposed with on one extreme the 'developmental state' – where technocrats dominate, and intervention and allocation are extensive – and on the other side 'sillicon valley capitalism' – where state intervention and credit allocation are relatively small. State intervention without strategic resource allocation points to 'corporate-led strategic capitalism' – wherein the private sector dominates – while the reverse characterizes a 'clientelized state' – with fragmented state administrative controls over industry and finance, and no strong political executive to integrate policies. Obviously, few countries are perfect examples of any one of the above types and most countries have some form of hybrid economic management. Still, Calder's typology is useful in highlighting differences between states.

Domestic structures and organization influence foreign policy and the way a state goes about projecting power, as well as the role of economic instruments and purposes herein. If the public and private sectors are more closely aligned domestically, they are better positioned to act in tandem in foreign relations when desiring to do so – and vice versa. Indeed, the stronger states in China, Japan and France display a greater tendency toward economic realism and have a relatively strong capacity to embark on forceful economic diplomacy. The differences in domestic

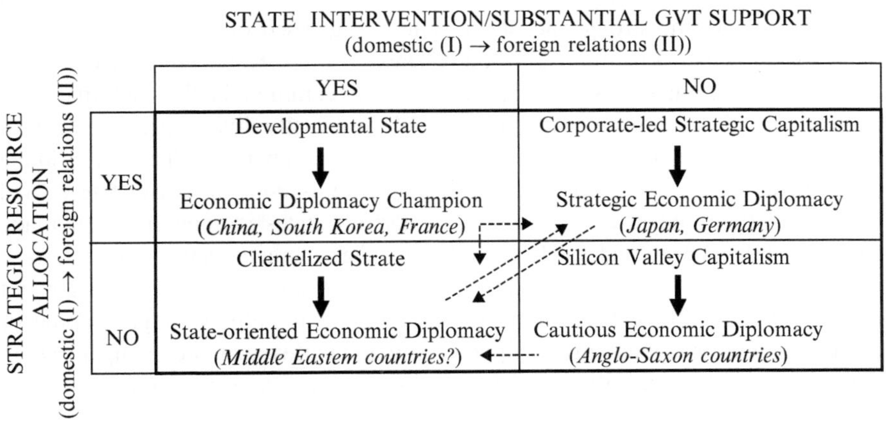

Fig. 14.1 The state and industrial transformation (I), the state and economic diplomacy (II) (Source: Calder (1993) (I) and author's compilation (II))

organization of politico-economic life between these countries, however, make for variations in economic diplomacy as well.

The analysis implicit in Calder's typology can thus also be applied to the relationship between domestic economic policy and foreign policy. Such an approach improves understanding of the relationship between state efforts at intervention in the domestic economy and strategic allocation of economic capabilities in foreign relations. Figure 14.1 (II) illustrates this, albeit in oversimplified form.

Three of the four quadrants of Fig. 14.1 represent states that adhere to some form of economic realism. This immediately and correctly illustrates that not *only* governments of emerging countries adhere to such an approach; China, France and South Korea are but three examples where state intervention in the economic sphere is prevalent and includes development of infant sectors, while Japan and Germany adhere to other ways to steer their economy – including strategic resource allocation – and in doing so commonly appear to respond strategically to external events (Calder 1993: esp. 109, 263–265). An important point alluded to in this figure, is that the lower right quadrant does *not* include *any* (advanced) developing countries while the majority of industrialized states in the West fall into this category.

While early developers as diverse as the US, the United Kingdom (UK) and the Netherlands adhere to a 'laissez-faire' strategy, two fundamental differences exist between the first and the latter two. First, the UK and the Netherlands are more dependent on foreign trade and capital transfers, and thus have a smaller base of economic power. Furthermore, the political and economic capacity of these countries to act is divided; while the former remains largely at the national level, the latter is mostly delegated to the European Union. This hampers a successful comprehensive economic diplomacy of these countries, both at the EU and the national level.

By contrast, governments in Asian countries are relatively more willing and able to intervene in domestic and international economic relations. They do so in different ways and to varying extents. One important difference amongst Asian states is whether the strong role of the state is organised in formal ways (China, Vietnam, Singapore) or more informally (Japan, South Korea, Indonesia). What governments of many Asian countries have in common is the fact that they strategically allocate resources to spur growth of a vastly diverse private sector at home and abroad. This may be the largest difference compared with countries in the Middle East and Russia, where the private sector is dominated by state-owned natural resource industries – making for a narrow, state-led economic diplomacy focused on the energy sector. Thus, while countries characterized by a clientelized state/state-oriented economic diplomacy guide and assist industries that are not necessarily cost-efficient or in need of government help, strategic capitalist/economic diplomacy countries support only industries that are competitive in their own right but are still helped further by government credit – for example to make long-term investments that are expected to improve competitiveness but involve greater risk.[12]

It deserves emphasis that putting a (regional) label on the economic diplomacy practice of key players in the international debate, is not to suggest that each is unanimous in the understanding of a particular approach. Nor does it suggest that each strategy is only adhered to within one region, or that a particular approach is applied consistently. The dotted lines point to such policy variations within countries/regions. Importantly, the labels do reflect each country's/region's political history. This contributes to the tensions between the different conceptions, since '[t]he historical socialization of each region promotes the commitment to a particular code of conduct of regional and international relations and reinforces the legitimacy of each model with a particular region' (Dunn et al. 2010: 297).

The point that is alluded to here – and an early conclusion to be drawn from this simplified typology – is that while *variations in the degree* of government intervention in the domestic economy and in international relations are many, the *common view* of the role of the state in Asian countries bridges national differences in political and economic systems and stages of development. This suggests that it is an illusion to think that the use of economic tools for political purposes, or of political tools for economic purposes will necessarily or proportionally decrease in the process of industrialization or with a change in economic model (from state- to free-market capitalism) or political system (from authoritarian to democratic).

From Theory to Practice

The rather theoretical observations above need to be applied to foreign policy practice in order to test their usefulness and accuracy. A first step to advance the theory-practice dialogue is to refocus attention away from International Relations-assumptions and towards foreign policy practice. That is to ask the question: How is economic realism exercised in international relations? This suggests a shift towards economic diplomacy; a foreign policy practice and strategy that are based on the premise that economic/commercial interests and political interests reinforce one another, and should thus be seen in tandem. At stake are broad national interests that include political and strategic as well as economic dimensions.

While numerous studies of different economic diplomacy expressions exist, few attempts have been made to bring order and meaning to the mass of phenomena that economic diplomacy encompasses. Indeed, most studies address one or a few particular element(s) of the whole, without providing the bigger picture.[13] Differentiation

[12] This illustrates why Japan, which also heavily subsidizes its inefficient agricultural sector, can – to a certain extent – be characterized as a clientelized state.

[13] For example Garten, Zoellick and Shinn (1998), van Bergeijk (2009), Arase (2005), Blanchard and Ripsman (2008). A notable exception is Bayne and Woolcock (2007/2003).

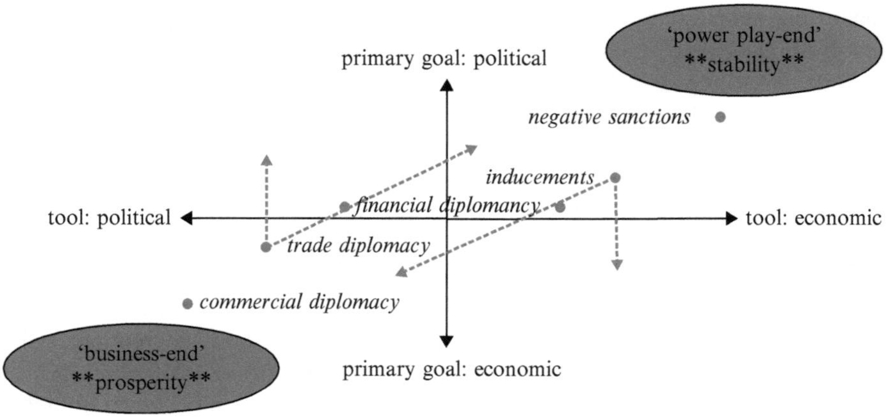

Fig. 14.2 Strands of economic diplomacy (Western countries) (Source: Okano-Heijmans (2011))

between the importance of specific factors in a particular country, case or situation is thereby lagging, while the distinctiveness and overlap between specific policy expressions, tools and purposes remain blurred. In other words, the concept of economic diplomacy needs to be unpacked and the various strands need to be placed along a continuum if actual happenings are to be analyzed in a coherent matter.

A conceptual framework of economic diplomacy helps to recognize and interrelate diverging strands – and thereby broad categories of perspectives from which economic diplomacy can be studied. The framework used here distinguishes a 'business-end' and a 'power play-end', and positions policy expressions along two axes that represent the tools (instruments) and goals of activities.[14] Certain overlaps notwithstanding, policies can thereby be grouped based on a reasonable judgment as to which of the categories is the *primary* goal or basis of a certain economic diplomacy expression. The point is that all expressions can be placed along a continuum, along which policies may evolve and through which governments' policies can be compared. This is expressed in Fig. 14.2.

At the 'power play-end' are instruments that generally involve actions and negotiations of a primarily political character, such as sanctions (and lifting thereof). Activities aim primarily to contribute to a stable international environment (security) and are often referred to as economic statecraft. Underlying cost-benefit calculations follow a political logic. At the 'business-end' of economic diplomacy are cooperative efforts by government and business that aim to achieve commercial objectives that advance national interests,[15] including trade and investment promotion (commercial diplomacy). Here, cost-benefit calculations primarily follow an economic logic and maximizing business opportunities is the primary driver behind

[14] This conceptual framework is expounded in Okano-Heijmans (2011).

[15] This definition follows Kopp but distinguishes more explicitly between ODA and other commercial activities in which the government is involved (2004: 1).

activities. In between these ends are activities that may be more or less economic or political, such as economic or development aid (and aid suspension), bilateral and multilateral negotiations on trade agreements (trade diplomacy), and financial and monetary policies (financial diplomacy). While this sketches out the general pattern, the distinction between the different strands is obviously fluid and strands may (and often do) overlap.

Figure 14.2 shows the continuum of expressions that characterizes the economic diplomacy practice of the majority of Western countries, while the dotted lines represent possible variations between countries, especially in other regions. This elucidates the fact that Asian countries are more inclined to use trade diplomacy for political rather than commercial goals (striving for influence in the region), while development assistance (inducements) of these countries generally considers relatively more commercial rather than political purposes (economic growth of self and the other, rather than promotion of human rights).[16]

The more a government manages to interrelate the different strands of economic diplomacy, the more comprehensive a country's strategy becomes. But while a broad, inclusive strategy is an important requirement for success, it is not a guarantee; it denotes the capabilities and intentions, but – in and of itself – says little about the actual impact of policies, which depends on the context in which the undertaking is pursued.

Empirical Testing

The above reflections on the theory and practice, as well as challenges and opportunities of economic realism and economic diplomacy, are meant to contribute to improved policy responses of any government that operates in today's environment of gradually shifting power balances. As history shows, economic diplomacy takes a more prominent place in foreign policy during such periods of change (Coolsaet 2001). It is thus no coincidence that – against the background of a (re)emerging China as an economic and political power, and relative decline of the trans-Atlantic powers[17] – economic diplomacy is gaining in importance again. The main challenge today may be the fact that variations in domestic political cultures and ideologies of countries, as well as level of development (particularly between the established powers and the various challengers) are now larger than at any earlier time in history. This is foretelling of a turbulent period, in which criticisms on perceived misuse of economic diplomacy will not be off the hook.

This section adds some empiricism to the preceding elaboration on theoretical assumptions and the practical application of the economic dimension of power.

[16] More on this in the empirical section.

[17] For more on this, see Ikenberry and Inoguchi (2010: 383–388).

The case of China is considered, as this country is rapidly enhancing its capabilities in the economic, military and political spheres and thereby poses the biggest challenge to the existing international system. Questions to be addressed are: When has China used or tried to use economic diplomacy in overt ways with discernible and directly attributable results? How is the Chinese approach different from (many) industrialized countries? To delineate the differences, this empirical case study addresses the degree to which economic power and economic diplomacy is adhered to (compared to other forms of power – mainly political and military[18]); differences in organization; bargaining versus negotiation; as well as quid pro quos in dealings with target countries.

Taking Centre Stage: China

China's role in reshaping international relations is of crucial importance, and can be viewed from two perspectives. On the one hand, China's international actions originate in factors that are specific to the country. On the other hand, China's way of practicing international politics can be understood as an exponent of the Asian mode of conducting international relations. Put differently, China is 'merely' the most recent example that generates the most attention today – because it is the main challenger to US hegemony.[19]

China's economic influence has a global reach, in fields ranging from international trade and finance to green innovation. Its economic diplomacy covers all strands along the business – power-play continuum, although Beijing – like other Asian governments – is hesitant to resort to economic sanctions in the Western sense; that is, to impose official trade or financial restrictions through bilateral or multilateral regulation. As will be shown, this is not to say that it is hesitant of transmitting negative incentives in more ambiguous ways.

On the 'business-end' of China's economic diplomacy, Beijing's active stance in the fields of commercial diplomacy (largely comprised of trade and investment promotion, and business-advocacy) and economic cooperation/development aid stand out. In the fields of market access, the availability of cheap labour, the import of Chinese products or Chinese investments and capital, the policies of the Chinese state are of the utmost importance. Chinese investment funds, banks and most multinationals are all directly controlled by the state. Direct foreign investments by Chinese companies overseas need to be approved by various government institutions, including the Chinese embassy in the recipient country. Moreover, the government has a profound influence on the extent to which foreign companies

[18] The political dimension of power stems from influence in international governance, for example the International Monetary Fund or the World Bank. This is different from but complementary to political power gained through economic and military capabilities.

[19] This paragraph builds on Okano-Heijmans and van der Putten (2009b).

gain access to the Chinese market. In contrast with western countries – but similar to neighbouring Japan and South Korea – , China's development aid/economic cooperation also follows the logic of the 'business-end' of economic diplomacy. Rapidly rising from relatively low levels, China's aid is conflated with foreign trade and investment, and explicitly aims to enhance also China's commercial strength. Although criticized by traditional donors that wish to separate aid from business, the adoption of the 'Seoul Consensus for Shared Growth' at the G20-meeting in November 2010 signalled growing acceptance for this development approach. This in itself may be seen as an indication of new political leverage that comes with the rising economic clout of Asian countries, especially China.

It should be emphasised that Chinese economic affairs do not *primarily* aim to gain political influence abroad. Continued economic growth and, by extension, legitimacy of the Communist Party are core national interests in the eyes of Chinese political leaders. The most effective instrument available to Beijing to protect these interests is its economic relations. This also goes for the defence of China's foreign security interests at large.

This does not mean, however, that the Chinese government will refrain from using its economic clout for political goals, when deemed necessary. A gentle example of this concerns Beijing's negotiations on bilateral and regional trade agreements, which primarily aim to further not so necessarily commercial ends but, rather, political goals. An illustration of this is the willingness of the Chinese government to make (short-term) commercial concessions in negotiations on trade and investment agreements. The aim is to alleviate concerns, especially of neighbouring countries, of China's rise and to strengthen China's position in the competition for influence in the region with Japan, and to a lesser extent India. One such example were the 'early harvest' provisions in the China-ASEAN free trade agreement, which immediately eliminated tariffs on certain agricultural goods, expected to benefit ASEAN-countries in particular.[20] Arguably less benign economic diplomacy at the 'power play-end' relates, first and foremost, to those political interests that the Communist Party regards as Chinese domestic issues. The endeavour to isolate Taiwan internationally and to undermine international support for the Dalai Lama and domestic dissidents illustrate this point. At the same time – and contrary to common understanding – it should be noted that China is not entirely unwilling to flex its economic muscles to achieve political change abroad. Norway learnt this the hard way after the (non-governmental) Nobel committee in 2010 awarded its peace prize to Chinese dissident Liu Xiaobo. China's foreign ministry responded by saying that the award would 'damage Sino-Norwegian relations' and derailed ongoing negotiations between the two countries on a bilateral trade deal. Further exemplary of Chinese willingness to use economic power for political purposes were its actions amid a territorial and political dispute over Tokyo's detention of a Chinese fishing boat captain in the Senkaku/Diaoyutai

[20] In hindsight, the actual benefits of this clause to ASEAN-countries have been disputed by many analysts. See for example Bello (2010).

Islands in autumn 2010. China imposed an informal ban on exports of rare earth minerals to Japan – and, later, to the US and European countries – , thereby causing severe unrest in industrial and government circles in those targeted countries. These depend heavily on exports from China in their supply of these natural resources, crucial for advanced manufacturing such as in next-generation vehicles and nuclear plants. Beijing's apparent readiness to use a strategic economic commodity as a political tool was only one in a series of alarming incidents.[21] Amid rising tensions, Chinese authorities also detained four Japanese employees of a construction company on ambiguous charges of entering a military zone in Hebei Province without authorization and videotaping military targets (Soble and Hook 2010). Another example is the clash between Australia and China, which in July 2010 had arrested and sentenced an executive with Australian nationality (but of Chinese background) of mining company Rio Tinto, without granting Australian consular officials access to the individual.[22] This incident occurred 1 month after Rio Tinto unilaterally scrapped a joint venture with state-owned Chinalco (the Aluminium Corporation of China), as the Australian Foreign Investment Review Board was reviewing the case. Each of these instances illustrate that the potential for flexible and arbitrary enforcement of Beijing's state and trade secrets laws raises questions about the ability of foreign firms to operate safely in China.[23] This points to relatively far-going willingness on the part of the Chinese government to engage in forceful economic diplomacy under ambiguous circumstances.

Formally, respect for national sovereignty is one of the main pillars of China's foreign policy, but in practice the Chinese government is quite flexible about this. Beijing's aim of protecting Chinese 'domestic' interests, such as those relating to Tibet or Taiwan, often results in attempts to interfere in matters that are part of other countries' sovereign rights. One such example was the rather explicit warning of the Chinese ambassador to the Dutch Parliament that a meeting with the Dalai Lama could seriously harm bilateral relations (Letter by ambassador Zhang Jun, dated April 9. NRC International 2010). The idea that countries officially receiving the Dalai Lama at the highest political level are punished through a reduction of their exports to China is supported by empirical evidence. This so-called 'Dalai Lama Effect' is found to be 8.1% on average, only observed for the Hu Jintao era (that is, from 2002), and disappears 2 years after a meeting took place (Fuchs and Klann 2010).

---

[21] To Beijing's credit, it may be added that the Chinese government in July 2010 had announced plans to cut rare earth export quotas for the second half of that year, leaving the theoretical possibility that this caused the sudden drop in exports in the case of the US and European countries.

[22] This violated a bilateral agreement on consular relations between the two countries (Ching 2010).

[23] For a critical US perspective, see US-China Economic and Security Review Commission (2010: esp. 257–266).

China increasingly has an interest in international stability and in playing the role of a 'responsible' great power – but here also, politics and economics are conflated.[24] The Chinese government has used its economic influence to pressure the Sudanese government into allowing a United Nations peacekeeping mission to work in Darfur, while at the same time using economic incentives to strengthen its access to raw materials and to shipping routes in a great number of countries. In principle, any issue seen by Beijing as directly relevant to its vital security needs can be addressed through economic means. As some of the above examples illustrate, respect for other countries' national sovereignty does not necessarily form a boundary that Beijing will not cross.

As Chinese capabilities to exert economic influence rise, and little doubt is left about Beijing's willingness to use them, the question remains how much power its economic clout really gives the Chinese leadership. That is to point to the distinction between active and passive power, and between positive and negative economic diplomacy, as well as to distinguish between targets of influence attempts. Failure to address the former issue leads to an exaggeration of China's economic power – including the 'power of credit between great powers' – that has been prevalent especially in policy circles in the US (Drezner 2009). For example, Beijing can use its financial power to resist US entreaties, but cannot coerce Washington into changing its policies.

In less powerful target countries, China's active influencing power is more substantial. One such example concerns that of certain European countries in the wake of the global financial crises. That is to say that it would be naïve to think that China's 'bailing out' of European countries – by investing in government bonds in Greece, Italy and Ireland – will have no political ramifications. An early sign of this came as Chinese premier Wen Jiabao admonished EU leaders not to pressure China on appreciation of its currency. The challenge for European countries – and other target countries, for that matter – is compounded by the lack of information about the pervasiveness of Chinese Communist Party influence in the daily operations of state-owned enterprises and their subsidiaries. Even if China's success at reducing the political room for manoeuvre of European countries may be limited for now, its investments effectively advanced the 'going global' strategy of Chinese companies. Illustrative of this is the 3.6 billion credit line from Beijing that troubled Greek shipbuilders could tap – almost exclusively to purchase Chinese-made ships (Alderman 2010). All of this enhances the image of a Chinese government skillfully exercising a comprehensive economic diplomacy that integrates power play and commercial purposes and expressions.

[24] On this front, policies of established powers – the US and, to a lesser extent, European countries – are not so different from China's, although the political objectives differ.

Conclusion and Future Research

Empirical research on economic realism and economic diplomacy, based on solid conceptual and analytical foundations, is at an early stage. While economists are making headway with cost-benefit analyses of various economic diplomacy expressions (including the trade-enhancing effects of summitry and diplomatic representation abroad), structured political science research in particular is lagging. A clear analytical framework for research is required, if shifts along the continuum of political and economic instruments and purposes are to be unveiled, and comparisons to be made between countries, regions and industries. The framework introduced in this chapter is a beginning, and there are several areas of particular interest for future research. This includes applying typologies, such as the one proposed here, to other questions of economic diplomacy; establishing links to alliance and agency theories; supplementing political science research with financial and commercial cost and benefit data; and industry-specific research.

The use of economic (as an alternative to military and political) means to enhance a country's position in the international system is increasingly prevalent as the potential of China and other (advanced) developing countries to exercise economic power grows and the legitimacy of war as a policy tool has waned. This should urge European countries to rethink the balance between political, economic and military capabilities. Such a call to interrelate economic and political external policy in answer to growing economic realism is not a call for protectionism, however. Rather, it is important that European countries make clear choices about where their priorities lie, for example concerning welfare, safety, environment, human rights and development cooperation. Clarity about priorities is at the basis of an effective response to the changing rules of the game in international relations. At risk is a betrayal of the political-economic model that took European countries years to develop – where structural adjustments that keep the attraction of the European approach in place would suffice.

References

Alderman, L. (2010). Beijing seen striving for influence in Europe. *International Herald Tribune*, 1 November.

Allison, G. T. (1999/1971). *Essence of decision: Explaining the Cuban missile crisis*. Boston: Little Brown.

Arase, D. (Ed.). (2005). *Japanese aid in the new millennium*. London: Routledge.

Baldwin, D. A. (1985). *Economic statecraft*. Princeton: Princeton University Press.

Bayne, N., & Woolcock, S. (2007/2003). *The new economic diplomacy – Decision-making and negotiation in international economic relations*. Hampshire: Ashgate Publishing Limited.

Bello, W. (2010). The China-Asean free trade area: Propaganda and reality. *UNSBIZ.com*, 15 January.

Blanchard, J.-M. F., & Ripsman, N. M. (2008). A political theory of economic statecraft. *Foreign Policy Analysis, 4*(4), 374–398.

Calder, K. E. (1993). *Strategic capitalism: Private business and public purpose in Japanese industrial finance*. Princeton: Princeton University Press.

Chang, H.-J. (2003). *Kicking away the ladder: Development strategy in historical perspective*. London: Anthem Press.

Ching, F. (2010). Did China trash a treaty? *Japan Times*, 3 April.

Coolsaet, R. (2001). Historical patterns in economic diplomacy, from protectionism to globalization, International Studies Association Convention. http://isanet.ccit.arizona.edu/archive/coolsaet.html. Retrieved 30 July 2008.

Drezner, D. W. (2009). Bad debts. Assessing China's financial influence in great power politics. *International Security, 34*(2), 7–45.

Dunn, L., Nyers, P., & Stubbs, R. (2010). Western interventionism versus East Asian non-interference: Competing 'global' norms in the Asian century. *The Pacific Review, 23*(3), 295–312.

Fuchs, A., & Klann, N.-H.(2010). Paying a visit: The Dalai Lama effect on international trade, center for European, Governance and Economic Development Research, Discussion paper no. 113, 20 Oct 2010.

Garten, J., Zoellick, R., & Shinn, J. (1998). *Riding the tigers: American commercial diplomacy in Asia*. New York: Council on Foreign Relations.

Gilpin, R. (1981). *War and change in world politics*. Cambridge: Cambridge University Press.

Heginbotham, E., & Samuels, R. J. (1998). Mercantile realism and Japan's foreign policy. *International Security, 22*(4), 171–203.

Ikenberry, G. J., & Inoguchi, T. (2010). Introduction. *International Relations of the Asia-Pacific, 10*(3), 383–388.

Kaletsky, A. (2010). *Capitalism 4.0 – The birth of a new economy in the aftermath of a crisis*. New York: Public Affairs.

Keohane, R. O., & Nye, J. S. (1977). *Power and interdependence: World politics in transition*. Boston: Little, Brown and Company.

Knorr, K. (1975). *The power of nations: The political economy of international relations*. New York: Basic Books.

Kopp, H. W. (2004). *Commercial diplomacy and the national interest*. Washington: American Academy of Diplomacy/Business Council for International Understanding.

Lukes, S. (2005). Power and the battle for hearts and minds. *Millennium, 33*(3), 477–493.

Morgenthau, H. J. (1968/1948). *Politics among nations: The struggle for power and peace* (pp. 28–29). New York: Knopf.

Nye, J. S., Jr. (2004). *Soft power: The means to success in world politics*. New York: PublicAffairs.

Okano-Heijmans, M. (2010). Troubled neighbours: Japan's negative economic diplomacy towards North Korea. *European Journal of East Asian Studies, 9*(2), 363–394.

Okano-Heijmans, M. (2011). Conceptualizing economic diplomacy: The crossroads of international relations, economics, IPE and diplomatic studies. *The Hague Journal of Diplomacy, 6*(1&2), 7–36.

Okano-Heijmans, M., & van der Putten, F.-P. (2009a). China's rise and the changing rules of the game in the international order. *CEPS Commentary*, 29 June.

Okano-Heijmans, M., & van der Putten, F.-P. (2009b). Economisch Realisme van Azië verandert de spelregels van de internationale betrekkingen [Economic realism of Asia is changing the rules of the game of international relations], *De Nieuwe Wereld*, Christen Democratische Verkenningen (summer), Amsterdam: Boom Tijdschriften.

Pilling, D. (2010). Poised for a shift. *Financial Times*, 23 November.

Radtke, K. W. (2008). Security in Chinese, Korean, and Japanese philosophy and ethics. In H. G. Brauch et al. (Eds.), *Globalization and environmental challenges: Reconceptualizing security in the 21st century* (Hexagon Series on Human and Environmental Security and Peace, Vol. 3). Berlin/Heidelberg/New York: Springer.

Smith, M. J. (2009). *Power and the state*. Hampshire/New York: Palgrave Macmillan.

Soble, J., & Hook, L. (2010). Japan sees Chinese ban on mineral exports. *Financial Times*, 24 September.

Strange, S. (1992). States, firms and diplomacy. *International Affairs, 68*(1 January), 1–15.

Tilly, C. (1990). *Coercion, capital, and European states, AD 990–1990*. Cambridge: Basil Blackwell.

US-China Economic and Security Review Commission (2010). Annual report to congress, Washington, DC, 29 October.

van Bergeijk, P. A. G. (2009). *Economic diplomacy and the geography of international trade*. Cheltenham: Edward Elgar Publishing.

van Wolferen, K. (2003). Sorting out the conceptual muddle: The role of the Japanese economy in the Asian financial crisis. *Cambridge Review of International Affairs, 16*(1), 57–58.

Zhang, J. (2010). Dalai lama meeting cannot [sic] be state visit. *NRC International*. 17 April, dated April 9.

Chapter 15
Exploring China's Rise as Knowledge Power

Maximilian Mayer

Introduction

The rise of China is a dominant theme in international politics. While factors such as demographics, geography or the skyrocketing Chinese Gross Domestic Product (GDP) have received persistent attention from researchers, this article points to a different and neglected aspect of China's ascent: knowledge und technology. I argue that a truly comprehensive understanding of how China could (again) become a hub of world politics requires an historical exploration of the Chinese position within the global political economy of knowledge. Few authors have emphasized China's blossoming technical and scientific capacities as a critical source of its growing influence (but see Lampton 2008). Their arguments strongly resonate with quantitative indices, which demonstrate the accelerating strengthening of China's output of publications, basic research capacities, and scientific networks (Royal Society 2011). Recent research also points to the possibility that a number of emerging economies, including China, are transforming into genuine commercial innovation hubs (Altenburg et al. 2008; Ernst 2011; CGS-Forschungsgruppe Wissensmacht 2011). Already, the concern with "the race to the top" in research and technology permeates policy discourses all around the world. Due to the advent of the global "knowledge economy" (OECD 2010; cf. Moldaschl and Stehr 2010), the importance of innovativeness is poised to increase only further.

But is China indeed approaching the first-tier circle of knowledge powers as various studies and reports appear to suggest (e.g. Adams et al. 2009; Lord Sainsbury

Thanks for support and precious comments to all members of the CGS-Forschungsgruppe Wissensmacht, Peer Schouten, Ruth Knoblich, Jared Sonnicksen, and the editors. All remaining errors are my own.

E. Fels et al. (eds.), *Power in the 21st Century*, Global Power Shift,
DOI 10.1007/978-3-642-25082-8_15,

of Turville 2007; Segal 2010)? The answer to this question needs to be based on diverse empirical data, but one also has to apply a theoretical framework, which construes the complex linkages between "knowledge", economic processes, and political dynamics at work appropriately. This kind of qualitative theory-driven analysis however, is lacking from many recent accounts that conceptually do not seem to reach beyond the conventional wisdom that the command of knowledge conveys positive effects upon a country's economic and military power. As such "knowledge power", to provide a preliminary definition, describes a tool that can be both applied to political ends and deliberately got manufactured. To quote from U.S. President Obama's 2011 State of the Union Address:

> Half a century ago, when the Soviets beat us into space with the launch of a satellite called Sputnik, we had no idea how we would beat them to the moon. The science wasn't even there yet. NASA didn't exist. But after investing in better research and education, we didn't just surpass the Soviets; we unleashed a wave of innovation that created new industries and millions of new jobs. This is our generation's Sputnik moment. Two years ago, I said that we needed to reach a level of research and development we haven't seen since the height of the Space Race. (White House 2011)

In the prevailing view innovation and technology serve as national power resource and are a driving force behind international competition. But to thoroughly evaluate China's knowledge power neither alarmist wording nor sophisticated econometrics alone will be sufficient. The following argumentation instead proposes to theoretically reconsider the role of "knowledge" in order to improve our comprehension of the course of contemporary international affairs and the rise of great powers in particular. Firstly, whereas the majority of International Relation (IR) scholars do not assume knowledge or technologies as substantial building blocks of the puzzle of global politics[1], three approaches of International Political Economy (IPE) are presented that provide a reasonably consistent conceptual understanding of the interplay between *knowledge* and *power*. Secondly, drawing from the ideas of Susan Strange, Robert Gilpin, and Joseph Schumpeter, the subsequent two sections explore the *global knowledge power politics,* in which China's rise is embedded, bringing the national pursuit and usage of knowledge into the analytical limelight. In the context of a realist narrative other possible relevant aspects of knowledge and technology are not included in my analysis.[2] Finally, the concluding section provides a case summary, scrutinizes the applied theoretical approaches, and briefly addresses further issues for the conceptualization of knowledge power in today's world politics.

[1] Due to space constraints this chapter cannot provide a comprehensive overview. For an excellent review see Fritsch (2011).

[2] This chapter built on concepts from IPE and thus remains a limited contribution to the ongoing conceptualization work. Constructivist and post-structuralist perspectives on knowledge and technology (see for instance Haas 1992; Litfin 1994; Mayer 2012; Miller 2007) are deliberately excluded from the analysis and will subsequently be dealt with elsewhere.

Theorizing Knowledge, Technology, and Power Shifts

The rich body of work that explores the history and sociology of science and technology has shown how knowledge, technology, and innovation have been intricately intertwined with the political economy, especially in the modern era, including modern statehood and social order (van Crefeld 1999; Rosenau 1990; Jasanoff 2004), the evolution of capitalism and economic globalization (Fischer 1982; Smil 2010; Rosenberg et al. 1992) as well as international relations (Ruggie 1975; Haas 1975; Keohane and Nye 1998). This interdisciplinary literature does greatly differ with respect to the suggested understandings and definitions of knowledge and technology, yet it usually is organized into two different groups. One variety of approaches believes that technical factors are overriding social forces – known as technical determinism. The other group, conversely, understands technologies as shaped by conflicting social forces or economic interests (Fritsch 2011; Law 1987) The authors I will mainly refer to for the purpose of this article can be differentiated along different lines. Schumpeter is exploring the dynamics of innovation mainly at the micro-level, whereas Gilpin and Strange are pointing to the macro-level. The central lessons of this literature will be distilled and then applied to the case of China.

The Power of Technology

Robert Gilpin points to the crucial role of technology for the occurrences of major wars. In his seminal work *War and Change in World Politics*, he argues that on the most profound level new technologies of communication, weapons, and transport lead to the transformation of the basic units of the international system. The evolution of the size and organization of political units have thus historically been related to evolving technologies. Furthermore, technology is at the core of Gilpin's central theoretical claim regarding the mechanisms that lead to major war. Namely, that rising powers will become expansionist when the expected gains of expansion outweigh the losses. States accordingly are in search of advantages that might result from various sources. Gilpin holds that "most frequently this advantage, especially in the modern era, has been conferred by technological innovations in the areas of military weapons and/or industrial production" (Gilpin 1981: 54).

The transfer of critical technology hence is able to trigger the demise of dominant powers and add to the capacities of their challengers. Subsequently, the advent of new military technologies leads to increased risk of hegemonic war and alters the nature of war itself (van Crefeld 1989). The hegemonic state will always try to hinder technological diffusion, especially of its latest military or dual use technologies (Gilpin 1981). Major powers will keep technological inventions and related know-how secret and under their exclusive control. For this purpose, governments often exercise a ban for high-tech weapon exports – as currently between the US and China – and apply conditions of secrecy usually to researchers, scientists, and their projects. Critical technology and tacit knowledge sometimes is not even shared with the closest allies.

Barry Buzan has proposed another technology-related factor in international affairs that he names the "technological imperative": This is the constant progress of technological inventions both in the civilian and the military realm that compels states to adapt to and anticipate further progress (Buzan 1987). Due to this dynamic, states have to spend a huge part of their budgets to remain ahead of their rivals and to compensate for possible diffusion – as illustrated most obviously during the battleships competition in the 1920s (cf. McBride 1997) and the Cold War. In the year 1957, the successful Soviet space mission revealed that the US led nations were technologically lacking behind the communist camp. In response to the surprise launching of Sputnik the US administration established a national centralized research agency (today's Defense Advanced Research Projects Agency, DARPA) and quadrupled the annual funding for the national science foundation (Divine 1993).

Consequently, the two super powers were logged into a scientific and technical battle that included massive state investments in the build-up of research cities, monitoring systems, and space programs (O'Mara 2004; Dickson 1988). The military "dominated the US federal R & D budget" between 1960 and 1990: Only 3 years saw less than 50% for this cause (Mowery 1992: 136). Defense related research in the US gave not only birth to the invention of computer chips, the internet and the following shift to network-centric warfare, but was also spurring the scientific and technical race towards virtualization and robotization (Der Derian 2009; Singer 2009). The institutionalization of the military-industrial complex, and particularly the DARPA, is a key to understanding the current global US military predominance (Paarlberg 2004).

To summarize, technological progress, national security and state power are inseparably tied to each other. On the one hand, scientific progress and its technological fruits enhance a state's "power capacity" and represent important tools of power politics. On the other hand, technology is inherently powerful since it could easily be used by adversaries against the very state that has created it. This forces all states to pursue cutting-edge research and development (R&D) covertly. If we want to explain the rise of great powers the presented perspectives urge us to direct our attention to the innovational capacities and the state policies that try to prevent the spread of (military) technologies.[3] Rising powers, in contrast, can be expected to try circumventing those barriers against the diffusion of technology and keen on developing their own strong innovation capabilities.

---

[3] Kennedy (1987) additionally points to the financial underpinning that might hamper a hegemon's ability to preserve his innovation leadership and technological advantage over his rivals.

Macro Structures of Knowledge

Susan Strange offers a broader perspective on knowledge power including information as well as ideological aspects. She advances four main global structures encompassing finance, production, security, and knowledge, which evolve in a constant interplay. The knowledge structure has insofar an underlying function as it entails both the conveying and exclusion of others from information or know-how that is highly relevant for the other three structures (Strange 1988: 119ff.). It co-determines the processes in the financial, production and security spheres since "the power exercised over the nature of knowledge to be acquired, and over the means used for its storage and communication, is a necessary complement to power exercised through the other three structures" (Strange 1989: 166). Whichever state is powerful in a structural sense will control a significant share of this structure. The dominant player in the knowledge structure automatically will be powerful in the other structures. Moreover, Strange claims that the knowledge structure has historically emerged as the main arena of international affairs:

> . . .the competition between states is becoming a competition for leadership in the knowledge structure. The competition used to be for territory, when land and natural resources were the major factor in the production of wealth and therefore the acquisition of power for the state. Then the competition was for industrial 'sinews of war' provided by the manufacture of steel, and later for chemicals, and petroleum and electric power. Today, the competition is for a place at the leading edge (as the jargon has it) of advance technology. This is the means both to military superiority and to economic prosperity, invulnerability and dominance. (Strange 1988: 132)

Power shifts may occur caused by diverse changes in the knowledge structure. According to Strange, three core dynamics are discernible. First, new actors take control over the information flux and global communication systems. Second, the internationally dominant language erodes and third the fundamental perceptions and beliefs about the human condition change (Strange 1988: 120). The consequences of these shifts include an increasing asymmetry between states in terms of access and acquisition of knowledge as well as a new distribution of power, social status, and influence within and across nations. Strange emphasizes that 'information rich' economies and, below the national level, social groups are especially profiting from the ongoing evolutions of the knowledge structure (Strange 1988: 133ff.).

According to Strange (1987), one must therefore look beyond the mere numbers of GDP, military spending, et cetera – that are in neorealist eyes reflecting national power capacities – to analytically and empirically grasp power shifts. She argues with respect to the alleged decline of US power in the 1980s, only a comprehensive analysis of all four structures reveals whether a power shift is really occurring. Strange draws the opposite conclusion, namely that technical changes and particularly the rising importance of information and globe-spanning communications have led to greater concentration of power in the United States. Ten years later, Joseph Nye has proposed an essentially similar chain of arguments:

> Knowledge, more than ever before, is power. The one country that can best lead the information revolution will be more powerful than any other. For the foreseeable future, that country is the United States. (...) This advantage stems from Cold War investments and America's open society, thanks to which it dominates important communications and information processing technologies – space-based surveillance, direct broadcasting, high-speed computers – and has an unparalleled ability to integrate complex information systems. (Nye and Owens 1996: 20ff.)

What Strange and Nye by their vigorous emphasizing of the persistence of US hegemony implicitly suggest is that rising powers have a hard time making the knowledge structures work in their own favor. In other words, the assumed existence of macro structures implies inertia and path-dependency both in global communication systems and evolution of national innovative capacities – resulting in an "evolutionary" (Dicken 2007: 74ff.) type of change.

An additional reason for the prevalence of slow changes is that economies with a sustained technological edge enjoy a comparative advantage allowing them to shape the regulations of intellectual property rights (IPR) under which technology is transferred to less innovative economies (Singleton 2008: 200). As such, the current shape of the global intellectual property system reflects the preferences of the industrial countries in general and the large multinational corporations in particular (Wissen 2003).[4] Many scholars and experts claim that this powerful component of the knowledge structure actually inhibits the economic rise of developing nations (May 2009; Taplin and Nowak 2010).

However, this does not mean that change is impossible. States can alter the knowledge structure through their educational policies producing more or better-qualified human capital. However, to establish a full-fledged educational system, including world-class universities, typically requires decades or even centuries. Furthermore, states can promote innovation-friendly institutions, technical standards, and regulations for IPR that profoundly impact processes of knowledge creation (Juma et al. 2001; Fagerberg and Srholec 2008), as the Asian "Tigers" exemplify (Evers et al. 2010; Hornidge 2006). The history of IPR shows how the dominant states have tried to extend their distinct regulations beyond national borders promoting international organizations and binding rules (Kindleberger 1988). In response, late-developing states almost automatically have broken the international rules for knowledge transfer, since these rules usually favor the

[4] Archibugi's (2010) conclusion that the current IPR are in the interest of a small number of multinational enterprises, yet not necessarily conducive for the national economies as a whole, corresponds with earlier assertions that the accelerating development of technologies is a "prime cause of the shift in the state-market balance of power" (Strange 1996: 7). The balance of the global knowledge structures appears to increasingly tilt towards the big corporations at the expense of states. For others patents and copyrights are unnecessary for innovation to happen at all. See Boldrin and Levine (2008).

leading knowledge powers. To circumnavigate restrictive IPR can even become a (secret) deliberate national strategy (Chang 2002).

Corporations can also function as agents of change in the knowledge structure by their innovations regardless whether learning processes, technology absorption, imitation or plain plagiarism are at play. Once successfully commercialized, they will secure or enlarge their market power in certain segments and sectors. The newly generated revenues can be further invested in the realization of more complex and costly innovations. This then leads to a self-amplifying circle (Ali et al. 2011), which can be assumed to also increase a states power over the economic and security structures. Within the global productions networks, knowledge power can be measured through the flux of royalties' payments and fees based on the ownership of technology and know-how according to international and national IP laws. Profiting from the increasing control over the other structures following the increasing share of the global knowledge structure, a state gains in turn more knowledge power as the example of rising Japan at the end of the nineteenth century illustrates (Morishima 1982).

Micro Dynamics of Innovation

Joseph Schumpeter – the founding father of innovation economics – proposed a theory of drastic and sudden changes of the economy. According to Schumpeter, "creative destruction" is not only inherent to capitalism, but is one of its main driving forces (Schumpeter 1947). Radical innovations give birth to new industries, companies and markets (Diamond 2006). He strongly emphasizes the role of creative and risk-seeking entrepreneurs for these kinds of innovations (Schumpeter 1926), while preexisting companies often have trouble even to survive with profound impacts on their 'host countries'. The invention and commercialization of new path breaking technologies can lead to a far-reaching restructuring of – to use Strange's term – the four "structures". This is because "Schumpeterian industries" that arise out of these revolutionary processes involve economies of scale and function after the winner-takes-all competition with profound consequences for governments operating in this sort of innovational environment:

> ...the location of that dominant firm is of paramount concern. In order to foster the development of national champions that dominate Schumpeterian industries, mercantilist-minded policymakers will put in place industrial policies that marshal the resources and power of the state to this end. (Singleton 2008: 200)

As such, Schumpeterian innovations[5] are real game changers. Corporations that can make use of this kind of innovations often immediately gain market dominance or monopolies. Transferred to the political arena, states can too be assumed to act

[5] For a discussion of the renaissance of Schumpeter's ideas see Freeman (2003).

like innovators. They may not only increase their military power projection, but new technologies also can open up the range of possible instruments, actions and the leverage of states more generally. For instance, new technologies may allow certain states to enter and subsequently govern unknown or unoccupied spaces like the deep sea, the outer space, and subatomic environments. Weapon systems originating from Schumpeterian innovation fundamentally change the way war is fought and security is guaranteed. For example, nuclear weapons had "world-transforming effects" that did sustainably alter global power politics (Schouten 2011).[6] More recent examples include technologies in energy or communication systems (like the World Wide Web, wind power, or photovoltaics) that spurred few companies to dominate their respective market. Search engines, software, and other social media technologies have enabled tiny companies to grow to astronomical sizes. On the other hand, the juridical governance of these technologies confers to the states in which those companies operate a decisive leverage over their peers. Hence, it is not surprising that states increasingly try to fence the global cyber space by "emerging cybered territorial sovereignty" (Demchak and Dombrowski 2011: 35).

Theoretically, rising powers can be assumed to aim at profiting from Schumpeterian innovations. Instead of sunk-investment in existing systems, they want to harvest the fruits of rapid innovation and leapfrogging. Yet, governments cannot simply "produce" Schumpeterian innovations. Although the probability of their occurrences requires the existence of certain social institutions and dynamics – typically given in successfully industrializing nations as Gerschenkron (1962) argues in retrospect – the most important role is played by individual inventors and entrepreneurs who develop bright visions and accept to take huge risks. To phrase it differently, this type of alteration in knowledge power cannot be fabricated, but does rather resemble a rare and unforeseen event. Once it happened though, the risk seekers – states or companies – will be rewarded.

Other actors instead experience the downside of an evolving zero-sum game that Schumpeter has coined "creative destruction". Firms are rapidly losing market shares or are incapable of entering dynamically growing markets. Likewise, states suffer from a sudden irrelevance of their most precious defense systems or from the unexpected erosion of their position in the global knowledge structure. In sum, technological innovation also can, in contrast to the subtle and slow processes described in the former section, lead to rapid shifts in knowledge power. Corporate product innovations and the social recombination of new technological applications or whole technical systems substantially can influence the macro-level of the global knowledge structure with profound implications for the security, production, and financial structures.

[6] Robert Jervis (1989) among others has argued that the "nuclear revolution" did alter statecraft and war fundamentally because of the mutual vulnerability it has created. See also Frühling and O'Neil in Chap. 5 of this volume.

Theoretical Lenses Combined

The insights from Gilpin, Strange, and Schumpeter are of great help for the conceptualization of the relationship of knowledge and power in international affairs. I argue that we need to combine these three approaches using them eclectically as analytical lenses. As a consequence, however, theoretical parsimony is not as perfect as we perhaps might wish because the three scholars shed light on different aspects of *knowledge*, *power*, and *change*. Neither do they share a similar ontological underpinning of "knowledge", nor the same level of analysis. Furthermore, Strange and Schumpeter do not agree on the pace and the timescale of innovational processes. The idea of "structure", by definition, implies a relatively high degree of path-dependency, inertness, and offers well-positioned actors possibilities for blockades. Revolutionary entrepreneurial innovations, in contrast, often lead to the fast growth of firms and new industries that radically rearrange national and global markets.[7] If we nonetheless want to merge Schumpeter's and Strange's ideas, we have to assume that slow and fast dynamics of innovation are operating at the global, the national, and the firm level in parallel.[8] Theoretically, all countries, and emerging powers in particular, can be expected to try to change the knowledge structures incrementally *and* to bet on "Schumpeterian industries" while supporting both goals with strategic industrial and research policies.

Accordingly, in the next section two different analytical lenses are employed to explore China's knowledge power. Stretching Gilpin's assumptions to their limits, one can assume that states persistently pursue a national knowledge strategy (NKS) in order to increase or maintain knowledge power. This notion mirrors what has been a matter of fact for modern great powers (cf. Hobsbawm 1987; Chang 2002). Today, the transition towards knowledge economies has led numerous governments within and beyond the Organization for Economic Co-operation and Development (OECD) to draft and implement ambitious strategies to enlarge their national research and innovations capacities. To summarize, without knowledge and innovation there is no development (Evers et al. 2010; Archibugi and Michie 1997), and consequently what we could label "global knowledge power politics" comes into view. We thus have to analyze how great power politics have influenced the political and economic environment of China's NKS or, put differently, the formative environment of Chinese knowledge power.

Additionally, following Strange's and Schumpeter's advice, we will inquire into the processes of innovation at the entrepreneurial level as well as the changes of the global knowledge structure related to China. Conceptually, the respective concept of knowledge used for this enterprise is rather broad in its meaning. Following

[7] Once established, however, these industries become huge players that are inclined to slow down developments and sustain the existing structures.

[8] The crucial difference between my argument and the literature on "varieties of capitalism" is that the latter contrasts diverging innovation processes assuming the differences being caused by differing structures of national cultures and institutions. See Hall and Soskice (2001) and Allen (2004).

Russell (1997) "knowledge" encompasses industrial know-how and scientific expertise as well as technical artifacts or generic technologies, ontologically equaling an objective instrument – a means for a state's ends that can be exclusively possessed.[9] "Power" subsequently is defined in terms of structures. The actors in control of the latter can determine "what knowledge is discovered, how it is stored, and who communicates it by what means to whom and on what terms" (Strange 1988: 117). This is the reason for which states do not simply want access to new technologies, but ultimately try to increase their share of the global knowledge structure. Only in this way can the technological advantage of states be maintained over longer periods. Consequently, "knowledge power" entails two elements: (1) the access to know-how and state-of-the-art technologies and (2), the control over a significant share of the global knowledge structure.

China and the Global Knowledge Power Politics

China is believed to have emerged as a technology hotbed. Whereas this phenomenon certainly needs a historical account[10], the following section sheds light on China's position in the international knowledge politics since the foundation of the People's Republic in 1949. The alleged increase in knowledge power will be explored in the subsequent section.

After the Communist Party had won the civil war in 1949, China became part of the eastern camp in the Cold War. As a huge, but backward economy and due to the US embargo it was heavily dependent on technology and know-how transfer from the Soviet Union (Zhang 2001). While the Soviet support expanded rapidly ranging from plant design for basic industries to various research fields such as computation, the underlying leitmotif was the concern for national security. Russian scientists did not only help the Chinese to develop their "indigenous" nuclear facilities as well as rocket and missile science, but the Chinese leadership – even in outright contradiction to Mao's aversion against intellectuals – redesigned the national higher education system as well as the architecture and the practice of research and scientific basically copying the Soviet example (Zhang et al. 2006). Moreover, during the late Qing period and in early decades of the Chinese republic, foreign companies had mainly facilitated technology transfer to China (Spence 2001). With the Chinese-Soviet collaboration it became an issue of

[9] This reductionist definition of "knowledge" certainly will not meet the consent of many scholars, but it resembles an umbrella concept for pragmatic use rather than a concise and exhaustive terminology.

[10] Joseph Needham's work shows that for millennia Imperial China had been the world's technological leader and many Chinese innovations in agriculture, defense, navigation, transport and power precede their European 'rediscovery' for centuries (Needham 1982).

"technical assistance" wholly organized by state organs completely excluding private enterprises and IP regimes.

How closely the transfer of knowledge and the security alliance were connected became clear when the Sino-Soviet split occurred. The support for high technology and nuclear weapon development were among the first things abandoned. By 1960, mirroring the deteriorating bilateral relations, almost all Soviet experts, engineers, and technicians had left China (Zhang et al. 2006; Westad 1998). Nevertheless, in only 4 years Chinese scientists won prestige by detonating the first "Asian" atomic bomb constructed from the remaining Soviet blue prints. For the subsequent decade however, the country largely remained without meaningful access to advanced military, not to mention commercial technology.

From the 1950s onwards Chinese innovations processes and knowledge production overall were heavily shaped by security considerations – both in terms of the content of knowledge, the preferred types of technologies, and even with regard to geographical arrangements. The fear of super power hostilities from two sides led to Mao's decision to further spread industrial production and research activities to remote places in central and southwest China. To withstand an anticipated attack, China's paramount leaders planned a secure industrial base far from the easily accessible shores and northeastern plains. The famous "third front" required a large-scale buildup of the entire industrial infrastructure, relying almost entirely on indigenous know-how. Economically and financially, this immense project had astronomical costs and significantly reduced the overall investment efficiency in China's economy due to various design problems both in single projects and the program as a whole (Naugthon 1988).

During the 1970s, the formative environment did dramatically change causing China's NKS to turn away from its security orientation. When the Chinese-US rapprochement started in 1972 the former "top priority construction of the Third Front no longer made sense" (Naugthon 1988: 372). The Carter administration's decision to gradually allow for bilateral trade and high technology exports to China between the year 1972 and 1979 marked a fundamental shift and has changed the government's options to access external knowledge (Long 1991). The revision of China's NKS embedded in Deng Xiaoping's "opening and reform policy" was enabled by this development. The Chinese leadership decided to rely on market mechanisms as the main transfer instrument for technology, substituting military alliances and ending the technological isolation that had hampered the Chinese economic development.

> From viewing imports as a necessary evil, the approach has swung to an acceptance of much greater trade flows and closer integration with world markets. Imported technology was seen to hold an extremely important position in China's modernisation strategy, as it become increasingly clear just how backward its technological base had become since the 1960s, and how disorganised and weak its domestic S&T resources are. (Conroy 1986)

In this new climate, the priority of the Chinese leadership shifted away from military modernization and defense industries towards commercial interests and consumer-driven technologies (US Congress 1987). The Chinese government hoped that the commercial interest and foreign direct investments by Japanese, European and US enterprises would become the crucial drivers for the much-needed diffusion of technology. Thousands of Chinese collectively and privately owned small and medium enterprises, whose activities were less controlled by the state following the economic reforms in the early 1980s, and began to integrate foreign technology such as heavy machinery, sets of equipment, and assembly lines into their business models.[11]

The massive engagement of foreign firms, furthermore, again led to a rearrangement of the geographical patterns of the knowledge production. The manufacturing and innovation clusters evolved within the export oriented special economic zones that the provincial governments had established in proximity to the Chinese coast with direct transport connection to the global markets.[12] Meanwhile, the Chinese education and research system was reopened allowing for substantial scholarly exchanges and collaboration. Since 1978 millions of young Chinese students have been staying at universities abroad, echoing the tradition from the late Imperial and early Republican period. The reorganization of the education system and the universities in particular now tends to follow the Anglo-Saxon model.

With China's integration into the world economy (and most significantly the admission into the World Trade Organization (WTO) in 2001) the accusation of "piracy" as being a strategy or at least the outcome of a deliberate neglect on the side of the Chinese authorities turned into a central critique. On the one hand, China has pursued certain policies that force foreign companies into forming joint ventures with local companies often *de facto* giving technologies and know-how out of effective control.[13] On the other hand, the central government has – in the beginning mainly upon US pressure – adopted regulations and laws for protecting intellectual property (Mertha 2005). In 1995, roughly 19,000 patent applications have been filed throughout China. Only 15 years later, this number had risen to more than 314,000 in 2009, leaving China only behind of Japan and the US while Chinese companies have also sharply increased their international patent applications.[14] Since Chinese companies increasingly have to rely on their own IP for profits in their home market and abroad, the Chinese government began revising the existing IP laws and regulations in order to strengthen the protection of IPR and the harmonization with international patent treaties.

Although after the mid-seventies Chinese and foreign private companies steadily moved towards the center stage of the knowledge creation processes, and the Chinese knowledge structure at large (Sun 2002), non-commercial structural

---

[11] For a detailed account of the success and flaws of technology import and absorption policies in the 1980s see Shi (1998).

[12] Breznitz and Murphree (2011) illustrate this aspect in their study of the Chinese IT industry.

[13] The Bureau of Export Administration (1998: V) openly states that "[t]he transfer of advanced US technology is the price of market access in China for US high-tech companies."

[14] Data derived from the WIPO under http://www.wipo.int/ipstats/en/statistics/patents/.

influences were not absent. In 1989, many governments did reduce their exports of dual-use items, high technology, and weapons to China. Initially, the ban had been imposed responding to severe human rights violations. Yet after the 1996 Taiwan crisis, the transfer of technology towards China has been increasingly discussed in terms of national security concerns, especially in the US (Feigenbaum 1999).[15] Many observers are warning against the unrestricted access to high technology, which might not only undermine the innovational advantages of American companies due to limited IPR enforcement in China, but is possibly also nurturing the power projection capabilities of a serious future adversary (Ikenson 2011). The Chinese government for instance is pursuing a "deliberate policy" to augment the PLA Air Force's capabilities with commercially migrated foreign aerospace technology (Shobert 2011).

During the last six decades, two dominant formative environments have influenced China's NKS. By the end of the 1970s along with China's détente with the United States, there has been a fundamental shift from security to an economy determined knowledge power politics. Although after the 1990s the formative environment of China's NKS is increasingly composed of both economic and security factors, the economic structure clearly remains the decisive determinant of technology diffusion and the Chinese NKS.

Is China's Knowledge Power Growing?

In the theory section, two dynamics have been suggested that can lead to the increase of knowledge power: incremental changes in the knowledge structure and rapid innovational dynamics that enable the flourishing of new technological systems, companies, or industries. Although the former type can be observed in China across multiple areas, it still remains heavily dependent on foreign technologies, while the latter type of change has not been occurring thus far.

The Communist Party views innovation as the "soul" of economic progress (Baark 2007: 337). China represents the "world's largest technocracy: a country ruled by scientists and engineers who believe in the power of new technologies to deliver social and economic progress" (Wilsdon and Keeley 2007: 6). Consequently, the Chinese state began to make huge investments to form one of world's most formidable agglomerations of human capital. Starting from literally nothing, China has in less than 100 year's almost exterminated illiteracy, producing hundreds of millions of educated people and dozens of millions of excellent engineers, researchers, and scholars, though the astonishing numbers may often reflect more quantity than actual quality (Gereffi et al. 2008). The state expenditure in R&D has been steadily increasing since the 1980s (it stood at 1.4% of the GDP in

[15] For the restrictive US policy with respect to space technology see Guo (2006).

2007 up from 0.6% in 1996), narrowing the gap to the industrial countries considerably. According to official planning, the national budget for R&D will reach up to 2.5% of the GDP until 2020. At the same time, multi-national companies began to relocate parts of their R&D facilities into Chinese campuses and science parks (Sun et al. 2007).

Clearly, the sum of these developments has changed the global knowledge structure, and subsequently the processes of knowledge creation in China as illustrated by the rising share of journal articles, citations, and patents (Adams et al. 2009; Luan and Zhang 2011). China already has achieved pockets of excellence such as in super computers, ultra-supercritical coal power plants, shipbuilding, or information and space technology. The country has turned into a leading technology exporter. Chinese enterprises are building dams (McDonald et al. 2009), communication systems, oil refineries, and power plants in developing countries all around the world. Meanwhile, the telecommunication giant Huawei has launched an operable technology using the new global Long-Term-Evolution (LTE) communication standard. By the end of 2009, Huawei employed the first complete LTE-based commercial network in Oslo, while a Chinese consortium around the Beijing-based CSR is expected for bidding to supply the bullet trains for the planned high-speed rail system in California.

These developments of technological catch up are strongly backed by various policies and public spending, since Chinese leaders intend to significantly improve their country's knowledge power. The Medium- and Long-Term Development Program (MLP) for Science and Technology Development (2006–2020) calls for several central areas, technologies and scientific fields to be mastered and implemented until 2020 focusing on clean technologies, energy efficiency, transport, environment, and agriculture. The MLP also puts emphasis on the national mastery of core technologies (Wilsdon and Keeley 2007; Naughton 2011) and pictures the dependence on imported technologies as a "threat to Chinese national and economic security" (Segal 2010). Under President Jiang Zemin a program had been installed to persuade as many Chinese scholars and scientists abroad (the "sea turtles") as possible to return back home in order to reverse the "brain drain" of the 1980s and 1990s (Zweig et al. 2004). The official push for homegrown innovation is additionally propelled by a growing sense of "techno-nationalism" among many bureaucrats, scientists and entrepreneurs (Suttmeier et al. 2004).

The expanding financial resources allow the Chinese central government to make large investments into prestigious infrastructures such as high-speed trains, telecommunications and Internet technology, and intelligent power grids. Even a Chinese space station is in planning. Meanwhile, Chinese high-technology exports per year have reached roughly 350 billion US$ – grossly overtaking the combined exports of Germany and the US. Considering the data about the national distribution of global technology exports as shown in Table 15.1, one could easily get the impression that China has reached a dominant position already.

The reality, however, is rather different from this superficial assessment. Chinese companies came to occupy prominent positions in various global production

Table 15.1 High-technology exports (in current US$) (Source: Data from http://data.worldbank.org/)

	1995	2009
China	13.2	348.3
Germany	57	142.4
Japan	110	99.2
UK	52.2	57.2
USA	128.8	141.5

networks and chains.[16] Especially in crucial components markets such as wind turbines, photovoltaic modules, IT, and increasingly automobiles, they have gained a dominant market position in very short time (de la Tour et al. 2011; Lewis 2007; Chu 2011; Breznitz and Murphee 2011). However, despite the official government goal of breeding cutting-edge innovation, the majority of Chinese enterprises instead moves to the technological frontier in the low- and medium-technology industries at best (Fu and Gong 2011; Ernst 2008). Export-oriented industries have chosen to remain one step behind the forefront of product innovation buying foreign technology or simply relying on licenses for producing high-technology components in the context of production networks. The competitive advantage, thus, is largely derived from cheap labor or process innovations.

This business strategy has to be understood against the backdrop of global processes of fragmentation and regional specialization that result in "production-stage economies of scale and scope". Whereas this kind of business model thus far has been extremely successful in terms of growth and turnover[17], it has not yet led to large absorption of technologies or the infusion of genuine inventiveness (Tang and Hussler 2011; Breznitz and Murphee 2011). The decomposition of China's trade further illustrates this point. Between 1996 and 2009, the share of processing trade was well above 80% of total high-technology trade, implying that China remained a genuine production and assembling site, not an innovation hub (Xing 2011b: 5). The data on royalty fees and payments fully reveal the current stage. In the year 2009, the Chinese economy has received about 430 million US$, whereas it had to pay to foreign patent and copyright holders more than 11 billion US$. These numbers show how much Chinese companies – from shipbuilders and turbine manufactures to the IT and telecommunications branch – rely on foreign licensed technology. The gap between fees and payments is rapidly growing. This means that China's share of the global knowledge structure is de facto shrinking. Figure 15.1 illustrates that, with the exception of the United Kingdom, China has the balance sheet with the highest negative proportion, while knowledge powers such as the US and Japan display positive balance sheets.

[16] For a critical analysis of the "Chineseness" of Chinese companies see Pan (2009).

[17] Chinese enterprises have acted perfectly rational because their strategy responds to the generally uncertain climate in China that prohibits risky long-term investments in innovation because laws for intellectual properties are absent, unclear, or loosely enforced (Breznitz and Murphree 2011: 13ff).

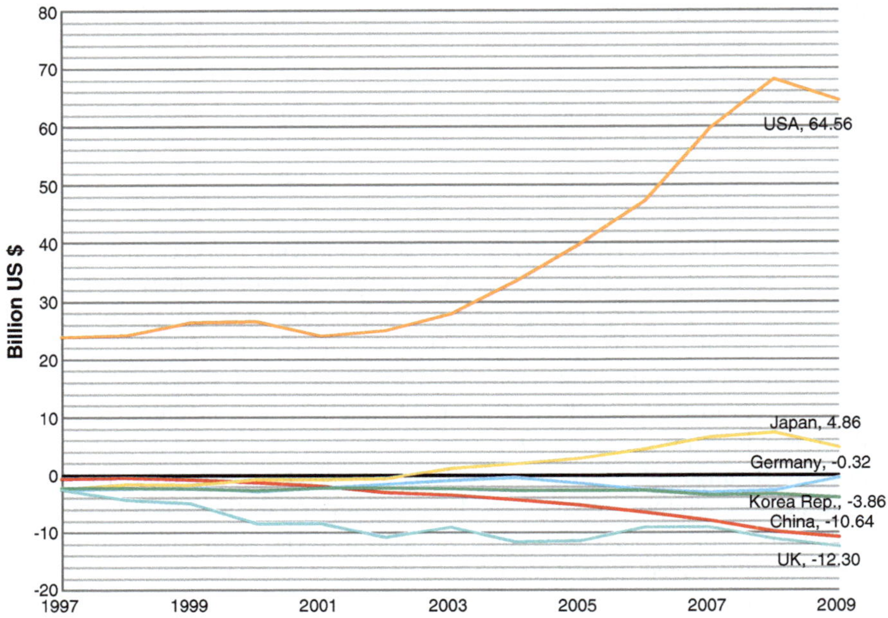

Fig. 15.1 Balance of royalty fees and payments (1997–2009) (Source: Data from http://data.worldbank.org/)

From this perspective, it appears natural that the Chinese government stresses "indigenous innovation" and tries to reform the existing IP laws. Whether China can reverse the current trend depends on how much it is able to implement a meaningful and strict protection of IP and private property in general. Trade partners and leading economic powers have constantly pressured China to upgrade and enforce its respective laws and regulations according to WTO principles (Bosworth and Yang 2000: 461ff.). Due to mounting complaints from foreign enterprises and governments, the Chinese government has stepped back from its recent attempts to use discriminatory IP laws and procurement rules for privileging and invigorating "indigenous innovation" (Lubman 2011). The reason though is not only the mounting external pressure, but also the changing internal interest constellation. While both government and companies have to a certain extend for a long time effectively circumvented the institutional structure of the IPR to support the nation's swift economic development (and still hold a generally critical stance towards Anti-Counterfeiting Trade Agreement (ACTA) and the TRIPS-PLUS agenda), China seemingly has entered a transitional phase now. Intellectual property is increasingly perceived as an important tool for promoting economic growth and innovativeness (Wechsler 2011); its lack is seen as severely hampering the Chinese technology champions.

The long-term effects of weak IP laws or their lacking implementation also disabling the bulk of enterprises to compete on foreign markets because most of them have never been really innovative in terms of ideas, inventions, and core technologies (Guan et al. 2006; Gilboy 2004).[18] Despite recent progress the same holds true for the Chinese defense industries as well.[19] Impressive as the growth of patent applications and grants by the Chinese patent office may appear, it hides the fact that the IP surge mainly consists of utility models and industrial designs with very low application requirements (WIPO 2010; Li 2008). Very few Chinese firms such as Huawei, Lenovo or ZTE own significant patents in mature markets.

Conclusion

The majority of theorizing in IR has treated knowledge as an "esoteric topic" (Weiss 2005: 309) that is at best capable of increasing complexity. Given the broad political attention paid to the creation, possession, and diffusion of "knowledge" today such views are anachronistic. We should aim to replace the merely additive treatment of knowledge with an empirically dense and theoretically coherent understanding of knowledge power. The present chapter intends to contribute to this project. Undoubtedly, the realist IPE approach presented here displays shortcomings and deficiencies such as the deliberate neglect of the many reflexive and social dimensions of knowledge. Furthermore, it cannot do full methodological justice to the discussed theoretical concepts due to an eclectic practice. Nonetheless, it is able to direct our attention to alternative phenomena and intriguing empirical puzzles. The lens of *global knowledge power politics* conceptualizes the ways global shifts in power are related to processes of knowledge creation and the knowledge structure. Applied to the case of China it provides us with a nuanced picture of the phenomenal Chinese development and promotes new elements for further studies beyond the classical factors such as resources, trade or military power.

In sum, China's knowledge power obviously has increased; yet not to such a great extent as many observers claim or fear. On the one hand, the country has enlarged its share of the knowledge structure and enjoys almost full access to the latest technologies.[20] This has strengthened China's position in global production networks significantly, rendering many countries, companies, and consumers dependent on Chinese process innovation. On the other hand, the weakness of Chinese IP regulations and the prevailing entrepreneurial strategy have hindered

[18] The cooperation between universities and start-up firms, which is among the main engines of growth and innovation in the US, does not work fully efficient without clear and effective IPR either.

[19] The People's Liberation Armey's military technology usually is one or two decades behind its competitors (Cheung 2011). For the case of maritime technology see Kirchberger in this volume.

[20] The defense sector suffering from prolonged export bans from Europe, Japan, and the U.S. is the critical exemption in this regard.

the emergence of true product innovation on a broad scale. In other words, China largely relies on creeping processes of knowledge creation that neither reduce its technological dependence nor result in a sharp increase of knowledge power. As Gupta and Wang (2011) put it in *Wall Street Journal*: "Yes, China is making rapid strides in some areas such as telecommunication technology. However, on an across-the-board basis, it still has quite some distance to cover before becoming a global innovation power."

As a matter of fact, large-scale rapid innovation dynamics have not yet occurred. The digital age still is dominated by US firms such as Apple, Google, and the likes that have led the way to Internet commerce and social networking, whereas Chinese companies – aside from a few exceptions (Chen and Li-Hua 2011; Fan 2011) – resorted to pragmatically copying foreign business models.[21] It remains to be seen whether the next wave of Schumpeterian industries will indeed originate from China. There are various fields in which this landslide type of change could be expected such as e-mobility, telecommunications or genetics, which are all powerfully supported by the Chinese government at the moment. The probability for this event is currently overestimated, albeit it is rising from a very low level.

This case study illustrates that, despite the alleged conceptual elusiveness of knowledge, a reasonably coherent and differentiated assessment of qualitative and quantitative alternations of knowledge power is possible. However, there is still a great deal of work to do in order to improve the methodical and theoretical tools we have at our disposal. First of all, "knowledge" is still not firmly established as a significant factor in IPE not to mention IR theory. Second, central concepts need further refinement. For instance, as Gilpin emphasizes and this study illustrates: great powers indeed do matter for national knowledge strategies. What cannot easily be grasped though are qualitative alternations of "formative environments". For a deeper understanding – not only of the Chinese story – the notion of "structures" should be closely connected with the idea of NKS. Theoretically, formative environments seem to be either economy or security-conditioned, each displaying specific logics as Table 15.2 illustrates. Accordingly, the NKS diverge with respects to the type of knowledge that is legitimately sought, as well as policy measures, and underlying institutional mechanisms.

How can we imagine these ideal type national knowledge strategies? A security-conditioned NKS is focused on military technologies and weapon systems, which is superlatively exemplified through the 'war economies'. Its primary goal is to enhance a nation's defense/offense capabilities. The range of socially valuable technologies is probably reduced to security-related applications, while the state centrally exercises the planning and funding of processes of knowledge creation. Typically, information and know-how are publicly or commercially hardly accessible since secrecy is the institutional logic that regulates the diffusion. In contrast, an economy-conditioned NKS is focused on commercial technologies and

---

[21] Chinese Internet firms possible could be among the first to change this pattern. See *Economist* (2011).

Table 15.2 Formative environment of national knowledge strategies

National knowledge strategies	Conditioned by security structure	Massive public funding for research, secrecy	Focus on military technologies
	Conditioned by economic structure	Private funding of research, market driven innovation, IPR	Focus on commercial technologies

knowledge is deemed to expand wealth and to foster economic growth. Innovation and technology diffusion is based on market dynamics by means of patents, copyrights, and trademarks and would not stem from military contest. In this picture, private enterprises develop and commercialize technologies and states are less able and willing to exert direct control over the diffusion process. In practice, the actual national knowledge strategies are mixed, somewhere in the middle ground between these two extremes[22]; nonetheless, this dichotomist typology allows us to conceptually differentiate between historic patterns of global knowledge power politics. In this line, it should be possible to explore the evolution of national knowledge strategies along with their formative environments in the context of a general realist framework.

Moreover, the increase of China's knowledge power questions the way in which the conceptual relationship between changes at the macro-level and rapid dynamics at the micro-level are construed. Incremental structural changes leading to the long-term reorganization of global and regional product chains are indeed significant for China's emergence as a world-level player – causing new economic vulnerabilities and technological interdependencies. China's industries have gained a prominent place within various global and regional production networks at the expense of Southeast Asian countries and even some of the "tiger states". This can be viewed as the effect of a shift of knowledge power among semi-peripheral states (cf. Xing 2011a). In the global geography of innovation and production of high technology, however, Japan, Europe, and the US have retained their dominant positions (Ernst 2009).

The first and foremost question stemming from a realist concern for rivalries or conflicts, which often dominates debates about China's future, is whether these alterations of knowledge power inevitably are leading to zero-sum scenarios. In what ways is this connected with different scales and dynamics of the global knowledge structure? In this regard, further theorizing far beyond what has been proposed in this article is needed. The Chinese case offers some evidence that rising knowledge powers do not simply substitute existing ones since they position themselves in niches in the global knowledge structure. Incremental changes

[22] A mixed NKS combines state and commercial funding of research and innovation, market dynamics and strategic national innovation policies. With respect to technology transfer dominant powers will rely on both regulation of IPR and secrecy. The diffusion of critical dual-use items could for instance be object to export restrictions.

therefore seem not to imply zero-sum games. Instead, as already has been mentioned above, national economies in different developmental stages can profit, while at the same time new interdependencies arise and old dependencies shift. Ultimately, emerging powers such as China might aim at greater technological autarky and certainly will not hesitate to invest into the most prestigious and expensive technologies. When they are finally near to catching up with established knowledge powers, fundamental rearrangements of the international security and economic structures may occur. In order to explore these potential developments conceptually requires the connection und eclectic recombination of different theories of innovation, national innovation systems, and global production networks with notions of structural power in IR. To understand the power-political consequences of incremental as well as rapid shifts of knowledge power on the one hand, and, conversely, how given power relations/structures shape evolving processes of knowledge creation on multiple levels and across different scales on the other hand, remains paramount to the unresolved challenges for the theorization of 21st global politics.

References

Adams, J., King, C., & Ma, N. (2009). Global research report China. Research and collaboration in the new geography of science. Leeds: Thompson Reuters.

Ali, M., Aleem, M., & Park, K. (2011). A spiral process model of technological innovation in a developing country: The case of Samsung. *African Journal of Business Management, 5*(7), 2874–2889.

Allen, M. (2004). The varieties of capitalism paradigm: Not enough variety? *Socio-Economic Review, 2*(1), 87–108.

Altenburg, T., Schmitz, H., & Stamm, A. A. (2008). Breakthrough? China's and India's transition from production to innovation. *World Development, 36*(2), 325–344.

Archibugi, D., & Michie, J. (Eds.). (1997). *Technology, globalisation and economic performance*. Cambridge, NY: Cambridge University Press.

Baark, E. (2007). Knowledge and innovation in China: Historical legacies and emerging institutions. *Asia Pacific Business Review, 13*(3), 337–356.

Boldrin, M., & Levine, D. (2008). *Against intellectual monopoly*. Cambridge, NY: Cambridge University Press.

Bosworth, D., & Yang, D. (2000). Intellectual property law, technology flow and licensing opportunities in the People's Republic of China. *International Business Review, 9*, 453–477.

Breznitz, D., & Murphree, M. (2011). *The run of the red queen: Government, innovation, globalization, and economic growth in China*. New Haven: Yale University Press.

Buzan, B. (1987). *An introduction to strategic studies: Military technology and international relations*. New York: St. Martin's Press.

CGS-Forschungsgruppe Wissensmacht. (2011). Sind die BRIC-Staaten aufsteigende Wissensmächte? Herausforderungen für die deutsche Wissenspolitik. Januar 2011, http://www.cgs-bonn.de/pdf/DP-3_BRIC_Wissensmacht_Final.pdf.

Chang, H.-J. (2002). *Kicking away the ladder. Development strategy in historical perspective*. London: Anthem Press.

Chen, D., & Li-Hua, R. (2011). Modes of technological leapfrogging: Five case studies from China. *Journal of Engineering and Technology Management, 28*(1–2), 93–108.

Cheung, T. M. (2011). The Chinese defense economy's long March from imitation to innovation. *Journal of Strategic Studies, 34*(3), 325–354.
Chu, W.-W. (2011). How the Chinese government promoted a global automobile industry. *Industrial and Corporate Change, 20*, 1–42.
Conroy, R. (1986). China's technology import policy. *The Australian Journal of Chinese Affairs, 15*, 19–56.
van Crefeld, M. (1989). *Technology and war: From 2000 B.C. to the present.* New York: Free Press.
van Crefeld, M. (1999). *The rise and decline of the State*. Cambridge, NY: Cambridge University Press.
Demchak, C. C., & Dombrowski, P. (2011). Rise of a Cybered Westphalian Age. *Strategic Studies Quarterly, 5*(1), 32–61.
Der Derian, J. (2009). *Virtuous war: Mapping the military- industrial-media-entertainment network.* London: Routledge.
Diamond, A. M., Jr. (2006). Schumpeter's creative destruction: A review of the evidence. *Journal of Private Enterprise, 22*(1), 120–146.
Dicken, P. (2007). *Global shift. Mapping the changing contours of the world economy* (5th ed.). Los Angeles/London: Sage.
Dickson, D. (1988). *The new politics of science*. Chicago: The University of Chicago Press.
Divine, R. A. (1993). *The Sputnik challenge*. New York: Oxford University Press.
Evers, H.-D., Menkhoff, T., & Wah, C. Y. (Eds.). (2010). *Governing and managing knowledge in Asia* (2nd ed.). Singapore/London: World Scientific Publishing.
Ernst, D. (2009). *A new geography of knowledge in the electronics industry? Asia's role in Global innovation networks* (Policy studies, Vol. 54). Honolulu: East–west Center.
Ernst, D. (2008). Can Chinese IT firms develop innovative capabilities within global knowledge networks? In M. G. Hancock, H. S. Rowen, & W. F. Miller (Eds.), *Greater China's quest for innovation* (pp. 107–216). Stanford, CA/Washington, DC: Shorenstein Asia Pacific Research Center/Brookings Institution Press.
Ernst, D. (2011). China's innovation policy is a wake-up call for America. In *Asia Pacific Issues*, No. 100. http://www.eastwestcenter.org/fileadmin/stored/pdfs/api100.pdf. Accessed on 10 December 2011
Fagerberg, J., & Srholec, M. (2008). National innovation systems, capabilities and economic development. *Research Policy, 37*(9), 1417–1435.
Fan, P. (2011). Innovation, globalization, and catch-up of latecomers: Cases of Chinese telecom firms. *Environment and Planning A, 43*(4), 830–849.
Feigenbaum, E. A. (1999). Who's behind China's high-technology 'Revolution'? How bomb makers remade Beijing's priorities, policies, and institutions. *International Security, 24*(1), 95–126. Summer 1999.
Fischer, M. (1982). Tensions from technology in Marx's communist society. *Journal of Value Inquiry, 16*, 117–129.
Freeman, C. (2003). *A Schumpeterian renaissance?* (SPRU electronic working paper series, Vol. 102). Brighton: University of Sussex.
Fritsch, S. (2011). Technology and global affairs. *International Studies Perspectives, 12*(1), 27–45.
Fu, X., & Gong, Y. (2011). Indigenous and foreign innovation efforts and drivers of technological upgrading: Evidence from China. *World Development, 39*(7), 1213–1225.
Gereffi, G., Wadhwa, V., Rissing, B., & Ong, R. (2008). Getting the numbers right: International engineering education in the United States, China, and India. *Journal of Engineering Education, 1*, 13–25.
Gerschenkron, A. (1962). *Economic backwardness in historical perspective, a book of essays.* Cambridge, MA: Belknap.
Gilboy, J. G. (2004). The myth behind China's miracle. *Foreign Affairs, 83*(4), 33–48.
Gilpin, R. (1981). *War and change in international politics* (p. 54). Cambridge, NY: Cambridge University Press.

Guan, J. C., et al. (2006). Technology transfer and innovation performance: Evidence from Chinese firms. *Technological Forecasting and Social Change, 73*, 666–678.
Guo, X. (2006). Blockade on China or the United States? U.S. regulatory policies on space technology exports to China. *WSI China Security, 2*(1), 73–83.
Gupta, A. K., & Wang, H. (2011). China as an innovation center? Not so fast. *Wall Street Journal*, 28 July 2011.http://online.wsj.com/article/SB10001424053111903591104576469670146238648.html.
Haas, E. B. (1975). Is there a Hole in the whole? Knowledge, technology, interdependence, and the construction of international regimes. *International Organization, 29*(3), 827–876.
Haas, P. M. (1992). Introduction: Epistemic communities and international policy coordination. *International Organization, 46*(1), 1–35.
Hall, P. A., & Soskice, D. (2001). *Varieties of capitalism: The institutional foundations of comparative advantage*. Oxford, NY: Oxford University Press.
Hobsbawm, E. J. (1987). *The Age of Empire 1875–1914*. London: Weidenfels and Nicolson.
Hornidge, A.-K. (2006). *Singapore: The knowledge-hub in the straits of Malacca* (ZEF working paper series, Vol. 14). Bonn: Center for Development Research, University of Bonn.
Ikenson, D. J. (2011). U.S. leaders learning the wrong lessons from China's rise. *China-U.S. Focus*, 15 March 2011. http://www.cato.org/pub_display.php?pub_id=12882.
Jasanoff, S. (Ed.). (2004). *States of knowledge. The co-production of science and social order*. London: Routledge.
Jervis, R. (1989). *The meaning of the nuclear revolution: Statecraft and the prospect of Armageddon*. Ithaca: Cornell University Press.
Juma, C., Fang, K., Honca, D., Huete-Perez, J., Konde, V., Lee, S. H., Arenas, J., Ivinson, A., Robinson, H., & Singh, S. (2001). Global governance of technology: Meeting the needs of developing countries. *International Journal of Technology Management, 22*(7/8), 629–655.
Kennedy, P. (1987). *Rise and Fall of the Great Powers: Economic Change and Military Conflict from 1500 to 2000*. New York: Random House.
Keohane, R. O., & Nye, J. S., Jr. (1998). Power and interdependence in the information age. *Foreign Affairs, 77*(5), 81–94.
Kindleberger, C. P. (1988). *The international economic order: Essays on financial crisis and international public goods*. New York: The MIT Press.
Lampton, D. M. (2008). *The three faces of Chinese power: Might, money, and minds*. Berkeley: UC Press.
Law, John. (1987). Technology and heterogeneous engineering: The case of Portuguese expansion. In W. E. Bijker et al. (Eds.), *The social construction of technological systems. New directions in the sociology and history of technology* (pp. 111–134). London/Cambridge, MA: MIT Press.
Lewis, J. I. (2007). Technology acquisition and innovation in the developing world: Wind Turbine development in China and India. *Studies in Comparative International Development, 42*, 208–232.
Li, X. (2008). *Patent counts as indicators of the geography of innovation activities: Problems and perspectives*. Research Papers 18. South Centre. http://www.southcentre.org/ARCHIVES/index.php?option=com_docman&task=doc_download&gid=1221. Accessed on 10 December 2011
Litfin, K. T. (1994). *Ozone discoures. Science and politics in global environmental cooperation*. New York: Columbia University Press.
Long, W. J. (1991). Economic incentives and international cooperation: Technology transfer to the People's Republic of China, 1978–86. *Journal of Peace Research, 28*(2), 175–189.
Lord Sainsbury of Turville. (2007). *The race to the top. A review of government's science and innovation policies*. HM Treasury. http://www.rsc.org/images/sainsbury_review051007_tcm18-103116.pdf. Accessed 10 Jan 2011.
Lubman, S. (2011). Changes to China's 'indigenous innovation' policy: Don't get too excited. *The Wall Street Journal*, 22 July 2011. http://blogs.wsj.com/chinarealtime/2011/07/22/changes-to-chinas-indigenous-innovation-policy-dont-get-too-excited/.

Luan, C., & Zhang, T. (2011). Innovation in China: A patentometric perspective (1985–2009). *Journal of Knowledge-based Innovation in China, 3*(3), 184–197.

May, C. (2009). *The global political economy of intellectual property rights. The new enclosures* (2nd ed.). London: Routledge.

Mayer, M. (2012). Chaotic climate change and security. *International Political Sociology* (forthcoming).

McBride, W. (1997). The unstable dynamics of a strategic technology: Disarmament, unemployment, and the interwar battleship. *Technology and Culture, 38*(2), 386–423.

McDonald, K., Bosshard, P., & Brewer, N. (2009). Exporting dams: China's hydropower industry goes global. *Journal of environmental management, 90*(Suppl. 3), 294–302.

Mertha, A. (2005). *The politics of piracy: Intellectual property in contemporary China*. Ithaca: Cornell University Press.

Miller, C. A. (2007). Democratisation, international knowledge institutions, and global governance. *Governance: An International Journal of Policy, Administration, and Institutions, 20*(2), 325–357.

Moldaschl, M., & Stehr, N. (Eds.). (2010). *Wissensökonomie und Innovation. Beiträge zur Ökonomie der Wissensgesellschaft*. Marburg: Metropolis.

Morishima, M. (1982). *Why has Japan 'succeeded'? Western technology and the Japanese ethos*. Cambridge, NY: Cambridge University Press.

Mowery, D. C. (1992). The U.S. national innovation system: Origins and prospects. *Research Policy, 21*, 125–144.

Naugthon, B. (1988). The third front: Defence industrialization in the Chinese interior. *China Quarterly, 115*, 351–386.

Naughton, B. (2011). China's economic policy today: The new state activism. *Eurasian Geography and Economics, 52*(3), 313–329.

Needham, J. (1982). *Science in traditional China*. Boston: Harvard University.

Nye, J. S., Jr., & Owens, W. (1996). America's information edge. *Foreign Affairs, 75*(2), 20–36.

OECD. (2010). *OECD science, technology and industry outlook*. Paris: OECD Publishing.

O'Mara, M. P. (2004). *Cities of knowledge: Cold war science and the search for the next Silicon Valley*. Princeton: Princeton University Press.

Paarlberg, R. L. (2004). Knowledge as power: Science, military dominance and U.S. security. *International Security, 29*(1), 122–151.

Pan, C. (2009). What is Chinese about Chinese businesses? Locating the 'rise of China' in global production networks. *Journal of Contemporary China, 18*, 7–25.

Rosenau, J. N. (1990). *Turbulence in world politics: A theory of change and continuity*. Princeton: Princeton University.

Rosenberg, N., Landau, R., & Mowery, D. (Eds.). (1992). *Technology and the wealth of nations*. Stanford, CA: Stanford University Press.

Royal Society. (2011). *Knowledge, networks and nations*. London: Royal Society.

Ruggie, J. G. (1975). International responses to technology: Concepts and trends. *International Organization, 29*(3), 557–583.

Russell, A. (1997). Technologyas knowledge. Generic technology and change in the global political economy. In M. Talalay, C. Farrands, & R. Tooze (Eds.), *Technology, culture and competitiveness. Change and the world political economy* (pp. 41–57). London/New York: Routledge.

Schouten, P. (2011). Theory Talk #40: Kenneth Waltz – The Physiocrat of International Politics. Theory Talks, http://www.theory-talks.org/2011/06/theory-talk-40.html (04-06-2011)

Segal, A. (2010). China's innovation wall. Beijing's push for homegrown technology. *Foreign Affairs,* 28 Sep 2010. http://www.foreignaffairs.com/articles/66753/adam-segal/chinas-innovation-wall.

Shi, Y. (1998). *Chinese firms and technology in the Reform Era*. London: Routledge.

Schumpeter, J. A. (1926). Theorie der wirtschaftlichen Entwicklung.

Schumpeter, J. A. (1947). *Capitalism, socialism and democracy*. New York: Harper.

Shobert, B. A. (2011). Fly China, risk included, *Asiatimes*, 29 April 2011. http://www.atimes.com/atimes/China_Business/MD29Cb01.html.
Singer, P. W. (2009). *Wired for war: The robotics revolution and conflict in the 21st century*. New York: Penguin Press.
Singleton, R. (2008). Knowledge and technology: The basis of wealth and power by Ross Singleton. In D. N. Balaam & M. Veseth (Eds.), *Introduction to international political economy* (4th ed.). Prentice Hall: Upper Saddle River.
Smil, V. (2010). *Prime movers of globalization: The history and impact of diesel engines and gas turbines*. Cambridge, MA: The MIT Press.
Spence, J. (2001). *Chinas Weg in die Moderne*. München: DTV.
Strange, S. (1987). The persistent myth of lost hegemony. *International Organization, 41*(4), 551–574.
Strange, S. (1988). *States and markets – An introduction to international political economy*. London: Pinter Publishers.
Strange, S. (1989). Towards a theory of transnational empire. In E.-O. Czempiel & J. N. Rosenau (Eds.), *Global changes and theoretical challenge*. Lexington: Lexington Books.
Strange, S. (1996). *The retreat of the state. The diffusion of power in the world economy*. Cambridge, NY: Cambrige University Press.
Sun, Y. (2002). China's national innovation system in transition. *Eurasian Geography and Economics, 43*(6), 476–492.
Sun, Y., von Zedtwitz, M., & Simon, D. F. (2007). Globalization of R&D and China: An introduction. *Asia Pacific Business Review, 13*(3), 311–319.
Suttmeier, R. P., Yao, X., Tan, A. Z. (2004). China's post-WTO technology policy: Standards, software, and the changing nature of techno-nationalism. NBR Reports (May 2004).
Tang, M., & Hussler, C. (2011). Betting on indigenous innovation or relying on FDI: The Chinese strategy for catching-up. *Technology in Society, 33*, 23–35.
Taplin, R., & Nowak, A. Z. (Eds.). (2010). *Intellectual property, innovation and management in emerging economies*. Oxon: Routledge.
The Bureau of Export Administration (1998) US Commercial Technology Transfer to the People's Republic of China. Washington
The Economist. (2011). An internet with Chinese characteristics. *The Economist*, 30 July 2011. http://www.economist.com/node/21524821.
de la Tour, A., Glachant, M., & Meniere, Y. (2011). Innovation and international technology transfer: The case of the Chinese photovoltaic industry. *Energy Policy, 39*, 761–770.
U.S. Congress, & Office of Technology Assessment. (1987). *Technology transfer to China. OTA-ISC-340*. Washington, DC: U.S. Government Printing Office.
Wechsler, A. (2011). Intellectual property law in the People's Republic of China: A powerful economic tool for innovation and development. *China-EU Law Journal*. doi: 10.1007/s12689-011-0001-x. http://www.springerlink.com/content/8810u786670m3472/fulltext.pdf. Accessed on 10 December 2011
Weiss, C. (2005). Science, technology and international relations. *Technology in Society, 27*, 295–313.
Westad, O. A. (Ed.). (1998). *Brothers in arms: The rise and fall of the Sino-Soviet Alliance, 1945–1963*. Washington, DC: Woodrow Wilson Center Press.
Wilsdon, J., & Keeley, J. (2007). *China: The next science superpower?* London: Demos.
Wissen, M. (2003). TRIPs, TRIPs-plus und WIPO. Konflikte um die Eigentumsrechte an genetischen Ressourcen. In *Christoph Görg: Postfordistische Naturverhältnisse. Konflikte um genetische Ressourcen und die Internationalisierung des Staates* (pp. 128–155). Münster: Verlag Westfälisches Dampfboot.
White House. (2011). *Transcript: Obama's State of the Union address*. http://www.npr.org/2011/01/26/133224933/transcript-obamas-state-of-union-address. Accessed on 10 December 2011
WIPO. (2010). *World intellectual property indicators*. Geneva: WIPO.

Xing, Y. (2011a). China's exports in information communication technology and its impact on Asian countries. *Economic Change and Restructuring, 44*, 135–147.
Xing, Y. (2011). *China's high-tech exports: Myth and reality*. GRIPS discussion paper 11–05 (June 2011).
Zhang, B., Zhang, J., & Yao, F. (2006). Technology transfer from the Soviet union to the People's Republic of China 1949–1966. *Comparative Technology Transfer and Society, 4*(2), 105–167.
Zhang, S. G. (2001). *Economic cold war: America's embargo against China and the Sino-Soviet Alliance, 1949–1963*. Washington, DC: Woodrow Wilson Center Press.
Zweig, D., Changgui, C., & Rosen, S. (2004). Globalization and transnational human capital: Overseas and returnee scholars to China. *The China Quarterly, 179*, 735–757.

Index

E. Fels et al. (eds.), *Power in the 21st Century*, Global Power Shift,
DOI 10.1007/978-3-642-25082-8,

MIX
Papier aus verantwortungsvollen Quellen
Paper from responsible sources
FSC® C105338

If you have any concerns about our products,
you can contact us on
ProductSafety@springernature.com

In case Publisher is established outside the EU,
the EU authorized representative is:
Springer Nature Customer Service Center GmbH
Europaplatz 3, 69115 Heidelberg, Germany

Printed by Libri Plureos GmbH
in Hamburg, Germany